THE LAST LETTER
A *Sgt. Parks* Novel

by

SSgt. Jacob Parkinson

DORRANCE PUBLISHING CO
EST. 1920
PITTSBURGH, PENNSYLVANIA 15238

The contents of this work, including, but not limited to, the accuracy of events, people, and places depicted; opinions expressed; permission to use previously published materials included; and any advice given or actions advocated are solely the responsibility of the author, who assumes all liability for said work and indemnifies the publisher against any claims stemming from publication of the work.

All Rights Reserved
Copyright © 2024 by SSgt. Jacob Parkinson

No part of this book may be reproduced or transmitted, downloaded, distributed, reverse engineered, or stored in or introduced into any information storage and retrieval system, in any form or by any means, including photocopying and recording, whether electronic or mechanical, now known or hereinafter invented without permission in writing from the publisher.

Dorrance Publishing Co
585 Alpha Drive
Suite 103
Pittsburgh, PA 15238
Visit our website at www.dorrancebookstore.com

ISBN: 979-8-88925-270-2
eISBN: 979-8-88925-770-7

TO THE READER,

First off, thank you; I am hoping to take you on a dark adventure of my life, while you read this at your leisure. This novel is a purely fictional narrative of fantasy, if you will, that I have created as way to tell of the misadventures of my squad during one subsequent combat tour to Iraq. Think of me as the bard to the men of 1st Squad 2nd Platoon.

This novel is not an ode to masculinity, nor do I follow any hardline political agenda; the purpose of the book is to give you, *the reader*, a glimpse into a bond forever forged, one that endears and haunts one another to this very day. That is the life of a Marine combat Veteran, a series of lifelong memories that never let go, ever. This book's narrative is pure fantasy, but all stories and memories of Iraq and my time as a *Grunt* in the United States Marine Corps are fact, as per the accounts of myself, members of 1st Squad and those that served alongside us in the Al Anbar Province, Iraq, the *Red Triangle*.

I am but one of hundreds of squad leaders that look upon the young miserable, dirty, exhausted, rough, weathered faces of their men and ask of them the impossible—"*gear up,*" another patrol into the unknown. My time spent in the Marines ('97–'09 active and reserve) is a fraction of those I served with and my combat tour: one of peril, action, dread, undying brotherhood and loneliness; it is but a pebble compared to other infantry unit leaders. My kids have often asked me over the years, *"Dad, what is your dream job?"*; my answer always remains the same, *"Kids, I have already had my dream job; an infantry squad leader in combat;"* there is truly no more rewarding position in the world. All live action, tactics, and training described throughout the novel are real-world applications and can be deployed by any Marine infantry unit at a moment's notice. *The Marine Infantry*, known as the *Grunts*, are the unheralded warriors of every American war dating back to 1775, yet there is no solid recognition for these *sledgehammers* of combat, the true *door-kickers*. We are miserable, filthy, angry, drained, and rely on no one but each other; that is what makes the *Marine Infantry* so damn effective. By writing this novel, I hope to honor not only the men of my squad, but all *Grunts* who have served and looked to the stars at *zero dark thirty*, freezing in the cold ocean on a Zodiac, pissing yourself to stay warm, or exhausted on some sand-ridden rooftop and asked yourself *"what the fuck was I thinking?"* then you look to the miserable son of a bitch next to you, *"but I wouldn't have it any other goddamn way."* Yut.

TO THE MEN OF BRAVO CO. 1/23,

I am not a historian or a journalist; one day the story of our unit will be told by a writer who can bring our tour some justice. We were but one of many untold stories of Marines that are overlooked and are never to be remembered, except by the lonely few that were there. Bravo Co. was a part of history, fighting alongside the very best warriors the Marines could throw at the enemy. The tale will be told one day of the *"Bastards of Anbar,"* along with the other infantry units of that fateful operation in 2004. I am not the one to tell that story. It was an honor to have served with you, the men of Bravo Co.

TO THE MEN OF INDIA CO. 3/5,

We were a boat company, yet the first infantry Marines to test the new Osprey program on some hot miserable desert night: April 8, 2000. We thought it an honor. Here is to the forgotten, gallant men myself, Sgt. Jackson, India Co., and the *United States Marine Corps* lost that fateful night:

- **India Co:** 2nd Lt. Clayton Kennedy, 24, Sgt. Jose Alvarez, 28 (posthumously awarded SSgt), Cpl. Adam Neely, 22, Cpl. Can Soler, 21, LCpl. Jason Duke, 28, LCpl. Jesus Gonzalez, 27, LCpl. Jorge Morin, 21, LCpl. Seth Jones, 18, Pfc. Kenneth Paddio, 23, Pfc. Gabriel Clevenger, 21, Pfc. Alfred Corona, 23, Pfc. George Santos, 19, Pfc. Keoki Santos, 24, Pvt. Adam Tatro, 19
- **Miramar:** Cpl. Eric Martinez, 21
- **Quantico:** Maj. John Brow, 39, Maj. Brooks Gruber, 34, SSgt. William Nelson, 30, Cpl. Kelly Keith, 22

TO MY MEN, 1ST SQUAD 2ND PLATOON,

I have no words, I love you. The novels are for you; I hope your names now live in honored infamy.

For my mom

THOSE FIVE LITTLE WORDS

"Thank you for your service," those *five* little words, are what is uttered by you when you see a Veteran plate or Veteran marking of some kind on an individual going on about their day. The Veteran walks with purpose, stoically but with a little bit of a cloud. A fog. A haze.

"Thank you for your service," those *five* little words, fills you with a sense of pride or patriotism for doing your part for this country by thanking a Veteran for his or her service. You leave feeling warm inside as you watch the Veteran awkwardly try to force out a *"you're welcome"* or a *"thank you."*

"Thank you for your service," those *five* little words, makes your meal a little bit better or your day a bit brighter. If you are with children, you explain to them why it is a good thing to thank a Veteran for their service. It is American or Patriotic.

"Thank you for your service," those *five* little words, entitles you to try and engage with us, as we shyly back away graciously. For the Veteran knows the questions that usually accompany those *five* little words. The conversation will be monotone, but we will force our best smile as you ask the questions.

"Thank you for your service," those *five* little words. We see it coming out of our peripheral vision, like a tracer round piercing the night sky. We have our prepared reply, but it will tumble out of our mouths forced or mumbled. We sheepishly duck our heads and politely reply *"thank you"* or *"you are welcome"* once again, all the while looking for an escape route, any way to keep moving.

"Thank you for your service," those *five* little words, are left hanging in the air as we escape and watch you carry on about your routine or meal. Smiling. We know what is coming after those dreaded words, whether we want it to or not. *It is coming.*

"Thank you for your service," those *five* little words, as you leave feeling warm, a cold of darkness floods over the Veteran, as it has arrived. Our spouses or loved ones know this dreaded storm is building; they see the cloud drop over the Veteran's face. We will be lost to a flood of memories like a tsunami crashing on shore.

"Thank you for your service," those *five* little words. We lose focus or train of thought for a split second. The wind momentarily knocked from our lungs. Bearings are eschewed, mind needs to be refocused. Trying to stall the inevitable.

"Thank you for your service," those *five* little words, bring: remembrance, pain, sorrow, joy, triumph, loss, regret, hopelessness, and anger in a roaring flash flood. It is not directed at the innocent smiling grateful you, but inwardly as the storm builds. The *"what ifs"* or *"had I done that"* break the dam and envelope our consciousness. We are then at that moment, lost.

"Thank you for your service," those *five* little words. We will have no slumber. We know the dreams will come whether we remember them or not. The bed shakes violently as we convulse in our fragmented sleep. The dreams consist of familiar faces from our time in the dirt. The smiling and laughing faces of the men, dirty and miserable. The faces get blurred or distorted, the laughter gives way to yells or screams.

"Thank you for your service," those *five* little words. The words will still echo within us the next day. Lingering in the air like a haze. We know it will happen again, maybe today or tomorrow but *"thank you for your service"* will come again and again and again. A tireless cycle of exhaustive emotion brought on by a gesture with the best of intentions.

"Thank you for your service," those *five* little words. Are a noble and thoughtful gesture, wrought with gratitude, patriotism, and support. It is one-sided. It is self-serving. 12, 3, 6, and 9 o'clock. Every man at those positions is who we fought for. *Our men.*

The Last Letter

"Thank you for your service," those *five* little words, are better demonstrated through action and policy for Veterans. Ensuring that lawmakers are held accountable for violations against our Constitution and our citizens, all citizens. That is how you thank a Veteran. For, that is all we have left of our time serving, haunted memories and our oath to this great nation.

SSgt. Parkinson Infantry Unit Leader/USMC

CH. 1
INTO THE FOREST

Deep in the lush, green, woods outside of Clear Creek, Idaho, the trees, thick and beautiful, the air smells crisp with the hint of rain, three silhouettes emerge amongst the natural serenity. The men dressed in camouflage, move in a somewhat military style tactical column. Be it on purpose or by experience, the three move in this formation haphazardly with confidence. All have various stages of beards, and all seem lost in their own thoughts, seemingly moving with no particular urgency.

The point man upfront throws up a closed fist, the military sign for *freeze*. All stop.

"Good place for a break and enjoy some nature," the point man suggests. The three drop where they are standing and lean back on their packs for a breather. The terrain is rugged and steep. The view of valley below made the trip worth it in the point man's eyes.

Hydrating with their CamelBaks, the men seem to take in the view all at once and pause to soak in the beautiful terrain.

"Here's a bit of nature for you fellas," laughs the one of the heavily armed men, taking a piss next to a tree.

"You might want to drink more water, James. That's awful yellow." The taller of the three observes to the urinating tactically adorned man, putting more tobacco chew into his mouth, offering some to the leader.

"Fuckin plain nasty, you two. I don't know how you fellas can chew that shit," the point man replies.

"Oh, come on, Sgt. Parks, '*this will make you goddamn sexual tyrannosaurus…just like me*,'" Ian, more affectionately known as Doherty amongst his fellow warriors, replies quoting the movie *Predator*.

"Yeah well, '*strap this on your sore ass, Blain*,'" Parks counters, giving the middle finger to Doherty and quoting the very same movie, the three erupt into boisterous laughter. As each laugh dies off, the men seem once again to drift off into their own private thoughts, soaking in the nature and enjoying the tranquility of it all.

The three served in Iraq together in the same squad. All were infantry Marines, otherwise known as *Grunts*, with Bravo Co. 1/23 out of Louisiana and Texas. That unit would go on to be dubbed the *"Battlin Bastards of al Anbar,"* later shortened to the, *"Bastards of Anbar."* This outing is a planned getaway that only these three could make due to the other members of the squad having obligations to family/careers and could not make the excursion. The point man, the one the other two call Sgt. Parks, a lean, old, bearded *Grunt*, leans over to give his shoulders and back relief from his ruck. The relief is brief, as any infantryman would know. He moans loudly. "Fuck, I hate getting ancient," Parks complains sorely.

"What are you now, Sgt. Parks, sixty-four?" James chides him with an affectionate smile.

"Fuck you. Forty-six." He smiles while spitting his phlegm on the ground. The other two halfheartedly chuckle. Parks, as his men and colleagues would call him, is SSgt. Parkinson; dubbed *"Parks"* by his best friend in the fleet while serving with India Co. 3/5. It became easier for Parkinson's superiors to yell *"Parks"* when he was a boot, that it stuck. So, when he got activated off the *Marine Individual Ready Reserve (IRR)* to join Bravo Co. 1/23, a prior Marine from India Co. was there to continue the tradition. The name would stick. No fresh start for Parks.

"Hey, Sgt. Parks, how far we patrollin?" Doherty asks, wondering, while taking in the beauty of the stop, his easy Louisiana drawl adding to the calm.

"First off, quit calling me *Sgt. Parks* for the last fuckin time." Parks laughs at the continued use of his old title. "Secondly, probably one more click and then time to fuckin bivouac."

The Last Letter

"I'll quit calling you *Sgt. Parks* when you quit saying shit like '*clicks*' and '*bivouac*,'" Doherty says with a big smile, sweat pouring down his rugged face. They all burst out laughing, the sound of peaceful humor echoing down to the valley below.

"Roger that." Parks smiles coyly. "Man, fuck I needed this," The former squad leader exclaims while lighting a cannabis pre-roll. The other two nod in agreement, James shaking his head to Parks' invitation to join him.

Doherty calmly leans on his pack and soaks in the rays of the sunlight peeking through the forest canopy above. "No thanks, brother." Doherty waves his hand declining the joint offered to him by his old, tired squad leader.

The three sit peacefully against their packs, true *Grunt* fashion, and survey the forested, lush valley below.

"Fuck, I'm glad I was able to get away from the fam and the daily work shit to do this," James says to no one in particular. Known as Ryan in the civilian world, he will forever be James to his fellow Marines. He keeps the *James* side of his life hidden from those who know him. He, also bearded, with the gruff exterior of a hardened Marine but a childlike jovial infectious sense of humor that always makes him seem younger than his age; inhales the crisp clean air, a sense of warm relief washing over him. "This has been perfect."

"Shit, I've been run ragged for eight weeks straight. It was time to get out, enjoy some good company and nature. Sgt. Parks, your invite came at the perfect fuckin time," Doherty proclaims, inhaling a deep breath of crisp untainted mountain air.

"I wish more could have made it from 1st Squad, but I understand that all you fuckers have incredibly involved lives now, and stop fuckin calling me *Sgt. Parks*," The former Marine says with a sheepish, weathered smile.

"Fuck, sorry. It's fuckin hard, brother. The last time I saw you, you had picked up staff and then you left the unit. Just habit, Parks." Doherty makes an awkward noise as he tries saying his old squad leader's name. "Nope, don't like it, doesn't sound right." Doherty feigns disgust, all genuinely laugh in appreciation of the joke.

"Sounds like fuckin shit to me as well, Sgt. Parks." James joins in on the humor, giving his old squad leader a hard time.

SSgt. Jacob Parkinson

Parks inhales the clean air and exhales deeply. "Fuck ya both." He looks around the green scenery from under his dark sunglasses, enjoying the moment with his former troops. "You know who would've eaten this shit up? Ol' Delta," Parks says to the other two. James and Doherty nod in agreement.

"That devil would've had on every new piece of gear; his kit would probably be better than any *MARSOC* bubba. Shit, in Iraq he looked like a fuckin *SEAL*. Intimidating the local populace, while the rest of us looked like turtles," Parks continues, laughing at his recollection of one of his team leaders, Sgt. Heisinger, known affectionately by 1st Squad as *Delta*, due to his tactical arrangement of gear during their tour in Iraq. The locals gave Marines the nickname *turtles* due to their old, outdated woodland camouflage flak jackets and coyote brown desert digital uniforms: green body, brown extremities.

James follows up in his soft Texas accent, "Shit, that motherfucker would probably have a drone followin over head of us right now. Sweepin the area ahead." They laugh together once more at the hilarity of the one they call *Delta*.

"Fuck, I miss those days, the best time of my life," Doherty proclaims, stretching his arms up high and adjusting his pack.

"It was the absolute best of my times; nothing will ever top that experience I shared with you men and then *Time* came crashing the fuckin party," Parks states, staring up at the sun peeking through the tree canopy overhead, exhaling his smoke, welcoming the calming effect.

As the beads of sweat roll down their faces, each man seems to be lost in reflections of their tour together in Iraq. They sit quietly but all seem content within their individual reflections, each with a slight grin.

"Yeah, that *combat addiction* is a motherfucker; *she* is an elusive, beautiful, seductive mistress, whisking away in the middle of the night, leavin us yearnin for more," James exclaims. He, too, begins to stretch and get comfortable, his back providing him no relief.

"Look who comes from the *Field of Dreams* and delivers a perfect soliloquy." Parks smacks James proudly on the shoulder chuckling amongst the pines.

"Well, Sgt. Parks what's our plan of attack?" James smiles; he and Doherty laugh, Parks shaking his head at the persistent use of his old rank and name.

The Last Letter

"I really do fuckin hate you two. Do you want a fuckin five paragraph order as well, dickheads?" Parks responds, looking down with a slight blush under his greying beard. "Well, *LCpls*, I figure we head down to that valley below, camp inside the tree-line, across the small river and have the valley spread out in front of us. Hang out by the river, patrol around, enjoy this gorgeous nature for the next couple days."

"Sounds like a good goddamn plan to me," Doherty exclaims, ready to get moving once again. "How far in do think we've gone?"

"According to the GPS, about four miles," James answers his old friend's inquiry.

"That's it? Holy shit, I'm sucking hind tit," Parks says, exhaling his last puff of smoke, taking in the beautiful green of the forest surrounding the three. "Well, we definitely don't have service for jack shit out here," explains Doherty, knowing they would not, as he, too, takes in and absorbs the tranquility of the deep woods outside of Clear Creek, Idaho.

"That's a given. Well, at least you can still take pics for everyone back home, and I'll do the same. Speaking of which, let's do it. Picture time, douchebags." Parks tells them, expecting some resistance from the two, but Doherty and James offer none.

James agreeing to the pictures readily, "Yeah, it is. The guys will love to see this shit when we get back and send them."

Parks huffs slightly, "*'Three fucktards in the woods'* will be the caption the men of Bravo will tag the photos."

James ignores his old squad leader. "Well, no one is goin to fuckin believe how old and bald you got, Sgt. Parks. But hey, no gut and nice grey beard, brother. Thumbs up," James remarks with his trademark charismatic wit.

The group gather in front of the beautiful backdrop of an Idaho forest outside of Clear Creek. Each one taking turns propping up their phones on a fallen tree, setting the timers, then posing for various shots together, most with smiles on the ageing men's faces; all three seem genuinely to enjoy the moment. They gather their phones, sling the packs back over their chest rigs, and pick up their weapons, stacked neatly against a nearby tree; the three take a moment to look over the valley below them, each eager to set camp soon and call it a day.

"What made you pick this forest outside Clear Creek, in bum fuck Idaho?" Doherty asks as he adjusts his three-point sling. "Shiiiiiitttt!" he groans suddenly. "I forgot to get a protein bar out of my pack. Sgt. Parks, would you be a dear and grab one out of my pack for me?" Doherty pleads humorously with Parks.

Parks rolls his eyes at his old troop's request. "Well, if you must know, and I don't want to hear any motard shit from either one of you. I'm killing two birds with one stone on this trip," Parks grumbles, retrieving his friend's protein bar from the ruck. "Here's your shit." He gives a smiling Doherty the bar with a pat on the back of his tactical vest. Parks' annoyance is in reference to every *Grunt* hating those words muttered by another during a field op or a hump *"hey, will you grab something from my pack."* Every infantryman hates it, but they are all guilty of it.

Adjusting his own pack on his sore shoulders, Parks continues, "After the Osprey crash in 2000 my unit, India 3/5, was idle again and we were doing fuck-all but sitting in the field, training, distracting the unit after the crash; I can see that now and wisely so. Anyway, I was sitting with command in the field, all of us were laying against our packs, blouses open soaking in the ballshot SoCal sun, and then suddenly the RO gets a call from battalion instructing India to hump our ass back to the barracks. We didn't give a fuck how far, it meant early ENDEX for the company and getting the fuck out of the field." Parks fondly recollects the *end of exercise* on that hot day.

Both James and Doherty seem content to hear the rest of the story, absorbing the cleansing mountain air, rejuvenating their tired, aching bodies from the hike into the forest. The years have not been kind to bodies of the former infantrymen.

"Continue…." James urges Parks, stalling the inevitable movement down into the valley.

"Fuck, where the hell was I?" Parks asks himself. "Oh yeah, we get to the barracks late that afternoon, turn in weapons to the armorers and stand by, per fuckin usual." Parks inhales another round of smoke and exhales patiently. "We get word that Idaho has a massive wildfire, and they're shorthanded hotshot crews, so India Co. is going to get a crash course in basic wildland firefighting, wildfire safety, and critical lifesaving steps in case you get caught in

a firestorm. Which is a real fuckin thing, by the way. What the fuck did a bunch of Grunts know about fighting a wall of fire? We were excited because it meant leaving Camp Pendleton for a bit. Besides, I was almost out anyway at that point. *'Oh, man… and I was getting short. Four more weeks and out. Now I'm going to bite it on this rock. It ain't fair, man!'"* Parks smiles quoting the beloved Bill Paxton from the movie *Aliens*, a staple favorite among Marine infantry. James and Doherty immediately recognize the quote and laugh.

Doherty stretches. "Fuckin classic, Sgt. Parks." He smiles over to his old squad leader who always had a knack for remembering inconsequential movie lines.

James, staring ahead down into the green, open valley below, "What the fuck? That's crazy?"

"Yeah, man, I thought so. We get training for about two days, shipped up here to Clear Creek, Idaho and battled that fire for a month straight, cutting lines. It was goddamn amazing. The forest that was not burnt was absolutely majestic, yes, I said *majestic*, fuckers." Parks ignores the looks of the other two Marines and gazes down into the lush valley below. "I wanted to see what it looked like all these years later and as you can see it is breathtakingly beautiful. Idaho, who knew?" Parks finishes his recounting of India Co's adventure as wildland firefighters for a month in the Marine Corps.

"Well, the Idahoans, Sgt. Parks," James quips continuing his stare down below.

"Yut." Doherty seconds James's sentiment with the customary Marine response.

Parks exhales in faux frustration from the chiding at the hands of his two former Marines. "Yes, I suppose they do. The Clear Creek community welcomed us with open arms, and it was awesome to see that level of appreciation." His stare continues, Parks begins to lose focus into the blur of memory, "An absolute ass kicker of an assignment, though. The actual hotshots that led us were goddamn ironmen; fuckers could hike circles around us going up and down these mountains and they were around our age now," Parks concludes, looking out at the breathtaking view of the valley.

"Well, our age, right Sgt. Parks?" James replies with wry smile pointing at himself and Doherty.

"Fuck you." Parks says, smiling and flipping him off before he hunches over to adjust his pack straps one last time before they get going. Parks looks for that *Grunt sweet spot* of comfort that every infantryman tries to find for his gear before stepping off once more.

"No, thank you. You may be in shape, but you're beyond cougar age. Let's do this," James replies, adjusting his AR-15 and leg holster, housing his .45 cal Smith & Wesson M&P, to make both weapons comfortable for the downhill trek to base camp. Doherty and Parks wearing similar weaponry and gear, do the same.

"Hardee, hardee, har, har. I take back ever trying to write you up for a combat decoration." Parks laughs, rebuking James's insult.

The three enjoy the two-hour hike down farther into the valley, taking their time to enjoy nature and being together once again, a scene reminiscent of their long forgotten past. Approaching the valley floor and look over the expansive clearing laid out before them, they stop at the edge of the tree-line, soaking in the sights and sounds the three can detect. Pausing in silence, remaining concealed, listening for any sounds that might signal an anomaly amongst the serenity of this natural backdrop.

"I'll take point across the valley and river. We'll set up camp in the opposite tree-line." Parks whispers aloud; the other two chuckle to each other.

"Some things never change." James offers, with a shake of his head. Doherty pats his old leader on the back of his chest rig reassuringly.

"We made sure to come between deer seasons, we should be fine." Doherty knows it is instinct instilled from years of training and experience in the infantry realm.

"Hey, man, what if some fucktard with an itchy trigger finger is waiting for some movement to fire at? Fuckin poaching shitbags. So, let me get out about 200 meters then follow suit with sixty-meter dispersions on the flanks." They erupt with laughter after a pause, Doherty and James shaking their heads, Parks suddenly feeling overzealous and embarrassed.

The old squad leader heads out into the clearing about 200 meters and stops. Parks takes it all in, the green forest, clean air, and the calming sounds of the slow-moving river ahead. It is magnificent. Parks smiles slightly, a sense peace finally in years. His troubled past cannot follow him to this tranquility. Parks turns to signal the others to move forward.

Doherty and James follow suit; all three then make their way across the *danger area*, across the small clear river, then breaching the opposite tree-line of the meadowed clearing without incident. They begin to set up camp, each with one-man tents. Parks then begins to stack wood to build a fire. Having already dug a pit with his E-tool[1], another fabled *Grunt* staple.

"Fuck that was brutal. I'm about to die," James exclaims after setting up his tent and crashing down on his ruck next to the firepit. "You sure as shit don't look tired, Sgt. Parks, you old, in-shape, dick."

Doherty, too, crashes down on his ruck after setting up his tent, exhaling with exhaustion. "Yeah, what the fuck, Sgt. Parks?" The warm late September sun provides Doherty with much needed energy.

"Stop calling me, Sgt. Parks, dicks. I'm hurting, you assholes." Parks continues to stack the wood until satisfied; he then places a fire start and lights the package. It will not be long before the warmth is felt from the small inferno. He watches the fire-start begin to ignite the kindling; the tiny budding flames hold the old squad leader in a slightly comfortable trance. "When I first stopped drinking, I had all this extra energy and anger from the withdrawals; so, I took up boxing," Parks replies, spitting out some phlegm. James and Doherty look at each other with humored skepticism. "Oh, fuck you two, don't give me those looks."

"What look? Oh you, mean this look." Doherty gives Parks the *Kevin from Home Alone* surprise face.

"Yeah, that look, ass. No, I took up the training of a boxer, not the actual fighting and I'm way too old to get bent into a pretzel by some young buck learning MMA. My fuckin shoulders and joints would snap like twigs. Boxing is all about endurance; that killed my cravings for booze. I was way too fuckin tired to drink. I would box a couple of rounds, get my ass kicked by the younger, faster turds and repeat, wearing myself down," Parks counters, slowly and painfully lowering himself to the ground. "See, you fucks, I hurt too, just like your asses."

---

[1] Folding shovel issued to infantrymen

James looks over from under his boonie cover, "Well, whatever fuckin works. You're definitely not suckin hind tit, like we are. A little heads-up and my ass would have at least trained a bit for this excursion, Sgt. Parks." he says coyly, readjusting the boonie cover to lay over his eyes, nestling farther down on his pack, trying to find that *sweet spot* of comfort.

"Hey, I had to compensate for my bald head. At least the both of you have a beautiful full head of hair. You with your luxurious dirty-blond locks and Doherty's wavy, full brown hair. I look like a bearded Mr. Clean, fuck you both." Parks smiles to James. "I once sparred another Veteran, six two-minute rounds. I couldn't move my body for two goddamn days. Thought I was dead. Never fuckin again."

James comments dryly, "How many times did you have to stop the fight to pee?" James asks, referring to Parks' notoriously known small bladder.

"Once between each round, maybe. Fuck all that extra exertion shit, right, Sgt. Parks?" Doherty laughs, a hearty laugh at the expense of his old squad leader. He, too, has been looking forward to this outing with his old Marine buddies from Bravo Co. 1/23. To Doherty, this is a good close to his Marine past. He knows his focus must lie on his loved ones and their love for him. His life finally feels purposeful again.

"You two are dicks." Parks blushes under his thick grey beard, still entranced by the growing flames of the fire. The flowing breeze from the valley blows through the tree-line adding much needed fuel to the controlled inferno. The men settle in for what seems an eternity, staring out at the open valley from whence they crossed. It is all serene and calm. Everything the men need at this particular moment in their lives. The silence is welcome amongst the three; it is a comfortable, easy calm.

James suddenly laughs to himself, breaking the tranquility of the moment. "I remember big-ass Culpepper checkin into the unit. No one knew who the fuck he was. He had been *UA* since day fuckin one. Every formation for roll call, they would announce his name, then quickly followed by '*UA*' from his squad leader. Big-ass, scary son of a bitch." James again chuckles to himself, remembering his old teammate from 1st Squad. "Shit, there was even a rumor Culpepper was awaiting trial for manslaughter and decided to go to war in the meantime." The three chuckle softly at James's recollection of their former squad mate.

"Remember that fuckin door breacher we had with us? What did we call that fuckin thing?" Doherty asks the others, trying desperately to search his memory bank for the answer that eludes him.

Staying perfectly relaxed under his woodland camouflage boonie cover, James responds coolly, "The Bitch."

Doherty smiles slightly hearing the answer from James. "That's right, *The Bitch*. Fuckin thing was heavy; no one wanted to carry that heavy fuckin thing. Culpepper's monstrous ass picks up the damn thing and holds it out with one arm, like it was a paperweight. All of us troops right then instantly agreed not to fuck with his big ass. No sir." More subdued laughter erupts from the three friends, each settlin in for the night's stay.

"I remember you checkin into the unit, Sgt. Parks, after getting snatched off the street and activated." James begins the memory of his introduction for the first time to his old squad leader.

Parks keeps his gaze transfixed on the small fire as it grows larger, "Yeah, that was a surreal phone call to receive. '*Sgt. Parkinson?*' I knew then. 'Yes, sir?' '*You are activated off the IRR, report to Bravo Co. 1/23,*' at such and such time. Immediately, I thought, '*my mom is not going to like this,*' and she didn't. No mother did."

James peeks up from under his boonie, "Sgt. Parks shows up, tells us you're our new squad leader. You then go PT, and we see you doin curls in the squat rack, building up those .50 cal biceps back then." James smiles referring to his old squad leader's arm workout, another typical staple among infantry units, there is always time for physical training. "My skinny ass couldn't keep up with you in PT."

Parks turns to look at his old, relaxed troop, "James, I was angry for being activated to the goddamn reserves. I wanted to go back to my old unit, India 3/5. No offense, fellas, but back then no active duty Marine wanted to go to war with fuckin reservists."

Doherty feigns hurt feelings, by clutching his heart. "You say such hurtful things, Sgt. Parks."

Laughing at Doherty's faux hurt feelings, Parks tries to backtrack. "You know what I mean. You motherfuckers from 1st Squad, are the best damn *Grunt*s I have ever had the pleasure to chew sand with, I wouldn't trade my time with you men for fuck all."

"Aww. Sgt. Parks you shouldn't have." James mocks his old friend with his charismatic smile and wit. "I got pissed at you for puttin Perry as my team leader, I hated you for that. He and I did not get along, ever. But you eventually fired Perry as team leader, then put me and Culpepper with you as *Team OFP*. Me and Culpepper fuckin loved you for that; then he and I became cocky motherfuckers after." James grabs a cigar from his pack and begins to light up the flavorful tobacco. The aroma wafts over the campsite offering a pleasant smell to the tired men.

Parks keeps his focus on the clearing the men crossed as dusk begins to creep upon the valley. "Ah yes, your famed team *On Fucking Point*, moniker for us. Culpepper hated that bullshit."

James smiles, taking a deep inhale of his cigar. "Well, it was true. We were always on fuckin point, Sgt. Parks." He exhales a larger circular ring of smoke, amazing the other two.

"He's right, Sgt. Parks. You did always take point and you know that," Doherty seconds James' sentiment.

Parks hangs his head low to his chest, he then inhales deeply, he is tired of hearing his former title, how can he explain to his men, he is no longer *Sgt. Parks*, nor does he want to be.

"First, James, I did not fire Perry, he came back from his assignment at the haji prison after our first firefight in Hiit. By then the squad was not TO[2], there were only eleven of us, it was easier to roll Perry in with Delta's team. During a firefight a squad leader essentially takes command of the fire team he maneuvers with, anyway. Besides Culpepper was the RO, he needed to stick with me at all times, you were a floating SAW[3] gunner and I'm not goin to throw you in with another team with a SAW." He inhales the sweet tobacco fragrance hangin in the air from James' cigar. "It tactically made sense to break 1st Squad

---

[2] Typical ordinance
[3] Squad Automatic Weapon

The Last Letter

down that way. Secondly, you young devils had enough to worry about without the added responsibility of point man. It was just fuckin easier if I did it. If something happened, the fuckup was on me and not you. Simple."

"That's why we love you, you old bastard. Troop welfare is your number one." James lowers his boonie back over his eyes once again.

Doherty slaps Parks on the back of his chest rig, "Yut," he says softly to his former squad leader.

Parks keeps his gaze on the setting sun. "Yeah well, you men conquered every fuckin mission put before you; there was no need for me to worry about mission accomplishment. Gunny *Dickless* Daisy hated every fuckin tactical decision I ever made, POGe[4] motherfucker."

"Fuck that piece of shit. I remember *Dickless* tellin us he has killed many men in the line of duty on the police force. After further research of the pussy, turns out he actually went around undercover soliciting other dudes for hand jobs and glory hole fun, just so he could arrest the poor bastards for male prostitution. *#motherfuckinhero*," James grumbles, his everlasting resentment for his former platoon commander becoming palpable to the other two old Marines.

Doherty chuckles to himself at James' dismay, "Easy killer, why don't you tell us how you really feel about *ol Dickless*?" He pulls a cigar of his own from his ruck, smiles at Parks, and lights the sweet-smelling tobacco product. "Smells a whole of lot better than the shit you smoke, Sgt. Parks." Doherty points to the cannabis pre-roll in Parks' hand.

"I concur." Inhaling his own waft of smoke, Parks acknowledges his old troop with a turn of his head and a slight nod.

James continues to grumble from underneath his boonie cover, "I remember gettin to Fort Polk and some fuckin genius, *Dickless*, decided to give me the SAW, even though I'm a multi-champion competitive shooter with the AR."

Parks laughs aloud at James' frustrations persisting still over two decades later, being assigned the squad automatic weapon. "Devil, I tried to get you assigned the *sixteen*. I brought up that very fuckin fact about you being a competitive shooter to *Dickless* and it was a waste putting you on the SAW. You want to know what his exact fuckin response was?"

---

[4] *Person Other than Grunt. (p-oh-g)* Derogatory term used to describe non infantry personnel

"Man, fuck that dude," Doherty chimes in while exhaling a huge, beautiful plume of white cigar smoke into the fading evening air.

James competes with Doherty and releases his own large cloud of sweet-smelling cigar smoke, "Yeah, I want to hear this bullshit. Why wasn't I assigned the *sixteen*, Sgt. Parks."

Parks turns to face his angered troop, who is now looking up at him, "Brace yourself, Devil, and I quote, *'good then James will be able to provide accurate suppressive fire.'* There you go, that was *Dickless's* reasoning giving you the SAW."

"Accurate suppressive fire! What a fuckin idiot! Suppressive fire is not supposed to be fuckin accurate. It's supposed to be suppressive, so the accurate shooters can put down the targets! What the fuck? I hate that fuckin guy, so fuckin much, Sgt. Parks." James declares, bolting upright, seething with rage. Parks and Doherty burst out laughing at James's furious reaction, still sensitive about the SAW two decades later. The boisterous laughter echoes through the surrounding valley, the natural backdrop absorbing the positive energy being displaced.

"Relax, Devil, I know you do. We all fuckin hate that man. That right there is a prime example of why. He did that shit to be a dick to you, not because it was some great tactical decision, just pure immature spite from a little bitch of a man. In the fleet, I was given free rein to assign weapons as I deemed fit within my squad. *Dickless* was a POGe motherfucker through and through." Parks tries to alleviate James' fury on the subject.

"Fuck him. I remember openin the crates that the SAWs were in and finding them submerged in water. All of them completely fuckin rusted." James relaxes back down on his ruck and begins puffing on his cigar. "I find mine and you immediately chew my ass for having a rusted weapon, Sgt. Parks. Gave me fire watch for a week. Fuck me, right? Semper Fi."

"It made you stronger, brother," Parks replies with a wry smile, staring once again into the merging fire. The flames beginning to ascend higher than the pile of stacked forest wood, the warmth spreading to the men on the burgeoning Northern Idaho evening. "Besides, I carried that bitch for two years as a boot," Parks refers to his own experience with the SAW during his early career in the Marines.

James huffs in disagreement, "Not in combat, Sgt. Parks."

"He has you there, Sgt. Parks," Doherty agrees with his old squad mate, James.

Parks hangs his head in mock surrender. "Touché."

Continuing to exhale large amounts of fragrant cigar smoke into the forested air, James continues his tale of woe with the automatic weapon. "Anyway, I got really proficient with that fucker, no one could touch me." Doherty looks over to Parks, smiles and rolls his eyes, Parks does the same, as if to say, *"oh here we go."* The disgruntled former Marine catches the slight looks of his old friends, "Fuck you guys, I saw that shit. No one could touch me; we did that SAW gunner challenge on the firin line. Fire, run back to a different firin point, change barrels, fire some more. Sgt. Parks, you were behind me screamin your ass off for me to hurry the fuck up and change my barrel." James exhales his last puff of the cigar before throwing it in the fire, "I open the spare barrel bag, reach in and pulled it out, quick as shit without lookin; all of you fucks were laughin your asses off. It wasn't my spare barrel, you dicks put a big black rubber cock, the size of a fuckin pringles can in my spare barrel bag." James chuckles to himself, enjoying the growing warmth of the fire.

Parks smiles trying to remember the scene, and Doherty laughs his customary spirited laugh. "That was great. I forgot whose idea that was, but he is a fuckin hero for thinkin of it." Doherty lowers his own boonie cover over his eyes as the sun begins setting farther behind the ridgeline.

"Yeah, well, fuck that dude for thinkin of it. There is no tellin how many days I humped that damn thing around without knowin. Assholes." James once again smiles his blond-bearded smile, his Southern drawl becoming more pronounced the more relaxed he becomes. More subdued laughter from the three friends. Each relishing the chance to reflect on their memories without the judgment of others.

"You remember trainin at *29 Palms* in that balls-hot, death-dealin heat? Goddamn that was brutal," Doherty exclaims, exhaling heavily.

Parks agreeing with his old troop, says, "Yeah, man, that was. In all my years in the fleet, I had never trained at *29 Palms* in the summer until then. All my training was done for CAX in December and then it was death-dealin cold. I never experienced cold like that before, not even in mountain warfare training, not even freezing my balls off the coast of the Pacific in boat company. So, desert training at the *'Stumps'* in the summer was a new fuckin experience for me, Devils." He shivers from the memory of the cold at the Marine desert training center, commonly referred to as the *Stumps* by infantry Marines.

"Yeah, left over unexploded ordinance every-fuckin-where. Afraid if I dropped into the prone, I would detonate some old fuckin mine and then *Boom!* No more Doherty, Sgt. Parks be writin my mama. *Dear Ms. Doherty, your son is dead because the Marines are too lazy to police their own shit.*" Doherty scoffs at the memory of the live-fire ranges designed for infantry personnel.

James huffs along with his fellow Marine. "Ain't that the truth, brother. Unexploded ordinance and swarms of fuckin killer bees. I had no clue if I was allergic or not, never been stung by one. Little shits."

Parks chuckles slightly, "Those fuckin bees. Hanging out by the water bowls[5], swarming any Marine trying to refill their CamelBaks. Getting inside the drinking nozzles of our hoses." Parks suddenly getting the chills down his spine from the memory. "I remember having to pull fuckin bees out by their wings before I took a sip of my goddamn water. Marines getting stung in the mouth. Little motherfuckers."

"Culpepper on guard duty by the water bowl getting his ass swarmed by those little vicious motherfuckers. He starts panickin, swingin his weapon and flak jacket around wildly, tryin to keep the little bastards from attackin him." James fondly remembering his old squad mate's dilemma in the middle of the desert. All three suddenly laugh at the image of their massive squad mate running wild from the little winged creatures.

Doherty peeks up, looks out across the clearing they crossed earlier, "I remember seeing his big ass, running across the desert droppin his gear as he ran from the water bowl, screamin profanities. I turn to Sgt. Parks, *'would you look at that.'*" More laughter from the three ageing Marines.

"What the fuck was that all about? I'm goin to ask the big bastard at the next reunion for Bravo Co. I see him at," James exclaims from underneath his boonie.

Parks adjusts his own pack behind him and sits up staring into the trance-like flames, "Good times, brothers."

---

[5] Large, steel wheeled containers designed to carry large amounts of water to Marines in the field

The Last Letter

"Yut." Doherty echoes the sentiment amongst the two with that simple Marine phrase. He throws his cigar into the fire, then closes his eyes, soaking in the crisp evening mountain air.

The three sit in silence, listening to the crackling of the small fire, the sounds of their forested surroundings, and steady flow of the quaint river in the clearing. James finally breaks their doldrum, the other two welcome the distraction from their own thoughts, "Victorville Air Force base was pretty good real-world application trainin all around in prep for Iraq looking back with hindsight now. By this point we were really coming together as a squad. Good fuckin trainin, still don't know why we busted up every toilet in the houses or buildings, not sure how or why that shit got started. But I'm glad we left our mark." James smiles proudly to himself.

Parks keeps his gaze fixed on the dancing flames of the campfire. "Yeah, you men were coming together nicely as a squad. I remember on a night training evolution, the platoon got ambushed by the aggressors and 1st Squad repelled the enemy's assault by fire and maneuver, in true fuckin Marine rifle squad fashion."

"Yut," Both Doherty and James echo.

"During the debrief, the aggressors fuckin praise our actions and then *Dickless* gives all the credit to Stockwell's squad during his debrief, just to be an asshole," Parks concludes angrily.

Doherty looks over to his angry old squad leader, still harboring hatred for their platoon commander for two long decades. "*Dickless* was a true fuckin piece of shit." The other two nod silently in agreement.

James then quietly laughs, "That's where Culpepper came up with our platoon slogan. Remember that shit, Sgt. Parks?" He looks to his old squad leader for affirmation.

"Yep, you're right. The squad was taking a break on the backside of Victorville, away from *Dickless*. I remember discussing that it's going to suck when we get to Iraq, having to kick in doors, then listen to the loved ones scream and cry as we snatch up their military age males at *zero dark thirty*. And what did Culpepper say in response, in his slow Louisianan drawl?" the squad leader responds with a mischievous smile.

"*'They can get over it or die pissed.'*" Both James and Doherty recite joyously.

The evening finally emerges and begins to cast a dark shadow on the men's surroundings, offering more solace and reclusion from their troubles back home. "Thank you, Sgt. Parks for setting this up, I really needed to do this, get it all out of my system." Doherty warmly explains.

Parks continuing his gaze into the fire, offers his former troop, "Nothing to thank me for. Trust me, brother, I needed this more than both of you know. Thank you two for making an old squad leader feel at peace for once. It is appreciated beyond words."

Nothing need to be spoken, the solace is comforting and welcome, each begin to drift into their own memories of their time together in Iraq. Nature comes alive around the weary men as the night sky darkens. This is why the men came on the excursion, the promise of much sought after peace.

CH. 2
DOHERTY AND THE GOAT

"Man, I got to call the missus. I promised I would check in every night and say hi to the kiddos," James exclaims before digging out his satellite phone with a coy smile. "Never leave on an adventure without one." His full bearded smile becomes contagious as the other two smile as well, not at the quip but being in the moment and absorbing the camaraderie.

"Fuckin smart, man," Parks says still leaned against his pack, enjoys the fire's warmth on this fall Northern Idaho evening.

"Yeah, it is, can I use it to call mine as well, brother?" Doherty asks his old squad mate.

"Absolutely. Parks?" James replies cordially then gesturing to his squad leader if he would like to use the phone along with Doherty.

"No, I'm good. My kids expect me to call when I get out of the woods and have service, and no to the missus, I'm not suitable for fuck all." Parks states, suddenly emotionless and drained. It startles the other two Marines, the sudden change in tone from their ageing squad leader.

"Well, if you need to, feel free," James offers over his shoulder, heading towards the river to make his call to his awaiting loved ones back in East Texas.

"I should have got a fuckin sat-phone for this. I did get a new GPS; it took my son to help me figure out some shit and then a month for me to get comfortable with the damn thing. Technology today, brother, it's fuckin insane. The GPSs, the Marines issued back then were monstrous," Parks says, sitting back, leaning on his pack, lighting a joint, and stares after James by the river, then back at Doherty, "Hey, brother, thanks again for joining me on this bullshit outing. Means a lot."

"Aww, shit, Sgt. Parks, no worries. James and I both needed this shit too. I do wish some of the others had made the trip, some need this as well, brother." Doherty then erupts with laughter while turning to Parks, "Remember when fuckin Sgt. Heis got our team lost on that patrol because his batteries ran out on his personal GPS, and he didn't have his compass."

"Holy fuckin shit that was hilarious! Delta is damn lucky that Culpepper doesn't have an itchy trigger finger and didn't put a round through Heis's head at about 200 meters out, *zero dark thirty*, middle of Dulaab." Parks, laughing and coughing at the same time, reveling in the memory of one of his team leader's follies.

"Always *zero dark thirty*. I didn't know where we were goin, I just followed Sgt. Heis." Doherty chuckles softly at the humorous memory of his team leader.

Parks sits quietly to himself trying to remember the details from so long ago. "It was a simple patrol order, your team was to take the right side of Dulaab, I take the middle with Culpepper and James, and Morales's team heads left," He explains, still smiling broadly. "My team was the only one that had to go across any fuckin terrain. Your teams only had to shadow the roads that skirted the perimeter of Dulaab. That was it, simple. Delta's fuckin batteries die. Classic, Delta. See, technology does have a weakness, needs power. Hey, I can't talk, I fucked up sight alignment on that bridge a couple patrols later, when Heis told me the right direction before we stepped off." Parks chuckles to himself.

"Hey, we got it right sort of," Doherty defends his old team leader, Delta. "It was easy since we were familiar with Dulaab from day one or should've been. That was after Schick was blown up and you started taking us outside the wire of the fuckin place. How Schick lived through that is beyond me. Fuckin Russian anti-tank mines. Remember that crazy shit, Sgt. Parks?" Doherty is caught by the flames of the fire, getting lost in the orange glow.

Parks exhales heavily at the sound of his old title, "Yeah, I remember. The order that came down to me was that Major Miller wanted blood for what happened to Schick, and we damn sure were not going to get it sitting inside the wire of Dulaab. So, it was time to think outside the box. Besides complacency kills, remember." They both smile at the motto that was widely plastered all over Iraq: *"complacency kills."* Means be proactive at all costs or that was Parks' interpretation of the widespread slogan.

"Hey, what did I miss?" James asks, plopping down against his ruck, returning from his call to his wife and daughters.

"Fuckin reminiscing about how Culpepper almost blew Delta's head off at *zero dark thirty* on that simple patrol." Parks responds to James who is trying to find that *Grunt sweet spot* once again to rest.

James moans uncomfortably adjusting his back. "Oh, you mean when his batteries went out on his GPS. Fuckin Sgt. Heis and all his wonderful little toys." They all laugh in unison, warmly, affectionately at the memory of their beloved squad mate. "Hey, brother can I use your sat-phone to call the ol lady?" Doherty asks

James politely.

"Absolutely, Devil," James responds tossing the phone to Doherty. He stands up, heads off to the river, as James had done earlier; to gain some privacy and to soak in the beautiful scenery while talking to his dear loved one.

Parks stares ahead over the openness of the valley and revels in the changing of the colors of the grass, trees, and even the falling leaves have him distracted. The former infantryman looks off past the river, becoming transfixed by the appearing stars above. He marvels at the clarity and brightness of the balls of light flickering in the evening sky. Parks desperately wishes he could change so many things from his past, but he pushes that aside to be thankful for the moment he is in with his two dear friends.

"What're you ponderin on?" James asks, finally finding his comfort once again against his pack nestled by the warm fire.

"Oh, not really anything, remembering the last time I was here and how everything was scorched Earth back then. It really is amazing how nature recovers, as long as man doesn't fuck it up," Parks replies matter-of-factly.

"I'm lookin forward to kickin back, starin up at the stars, and tellin some bullshit," James offers, smiling from underneath his boonie cover. He welcomes the encroaching night air's comfortable embrace after a long day of hiking.

"I concur. Fuck, I wish more of the guys could've made it out for this." Parks watches Doherty pace back and forth by the river talking to his fiancée, listening to her encouraging, loving words.

Doherty returns from his call after about twenty minutes, smiling warmly, encouraged by the conversation. With the camp set inside the tree-line and the firepit built outside, the three have their rucks to lean on next to the warm, glowing flames. The men stare at the fire for a few minutes, not saying a word, indulging in the moment with old friends.

"What the hell was it like here durin the fire? Shit, I think I was still in middle school when that happened?" Doherty asks, staring at his surroundings in wonderous amazement at the recovery of the landscape.

"Shit, me too." James adds with a crooked smile.

"Yeah, I'm fucking old, I know. When we were here fighting the fires, man all I remember is the grueling up and down cutting of line in the mountains." Parks look about the scenery. "Those fuckin hotshots are the *Grunts* of firefighting. Endless days and nights, just cutting line, nothing else," Parks responds, staring into the fire. "All this was black and burnt." He waves his hand, motioning over the valley before the three tired men.

"Did you see some burnin bears and shit, like that one fuckin movie," James says with a chuckle at the absurdity of Hollywood portrayals.

Parks, staring up at the opposite side of the valley explains, "My whole platoon was resting one night with our Hotshot unit leader, in a valley much like this one. The other side was just fuckin ablaze, a monstrous wall of flame, and we were all mesmerized by this wall of fire that we were getting ready to start digging lines against. Then all off sudden we hear a horrible agonizing scream, never heard anything like it, ever; the Hotshot says, *'Look up, you guys see that darting fireball'*, we look and see this orange ball of fire zigzagging across the mountainside. *'It's an elk on fire, we'll hear the screams until he burns.'* It was goddamn terrible," Parks explains, looking into the hypnotic flames of the campfire.

"Thanks a lot for the *Debbie Downer* shit right there, Sgt. Parks," James quips, staring into the fire, imagining the scene.

"Hey, you fuckin asked," Parks states plainly.

James scoffs, "The fuck I did, Sgt. Parks. Doherty asked."

The Last Letter

"Had I fuckin known Sgt. Parks was goin to depress the shit out of us, I wouldn't have." Doherty laughs, slowly, his gaze is caught by the rhythmic dance of the flames.

The former Marine remains silent, still internally grimacing at the mention of his old rank, *Sgt. Parks*. How does he explain to his beloved men that he loathes that name and title. Parks has failed to live up to the standard set forth by his former self, the *Sgt. Parks*, everyone expects and remembers. "Fuckin movies. Just like in fuckin *The Hurt Locker* all the wires were this nice fucking thick bright red. Never fuckin saw that once, a damn nice bright red wire, all the wires I cut were fuckin comm wire[6], tricky little fuckers. Thank God, Del Vecchio has those eagle eyes of his." Parks retorts with a huff of grimacing disdain.

"How many IEDs we find that day, Sgt. Parks, sixteen or some shit?" James asks with pride, still hidden under his boonie, fighting the urge to drift off to a restful sleep.

Parks keeps his gaze fixated on the flames, "I stopped counting after the tenth one I cut." He lets out a deep sigh. "The scary ones were the triple stacks with the propane tanks. That was an eye-opener when I saw that for the first fuckin time."

"I still don't know how the fuck you just went up and cut those wires, Sgt. Parks, crazy-ass motherfucker." Doherty states, fondly remembering that day over twenty years ago.

Parks does not break his gaze from the fire, "EOD couldn't make it, I had no choice." He is emotionless, his face weathered and scarred; betrays nothing of his struggles within.

"Yeah, that whole day was fucked, Sgt. Parks." James lets out a deep sigh.

Doherty fixated by the flames, simply, quietly concurs with his old friend, "Yeah, that was a long fuckin day." The three sit in silence; it is a comfortable, withdrawn, silence, each lost in their own memories from that grueling day.

"How's the fam, Doherty?" James asks, breaking the silence after several long minutes.

"Good, brother. Thanks for the use of the phone," Dougherty answers. He rummages through his pack, pulls out an MRE, and begins to prep his dinner.

---

[6] Thin, copper, almost invisible wire used by the US military

"Look at that fuckin shit! That's some fancy shit right there! What flavor is that?" James asks, his eyes bugging out, looking at Doherty's MRE, propping his boonie cover up on his forehead.

"Fuck you, my woman found these on Amazon just for this trip. She was excited for me to go; says I haven't gotten excited for anythin in a long time, and it was nice for her to see. That made me tear up a little because I know I've been in a haze for a bit, and she just wants to see me smile. So, Cass got all into this shit. She started learnin how to work the GPS along with me and helped me get all my old gear together. To be honest, it was good to be in the moment with her; we even went to the range to fire my weapons, I was reluctant because I haven't fired a fuckin weapon since the Marines, but she made me relax. She's a damn good shot, man. Cass didn't want me missin a bear if it comes chargin at us, brother, I don't deserve her, I'm extremely lucky, and she's made me a better man for it." Doherty says with stoic conviction, his slow drawl softening a bit, reflecting on the fun conversation, he had with his fiancée on the rifle range.

"Good for you and her, man. That sounds really nice, brother. It's good to see. Hold onto that tranquility and don't take her love for granted because if you do, it'll be gone, and you'll have no one to blame but your fuckin self." Parks replies, staring off towards the dark banks of the slow-moving river.

James looks over to his former squad leader. "Goddamn, Sgt. Parks, you are the old man of regret. Smoke another, let's put a smile on that unhappy face." He winks at his old friend.

Parks smiles slightly, giving James the middle finger. He looks to Doherty. "You two planning on having kids?"

"Actually, Sgt. Parks, just found out she's pregnant with our first." Doherty replies with a large smile under his full scraggly beard.

"Holy shit, brother. That's fuckin great, man." Parks follows up emerging from the doldrum that was beginning to sap his energy.

"Congrats, brother. You better hope it's not a girl. I have two and it's nothing but 24/7 worry. You have to fear every man that comes into their lives as a potential threat. It's a beautiful nightmare." James deadpans about the daunting task of fatherhood.

Parks nods his head in agreement. "I concur. You have to protect them from men like myself. That's my biggest fear—my daughter will end up with someone like her father. It's a fuckin nightmare." He looks to the fire for escape from his trepidations.

"Thanks, dickheads, for the frightful pep talk. Damn, let me enjoy the moment, assholes." Doherty laughs at the two friends.

"So, what fuckin flavor, MRE?" James asks, trying to change the subject to keep his squad leader from traveling down a depressing path. He wonders to himself why Parks is seemingly trying to drive his persona into the ground. James shrugs it off hoping the change of subject will bring back his jovial friend.

"Chicken Catchatorre," Doherty exclaims in a horrible Italian accent. "You?"

"I have Vegetable Manicotti for the next few days. Why mess with what I know's in the package and will tolerate for three to four days?" James replies while ripping into his own MRE.

"Sgt. Parks?" Doherty asks, looking to his distracted squad leader.

Parks barely registers the question, his attention on the flames, "I have chicken and rice, as well as a variation of escalloped potatoes and ham." He smiles ever so slightly under his greying beard. "Which I used to love back when they came in the brown bags. Leftover MREs from the '80s. Chalky-ass M&Ms falling out as dust. Everythin a growing boy needs." He replies with a bit of nostalgia, feeling his mood changing for the better, snapping the grip his depression currently lords over him.

"Yeah, we know. All you former active-duty fucks would ever talk about is, how good we had it with the new pink MREs." James counters, he and Doherty laugh in agreement.

"Yeah, yeah. Touché. Broken fuckin record, I get it. Well, get used to it, ass. These next few days are going to be nothing but beautiful scenery and bullshit tales," a smiling Parks replies while lighting up a new pre-roll, hoping his mood will improve. With that, the three seem to settle into a trance of reflection, staring into the fire as a flood of similar memories wash over them simultaneously.

After a few peaceful, silent moments, James speaks up, still under the relaxing canopy of his boonie cover, "I was thinkin about that mounted patrol we went on outside of Dulaab, one of our first, and of course Sgt. Parks went off-script."

"Yeah, I remember that patrol, and I wasn't off-script. I was conducting a show of force in our AO[7]." Parks gives a coy smile into the hypnotic dancing flames.

James scoffs, "Call it what you want, Sgt. Parks, I call it *John Wayne* shit."

It is Parks' turn to scoff at James' suggestion. Parks always had a method for his madness and that was to ensure troop welfare. Which started by keeping his Marines alert and non-complacent, meaning to the former squad leader, going off-script was integral for the experience of his men. "Call it what you want, Devil."

James nods towards his old squad leader. "Yep, *John Wayne* shit, it is. Any-fuckin-way, I remember we do a security halt outside that shithole village after talkin to the Bravo Marines at the Dulaab gate. Just sittin there drinkin water, talkin shit about rollin through the village ahead, thinkin we're some badass spec ops force." James laughs to himself at the absurdity of the memory. He revels in the fact the squad thought they were invincible in the moment. "Goddamn, those were good fuckin times."

Doherty stares out at the dark banks of the small valley river. "Yeah, they were, brother. Damn, we really thought we were never goin to die. Fuckin crazy, man."

James peeks up and looks across the fire to see Doherty staring straight into the darkness of the valley, distracted, distant. "Hey, brother, you remember that little fuckin goat herder?" James asks his old friend.

Smiling slightly, Doherty breaks his trance from the darkness of the valley. "I remember that little shit. He was whippin the tar out of those goats. Just tearin their asses up." The old friends laugh together at the hilarity of the situation, only in the infantry can you find humor in the backdrop of combat.

Pulling his boonie back over his eyes, James continues, "Doherty, you look over at that goat gettin its' ass whipped by that motherfucker laughin his tiny balls off and turn to us, *'He won't be laughin when that goat turns around and bites*

---

[7] Area of operation

The Last Letter

his little tallywacker off.' Goddamn that shit was funny as fuck." James chuckles heartily. Parks and Doherty join in with their own laughter at the recollection. The men allow their laughter to trail off into the valley's autumn air, a comfortable isolation once again befalls the three old Marines.

"Oh, shit I almost forgot," Parks says rummaging in his pack. "I meant to give this to you when you and Culpepper were together." He pulls out a gift box of *Blanton's Straight from the Barrel Bourbon* from his rucksack. Parks then hands the box over to James. "It's for you men Swiss cheesing those fuckin hajis that ran the VCP[8] in Ak-Turba on our last operation. Those fuckers were trying to get to the CP[9], you men stopped them. I promised you and Culpepper a bottle of whiskey but that should do." Parks points to the box in James' hands.

"What the fuck! This is some amazin shit, right here, Sgt. Parks." James carefully unpacks the bottle and the two engraved drinking glasses, one reads *1st*, the other *Squad*. "Thanks, Sgt. Parks. Shit that was a platoon effort and annihilation." Smiling fondly, he pours two glasses of the fine bourbon, only after inhaling the luxurious sweet aroma emanating from the open bottle, he then passes the glasses to Parks and Doherty.

"Ah, no thanks, brother." Parks passes the engraved glass back to James. "Sober."

"Oh, that's right. How long's it been since you last drank, brother?" James asks, feeling somewhat embarrassed for passing his squad leader the drink. He then takes the glass politely back, smells the sweet aroma and sips the warm beautiful amber beverage. "Oh, motherfucker that's good, Sgt. Parks. Thank you."

Doherty follows suit with his squad leader, refusing a glass to James' dismay. Doherty does enjoy the sweet aroma of the warm amber liquid. "Shit, that smells damn good though." His eyes close as the smell of warm bourbon flows through his nostrils.

"You're welcome, James. The bourbon was for the whole squad, you men did the right thing that day in Ak-Turba." Parks offers, nodding his approval.

---

[8] Vehicle Checkpoint
[9] Command Post

"Too bad you weren't still our squad leader for that shit, Sgt. Parks," James says solemnly. "But we gave them one hell of a run when 1st Squad was together."

"Yes, we fuckin did, Devil," Parks acknowledges his former troop's assertion. "How long you been sober, Doherty?"

Doherty takes another puff of his sweet-smelling cigar, closes his eyes and leans back into the *Grunt sweet spot* of his pack, enjoying the spreading warmth of the fire, "Four years. You, Sgt. Parks?"

"Not near long enough. Just a little over eight years, I guess. I go by *Flag Day* in June." Parks smiles slightly to himself and inhales another waft of smoke, exhaling after a pause, watching the vapor dissipate into the flames.

"What the fuck, *Flag Day*?" Doherty asks perplexed. "What's so damn special about that day?", he continues, still trying to fathom the relevance of the holiday to his old squad leader's desire to stop drinking.

Parks laughs at himself, then looks at the other two. "*Flag Day* was the first holiday that was coming up I could mark a notable day of stopping, easy to remember, I knew I wouldn't make it to July 4th." He reflects on the day he woke up and decided that was it, no more. The former Marine would no longer drink and face his guilt about his past head-on, but first he needed to get sober; nothing was more important. "James wipe that guilty look off your fuckin face and enjoy the warm feel of the expensive, smooth bourbon wash down your throat, Devil. Please, I beg of you. I didn't carefully lug that fuckin bottle across the mountains and valleys just to have you feel all fuckin weird about drinking that shit. I'm going to smoke another pre-roll and I'll be good to go." He ends with a smile, motioning for his friend to raise his glass and enjoy.

"I was wonderin why you carefully set your ruck down at every stop. AA seems to work for you, Sgt. Parks," James comments. "Here is to 1st Squad and the rest of Bravo Co. 1/23." He takes a well-deserved swig of the exquisite bourbon. "Man, I could just fall asleep after that perfection." James adds with his eyes slowly closing beneath his camouflage boonie.

Parks takes a deep drag of his pre-roll and listens to a pack of wolves off in the distance. It is the first big game the old Marines have heard since the beginning of their trek. He reflects on James' comment; he does not want to disillusion his former Marine. "AA, no Devil, no AA for me. They put way too much fuckin pressure on the number of days. A full-blown fuckin alcoholic isn't going to be able to quit goddamn cold fuckin turkey. It takes struggle, pain, and fuckin messing up to successfully try to become sober. It's a fuckin everyday thing even if I don't consciously acknowledge it, talk to the fuckers that have been sober twenty-plus years."

The former squad leader inhales deeply, and continues his tirade, "You mean to tell me if that person even had a sip of whiskey or wine; that their twenty-plus years are fuckin wiped away. Fuck that. Those poor fuckers put in their time; it doesn't get wiped the fuck away because they had a single drink. That ladies and gentlemen is why I say fuck AA, but hey if it works for some people, it works, good for fuckin them, I won't begrudge them their fuckin salvation. Who the fuck am I to dictate to anyone? I smoke weed to curb those fuckin cravings for the drink. Fuck." Parks inhales another puff of smoke, keeping his gaze transfixed on the flames before him, knowing he's starting to go dark. "That last F-bomb was for you, James. I know your smartass had an accurate count on that shit." Parks smiles trying to lighten the mood after his rant on sobriety. He catches his troop counting on his fingers the number of *F-bombs* Parks let go on his mini-tirade.

"Sixteen damn times, Sgt. Parks. I think that's a record." James counters, needling his squad leader about his penchant to use the Fword, exceedingly.

The three settle into a laughter that is more about camaraderie than humor. Each Marine seems to reflect on some distant memory that embraces their shared collective of experiences together. It is a calm amongst the camp, each basking in the company of one another, no words need be spoken.

"We haven't really talked much in detail on 'ol Gunny *Dickless* Daisy, that piece of shit," Doherty chimes in angrily after a long subdued pause.

The other two seem to instantly freeze in their thoughts, their jaws clench unconsciously with rage; for that name had not been spoken in depth amongst the men in over twenty years. The name is sacrilege amongst the men of Bravo Co 1/23. That name is uttered amongst the Marines with disdain, contempt, and hatred. It is a name every man of 1st Squad has come to loathe. To Parks, that man's name is the bane of his miserable existence. "I fuckin hate that coward piece of shit," the former squad leader growls into the flames.

CH. 3
OUR SQUAD'S FIRST HVT

The name of their old platoon commander seems to transport all three back to the last patrol 1st Squad would ever be together for. A combat operation outside of Fallujah during a battle for that town in November 2004, an operation none of 1st Squad would ever forget. It is that one singular night that has bound these men for eternity. None of the former Marines speak; they let their minds wander to the deep recesses of hatred for their old coward of a platoon commander.

"Last I heard from Sgt. Mac before his second deployment was *Dickless* went back with another unit as a 1st Sergeant. Must have sucked to have been in that fuckin unit." Parks grumbles under his breath breaking the trance the fire has ahold of the old Marine.

"Those poor bastards would have nowhere to hide from his stupidity if he was their company 1st Sergeant." James replies, propping himself up to pour another libation of sweet, smooth bourbon. "God, that's some good shit, Sgt. Parks, can't believe the taste."

Parks keeps his teeth clenched, staring into the darkness of the valley. "James, last you and Bgame reported was that *Dickless* was trying to become a police chief of some small ass town in the middle of fuckin nowhere."

James laughs slightly, "Yeah, Bgame knows an officer at that department, and no one wants to partner up with that chickenshit. He says all of the cops there see through *Dickless's* bullshit stories of heroics."

"Fuckin pussy." Parks snarls under his breath, staring vacantly into the darkness.

"I fuckin hated *Dickless* and to mention it, I hated Sgt. Mac as well. Fuck them both." Doherty glares into the fire.

Looking back to Doherty, Parks remarks at the sentiment of his former troop. "Fuck, I wish the enemy would've fragged *Dickless* when they had the chance, fuckin pussy never left the Hummer during a firefight though." Then he laughs suddenly, keeping his smile fixed on his old friend. "I know you hated Sgt. Mac, because our first ball back, Doherty, you got absolutely shitfaced, well, we were all fuckin shitfaced."

"Ain't that the truth." Doherty rubs his temples trying to remember that evening so long ago.

Parks continues, a broad smile under his greying beard, "You and I were in line for the bar, you were buying me a drink and said, *'I love you Sgt. Parks, I love you, but I hate that fuckin guy, I hate Sgt. Mac, fuck him!'* All loud, slurred and shit, with your arm draped over me, while Mac was in front us; you horse's ass." Parks laughs, James joins in heartily with his squad leader. "We were at a Marine Ball, so technically on active duty. Sgt. Mac could've handed you your ass, right there. I had to defuse that situation, but I understand you men have your hatred of him from GITMO[10], but the man knew his shit. Sgt. Mac was Marine through and through. I get that pissed you off, but you men of 1st Squad miss the fact," Parks drops his smile and begins to become entranced once again in the warm campfire. "That night outside of Fallujah, Sgt. Mac backed my play before breaking his collarbone trying to relieve *Dickless* of command. So, you men of 1st Squad may want to take a moment and reevaluate your assessment of Sgt. Mac. Just food for thought, dickheads."

"Man, he was terrible to us, all you fuckin prior active guys comin to the reserves are. Then you expect us to be, all Marine, all the time. We're not the fleet, that should be the fuckin sign upon entry to a reserve unit. It's a joke to us, when at drill we see a new prior active NCO11[11] come to the unit. We then take bets how long it takes before said NCO blows his fuckin lid over our attitude. To reservists, it's a hilarious shit-show." Doherty explains, James nodding along with his old friend, eyes closed under his boonie.

---

[10] Guantanamo Bay, Cuba
[11] Non commissioned Officer

"I concur. "Don't think you were no different, Sgt. Parks," James says with a wry smile, sipping more of the bourbon and enjoying the warmth of the amber liquid flowing down his throat. "But we came to love ya, eventually, you old bastard."

"Thanks." Parks answers with a tired smile. "Yeah, I know I was the same. You must understand the fleet, it's a whole different animal. My team leaders and squad leaders were thrashing us all the fuckin time. So, when we leave the fleet and go to a reserve unit, we go full *motard* on reservists. The fleet hates the reserves, especially us, *Grunts*, because we're jealous. You only have to do the shit once a month and two weeks out of the year, so it's pure jealousy from the fleet *Grunts*. We're stuck in the *suck* permanently until discharge day. Just pure jealousy, brothers. As we found out in *29 Palms*, how Bravo Co. was treated by the base command and its logistical staff. Calling us the *irregular Marines* on the chow hall sign. Shit, how we were treated our whole deployment by active command. So, I'll never turn my nose down on reservists again. You fuckers from 1st Squad were the best I ever served with." Parks looks over to each of his former troops with a prideful glow.

"Aww you shouldn't have." James mockingly wipes fake tears from his closed eyes; after again indulging in another small sip of the beverage.

"Fuck you. Way to turn my emotional opening into a joke." Parks replies with a huge grin on his tired face. The three chuckle exhaustively and stare back into the glow of the fire.

Continuing to sip his bourbon, James asks of his squad leader, "Here's a quick question. Why the fuck did I let you talk me into wearin *SAPI*[12] plates in my chest rig for this shit, Sgt. Parks?" He proclaims, with a smile, staring off towards the sound of the small flowing river.

"Hey, man, you know me. All the way or no way. Besides, if a bear attacks us, our vital organs are protected. Ever think about that." Parks replies, exhaling a cloud of smoke.

"Shit if we get attacked by a bear, Doherty's screwed. I know I'm not faster than you, Sgt. Parks, but I think I can goddamn outrun Doherty." James peeks up from under his boonie to look over in his friend's direction.

---

[12] Small Arms Protective Insert

Doherty breaking his trance from the fire responds accordingly, "The fuck you can, Devil. You were suckin hind tit this whole hump. Bear's got yo' ass." With the joke landed, the three erupt in genuine, comfortable laughter.

Moments of solitude pass before James speaks up again, "Fuck, I remember when we went to Fort Polk to train, before we shipped out to *29 Palms*, you were the only crazy bastard who brought their *SAPI* plates and put them in your flak to train with, Sgt. Parks. It was fuckin 95 degrees with 95% humidity, you crazy-ass motherfucker. You were the only one in the company to do that shit. I think you were our squad leader for all of one drill before that and it was a gear inspection for Fort Polk. Bgame's the one who knew you from the fleet, he told us some stories about you and the Osprey crash, that was fuckin nuts in itself, brother. Then when we saw you wearin your *SAPIs*, and 1st Squad all thought *'oh shit he's goin to be another of those motard fuckin squad leaders.'* But you didn't make us wear them. I never understood why not?" James asks of his former squad leader.

"It's true, Sgt. Parks we all thought that shit. We saw you wear the *SAPIs* right off the bat and rolled our fuckin eyes. It was goin to be a long deployment with this new asshole from the fleet for a squad leader. No offense, Sgt. Parks." Doherty reaches over to the falling asleep James and nudges him with a stick, much to the dozing man's annoyance.

Reflecting for a few motionless seconds, Parks tries to convey his thought process then, "Man, to be honest I wanted to acclimatize myself to the weight of the flak with *SAPIs*. Truth be told, we were headed to *29 Palms* to train, and I'd been there several times in the fleet, and knew what was coming. My plan was to make our squad acclimatize real fuckin quick when we got to the *Stumps*. There would be no excuses come time to hump the rucks with the fuckers in our flaks. I knew it was going to be hell on earth for you guys—*29 Palms* dead summer, holy fuckin shit." Parks, exhaling a large puff of smoke, enjoying the sudden calm wash over him.

"That was pure fuckin misery," Doherty laments, taking a slow inhale of the sweet cigar. He exhales a deep release of tension, absorbing the peacefulness of his surroundings of the autumn woods.

Parks nods his head in agreement and continues, "Besides, how the fuck was I supposed to make you men do all this shit if I fell out of a run or hump

The Last Letter

because of the weight. Would you have followed or respected a squad leader that did that shit? Nope, wasn't going to happen, not on my watch. But I'll tell you the truth; that little fuckin hump we did from the barracks out to the *MOUT*[13] facility at Fort Polk, almost dropped me. First time I ever felt that during a hump. Thank God, squad leaders bounce around the middle of hikes, like assholes, to check on their squads, shit gave me time to recover. Almost ripped those fuckin *SAPI* plates out in front of the whole damn company. Shit was brutal." Parks scoffs at the memory.

"Yeah, well, you were the only idiot to wear them, Sgt. Parks. Thankfully you didn't make us wear them right away. Man, like I said, all we heard were stories from Bgame about the fleet. The Osprey crash and how you lost half your men from your platoon. We honestly didn't know what to expect, brother." James responds carefully, concerned about stirring up too many memories for his ageing squad leader.

Parks begins to lose himself to that familiar *nothingness*, a vacant stare as his peripherals become an obsolete blur. "Man, the Osprey crash. That was something, alright." He takes another large inhale of his pre-roll, hoping to ease the approaching storm of memories from that night of the tragic crash. The dancing flames of the fire, reminding Parks of the engulfing inferno that claimed the lives of the Marines from India Co. Parks exhales heavily, dismissing the tragic memories for a brighter one. "Although, I do recall a battalion hump where a certain individual fell out carrying his SAW. James, any comments?" Parks mentions wryly with a smile, looking past the small fire to James, who is burying his head further under his boonie and taking another sip of the succulent bourbon.

"Hey, Sgt. Parks, I was done and had been downing beers with fellas the whole night before; I was never goin to finish. I know I'll never live that shit down. Fuck, the guys from the squad still give me shit to this day when I see them." James replies, lowering his head in mock shame.

Doherty laughs heartily, keeping his gaze transfixed on the dancing flames. "Of course, we do, brother. Fuck even Caruso made that hump." He winks coyly at his disgruntled squad mate; James gives his friend the middle finger in a defiant response. Doherty and Parks laugh together warmly.

---

[13] Military Operations Urban Terrain

SSgt. Jacob Parkinson

"Well, in all fairness, I had to skull-fuckin-drag Caruso to the finish. You were already on the seven-ton, James, or I would've done the same to you, brother." Parks looks to his old troop with a hearty smile, who still resides under his boonie, refusing to face the chiding from his two Marine friends.

Infantrymen take pride in not falling out of mandatory hikes (humps). It is an unrewarded sense of pride and accomplishment amongst the *Grunt* community. The longer and more grueling the hike, the sense of pride of the accomplishment increases. On the counter argument, if a *Grunt* does fall out of a hike, he is admonished, thrashed, hazed, ridiculed, and forced to do a remedial hike the following weekend. James knew this.

"Hey, James, don't worry about it, brother. You were a fuckin stellar Marine; the squad knew this. Shit, I had a buddy in the fleet, Dunn, who didn't give two shits, and would look up at me during a hump and say, *'fuck it Parks I'm done, the docs can give me the red rocket[14] up the ass; beats humping the last twelve miles of this bullshit.'* And Dunn would fuckin sit there, call *'corpsmen up'* himself and start dropping trou right there to prepare for the red rocket up the ass." Parks reflects fondly, remembering his friend from the fleet, patiently waiting, ass out for the Navy Corpsmen. "The fucker would go on to pay me a hundred bucks to do his remedial hump for him the next week." Parks chuckles softly.

Doherty looks over to his squad leader, puzzled, "Fuck that. I wouldn't have done it for five hundred, Sgt. Parks."

"We were *boots*, I needed the money, we all did. Spent it on alcohol for me and Dunn anyway. Wore his cammies and carried his SAW for the hump, James." Parks gives James a nudge with his boot at the mention of the automatic weapon. "When it came time to turn in weapons, I forgot I was Dunn for a moment, all the salt dogs were screaming for *Dunn* to turn in his weapon. I was standing there like a fuckin idiot with the nametape *Dunn* across my chest." Parks scoffs at the sudden memory. "Ended up getting thrashed for not paying attention. Thankfully we were boots and we all look alike to the salt dogs. Shit, that could've got ugly for us both." Parks puts his head own with a smile at the absurdity of his past hijinks in the Marines.

---

[14] A long thermometer inserted anally with a red tip, to measure core temperature

The Last Letter

Doherty looks slightly astonished. "Like I said, fuck that. Not worth the hassle."

"*It ain't easy having Pals*," Parks replies, quoting the movie *Young Guns*, a beloved film from their generation's formidable youth.

"Well, hell, I still look back and still feel like shit about it, Sgt. Parks. I thought I was done for when we got back to the barracks," James states matter-of-factly. "But you still let me go out, fuckin drink and do whatever," James wonders aloud.

"Listen, you were a locked on Marine and had a good head on your shoulders. At that time, I started to question my own leadership methods anyway. As much as us active-duty guys wanted the unit to be like the fleet, reserves cannot function that way. I was learning this aspect as we went, and watching Delta take his more laid-back approach to his team, and Attebery's leadership style with his mortar section, I realized I needed to adapt my leadership to suit the environment I was operating in. Besides, man, I realized we were going to fuckin war, worrying about a hump and punishing you just didn't make much sense to me, much to *Dickless's* dismay." Parks huffs slightly at the memory. "My troops that died in the Osprey crash deserved a better squad leader; it was time for me to be one for you men." He ends solemnly, the fire keeping the autumn night chill at bay.

"That was beautiful, man," James says, pretending to choke up and drop a tear, hoping to take Parks' mind off the gloomy past.

"Fuck you." Parks laughs slightly. A calm silence befalls the men, the sounds of nightlife amongst the forest begin to echo down into the dark valley.

Doherty asks the two, hoping for their help in the forgotten recollection, "You two remember our first *HVT*?"

"You mean the *lefty*, Sgt. Parks snatched off the rooftop in that shithole town outside Al Asaad." James chuckles, holding the bourbon glass securely on his rising chest. "Our first night raid, 2nd Squad assigned to cordon off the building, 3rd herd sitting in reserve for QRF[15]. 1st squad on assault, baby." James' smile brims from ear to ear at the memory. Parks cannot help but smile along at the sight of the relaxed former Marine.

---

[15] Quick Reaction Force

"You're goddamn right we were, Devil." Doherty raises his head towards his old squad mate and nods, James peeks up from under his boonie and returns the gesture.

James continues, slowly drifting towards sleepiness, the bourbon starting to do its' intended purpose, "First platoon was a couple of blocks away, gettin it on."

Doherty huffs quietly, "Those fuckers were always gettin into it since the day Bravo set foot in Iraq. They had their *combat action ribbons* before the rest of us. Man, I was fuckin jealous, key term *was*, until 1st Squad made up for lost ground."

"Yut!" James yells out, raising his glass again to the autumn night air.

Parks exhales patiently, watching the fire dance its' rhythmic dance against the dark backdrop of the forest. "Ain't that the truth."

"We roll up in the seven-tons, dismountin to hit the house and hearing sporadic gunfire. As we're runnin towards the target house, fuckin Doc Owens goes down. Everyone starts yellin, *'Doc's hit! Doc's down!'*", James' southern drawl becoming more pronounced as the bourbon begins to kick in. "Sgt. Parks, you yell *'Keep fuckin movin!'* We quickly scrum around Doc and rush him to cover." James laughs a boisterous laugh. "He tripped over a fuckin rock. He wasn't fuckin shot." The three erupt in subdued laughter at the shared flashback.

Doherty looks back into the flames, "And the Academy Award for best fall on a *HVT* raid goes to Doc Owens." More soft laughter at the comical moment during an intense situation.

"In his defense, Devil, Doc kept tryin to tell us he wasn't hit, that he was fine, but the squad thought it was just the endorphins talkin." James comes to the humorous defense of the Navy Corpsmen.

Parks adjusts his position on his pack by the fire, trying to find comfort for his ailing back. "There was no goddamn way we were going to let anything happen to Doc Owens; he's the man. Best fuckin corpsmen I ever served with. Love that dude," Parks ends his statement with conviction.

"Fuck yeah, we do." Doherty echoes his squad leader's sentiments about their endearing corpsmen.

The Last Letter

James keeps the flow of conversation going. "Team OFP[16] makes entry and begins clearing the target house." His smile starts to grow underneath his boonie cover.

Parks keeps his gaze fixated on the fire, but his grin begins to emerge as well. "You forget, young Devil, the trouble we had gaining entry into the target house."

James pushes up his boonie to look over at his old squad leader, "What the fuck are you talkin about, Sgt. Parks?"

"Remember. The fuckers barricaded the steel door. Sgt. Parks was tryin kick the shit out of it; fuckin thing wouldn't budge." Doherty interjects with a chuckle at the memory of his squad leader consistently trying to kick in a barricaded steel door to no avail.

Parks adds, grinning, "Precisely. That's when I discovered every Iraqi understands goddamn English." Again, another slight smile from the old squad leader. "I turn to Delta and yell, *'give me a fuckin grenade, I'm blowin' the fuckin door open!'* Next thing I hear is the sound of the barricade coming off the door and opening to the screams and pleas of the women and children. Fuck, I hated that." Parks' smile fades as the long ago wails return for justice.

"Shit, how'd I forget that. Doesn't matter, entry was gained." James lowers the boonie back over his eyes, careful not to spill his drink resting on his tired chest. "I was posted up at a stairwell to the right by the entrance, while you and Culpepper start goin room to room. As I'm waiting for you and big ass Culpepper to come back, so we can head topside, I start to hear strugglin sounds from the second story." James pauses to take another sip of his beautiful amber bourbon. He sighs deeply, "Just then the door I have my SAW trained on, rips open and this guy comes flying down the stairs and rollin the fuck down to my feet. More movement at the top of the stairs, I aim back up top and see you, Sgt. Parks, rifle slung across your chest and a big 'ole smirk on your face. I almost shot your old ass." James laughs at the humorous memory.

Parks smiles into the fire, "Hey the fucker ran when I finally got in the door. Cooley's the one who spotted the shithead trying to escape across the rooftop, *'Hey, Sgt. Parks, you got movement on the roof!'* Morales and I give chase through the house and up we go. Would've shot the fucker too, had he not thrown his

---

[16] On Fucking Point

fuckin hands up immediately when we caught up to his ass. Culpepper joined us on the rooftop to help me guide the haji down the stairs, James; *guide* is the key term," Parks emphasizing the word with his weathered smile.

"Whatever helps you sleep at night, Sgt. Parks." James counters, the three laugh again, a restful laugh. None of the group have had a chance to really talk amongst one another completely since that night outside of Fallujah.

Doherty takes another puff of the expensive cigar, gazes approvingly to his two old friends, *this is exactly what we three needed*, he ponders to himself before speaking up. "Man, I remember us findin jack shit and what a letdown that first raid was."

"Hey, brother, the platoon was given six-month-old intelligence; the only reason Bravo Co. got the raid was because Marine Recon bitched about the intel being too old and passed it down to us. Recon did the same shit at the *Battle of Hiit*, they passed on the operation because intel was too old and the next thing you know Bravo Co. is in its' first full multi-day battle," Parks angrily recounts the lack of urgency on the part of Special Forces during Bravo Co's rotation in the Al Anbar Province, Iraq.

Doherty, also disgruntled with the lack of help from Marine Recon, adds, "Lazy-ass bitches, we do all the work, and they get all the glory. Shit, Recon even jumped on Bravo's coattails for Hiit, showin up at the end and firin off a few rounds after 1st and 2nd Platoon had already secured the area, especially 1st fuckin Platoon."

"Well, they didn't miss anything that night, brother." James continues with his tale of the first HVT the squad encountered. "Sgt. Parks, you call *HET*[17] team in to start working on this fuckin shithead. We're just waitin for them to be done and I notice another guy in a room by himself. Bgame had come in to see what's happenin; I tell him there's a guy in a room by himself and don't know if he's been cleared. We go in, weapons at the ready and this angry old man holds his hands up, except the fucker has no hands, just goddamn stumps. Bgame starts askin him, '*Kalashnikov?*' '*Kalashnikov?*', makin the trigger pulling motion with his fingers." James pauses, takes another sip, relishing the moment of memory and huffs slightly. "The old man looks at the

---

[17] Human Exploitation Team

two of us funny and then started yellin' shit in Arabic, wavin his fuckin stumps in our faces. Bgame shrugs, looks at me and says, *'Fuck it, Devil. If this guy can figure out a way to grab a gun and shoot us with no hands, the fucker has earned the kill.'* Then he walks out." The three cannot help but burst into laughter at the memory of their old friend Bgame's perfectly quipped combat dialogue.

"Only fuckin Bgame. The man's an old dirty warrior." Doherty exclaims with a smile, fondly remembering the 3rd Squad leader.

"Yut." James and Parks respond with the typical Marine vernacular for such a situation.

James adjusts his head on the pack behind him. "The *HET* guy, who speaks perfect fuckin Arabic, yet has a thick Boston accent tells us, *'Yeah, this guy's fahking retahded. He's a fahking retahd. Literally. He has no clue what the fahk is going on. Good work guys, you captured a lefty.'* Bravo 6 actual, this is Bravo 2. Mission complete. We are *RTB* at this time." James mockingly imitates the radio chatter of a *SITREP*[18]. More laughter from the three camouflaged adorned men. Each absorbing the energy provided by the company they are in and the collective reminiscing.

"That's a fuckin good one, James." Parks continues to stare at the welcoming fire, content with his memory of events long past. "I forgot about the guy with no hands. It makes sense to me now two decades later."

"What's that, Sgt. Parks?" Doherty asks his tired squad leader, breaking his own trance from the dark valley they had crossed earlier in the day.

Parks ponders the details of James' memory, "Well, HET team did find a box of triggers, comm wire, and a couple cell phones in a shoebox under the bed in the room. The HET team leader told me it was common bullshit found in these homes. Now hearing about you and Bgame finding that fucker with no hands. I'm thinking he blew his fuckin hands off making an IED[19] then he began to train the *lefty* because he's expendable." Parks stares into the fire admonishing himself for not making the connection then while in the moment.

Doherty laughs slightly. "Fuck, Sgt. Parks, we were never trained for shit like that, a guy with no fuckin hands. No one told us *'look for guys with no hands or missin*

---
[18] Situation Report
[19] Improvised Explosive Device

fuckin digits.' I didn't realize that until the movies started talkin about that shit. We were not EOD and you, Sgt. Parks, were damn sure not supposed to be fuckin around with the wires when you did come across them, motivated ass."

James laughs from under his boonie, "Yut." He takes another sip, then refills the glass.

"Fuck ya both." Parks smiles broadly. He looks to James refilling the glass again. "You going to finish that all, not save any for the rest of excursion?"

"It's fuckin smooth Sgt. Parks. And what better setting than to enjoy an almost $300 bottle of bourbon?" James exclaims, slowly stretching his aching shoulders from the hike in.

Parks huffs, "Roger that. Damn, I do wish more of 1st could have made it out. I think they would've loved this." His gaze not breaking the fire, knows this may be the last time they are ever together.

"That would've been pretty damn cool if they had. Pretty damn cool…." Doherty begins to trail off to a semi-state of slumber. The three friends begin to fall into their own state of solace, listening to the crackle of the fire and the sounds of the forest surrounding them. It is a moment the men will treasure for the remainder of their lives.

CH. 4
A SHIT CANAL & THE PLAYBOY MANSION

The air is crisp and warm on the autumn evening, the campfire mesmerizing the three men, not letting them focus on the present but seemingly drawing them back to their shared past. The smell of true, fresh unsaturated air refreshes the former Marines after their long trek through the mountainous terrain. "I was thinkin on when we got ambushed outside of *Fallujah*, on that last operation 1st Squad was together for?" Doherty begins, still entranced by the dancing flames.

"I try to forget that shit every damn day, brother," Parks states solemnly about the last time he would lead his men into combat as a squad.

"Any-fuckin-way, like I was sayin, when we got ambushed outside the city, which will remain nameless, and James, you were firin your SAW at that fuckin haji with the RPG, literally walking the rounds right onto target. I mean you unloaded from your boots all the way to up to the haji." Doherty mimics the action of James firing wildly and all erupt into unison laughter.

"Fuck you. I got the SAW on target, didn't I? Tell him, Sgt. Parks."

Parks huffs slightly, "Oh yeah, you got them on target alright, after about sixty rounds walking them onto the goddamn target." He deadpans in response; Doherty laughs at his old squad leader's unbiased assessment.

"You know what? Fuck you too, Sgt. Parks. Besides, by the time my rounds found the target the Abrams had turned that haji into a fine, sandy, pink mist." James replies with a smile, stretching from ear to ear.

SSgt. Jacob Parkinson

"Yeah, that was fucked up, brother. Holy shit that was a hell of day. Sgt. Parks, If you had included in the frag order[20] that we would get mortared, ambushed, secure a downed helo, find God knows how many IEDs, which we cut ourselves, and do what we did to *Dickless* all in a span of twenty-four hours; I would have still said, sign me the fuck up." Doherty scoffs slightly at the thought of that shared day long since passed.

"I concur" James grunts, refilling his glass a quarter of the way and lays back on his pack, lowering his boonie cover over his eyes once again, allowing the warmth of the fire to relax his aching bones.

Parks' stare widens with each rhythmic dance of the orange flames, his peripherals turn to haze. The old *Grunt* is caught once again in the trance of the *nothingness* hovering over him. "That was a long fuckin day."

"Shit, yeah it was. Not to mention *Dickless* kept sending 1st Squad out on patrol before that because he hated us... well, at least hated you, Sgt. Parks." James grumbles, recalling his platoon commander's cowardly actions.

He does not dare break his gaze from the distant *nothingness*, Parks enjoys the momentary trance of an emotionless state. "The feeling's mutual," Parks replies without a hint of emotion.

"Holy fuckin shit!" James shoots upright onto his left elbow and looks to his squad leader hypnotized by the flames. "Sgt. Parks, you remember a couple days before the *incident*, when you fell into the shit-canal takin point on patrol with HET team at zero dark thirty?" James's laughter is soon joined by Doherty's; both their hearty sounds fill the valley with a sense of jubilation. Parks slightly smiles, he does remember the event but not to the humorous extent as his former troops. "Sgt. Parks, I was right behind you when that happened. One second, I see your silhouette, the next it fuckin disappears, and I hear a *splash*." James recalls, more subdued laughter ensues from the two former troops. "Culpepper and I rush to the edge of the canal, to find you standin with your rifle extended over your fuckin head, shit water up to your neck. The two of us had to pull your miserable ass out by your pack straps." Both James and Doherty explode into laughter, echoing throughout the dark valley surrounding the warm-hearted Marines.

---

[20] Fragmentation Order

The Last Letter

"Shit, we heard the splash all the way back at the rear of the patrol. Delta looks at me and gives me the *'what the fuck was that'* motion." Doherty enjoying the moment of banter between the three, he, too, is reveling in the flashback.

Parks gives a huge smile and slight patronizing chuckle, keeping his gaze affixed to the warm flames, enjoying the sound of laughter from his former troops at his expense. This is exactly what Parks is hoping to come of this trip, one final bond between he and his men. "I was not a happy little Marine after that shit."

"I've never seen you so pissed. All you did was start fuckin swearin up a cuss storm on a level I never heard. *Zero dark thirty* and Sgt. Parks is droppin every version of the f-bomb at the very beginning of our patrol, it was fuckin great. If we only had Go-Pros back then, that moment would be enshrined as the patrol fail of all time." James utters, winking at his tired squad leader.

Parks break his trance from the *nothingness* that has ahold of his consciousness and shoots the middle finger to James. "Yeah, well fuck you, man. That shit was nasty. I'm lucky it was shallow and only went up to my neck and you're goddamn right I was fuckin pissed. Fuckin shit canal." Parks grits his teeth, recalling the smell and feel of the sewage in the channel. "I'm lucky you and Culpepper plucked my ass out of there when you did. The fuckin mecca and cradle of civilization, my ass." The angered Marine states, mocking Iraq's biblical place in history. His demeanor changes into a grimace, his mind is swept back to that moment of pure, unfiltered disdain for his environment. "Being pissed doesn't even begin to describe my feelings that night. I don't know what that feeling was, but it was beyond pissed. I hated that fuckin country so much after that moment." Parks clenches his jaw ever tighter.

"Shit, Sgt. Parks, we heard you at the rear of the formation, the rest of the squad had no clue what the hell was goin on. Morales and Delta are tryin to figure out what the fuck happened as you halted the patrol. Everyone is takin a knee except you, Culpepper, and James, here." Doherty's smile still working across his weathered face.

"Of course, me and Culpepper were movin, we had to get Sgt. Parks' ass out of the shit-canal. We didn't know if he was drownin or what. He just disappeared and there was a *splash*." Again, the three laughter in unison The autumn night air providing a sense of comfort and security for the men.

SSgt. Jacob Parkinson

"Delta comes over the PSR[21] *'Sgt. Parks, HET team leader thinks we should go silent.'* I'm covered head to toe in Iraqi shit and this motherfucker wants me to be silent, fuckin tagalong HET team." Parks grumbles into the welcoming flames. "I lose my shit, *'Tell HET to get their asses up here and lead the fuckin patrol then!'* Delta's only response, *'Roger that, Sgt. Parks,'*" He adds, the other two men listen happily along. "And that was on day two of *Operation Phantom Fury*, we were told the operation would last at most seven fuckin days. Not a damn one of us, out of the whole company, packed extra cammies, all we took were extra socks and skivvies. The rest ammo and chow. Seven days, my ass. Almost thirty days later and I'm still fuckin wearing the same shit-soaked cammies. That smell never left. I can still smell that shit to this day. It permeated my fuckin skin." Parks snarls into the flames, his experience bringing back the rage he felt that night.

"Don't feel bad, Sgt. Parks, I couldn't smell you over the rest of the fuckin country." James coyly states with his sheepish grin, continuing to nurse his smooth bourbon.

"Hey, but you tried to get that shit smell off, Sgt. Parks. Later, after we dropped off HET team at the patrol base, you briefed us, that we still had about six more hours of patrol to do. We get to this office complex, Sgt. Parks, you kick in that office door and told everyone to rest. Everyone is groanin and droppin in place, you find that fuckin hose attached to the sink, then proceeded to hose yourself off, gear and all. Crazy fucker." Doherty says, shaking his head, watching James finish another quarter glass of smooth bourbon.

Parks sighs tiredly, "That was after 1st Squad had already kicked in the doors to that village, so HET team could do their interrogation thing. Looking back, I feel bad for that haji woman, on her hands and knees following me around the house, wiping up the shit that was flowing off my body, as I'm kicking in doors and snatching every male I see, only to have you men flex cuff and slam their asses against a wall. Poor woman the whole damn time following me and wiping up the shit I trampled all over her fuckin house. She didn't deserve that. Man, I was so fuckin pissed." Parks tries to hide his emotions, but his face is getting red at the thought of falling into that canal and the guilt of treating the locals awfully.

---

[21] Piece of Shit Radio, dubbed by Marine infantry

"Look, Sgt. Parks' face is red under that grey-ass beard." James laughs, pointing for Doherty to look at their angry squad leader's face.

"Hey, man, it would've been one thing if I had an extra set of cammies. Higher said seven fucking days not twenty-seven." Parks replies, trying to rationalize his lack of preparedness for the operation. He keeps his gaze transfixed on the flames. "Fuck, I'm shocked I didn't die of some horrible goddamn virus from that actual shit. After I hose off, still smelling like shit by the way; fuckin Jackson comes up to me '*hey Sgt. Pawks*'" The three laugh at Parks' southern drawl imitation of their humorous 1st Squad member. "'*We found a safe back there, can we get into it?*' I lay there in that fuckin leather office chair soaked and miserable, I offered only two words to you eager men, '*Fuck yes.*'" The flames silhouette Parks withdrawn face, his contemplation solely on the regrets of his life.

Doherty and James both smile at the memory of their feces-covered squad leader giving the command without hesitation. "Yut."

Laughing somewhat to himself Doherty reveals, "We tried the safe, nothin there. It wasn't even locked." Doherty trails off staring into the fire. The three tactically dressed men seem to once again drift away into their own recollections of the past.

"Fuckin safe was a letdown. You hear all those stories and then nothin." James relays with disappointment, his Texas drawl becoming more pronounced, as the long-awaited sleep begins to take hold of the tired Marine.

The men seem to settle in around the fire, James and Doherty enjoying another fresh cigar each, Parks quietly resides motionless, lost to the flames. All perfectly content in the blissful sound of the crackling wood burning.

"Damn I wish more of 1st could have made it; those fuckers are missin out. This is absolute heaven right at this moment, fellas." James contemplates, breaking the silence with a buzzed smile. The other two men nod in agreement.

Doherty looks about the dark valley the men traversed earlier that day, "Who fuckin knew Idaho was so beautiful, I mean really?"

"I sure as fuck didn't." Parks answers matter-of-factly. "When command pulled India Co. out of the field and said were going to fight wildfires in Idaho as hotshots; all of us were trying to contemplate Idaho having forests. We couldn't picture it. The jokes about potatoes and French fries were aplenty." James and Doherty give a slight humorous scoff. "Then we get to Clear Creek and there's nothing, but this beautiful landscape set ablaze. Fuckin crazy." Parks still entranced by the fire does not look about the landscape as it is now but only reflects on the past state of the forest.

"Well, the woods rebounded like a fuckin warrior. It's beautiful." James chimes in almost nodding off, the bourbon finally giving him peace and comfort.

"Hey, man, you about to go down?" Parks asks James, looking over to his old troop resting under his boonie cover.

"Brother, you drag us all over this beautiful landscape, ply me with the best tastin bourbon I've ever had. Nope, I'm not about to go down, I'm just gettin started, Sgt. Parks," James responds slowly closing his eyes.

Parks grimaces once again at his former title but does not protest. "He's going out." He looks to Doherty.

"Yep, I give him about four and he'll be out." Doherty chuckles, nodding towards James.

"Fuck ya, both." With that James drifts off and begins to snore almost immediately, his bourbon glass secured in his iron grip, lying upon his gently rising and falling chest.

Parks starts chuckling softly. "He's going to attract bears."

"Well, at least we're armed to the teeth. Although that game warden we talked to in town would be none too pleased if we smoked checked a bear. She didn't look like a person I would want to piss off." Doherty mentions, settling in on his own pack by the fire.

Parks nods, "Me either. Thankfully we have her number in case shit goes south out here."

Doherty nods silently along in acknowledgment, "Shit, man, I'm about to be out myself, you think James will mind if I call Cass really quick?" he asks, looking at his watch quickly and over to the sleeping James.

"No, I don't mind, go right ahead, Devil." James offers, raising the satphone without ever opening his eyes, through mid-snore.

Doherty stands gingerly, strides over and receives the phone from James. "Thanks, brother." He grabs his AR-15 and then makes his way towards the

The Last Letter

small, babbling river the men crossed earlier. Doherty hopes to catch his loved one before she turns in for the night, to tell her goodnight and he loves her.

As Parks watches the former Marine disappear into the black of the valley, his mind begins to drift to all the horrible moments in his life, the impasses start to flood his consciousness. Perpetuated by himself; these horrible moments do not leave but linger in his mind unable to release their grip on his waking concentration. Parks always hates these silent recalls, left to his own guilt and shame. He is to be lost to the dark thoughts of the past, not of his time in the Marines but of his actions after the fact. The subsequent 24/7 drinking and violence directed towards any and everyone, especially toward the one he was charged with protecting and supporting the most, his 2nd wife. To Parks there is no amount of time lapse or years of sobriety that will ever erase his treatment of Katie; she wanted his love and cherishment, but he gave her abuse, drunkenness, and shame, culminating in his arrest for domestic violence, the absolute lowest he could fall. She deserved a better version; Katie deserved everything better. All his loved ones did.

That is the purpose of this trip with the men; to finally relay the shame, the guilt and regret he carries with him; that the *Sgt. Parks*, the 'hero' according to them, is nothing. *Sgt. Parks* is no more, he never returned from Iraq with his men, a shell came home; one that is not worth the effort. No, Parks came here to tell his men to bury their vision of a beloved squad leader.

The sounds of the forest distract Parks from becoming lost in his troubled past; the noise slowly grows into a persistent distraction. A distorted whistling of some nature. Parks cannot quite place the sound. The sound begins to become steadier, growing louder. Parks turns his head in time to quickly catch James' glass of bourbon falling from his slumbering chest. He sets the glass down on the ground safely, watching as James' snores grow louder and louder. Parks smiles to himself and stares back into the fire; for the briefest of moments, there is levity and humor he feels.

The former Marine tries to remember if any of his men snored while in Iraq. Culpepper being the only one he can remember doing so. He stares off into the beautiful dark landscape ahead of him with a smile on his face, listening to his former troop snore. Parks reflects on the rest of the squad, wishing they could be here at this moment witnessing all this natural beauty to be interrupted by James' incessant snoring. The squad leader's smile broadens ever so slightly.

After a few tranquil moments, Doherty returns from the river with the sat-phone in hand and a glow about his bearded face. He assumes his old position of leaning back against his ruck, staging his weapon carefully, and nestling back into his comfort zone. "Shit, I could hear James 100 meters in. Cass and I had a good laugh at his expense."

"How are things?" Parks asks Doherty politely.

"Good, man. Real good. Just wanted to say goodnight to her." Doherty replies with a huge grin, staring into the soft fire.

"Hey, man, that's great, brother. Hold onto that feeling, don't take her for granted, be that caring loved one." Parks replies solemnly. He feels a constriction of emotion forming in his throat.

Doherty looks to his troubled squad leader, "I am, Sgt. Parks. She's my rock. Being here with y'all is exactly what I need to close that chapter of my life, finally, and begin fresh with Cass. No more livin in, *the what happened and what has been*, my future is with her and startin a family." Doherty takes a small puff of his cigar exhales and tries to push the memories of his own troubles after returning to the recesses of his mind.

"I'm happy for you, brother. Don't end up looking back wishing you had done everything sooner or differently, wanting to take it all back. It will eat you alive, every fuckin day." Parks states, staring blankly into the fire, the *nothingness* taking hold.

"What the fuck, Sgt. Parks, way to kill the mood." James chimes in, suddenly arising from his snoring slumber and lifting his boonie cover to look over to his distraught squad leader.

"Shit I'm sorry, Doherty. I mean, savor this because you don't get a second chance. This is it. You're in a good place and have overcome so damn much; I can see you will truly appreciate every drop of your time with your loved one." Parks explains softly, feeling the emotional constriction grow tighter in his throat. He knows he lost that chance long ago and deservedly so.

"And with that folks, Sgt. Parks knocks it out of the park." James smiles towards his former squad leader. "Welcome back to positivity, sort of."

The Last Letter

"You're a fuckin douchebag," Parks replies, sheepishly smiling while poking the fire with a stick for amusement.

The three reside once again in silence, letting the crackling of the fire and the sounds of the forest be the only chatter heard. Parks suddenly feels the weight of his guilt and regret begin to take hold. He does not want to travel down this abysmal road of consciousness. Parks wants to remain in the moment with his men, but the *nothingness* has other plans. *Not now*, he begs himself. The emotional constriction in his throat gripping ever tighter.

Sensing his old squad leader's distraction, Doherty tries to bring some levity to the campfire, "Sgt. Parks, there's somethin I have been meanin to ask you after all these years."

Parks does not break his gaze of the flames, the emotional constriction loosening enough allowing him to softly respond, "What's that, Devil?"

Doherty exhales cigar smoke, watching it rise into the blackness of the night sky. "How in the fuck did you get us invited to the Playboy Mansion when we got back from Iraq?"

James perks up from his semiconscious state. "I forgot about that shit. Damn, I wish I had made it out for that one."

"You didn't miss shit." Parks grumbles into the flames. His jaw beginning to clench with anger, the emotional constriction all but disappearing.

"It still would've been nice to say, *'I've been to the Playboy Mansion.'* Pretty damn cool if you ask me." James counters inquisitively.

Doherty chuckles slightly. "You really didn't miss shit, brother. Fuckin pussyass Hefner didn't want any girls around returnin battle-hardened Marine *Grunts*, so there was nothin really to brag about. It was empty. Still, Sgt. Parks, how'd you get the invite?" Doherty looks over to his distracted friend.

"I wrote the company a shitty letter, bitching about all the parties they throw at the mansion for douchebag celebrities but the ones that buy their magazine, the people on the front, don't receive any recognition or parties thrown in their honor." Parks continues angrily grumbling.

James looks up confused, "That got you an invite to the mansion, an angry fuckin letter?"

"I guess so. I received the invite in the mail at Al Asaad right before Bravo shipped home. I forgot who from Bravo Co. made the trip to the mansion, I did it for you fuckers from 1st but only Delta and Doherty made the trip from 1st Squad. Of course, Stevenson and Frazier drove out with Doherty. Attebery from Weapons; can't really remember the rest. Again, you didn't miss a fuckin thing. No playmates to give autographs or take pictures with. No, souvenirs or mementos. Not even fuckin Hef to say, *'welcome home,'* because that would be seen as taking a stance as "pro-Iraq war," is what I was told. Mind you this is when we got back in '05, when people actually gave shit about Marines. Nope you missed jack shit, brother. It was a waste of a trip," Parks growls from underneath clenched jaws.

Doherty exhales another puff of the sweet-smelling Cuban cigar, "Sgt. Parks is right; it was a waste. The infamous '*Grotto*' was this giant maroon futon pad and, I shit you not, cum stains all over the fuckin thing. We weren't allowed to take pictures of the grounds or that shit would have gone viral even back then. Let's see what else." Doherty inhales and exhales the sweet smoke once again, "Oh, the *Van Room* was pretty fuckin cool."

"What the fuck is the *Van Room*?" James asks, suddenly no longer tired.

Taking another puff of his cigar, Doherty looks to Sgt. Parks, who in turn nods for him to proceed, "Brother, it's this large arcade room that's designed to look like the interior of a '70s porno van. You know plush flooring and paneling, shag carpeting, the basic '70s bullshit. I think even beads, maybe, right Sgt. Parks?"

Parks nods in agreement. "Like we said, you didn't miss fuck all. The real story of the trip is when we got back to Tucson. That's when all hell broke loose. Stevenson gets blacklisted from a bar before even stepping foot in the fuckin place. Delta passes out in an ant bed and then later proceeds to jump out of a moving fuckin vehicle. Not to mention Doherty's misadventure getting back to Louisiana with Frazier and Stevenson. You know, your run-of-the-mill Marine infantry drunken bullshit." Parks keeps his gaze attached to the fire, but as his anger is subsiding, the aftermath from the Playboy trip comes into focus.

"Semper Fi." Doherty laughs, the same memory falling in line with Parks'.

The Last Letter

James, now wide awake, trying to fathom what he is hearing for the first time, "Someone please explain Sgt. Parks' last statement. Stevenson and Delta did what the fuck?"

Doherty staring over to his squad leader. "Care to explain, Sgt. Parks?"

"I'll tell the Delta piece; you tell the Stevenson debacle and how you men got home." Parks responds, a smile begins to emerge across his bearded, weathered face. He knows the outcome of both tales and is awaiting the look on James' boyish face.

Doherty adjusts his position to face James more directly, "Okay, yes, the Playboy trip was a fuckin bust. We get back to Tucson, where Sgt. Parks was staying with his gracious family, and decide to go get shitfaced to erase that trip from memory. We head to some fuckin bar, and as we're tryin to get in; the fuckin pussy-ass bouncers wouldn't let Stevenson in because he's '*slurrin*' his words. We haven't had shit to drink yet." Doherty laughs heartily. He sees the bewilderment on James' face, hearing the story for the first time.

"Sgt. Parks gets in their face tryin to explain Stevenson is from Louisiana and that's his accent. That didn't go over well with them, and Sgt. Parks was kicked out as well."

"Goddammit, I would have loved to have been there for that shit." James excitedly answers, staring at the two former Marines.

Parks scoffs at the remark. "You didn't miss anything. The bouncers were smart not to let us in. We did end up losing Delta later that evening in all of the drunken fuckery."

Doherty exhales another puff of cigar smoke, "Fuck yeah we did, high-speed bastard went MIA."

"Jesus, man down. How'd you lose track of Sgt. Heis?" James asks perplexed, trying to imagine that evening.

"It was either Stevenson or Doherty, here, that found Delta outside the last bar passed out in a fuckin ant bed. Just covered with the little fuckers, stinging the shit out of him for trespassing on their kingdom." Parks, finally feeling the humor of the situation dissipate his anger, begins to relax and ease back into his pack next to the fire. His laughter comes easily and is followed by the other two resting men.

James, no longer wishing to sleep, pours another glass, "Now I'm really pissed I missed this shit. How could I have not heard these stories already? What happened to Sgt. Heis after you found him?"

"The group decides to call it a night after that. Attebery and I get Delta into the front seat of the car we were riding in. My poor sister's friend that drove our drunk asses around that night deserves a medal for bravery and compassion. Jesus, we were fuckin nightmares. We as *Grunts* definitely fuckin deserve our reputations and stereotypes." Parks laments, remembering the poor young woman's shocked face at the reckless disregard the men had for their own lives. Looking back, Parks realizes that they were no different than any other returning infantrymen; they were not special in any way shape or form. All of them never truly wanting to come home.

"Yut." Doherty reaffirms softly, his squad leaders sentiment, for he is no longer smiling either. His own regrets and guilt coming to the forefront. "We were out of control."

Parks lowers his head towards his chest, "Yep. None more so than myself, Devil. I should've been more responsible for us all." He pauses a moment to remember his failure, the flames not releasing his gaze.

"What the fuck happened to Sgt. Heis?" James asks impatiently, sensing the mood shift towards the dark and wanting to find the humor once again.

Breaking his gaze from the rhythmic flames, Parks looks to James. He no longer wants to smile at the situation from the past, now viewing it as tragic. "Delta loses his shit for a moment. Starts yelling, *'You don't know, you weren't there,'* type crap, the driver is getting scared, I'm trying to calm Delta from the backseat, holding his shoulders telling him shit like, *'I was there, I was your fuckin squad leader, calm down, Devil. I love ya, man!'* He tells me he's *'sorry'* opens the fuckin passenger door and jumps the fuck out, without hesitation. Me and Attebery are losing our shit in the back of the car; the poor driver slams on the brakes and screams *'What the fuck?!'* I look back and see Delta rolling on the pavement of the street and suddenly stop, splayed out on his back. I'm thinking the motherfucker is dead." Parks is no longer smiling; a shadow regret washes over him. He finds no humor in this story; he finds failure as Delta's good friend and squad leader.

"Jesus! What the fuck happened next?" James asks with concern. He, too, no longer smiling.

Parks suddenly does not want to complete this story of his beloved team leader but knows he must, "Thankfully we were almost home and going only about eighteen miles an hour. I rush over, grab Delta's ass quickly; he is belligerent, of course, but okay. Minor scrapes and road rash. We throw his ass in the car and my sister's friend, losing her shit, gets us to the house, and disappears into the night at the double time."

"Goddamn, don't blame her. Was Sgt. Heis, okay?" James adds, looking to his old squad leader across the fire.

Parks keep his gaze transfixed, "Yeah, Delta was fine. His face was so damn swollen and red the next day from all the fuckin ant bites and road rash. Looked like a giant fuckin tomato. That part was truly funny, seeing him arise the next day, moaning and shit. Then all of us began our apology tour, to my mom and sister, her friend, sister's neighbors, to each other. It was truly a fuckin trainwreck. Looking back, I became the pathetic combat Marine stereotype almost immediately, I fuckin hate myself for that. Not realizing what a complete fuckin waste I was." Parks reflects with hatred upon his past actions. "*Sgt. Parks* stayed in Iraq. I don't know what the fuck came back, but I hate him."

"Fuck, Sgt. Parks. You didn't know. None of us did. They gave a one fuckin hour-long class on how to readjust to society. It was a joke. We thought we were normal, and the rest of the country was fucked. We did the only thing ever taught to us in the *Grunts*, drink until you drop and then repeat." Doherty tries to provide solace to his tormented squad leader. He, too, feels shame at some of his own actions from his return, like all returning combat Veterans. "We just didn't know, Sgt. Parks."

"Please stop calling me that." Parks, trying to fight the emotional constriction, is losing and can feel the tears starting to form.

James tries to lighten the mood, his most endearing characteristic, "Well, Jake, makes it sound like you work at State Farm. I start immediately looking for your khakis." He chuckles, exhaling another puff of white, thick cigar smoke to lift up to the beautiful clear night sky. James stares after the cloud, finding a sense of tranquility in the movement. Parks, appreciating his troop's distraction, gives him the middle finger. James smiles a bit and continues, "And just callin you '*Parks*' feels fuckin weird. '*Sgt. Parks*' feels natural to the men of 1st, can't help it, brother."

"Oorah." Doherty acknowledges James's sentiment.

Parks clenches his jaw, knowing it is futile to argue with his former troops, "The real heartwarming part that came of the whole trip to the mansion was how Doherty, Frazier, and Stevenson got back home to Louisiana. That in itself should be a short film on patriotism, respect, honor, pride, endearment, and humanity. All of the fuckin above. Truly inspiring sequence of events."

"Yut." Doherty offers again quietly, reflecting warmly on the memory of his trek home from Parks' house in Tucson. He has not thought upon those events since a Bravo Co. reunion ten years earlier, reminiscing fondly with Stevenson and Frazier.

James gives Doherty a perplexed look, Doherty smiles in return. "It's really nothin. Stevenson's 4-Runner broke down in New Mexico, a state trooper picked us up and gave the three of us a ride to the next jurisdiction, then another state trooper met us there and carried us to the next jurisdiction. That shit happened all the way across New Mexico, Texas, and finally Louisiana. No matter the stop, a state trooper was there to carry us home. It was fuckin awesome, brother," Doherty quietly relays, himself trying to fight back a solitary tear reflecting upon the kindness of the state troopers across the southern states.

"That's some motivatin shit, right there." James says upon hearing the conclusion of his friend's odyssey.

Doherty nods slightly, "Shit was an adventure." He smiles warmly but distant.

The dark of night engulfs the campsite only to be held at bay by the small smoldering fire. There is a collective solitude that befalls each man. Each sensing the other's presence and finding comfort from bonds formed decades ago. There has been enough nostalgic recollection for the time being, the three drift into their individual vacant *nothingness*.

CH. 5
A MISCOMMUNICATED PATROL

The three friends relax around the fire in perfect synchronistic harmony. The sounds of the forest and valley surrounding the men, almost seems to be lulling them to sleep. As if on que, a wolf begins it long and piercing, powerful howl through the beautiful crisp, clear Idaho night.

"Well, if that's not a little discouragin for my peaceful night's sleep." James quips, propping up on his elbows and checking that his weapons are within range. They are. His AR-15 set up on its bipod next to him and his Smith & Wesson .45 semi-auto in his bag.

"Well, after that close crazy-ass howl, I'm goin to ask the dreaded question: Are we standin fire watch[22]?" Doherty asks with a half-smile, knowing he does not want to have to stand post tonight. It has been over a decade since he last stood a fire watch, and it is plain boring when not in combat.

"Aww. What the fuck did you bring that up for, Doherty?" James grumbles, lying back down and pulling his boonie over his eyes to block the glow of the flames.

"Well for one, I don't want a fuckin wolf to attach itself to my throat while I'm sleepin and tear me to shreds, to become wolf shit in a day or two. Besides, you won't get first watch anyway, you just get your beauty sleep, *Snorin Beauty*." Doherty throws a small pinecone at James, hitting his old friend in the leg.

"Asshole. Shit, as long as I don't get second to last watch." James blurts out, adjusting his leg after the impact from the pinecone. "Anyway, point taken.

---

[22] Marine term for standing guard

I saw *The Grey* with Liam Neeson, I ain't goin out like that," James replies matter-of-factly.

"Well, whenever we do hit the rack, I'll take the first two hours, then Doherty, then you, *Snoring Beauty*. Great call sign for you, James. Too bad we didn't think of that shit in Iraq." Parks adds with a chiding smile over the flames.

"Yeah, shows what you remember, Sgt. Parks, I didn't snore then." James rebuts smugly.

"That you know of," Parks counters swiftly. "But you're right, I don't remember you snoring, I remember Culpepper snoring on that rooftop, after our first firefight in Hiit. I went to wake him up for his fire-watch, the big bastard tried to put a round through my head. Fucker jumped and went for his fuckin rifle when I shook him; had to slam my foot down on his weapon to keep the big bastard from grabbing it. Then, I had to soothe him like a child waking from a bad dream. It was like trying to soothe the Hulk, *'Hey big guy, sun's getting real low.'*" Parks relays to the two, imitating his best maternal tone.

The former Marines erupt in boisterous laughter, imagining the large Culpepper having to be reassured by Parks on a rooftop, *zero dark thirty*, Anbar Province, Iraq. It brings the whole group to peaceful, warm remembrance of that shared moment in time.

"Damn, I wish the others could have made this trip. I would love to see Culpepper's face when we tell some of his stories." Parks says softly. He knows these moments with his men will never happen again, all three know this trip will be the last time they see one another. The river of life will forever carry 1st Squad further apart, never to share their laughter with one another, only to live in pleasant, fond memories.

"Fuckin Culpepper reminded me of the Swede from *Heartbreak Ridge*," Doherty adds with a slight smile and laugh, keeping his gaze on the dwindling fire.

"Yeah, he did, big fuckin bastard. Which brings me to my next point, Sgt. Parks." James raises his cover to look to his old squad leader.

Parks looks to his former troop, knowing exactly where James is about to steer this conversation, "What pray tell is that, James?" He looks to Doherty, who rolls his eyes, acknowledging he, too, knows where James will steer their idle chatter.

The Last Letter

"Why the fuck did me, Jackson, and Cooper get stuck with the SAWs and not Culpepper, the big motherfucker that he is? Jackson was tall and lanky, Cooper, maybe I could see, he looked like a machine gunner, but I was an award-winning shooter with the sixteen." James huffs at Parks, in true disappointment. To James, it was an insult to carry the SAW in combat, he truly felt his talent was wasted during their deployment.

Doherty throws his hands up in mock surrender, "Oh, here we go again, Devil." He exhales in humorous frustration.

"Fuck you. You got the sixteen. You don't know the pain of that fuckin weapon," James fires back, still angry decades later.

Parks, tries to calm his old friend, "Brother, I carried that bitch for two long years in the fleet, in a boat company, so that fucker always needed the rust busted. I feel your misery."

James immediately fires back at his squad leader, "But you didn't carry the fucker in combat, Sgt. Parks."

Turning his head towards the flames, knowing his former troop has the superior argument, Parks concedes, "Touché, Devil."

Doherty launches another pinecone at James. "It's too late now, brother. Enjoy the *suck*." James fires his own pinecone back Doherty, then gives him the middle finger with his left hand. Doherty and Parks laugh at the irritation of their old squad mate.

"Listen, James, I brought all that shit up to *Dickless*. That fucker wouldn't let me do shit the *Grunt* way. Best suited man for the job regardless of rank. That's how it's done in the fleet, but he was a fuckin reservist POGe his whole career." Parks exhales a cloud of smoke into the night, watching it ascend. "Didn't you notice that all SAW gunners were the brothers of the platoon? Tell me Potter should have been assigned the SAW, fuck no, that Marine was designed for room clearing, he should have had *Dickless's* M4. Then he assigned you the SAW out of pure fuckin spite after I told him I wanted you to have a sixteen because of your marksmanship training. *'I will do what I want with my platoon, Sgt. Parks'*, is the only answer I received from *Dickless*. Orso too, that fucker went to RECON school, he got the SAW out of spite by *Dickless Daisy*. 1st squad was made up of all the *'problem children'* of the platoon?

Jackson, Cooper, Doherty here, Culpepper, Thomas, and you all had combined multiple UAs or missed drills, your attitudes were deemed unbecoming of Marines. I'm not trying to single you men out but that was what I was briefed when I was assigned to the unit and given the squad. I had never seen a *Grunt* reserve unit before; it was all a fuckin shock. Complete opposite of the fleet." Parks explains, still trying to remember the exact moment he arrived at Bravo Co. 1/23 and the culture shock he received.

"Oh, we know. That's all we hear about, *'It's not like this in the fleet.'* Drove us fuckin nuts." Doherty says, taking a puff of the sweet cigar and rolling his eyes.

James laughs excitedly, "Yes it fuckin did. It never fails. Fleet Marine comes to the reserve units, lasts two drills and then checks out because *'it's not like the fleet.'*" he mockingly whines.

"I know, I completely understand. It's like when a Drill Instructor comes from the drill field or a boot officer fresh from OCS, always wanting to drill and run everywhere and not listen to their sergeants. I'm well aware fleet Marines are dicks upon arrival at a reserve unit. I get that." Parks chuckles a little bit, reflecting on his own behavior upon arrival at Bravo Co.

Another howl of the alpha wolf interrupts the peaceful night of the three. "Man, I swear Sgt. Parks, if I end up as wolf shit, I will never forgive you in the afterlife." James begins eyeing the surroundings quickly.

"We're going to have a literal fire watch. We have enough wood collected to keep it going until morning. Just don't fall asleep on your watch and the big bad wolf won't come for you, sweetheart." Parks replies with a halfhearted laugh.

"Roger that, Sgt. Parks, literal fire watch, aye, aye." James answers with his charismatic wit.

"You dick." Parks replies, takes out another pre-roll and stands up, stretches his arms; and groans with the pain it induces. "I'm heading down to the river for a bit and smoke this. Be back in a few." With that said, Parks picks up his AR-15 and his Springfield 1911 .45 semi-automatic pistol; places the pistol in his right thigh holster and slings his AR across the front of his body with the three-point sling.

The Last Letter

"Shit, I'm surprised you're not throwing on your gear too. *Complacency kills*, Sgt. Parks." Doherty chimes in. Repeating the mantra used during their time in Iraq.

"Ass." Parks smiles to his old troop. "Don't talk too much shit while I'm gone. I already cringe at my past doucheness, you fuckers." He huffs, both men smile in return, knowing that is exactly what is going to happen once the ageing squad leader disappears into the darkness.

James looks up to his old friend, "Oh, you mean like that time in Ramadi, you had Delta take your picture to mimic our platoon T-shirt. You mean like that, douchebagness, Sgt. Parks?" James flashes his trademark boyish smile.

Parks gives James the middle finger. "Yes, like that time, dickhead." Parks smiles to his two former troops and disappears into the vast darkness of the valley.

Doherty turns to James who is still trying to fall asleep, "Shit man, this feels good, brother?"

"Yeah, it does." James replies, propping his cover back above his eyes, knowing he is not sleeping anytime soon. "I do wish more of the guys from 1st Squad could have made it, but this is still awesome to be here with only you and Sgt. Parks. Those times in Iraq with 1st are the best times of my fuckin life, brother. I wouldn't want to go through it without any damn one of you, especially that motherfucker over yonder by the river." James snaps his finger in the direction that Parks disappeared moments earlier.

"Yut." Doherty replies, following James's gaze. "No other motherfucker would have done what he did over there and under those circumstances. To the fucked up 1st Squad." Doherty holds up his cigar to mimic a toast to his friends.

James holds up his glass and takes a drink, "Fuck, that shit is oh so smooth." He exhales still admiring the taste of the beverage. "What do you think happened to him after he got in trouble at Lejeune?"

"I heard bits and pieces; he was supposed to go over with my unit in '07. Then the trouble." Doherty states, still gazing into the darkness in which Parks disappeared. "Shit, brother, I hadn't talked to Sgt. Parks in over fourteen years. I got his number from Bgame and even then Bgame didn't know if that was even his current one. But it worked and here we are after a couple more years of back-and-forth." Doherty recalls his failed attempts to track down his squad leader in the past.

James nods in slow agreement, his gaze returning to the fire, he adds another piece of wood. "He stopped goin to the reunions. Shit, maybe Sgt. Parks will tell us what he's been doin on another three-mile fuckin hump tomorrow." He takes another long drink of bourbon, "Tell me again, why the fuck I agreed to come in full tactical gear. This shit is for the young bucks. Goddamn everythin hurts. If that game warden wasn't a former Marine, there is no way she would let us fucktards do this." James grumbles, stoking the fire with a branch.

Doherty laughs under his breath, staring up at the stars and smoking his fine Cuban. "Yeah, she is definitely stone-cold, brother. She had that steeled, hardened look in her eyes. Fuckin no joke. We did promise no huntin." Doherty looks about his forested surroundings lazily, happily, "Although, one of those fuckin wolves get any closer on my watch, it'll become open season. I'm not havin cops explain to Cass that I became wolf shit all because I wanted to go play Marine one last fuckin time."

"No shit, brother, ain't that the fuckin truth." James replies, both men scoff at their own paranoia of the forest's wildlife.

The two Marines stare off into the direction they last saw Parks. The night air is warm enough to sleep under the stars, next to the fire without the need for one to seek shelter. "Shit, so how've you been doin, brother? It's good to hear you and your old lady are in a good place." James looks to his old friend across the tranquil fire.

"It finally feels good for each of us. She stuck through my bullshit, alcohol, drugs, you know our typical off-the-rails shit we do. Cass helped me through all that. Now I've finally found that purpose to be myself again and live, not for myself but for the happiness of someone else. That makes everythin fuckin beautiful, man." Doherty answers, staring off into the darkness in which his old squad leader departed. "Now, if only all of us wayward lost souls can find that purpose again before it's too late."

"It took me awhile. So many mistakes made, only to realize I was the problem, not the civilian fucks." James offers wearily.

Doherty laughs slightly, "I see you have made progress."

James tips his glass toward his old squad mate, "Like you, brother, I know I wouldn't be anywhere without my wife. She keeps my mouth in check and my ass in line. She is my purpose."

"That's actually quite beautiful, brother. How long have you guys been married now?" Doherty asks, the fire again attracting his attention.

"Shit, I met Jocelyn when we got back, so that was 2005. We've been together nineteen-plus years, married sixteen. Fuck, that's a long damn time when I say it aloud." James replies sarcastically of his math.

"I will remember to tell her that when we get back." Doherty says with a broad, relaxed smile.

"The fuck you will. She'll gut punch me on the spot," James replies to Doherty's suggestion. "What's said and done in these mountains, stays in these mountains. If Bigfoot himself opens a fuckin beer next to us and asks directions to town, we say fuck all to a soul." James laughs at his own joke and Doherty joins in because it is James, and he is relishing being in the company of his old squad mate. The men seem to settle into the fact that they both needed this excursion, it could not have come at a more opportune time for each. A chance to seal away their combined, shared past with one another once and for all, be together as a squad once again. But alas, it is not to be. The two cherish the moment with each other nonetheless.

"It would've been fun to reminisce with everyone." Doherty states with slight disappointment, nursing his little remaining cigar and starting to feel the weight of the hike into the valley.

James answers disappointed with a huff, "Yeah it sure would've been cool, brother. We'll never get this chance again." The absence of the rest of 1st Squad begins to weigh heavily. Each knowing this trip was the absolute last chance for the squad to come together again, one final time. To laugh, to smile, and say one final goodbye to each other.

"It really is too bad. We will have to make this count for the three of us, Devil." Doherty offers his old friend with a wink. After a brief solitary pause, "So, fuckhead, how's the family?" Doherty asks, trying to keep his old friend engaged in conversation, and from passing out.

"Oh, man, good. You know work, kids, wife. You try to keep all three movin harmoniously. That's been my goal and we're doin great, chaotic and wonderful all rolled into one." James heartfully expresses, instant visions of his family dance before his closed eyes. "It's nice to get out here and do some reflectin on where we've been and where we are now. The path for me has been beautiful and full of torment. I feel for the fellow Devils who can't find that balance because once you do; it's a beautiful fuckin thing."

Doherty nods his agreement. "It truly is, brother. It took me a minute to get there, but I'm now enjoyin the past while looking forward to the present and future. This trip was perfect timin. You're right, I needed the reflection to appreciate my present, if you know what I mean." Doherty contemplates the peace in which he has finally achieved.

"I do," James replies. They both finally find their comfortable positions and stare off in the direction of where Parks disappeared into the vast blanket of the dark valley. The two have found a sweet moment of shared solace.

. . .

Parks sits next to the bank of the river, listening to the sound of water smoothly slip by. He inhales on a pre-roll and begins to lift his head to the dancing stars above. Thus, begins his own reflection of failure to the ones he was supposed to love and support, none more so than Katie. He exhales solemnly, the constriction forms in his throat once more. All self-induced mistakes and cringeworthy moments that physically make Parks convulse with guilt and shame; *how did I make so many horrible decisions?*

He hates these moments, they become more frequent and hostile as time moves on; consuming his every waking moment he spends pacing his vacant house. Parks adjusts his rifle across his chest and releases a long exhale of smoke, but there is no calming effect anymore. He smokes now to slow his heart rate, keep the desire for alcohol at bay and to ease his tortured mind.

He contemplates how much to reveal to his men, no longer the man they remember. There is no more noble, *Sgt. Parks*. How does he explain what a waste of life he has become. The *should haves* and *would haves* never leave, not

The Last Letter

for a single solitary moment. The culmination in hurting the one he loved most long ago—Katie, but his wife endured so much more. *I should have fuckin ended it then*, Parks thinks to himself of his eventual arrest. He knows there is no coming back from what he has done or who he became, he accepts his fate to be damned. There is no forgiveness he can find for himself hurting her all those years ago; it is shame, horror, guilt, and pain he must carry the rest of his life, a constant reminder of his failure as a husband, man, Marine, and human being.

Parks sits next to the bank of the river, listening to the sound of water wash by, he is on a repeat of remorse. All the pain, self-induced mistakes, cringeworthy moments flash suddenly to his forethought. His mind flashes to the torment he caused Katie; her tears, her pleas for his love, her pleas for him to stop. *Her pleas.* Parks puts his face into his gloved hands and begins to sob. It was her love he vacated so easily as she tried so hard to make him see all he had before him. Parks hates these haunting, crippling moments, but they have become more frequent as years escape him. It would be easy to blame the alcohol, like so many do, but his actions can never be dismissed, the pain can never be dismissed, and the excuses should never be. He knows this and lives by this tortuous creed.

The old squad leader readjusts his rifle across his chest again and wipes the remaining tears from his weathered, scarred face. "Fuckin take me, aneurysm, right now, motherfucker." Parks angrily speaks to the stars above, as is if willing God to kill him on the spot. *Katie*: she will haunt his thoughts until he passes from this Earth.

He accepts this is how it should be; he deserves no compassion; it is a tenet he chooses to live with daily. "Fuck you, Jake, what a fuckin piece of shit you are." Parks growls to himself, staring at the dark slow current of the river flowing calmly by his position on the bank.

He begins to reflect what the impact of his horrible actions have had on loved ones; yet they still hold him in high regard. It is all bullshit he says to himself. He wants to put to rest the ghost of *Sgt. Parks*, to pass peacefully into the blackness and be done with this guilt, this shame. Parks crumples to his knees next to the silent, inviting dark river, reaching for his side-arm, using every muscle fiber in his body not in one swift movement to end it all. His hands do not shake but rest rather comfortably on the leg holster; almost peacefully beckoning for him to end his turmoil, regret, shame, and his pain. Parks instead slams his gloved fist into the bank of the slow moving river, his Kevlar knuckles leaving an indent in the soft earth.

"One day, brother, but today is not that day and not like that, never like that." Parks moans heavily. It is a familiar mantra that he repeats to himself when the *darkness* comes calling.

With a heavy sigh the broken squad leader finishes his smoke, carefully puts out the roach on a wet rock of the river and puts it in his pocket. *Grunts pack their trash*, so as not to let the enemy know their unit's disposition. Although in Iraq, they burned everything including the human waste, he recalls.

With that Parks sets out to circle back behind the camp, set trip flares along likely avenues of approach to the campsite for bears or other curious predators. He will set up the flares about 60 to 100 meters from camp, terrain willing. Parks hoping Doherty and James don't mistake him for anything worth engaging with rifle fire. He lets out a slight grumbled moan as his joints begin to function once again.

. . .

"Man, I do miss those days. Our squad was the shit while it lasted." Doherty says softly to James, becoming lost to the memories of days gone. "My second tour was jack shit compared to goin over with Bravo Co."

"Yeah, man, my second tour was to Africa. That command was fucked, nothing like Iraq." James pauses momentarily, scoffing at the memory of his second deployment. "Fuck yes, our squad was the shit, Devil. Those days were the best of my life, except of course carryin that fuckin SAW." Smiling broadly underneath his boonie, James takes another sip of his almost depleted 4th glass of bourbon.

Doherty shakes his head at James' constant aggression towards his designated weapon. "Of course."

The Last Letter

James exhales deeply, sleepily, "I didn't think it was goin to be that way at the beginnin. No offense to us, but we all had a *'do not give a fuck'* attitude about the reserves. Jackson, Cooper, Culpepper, Thomas, me, you. The only ones that gave a fuck was moto Perry, straightforward Del Vecchio, oh and, of course, dickhead Caruso." Doherty nods his agreement with his old squad mate. "Thank God, Sgt. Parks got rid of him." James finishes his glass of the soothing liquid and feels the warmth trying to cajole him to a peaceful rest. "Shit, if the guys in the fleet think we're a joke as reservists, why the fuck should we take it seriously? Those days will always be special, brother, but we must lay that shit to rest and today is as good as any." James explains, bouncing from point to rambling point.

"You're right, Devil. Holding on to that shit is what led me down the rabbit hole in the first fuckin place. All of us from 1st Squad need to put that night to rest, for good." Doherty says, sympathizing with James. He gazes back into the dwindling fire, then throws another log on to keep the warmth flowing throughout the campsite. The two sit in collective solitude, both reflecting on the last night they were together as a squad.

James does not lift his boonie but exhales the words, "Yeah, we do. Especially that man over by the river." He points in the direction Parks disappeared earlier.

Doherty's gaze follows James' motion, "Well, comin out here with you two has been great to help put that shit to rest. That's why Cass was so supportive of me comin on this little venture; she knew it would be a nice bow on top of a great present of fond memories."

"Well, at least we had Sgt. Parks for as long as we did." James replies.

The increasing warmth of the fire trying one desperate time to lull the former Marine into a deep, restful slumber.

"It was short-lived but what a fuckin ride." Doherty answers, a resurgent smile spreads across his bearded face. "You remember that time Sgt. Parks took us on patrol when we first got in-country and he kept tryin to re-enter friendly lines at Al-Asaad." Instantly the two former squad mates open with laughter, each knowing the outcome of said patrol. Doherty continues, calming his joviality, "He kept being denied re-entry to friendly lines and how fuckin pissed Sgt. Parks got. The second time he said fuck it and he forced the guard to open the gate, took us straight to that POGe PX[23] and let us fill up on goodies before we went back out." Doherty continues, with a broad smile.

James grumbles under his breath, "Fuckin camp guard bitches."

"Yeah, well *Dickless* didn't tell me in the order it was to be an eight-hour patrol." Parks explains, suddenly reappearing from the dark forest behind the two comfortable men.

"What the fuck, Sgt. Parks?!" James shouts, shooting straight up from his restful supine position against his pack.

"Holy shit! You just scared the ever-livin fuck out of me!" Doherty chimes in, dropping his almost finished cigar and choking on the escaping puff of smoke.

The former squad leader stands before them with a slight smile at having shocked his former troops. "Sorry, Devils, I thought you heard me coming up through the woods. I was not quiet," Parks apologizes with a coy smile, then sits down next to his pack.

"Well, fuck, that's a damn good way to get yourself killed, Sgt. Parks." Doherty continues, leaning back down against his pack after securing his cigar. There is laughter as the friends settle back down comfortably next to the fire.

Sipping warm water from his CamelBak to relieve his cottonmouth, Parks reflects on that patrol, "Yeah, those POGe guards were actually pretty damn cool. I told them my fuckhead platoon commander didn't tell me in the order it was an eight-hour patrol. POGs weren't supposed to let us back in friendly lines, but I told them we would bring them back some shit from the PX and we did. I did not force them, ass, I bribed them." Parks looks to James, who is still trying to find his *Grunt sweet spot*.

"Tomatoe, tomato." James responds nonchalantly.

Parks focusses on the orange, rhythmic flames once more, "If *Dickless* had told me eight hours in the patrol order, then there would've been no issue. That fuckin cocksucker, piece-of-shit coward. Goddamn I hate that man." he snarls into the flames, his teeth grinding feverishly.

---

[23] Post Exchange

The Last Letter

"That's good Sgt. Parks, open up, let all that shit out. Tell us how you really feel." Doherty mockingly takes the tone of an impromptu therapist, looking to his squad leader.

Parks does not break his gaze from the flames, flashes Doherty the middle finger, much to Doherty's delight. "Tell you one thing, I sure as shit was not going to do the same damn patrol route over and over and over again, just for us to be blown up on our tenth fuckin loop. Not on my fuckin watch." Parks explains, heavily exhaling, feeling every bit of his forty-plus years.

"Oh, is that why we went all over Allah's holy land that day?" James asks, nursing his last delicious sip of the expensive bourbon and slowly placing the glass on the ground next to him, feeling the effects of the now-four glasses.

Parks looks down with a chuckle, "*Complacency kills*, right? How boring and dangerous would that have been to do that same route repeatedly? I was so fuckin pissed. *Dickless*, POGe bitch, set me up on purpose to make me look like an asshole to higher. That's okay, fuckin joke was on them, I disconnected the blue force tracker[24] and command had to keep asking our location. I would report 1st Squad to be at a certain checkpoint, and we would be at another pos altogether." James props his cover up and along with Doherty give their squad leader quick looks. "Don't worry Delta always had our exact coordinates locked in his personal GPS." Parks clarifies, catching his former troops' sideways glances.

"Yeah, as long as Sgt. Heis has workin fuckin batteries in the thing." James chimes in with his timely sarcasm, followed by more subdued collective laughter from the old friends.

Gazing into the depths of the fire, Parks recalls more, "Hey, at least our squad didn't start the *Battle of Hiit*. You can say, technically, crazy-ass Attebery and his band of plucky mortarmen got the *Battlin Bastards* rolling. I was on COC[25] watch when all that shit went down in Hiit after Attebery's patrol *'buzzed the tower'* by driving his patrol smack dab in the middle of that shithole town. After Attebery's *'fly by'*, was when all fuckin hell broke loose." Parks offers with a huge grin, quoting the movie *Top Gun*.

---

[24] Early GPS location device on friendly vehicles
[25] Combat Operations Center

"What the fuck are you talkin about, Sgt. Parks?" Doherty asks with a puzzled look on his face. "All we were briefed by you, was a private contractor and a general's convoy was ambushed in Hiit and to standby."

"Yeah, I haven't heard this part of the *Battlin Bastards* lore, Sgt. Parks. Please enlighten these two old devils." James adds, comfortably nestled back in his *sweet spot* on his pack.

Parks lowers head at the mention of his old title, he knows the two men will not stop calling him by his former title, he must accept it. "It's not my story to tell. Next reunion of the *Bastards*, find Attebery's old ass and ask him about his patrol of Hiit. Attebery will smile and then wow you Devils with a fantastical tale of how a simple patrol had gone awry." Parks smiles into the dancing flames of the campfire. "I may have thought '*outside the box*' on our patrols, but even I knew better than to take us into that fuckin shitshow." The old squad leader's smile grows thinking of his buddy, Attebery, and the aftermath of his improvised patrol.

"Honestly, how have we not heard this story before now?" Doherty asks, while he, too, gazes into the fire with detachment.

"Like I said, fellas, it's Attebery's story to tell, and it's a damn good one." Parks relays, enjoying the moment of comical reflection. That is what a combat *Grunt* experiences; times of intense humor with your men through shared misery, followed by intense bouts of violence through the same shared misery. The cycle is lifelong and condemns many men to the vastness of isolation. Parks knows he is in this never-ending hellish cycle, but to him it is futile to fight the current. He does not have the strength to tell his men he has given up.

James, suddenly realizing something he missed years ago, speaks up, "Let me get this straight, Sgt. Parks, you didn't want to go check out the town of *Hiit* with our full fuckin squad armed to the teeth, but you will take Culpepper and me on a three-man patrol through a hostile village. Explain, please?" He asks with a perfectly placed humorous antidote to keep the mood jovial.

"Hey, brother, I asked the squad if they wanted to go or rest, purely voluntary. I fuckin knew you and Culpepper would go, because you two were my personal security detail." Parks begins to explain his decision-making from over twenty years ago.

"Goddamn right Culpepper and I were goin with you. Fuckin *Team OFP*." James huffs proudly.

Parks chuckles at James's lively response. "Exactly, but the rest of these shitheads wanted to rest their pretty little eyes and catch some Iraqi sun." He looks in Doherty's direction with a slight mischievous grin.

"Shit, I didn't know. I was followin the lead of my team leader. Sgt. Heis was layin there as well, shit all of us were. Lookin back, I wish I had gone with you three." Doherty replies staring at the fire, flicking his spring assisted knife's blade open and closed. It is common for infantry Marines to repeatedly open and close the blades on their knives, it is an equivalent of a nervous tick for *Grunts*.

"Why, you didn't miss anythin, only the thrill of the *'pucker factor'* of the ol' asshole, when those hajis tried to get us to go down some back alleys and shit. That's when Sgt. Parks here, did an about-face and said, *'fuck that'* and we moved out at a quick time." James laughs at the memory of hurriedly exiting the small village nervously, "Right, Sgt. Parks?"

Looking now towards the dark valley, Parks reflects fondly, "Yeah that was before *Hiit*. I remember telling Delta, *'you hear gunfire, you cut the wire, you come fuckin weapons free and hummers rolling to get us.'* No, *Black Hawk Down*[26] situation for us. Fuck that, that's all that flashed in my head when those fuckers started waving us down the alleys. No fuckin way I was going to let us end up hanging from some fuckin bridge, just to be plastered all over the fuckin news." Parks recalls, angrily staring into the darkness of the valley.

"That incident right there started the *'I'm goin to tell your mama what you did when we get back'* moments. Me and Culpepper would shout that shit to you when you did somethin crazy, Sgt. Parks." James remembers fondly of him and the large Marine always chiding their squad leader during patrols much to Parks tired chagrin.

"I remember, Devil." Parks states, emotionless.

The comfortable quiet befalls the three friends. The crackling of the fire, the distant sound of the slow-moving river, sounds of distant wildlife beginning

---

[26] Battle of Mogadishu Oct. 3–4, 1993

their usual night's trek for food, are the only auditory stimulus the men need to hear at this moment. It is not depressive, or lonely, or even sad; it is a vacant feeling each understands of the other. They see no need to interrupt one another's *nothingness*, so the three old friends sit in silence, awash in the orange glow of the fire.

CH. 6
THE ACCIDENT

Their silence of individual remembrance brings comfort of not knowing how much time has passed in isolation but the three not really caring. James is about to begin another fabled 1st Squad adventure, suddenly the breaking, snapping sounds of branches being crushed under foot can be heard some distance behind the campsite. The men immediately bolt upright with rifles at the ready. Weapons off safe and finger on the trigger. The three former infantrymen exercising fire discipline, patiently waiting to acquire a target. Years of training and muscle memory flow through their veins.

"What in the fuck was that?" James whispers calmly, scanning the eerily dark forest.

"Fuckin Bigfoot, maybe." Parks replies with a slight smile, he, too, scanning the darkness ahead.

"Yeah, real fuckin funny, Sgt. Parks. This is how every horror movie starts, three heavily armed assholes wiped out by some deranged hillbilly family, or some unstoppable fuckin alien kills them off one by one." James retorts, simultaneously replaying every classic horror movie he has seen throughout his life.

"Are you fuckin talkin *Predator* situation, here?" Doherty quietly smirks, he, too, not taking his eyes off the surrounding environment.

James feels a chill suddenly run down his spine. "You, my friend, are a dick and watch, we'll be strung up from a tree like a goddamn trophy and the hero game warden will save the planet."

Parks moves farther to point, edging closer to the tree-line. "Quiet," he orders quickly. "It's probably a bear or wolf smelling the MREs, time to put that shit far away and down wind," Parks relays over his shoulder to his eager troops. "Fuck, that means my trip flares didn't work." Parks adds, still keeping his voice low, hoping to decipher the noise ahead in the darkness. The night seems to cool rapidly, the hairs on the back of Parks' neck begin to stand. He becomes agitated.

"You fuckin put up trip flares, Sgt. Parks? What about forest fires, *Mr. Hotshot*?" James asks sarcastically, inadvertently scanning the treetops, thanks to Doherty's *Predator* comment.

"One, fuck you. You can stow that *Mr. Hotshot* shit; *Sgt. Parks* is bad enough. Two, dick, I put them up for this exact reason, we have plenty of water to dose the flare or surrounding area of sparks, if need be." Parks fires back over his shoulder, not taking his eyes off the forest ahead, waiting patiently to hear the sound again.

"Fuck, I think it was a hell of a good idea, Sgt. Parks. You just missed that avenue of approach. I think whatever the fuck that was is gone; I'll get rid of the refuse." Doherty affirms, returning his voice to conversational tone. He eases his finger off the trigger and leans over to grab the trash produced by the three men. Suddenly a shattering of the dark forest, as a massive bull elk barrels through their camp and bounds over the fire in an effortless glide.

"What the fuck!", the three shout instantly, jumping out of the way. Parks escaping being gored from the massive spread of the elk's antlers by inches.

James continues in shocked amazement, "What the fuck! What the ever-livin fuck! I almost shit my fuckin pants!"

"Quiet!" Parks barks his order, unintentionally reverting back to his squad leader tone of voice. His gaze follows the elk's path into the dark valley the men traversed that very morning. To Parks, that seems like an eternity ago. "He was running from something."

"Do you feel that? The rumblin?" Doherty asks, looking around the darkness of the forest from which the elk had suddenly appeared.

A fiery explosion over the treetops, sends debris and shrapnel of wood cascading down among the still shocked Marines, as they frantically scramble for

The Last Letter

cover. Suddenly a sleek, black private plane appears through the canopy of trees on its way to crashing on the far side of the river against the rising mountain range the men had descended earlier that beautiful day. The horrific sound of metal being torn apart by the unforgiving trees and treacherous boulders, ricochets throughout the once-peaceful valley. Finally, the plane comes to rest in a massive fireball on the opposite side of the solemn river.

Parks breaks his momentary flashback of the Osprey crash and the enormous fireball left in its' wake, calling out to the other two, "Get your gear on, let's move." The men immediately grab their chest rigs, strap them over their upper torsos and grab their helmets in a fluid almost coordinated effort.

"James, grab your sat-phone, you can call it in when we get to the exact location and can pinpoint coordinates." Parks orders. Each man pulls the bolt back slightly on their rifles and taps the forward assist to ensure their weapons are condition One[27]. It is instinct, nothing more.

James cannot help but smile through his rough beard. "Roger that, Sgt. Parks. Never a dull moment with you."

Parks huffs slightly to his old troop, "Yut."

"I know a place we can cross, quicker than before. I scouted it while talkin with Cass earlier, Sgt. Parks." Doherty tells his old squad leader. The former Marine has forgotten the feel of combat adrenaline, it is a welcome sensation flowing through his steel-like veins.

Parks nods to Doherty while holstering his sidearm after putting a round in the chamber, "Shit, even now you still call me *Sgt. Parks*."

"Fuck, now more than ever is this time to call you *Sgt. Parks*." James makes sure his weapons are perfectly situated for proper deployment. "Just no fuckin SAW this time, thank God. Let's move." James, happily joining the conversation, stowing his sat-phone on his gear.

"Let's hope there are survivors. Point me in the right direction, brother," Parks states to Doherty, staring towards the fireball of the crash site.

"Roger that, Sgt. Parks." Doherty pointing in the direction Parks should follow to the quick river crossing.

---

[27] Magazine inserted, round in chamber, bolt forward, weapon on safe, ejection port cover closed.

"Dickhead." Parks grumbles, still annoyed at the constant use of his former title.

James takes the position of tail-end *Charlie*, and the Marines then set out following Parks' lead to the crash site, under Doherty's direction. All three feel this sense of forgotten excitement, a sense of active purpose once again. Making their way across the danger area of the valley, a light rain begins to fall, helping to extinguish the faraway flames of the wreckage and silence the infantrymen's approach.

"Shit, just what we need," Doherty whispers, wiping the drizzle from his eyes, still moving smoothly in his combat glide.

James speaks softly from the rear of the formation, gliding smoothly over the terrain. "Hey, Doherty, you wanted a three-man patrol, now you have one."

Parks, eyeing the remaining fires amongst the wreckage not yet put out by the light rain in the distance, feels a twinge of caution flare up, "At ease." he orders the men to silence, while the three move effortlessly in their heavy gear. Age at this moment has no bearing on the former *Grunts*. As Doherty and James follow Parks across the river and begin to discover wreckage, they soon realize this was no commercial flight. The ground and trees are littered with twisted metal, seats, and personal belongings. The crash site is a carnage of destroyed trees and scarred landscape. The slight rain seems to keep the fire from spreading from the area.

"What the fuck, Sgt. Parks?" Doherty asks of his old squad leader, surveying the damage imposed on the landscape from the crash.

"Do not touch shit until we get to the cockpit or find the rest of the fuselage." Parks keeps his weapon at the ready, still fighting flashes of the Osprey crash struggling to grip his mind. Shaking the dark reminder away, Parks looks about. "Hopefully, we find some survivors." He listens patiently for any sounds of life.

"Let's hope, but it doesn't look good, Sgt. Parks." James responds gloomily, pulling up the rear, surveying the wreckage.

"Well, let's keep moving. Keep your eyes and ears open for any sound of survivors. We don't have much time before those wolves want to investigate." Parks reminds the men of their current surroundings.

"Fuck, I had forgot all about those fuckers." James reacts with a weary look over his shoulder back towards their camp. He can still make out the glow of the dying campfire. "Well, at least our fire is still goin."

"For now, this rain is goin to put that shit out soon. Come on, the main body and cockpit are just up ahead." Doherty proclaims, turning to make his way farther towards the wreckage. "If any needs rescuin, they'll be in that part of the wreckage."

"Let's hope we find people to rescue." Parks responds, moving cautiously farther up into the crash site.

The Marines continue traversing up the gradual incline, looking at debris and wreckage along the way. The rain slows to a drizzle, the forest seemingly becomes eerily quiet and isolated. Moving closer to the impact site, the men begin to gauge the enormity of the crash site. Freezing in position, weapons at the ready, now off of safe, scanning their surroundings carefully, they listen intently.

Parks continues into the heart of the impact area and soon the friends find themselves staring at the carnage of the cockpit and fuselage. The plane is ripped in two. The tail careening off about eighty meters to the right flank of the men. The cockpit and rest are displayed directly twenty meters in front of them.

Immediately they can see the bodies of four uniformed men sprawled in various positions across the wreckage and forest floor. The former Marines can also see into the cockpit and both pilots are dead. All bodies badly contorted from the impact. "Fuck, I don't think we have any survivors, Sgt. Parks." Doherty turns his head slightly to his squad leader, looking for affirmation of his consensus to the scene.

"Nope, I don't think so either." Parks answers, surveying the wreckage. "Check the bodies for any vitals but leave the searching of them to the authorities."

"Roger that, Sgt. Parks." James confirms, the rush of action flowing through him; it is a feeling long forgotten and most welcome by the Marine.

"Dick." Parks retorts, with a slight nod to James, he knows the feeling that courses throughout his friend's body.

The three move cautiously towards the plane to assess vitals of the flight crew strewn about the forest floor. After taking a couple strides towards the halved fuselage, a mutilated uniformed survivor appears suddenly in the hatch. It is a ghastly sight to behold for the combat Marines; the survivor is horribly mangled from the crash but yet he lives, to the shock of the three old friends.

"Hicimos lo mejor. No es culpa nuestra. Deja a nuestras familias en paz!" the injured man screams, firing at the three with a sidearm that seems to appear in the mangled man's hand out of the mist. His first shot misses his intended target, the survivor does not get a second. As soon as the survivor fires his first; Parks, James, and Doherty return fire, with controlled three-to-four-round bursts fired from each man's rifle. They fire calmly, emotionless, and with muscle memory. The survivor is no more as he is peppered with controlled, accurate fire and drops immediately in the plane's hatch.

"What the fuck was that about?!" Doherty asks after they all cease fire without a word being uttered.

"Fuck, be careful. Check the rest of bodies very carefully don't need any more fuckin surprises." Parks orders, looking about the surroundings, expecting the worst. "Wonder what the fuck he was shouting? I don't habla, wish I did, though, now more than ever."

James answers, standing over the man the three put down, "He said. *'We did our best. It is not our fault. Leave our families alone.'*" Both Parks and Doherty look at James with puzzled expressions. "My wife is a Border Patrol Agent, remember? She learned Spanish long ago. It's a lifesaving tool in her profession, and she has taught me well."

"That's fuckin impressive, James," Parks acknowledges his troops surprising knowledge of another language. "Shit, we stumbled upon something, fellas, that we should have no part of. Do not touch fuck all. Especially that fuckin case attached to our dead Rambo's arm, that's definitely some highspeed shit." Parks asserts to his former troops, both men registering their former squad leader's unexpected nervousness, something the two have never witnessed from the *Sgt. Parks* they remember.

James takes a momentary look around the wreckage. "I concur Sgt. Parks. Who the fuck knows what the hell's goin on? I tell you one thing; these men are not ours. No one carries a dumbass Desert Eagle as standard issue." James points to the dead man's weapon on the ground beside his limp body. "Lucky

The Last Letter

you weren't decapitated, Sgt. Parks." James looks at the damage to the tree behind the three men.

"Lucky." Parks keeps his gaze on the black case attached to the dead man's wrist. "What about the rest?" He asks Doherty.

Doherty, exiting the intact portion of the fuselage, containing the cockpit, answers grimly, "Yeah, Sgt. Parks, four more inside, all are dead, pilots too. I think it's time to call in the authorities."

"Sooner the police or the fuckin DEA get here the better, this has cartel written all over it." James waves his arm about the crash site. "Did I fall asleep and not realize it? This is some bullshit Hollywood B-action movie fuckery right here. What's next? Vin Diesel goin to parachute in?" James scoffs sarcastically at the situation the former Marines find themselves currently residing in.

The three friends stand looking over the wreckage and bodies. "The poor bastard must have thought we were some sort of death squad." Parks theorizes, pointing at the body of the shooter.

"Well, shit, Sgt. Parks, look at us. We look like a fuckin hit squad, except for being little bit out of shape, but he couldn't tell that in the dark." Doherty explains, still staring at the man lying dead on the ground. None of them feel any emotion about the deceased but all wish it had not come to the finality in which it did for the survivor.

"Poor bastard. Survives the crash just to be blown away by three fuckin douches out reliving their old times together." James responds, staring inquisitively at the deceased man on the ground; he feels not sorrow for the man but instead pity.

Parks nods his agreement, "Regardless we're stuck here pulling guard duty until the authorities arrive. James, head up above the wreckage and get a call out on your sat-phone."

By now James and Doherty are not referring to their old squad leader as *Sgt. Parks*, to playfully harass him, rather now it is a form of psychological safety net for the two former Marines. The three agitated men scan their surroundings in reluctant amazement.

"James, call the Sheriff's Office and the game warden. I figured she would know this country more than the sheriff and be able to pinpoint us sooner."

Parks directs his former troop, whose is readjusting his gear for the hike up the ridge.

"Roger that, Sgt. Parks. Provided we don't go to jail for killin a man." James gives the situation a slight pause of reality.

Parks looks over to the uniformed man slumped on the ground, deceased from the men's semiautomatic fire. "We're not going to jail. Just get your ass up that ridge and make the call. Doherty and I will stay put and watch the crash site, make sure no animals start tearing into the bodies."

James traverses up the steady incline, disappearing into the dark tree-line, hoping to get through to the proper authorities. Doherty and Parks begin to survey more of the wreckage without touching anything, moving silently together. "Man, Sgt. Parks, I got a bad feelin. This shit don't look right, brother. It's a clusterfuck out here." Doherty states, pausing to inhale the crisp mountain air, hoping the clean air will clear his head. He smells nothing but smoke and jet fuel.

"Yut." Parks confirms, staring at the bodies on the forest floor. The cloudy night sky gives way to the moon and stars after the slight rain moves away into the distance. The two men seem to be a bit rejuvenated by the break in the clouds and the sudden clarity of the night shines down upon the catastrophic scene. "Well, now all we do is wait; provided James can get ahold of someone and the availability of helos at this hour. I would say we're going to be pulling guard duty for several hours."

"Roger that, Sgt. Parks. I guess when James gets back, we devise a plan, where at dawn two of us go back, break down the camp and get ready to roll when the authorities get here." Doherty adds, looking back to see the tiny grey smoke of their extinguished campfire in the distance.

"Good plan, Devil. Hopefully, James gets ahold of someone," Parks responds, staring off into the darkness of the mountain where James disappeared moments earlier. The towering ridge the men traversed earlier that very day, seems to Parks a dark presence looming over the three, a chill runs the length of his spine.

On que, James emerges from the blackness of the forest, like a warrior apparition and makes a beeline straight towards the two men, with a look of seriousness on his face that Doherty and Parks are not accustomed to from their old squad mate. "Well, I have some bad news and then I have some bad news. Which do you want first?"

"Give us the bad news," Parks responds, letting out a sigh, knowing things are about to go from tragic to critical.

"Well, I did get ahold of the sheriff. He told us to stay put and not to touch a damn thing. He was very emphatic about that, then the fucker transferred me to his deputy."

Doherty looks at James incredulously. "No fuckin shit."

James nods his head in agreement with Doherty. "I agree but under the circumstances, I understand. The sheriff's deputy said she would contact higher and not to worry, but she did say it will be quite some time before the sheriff can get a helo out to us. Which I found odd," James replies, still staring at the wreckage.

"Yeah? How so?" Parks asks, following James's gaze.

"I called that federal game warden first because, like you said, she would know the area firsthand. She relayed to me, she get ahold of her own helo pilot from some other locale and get it up here ASAP[28]. I figured she and the sheriff would know the same fuckin pilots, out here in BFE[29]. Right?"

Parks' gaze falls on the man the three put down. "Right", he softly concurs with his former troop.

"Well, whatever, the bad news is we're stuck here for a few hours, I reckon." James follows Parks' glare at the uniformed man lying motionless, bleeding out from his multiple impact wounds from their rifle fire.

"I wonder what he meant by *'leave our families alone'*?" James asks no one in particular, hoping conversation will distract the three.

The former *Grunts* pause and stare at the dead poor soul on the ground riddled with rounds fired from their rifles. They do not feel remorse or sadness; the former Marines feel only pity. To them, the man died foolishly, needlessly. The men meant no harm. Parks, Doherty, and James will not lose sleep over the death; to the infantrymen; it is now fact.

---

[28] As Soon As Possible
[29] Bum Fucking Egypt

"Some cartel fucker probably has their family held captive somewhere and were forced to do this fucked-up run." Doherty states, still focused on the dead man. "Anyway, that's the cheesy movie scenario runnin through my mind at the moment; how that shit happens in real life is beyond my comprehension."

"It may be a cheesy movie scenario but not fuckin today. I'm afraid real life is about to get a shit ton more complicated than some fucktard *Michael Bay* movie." Parks grumbles, now focusing on the case attached to their victim's wrist. *"I have a bad feeling about this drop,"* Parks distractedly quotes the movie *Aliens*, transfixed upon the foreboding black case.

James responds quickly with the corresponding answer, recognizing the quote, *"We get back without ya'*, Sgt. Parks, *I'll write your mama."*

"Should we get a small fire goin on this side, Sgt. Parks?" Doherty asks of his old squad leader.

"Yeah, might as well, Devil." Parks agrees, knowing the three will be stuck there for some time and will need the warmth.

The men begin to gather up some kindling and fallen tree branches for a fire, the former squad mates freeze in their tracks simultaneously. "What the fuck is that Sgt. Parks?" Doherty exclaims, immediately dropping the wood he gathered at his desert boots.

"No fuckin way they're here already." Parks answers back, also dropping the wood he has gathered and stares back towards their campsite.

"Get the fuck out of here! That's the sound of an incomin helo. You're right, Sgt. Parks, there's no fuckin way they could've got here from the time I made the call to now. No fuckin way. The game warden seems very good but not that good, unless she was a helo pilot in the Marines." James follows his squad leader's stare back towards their camp.

"Hey, man, get my binos out of my butt-pack, I want to see where the hell that's coming from." Parks turns his back to James, allowing him to retrieve the binoculars from the pouch on the back of his chest rig. James hurriedly retrieves the binoculars and hands them to his old squad leader. Parks frantically starts scanning the night sky back towards the direction of their camp. "Now more than ever I wish the rest of the fuckin squad was here."

The Last Letter

He exclaims, not removing his eyes from the binoculars, hoping to find the source of the familiar sound.

"Yeah, me too. Delta would be eatin this shit up right now." Doherty declares, trying to pierce the darkness with his own sight, hoping to spot something, anything. "I have a feelin, Sgt. Parks, things are about to go south, fast," he states, following Parks' glare back in the direction of camp, all seem to agree that is the direction the helicopter sound is emanating from.

"Everything will be fine; we need to stand fast until the game warden gets here. She was a former Marine, we're good." Parks replies calmly for Doherty, never taking the binoculars from his eyes. The binos conceal the foreboding doom he fears is heading their way. Parks knows he and his friends will have no trouble engaging whatever may be descending, but he also knows that whatever is coming will be better equipped and better trained than they. James and Doherty both realize this scenario as well. They are three former Marine *Grunts* in their late thirties and forties, and although well-armed, have limited range with reflex sights and no night-vision equipment. Parks, James, and Doherty know if their situation gets worse, they are doomed.

"I guess we will find out soon enough." Doherty states, never releasing his fixated gaze on the direction of the approaching noise. His anger beginning to tense his muscles.

"This will definitely be one hell of a story to tell the fellas at the next reunion." James responds flatly, double-checking his gear on his chest rig, making sure his mag-pulls[30] are aligned where he wants them to be.

As Parks is about to respond, he sees the dark silhouette of the helicopter appear out of the black sky, a ghostly sight for the men. It immediately hovers above and behind their campsite. The sleek, all-black helicopter appears with no running lights, barely making a sound while hovering. Parks watches with disbelief, recognizing immediately something familiar from his days in the fleet; fast rope lines being dropped from the side doors of the craft. He begins to count the silhouettes dropping through his binoculars, but the tactical team drops too fast, and Parks loses count at ten, with more still dropping.

---

[30] Quick pull for ammunition magazines from their pouches

"Fuck. James, get your ass back up on the ridge and call the game warden and sheriff back." Parks turns to his troop with a look of dread on his weathered face.

"What the fuck did you see, Sgt. Parks?" James now begins to whisper, registering the look of fear on his squad leader's face; it is a look he has never seen from the man.

"Men fast roping out of that silent helo just beyond our camp. You have to move. Now!" Parks exhales, realizing the three of them are in dire need of assistance. "If they come this way, Doherty and I will hold them until you get help. Hopefully, they're FBI or DEA, and we'll be able to turn this over to them." Parks looks to James and Doherty, both expectantly waiting for the good news from their former squad leader; it does not come. "Men, I think this is officially gone south. Now go, James." Parks orders his former Marine.

James is getting ready to protest his squad leader's orders and suggest they should stick together, but before he can utter a word of disagreement, the trip flares Parks set up for bears and wolves ignite in four separate locations surrounding the perimeter of their campsite. The three begin to hear shouting in English, Spanish, and other languages that they cannot place.

"Fuck!" Parks whispers with anger, he knows the exact dispersion he placed the flares. The incoming tactical force is numerous.

The men have taken up cover behind boulders and broken trees from the impact of plane. "How many did you see?" Doherty whispers back to Parks, peering through the darkness in the direction of the camp.

"I lost count." Parks still looking at the flares in the sky as they burn and fade away into the dark of the forest. "They're well dispersed. That means they have more men than I thought, and they're on a mission to search and secure. James, you need to get going. Now, please." His look to James is one of desperation. Parks knows their time has run out.

"Roger that, Sgt. Parks," James replies, no longer joking or answering with his charismatic wit. He realizes the gravity of their desperate predicament.

"Also call your wife, tell her to get on the horn with anybody with Border Patrol and let them know our position." Parks adds, hoping for more law enforcement to show.

The Last Letter

"Trust me, she's the first person I'm going to call." James whispers back to Parks as he begins to head up the ridge again. James gives one last glance back over his shoulder to his two old friends, his eyes widen, James notices something dreadful. The hovering helicopter is turning their direction and heading towards their positions amongst the wreckage. "Shit!"

"I see it, James. Go! They have thermals!" Parks whispers angrily; he knows what is coming next. *The assault.* He has a quick flashback from when he was in the fleet with India Co. and a Cobra attack helicopter silently hovered above a night patrol he led during training at Camp Pendleton. The attack helicopter hovered quietly and moved its turret side to side at Parks and his men; signaling they were KIA. Parks at that moment stood up out of the reeds, *zero dark thirty*, and waved to the pilots acknowledging his defeat. Now he doubts such a gesture would be met with that same kindness. In other words, Parks knows they are fucked.

As the helicopter flies low across the valley floor, Parks looks through his binos with the illumination of the moon as aid, begins to see the silhouettes coming towards the river crossing. There were so many, and they move with such speed. This group are highly trained. The squad leader sighs deeply. "James, run! They'll be here soon," Parks repeats, keeping his eyes on the advancing tactical team.

"Fuck let's all go!" James pleads with his squad leader.

"They'll overtake us and quickly." Doherty replies matter-of-factly. No emotion, steeling his nerves for what is to come.

Parks, keeping his eyes on the advancing group and helicopter, says plainly, "Doherty's right. Tell your wife to send the fuckin cavalry." He, too, begins to shut down his emotions.

"Alright, brothers, I'll make the call and be right fuckin back. Hold 'em, goddammit." James begs of his two old friends, turning to head up the ridge. Suddenly the helicopter is above all three and bores its' floodlight right down upon their position. A rifle shot rings out and grazes James' pack. Stumbling back, James expertly throws his rifle into the pocket of his right shoulder and fires directly at the floodlight, destroying the enemy's illumination. Parks and Doherty likewise open fire on the helicopter and its' door gunner. The dark helicopter veers wildly to the right, trying to bank out of incoming rounds from the former Marines on the ground. James knows this has bought them some time and with one last nod to his old friends, he disappears up the forested ridge, with the little adrenaline he has remaining.

As soon as James disappears into blackness beyond the wreckage, shots begin to ping all around the remaining two, "Smoke check 'em!" Parks orders Doherty. Both men begin to fire at the shadows moving rapidly across the valley floor advancing on their position. The shadows move expertly into suppressive fire and maneuver operations to counter the Marines' rapid firing. The automatic machine-gun fire takes both men by complete surprise, it is the shock and awe the aggressors were hoping for. The sense of finality begins to creep into Parks' consciousness.

"Shit!" Doherty shouts, pinning himself to the forest floor behind the little cover he has in the downed tree.

"Motherfuckers used those initial rounds to locate our positions!" Parks screams over at Doherty from his cover behind a boulder.

The rate of fire keeps increasing as the semiautomatic rifles join in pinning the two men behind their cover. Then comes the telltale sound of an M-203 grenade launcher. Both men know the *thump* of the 203 well; their eyes lock with one another in defeat. The grenades explode around them, hitting the trees all about them and impacting the wreckage beyond, sending a cascade of shrapnel, consisting of wood and metal, down upon the two men's covered positions. He and Doherty are running out of time, Parks recognizes the basic tactics being employed against them. It will be over soon enough. The former squad leader sighs with a heavy heart. Yes, they would die bloody, both Parks and Doherty know there will be no last-minute heroics from 'ol *Sgt. Parks*.

Parks begins planning his and Doherty's next move. Bombarded by a barrage of ground fire and grenades, he then witnesses the dark helicopter, quietly fly overhead towards the ridge, the door gunner suddenly begins to open up into the darkness with semiautomatic rifle fire. To Parks' great relief, he and Doherty can hear James quickly returning fire. He would give anything for a grenade, the only thought Parks can hold on to—*one fuckin grenade, goddammit*.

The Last Letter

"Parks, they're goin after James!" Doherty turns his head to yell at his squad leader.

"Put in a full fuckin mag and unload over your position. I'll do the same and make a beeline straight into the darkness behind the wreckage. We're going to find James and make a fuckin stand, brother."

Doherty looks from his position, debris kicking up all around the pinned Marine, and gives Parks an emphatic, "Yut!"

"We'll have the advantage on the ridge. Get ready, Devil." Parks slaps in a fresh magazine, Doherty doing the same, watching his old squad leader for the signal to begin firing. "Now!" Parks put his weapon to the right of the boulder and open fires on the advancing death squad. Doherty instantly does the same. Parks signals for his troop to move as fast as he can back through the wreckage, still smoldering with grey smoke, to the other side and into the black of the forest, while providing the covering fire.

Caught off guard by the brazenness and suddenness of the counterattack the advancing enemy force drop into the prone position to return fire. This momentary pause gives Parks a chance to move through the crash site and towards the sound of James and the helicopter engaging in a remarkable battle. Rounds from the enemy pinging off the wreckage, explosions from the 203 grenades trying to find their mark. Parks and Doherty can hear the helicopter banking in different directions as James expertly picks his shot to drive them off.

The encroaching group lose their targets into the smoke of the crash site and the NVGs[31] they wear, are now useless until they are beyond the other side of the smoldering wreckage. The insurgent force still has not uttered an audible word, moving as one fluid beautiful extension of one another.

"Keep fuckin moving; we don't have any time to waste." Parks relays to Doherty, as Doherty turns to help Parks up the ridge. "I'll catch up. Find James. I'm right behind you. Meet up with James."

"Well, get the fuck up here, then! I hear James just up ahead; he's on the phone!" Doherty yells back to Parks, beginning to makes his way up the steep ridge towards James' frantic voice. He can also see the helicopter banking and beginning another run at his friend's position.

---
[31] Night Vision Goggles

Parks can see it too. They need to get to James quickly. He tries to stand and run, but it is of no use. He looks down at his right leg and sees a piece of wood sticking through his calf muscle. His cammies are soaked with blood and his desert boot is filled with the warm liquid as well. Parks grabs the shard of wood, pulls it out quickly with an unrelenting scream, and ties it off with his neck gaiter all in one swift, painful motion. He wishes he had grenades—the only thought keeping him from losing consciousness from the pain.

"Nope, not today, Sgt. Parks." Doherty appears from above, grabbing Parks by the shoulders and propping his squad leader up against him. "This is not the place you die. You die up there with us, as fuckin one."

"Roger that, Corporal." Parks answers his former Marine with a dry smile, trying to block the searing pain radiating in his lower leg.

"James. We're on our way!" Doherty yells up the ridge, hoping James can hear him. By now the men disregard being silent, they want to meet up with their squad mate and make a final stand, together.

"Good, hurry the fuck up then!" James shouts back down the ridge. He is closer than Doherty thought, which is good for them. He knows Parks is not getting up the ridge alone and he also knows Parks will tell him to leave his old squad leader behind to futilely make a stand by himself.

That's not goin to happen, Doherty vows to himself. "We're almost there, Sgt. Parks. Come on, lean on me." Doherty encourages Parks to move quickly up the ridge. With each step Parks can feel the blood pour into his right desert boot. The two men can hear the aggressors reach the wreckage below them; it is a matter of minutes before the group continues up the ridge in pursuit. This time the former Marines will have the advantage of being on higher ground, but it will be their last stand, and the three Marines know it. The old friends are running out of time.

Making their way up the ridge, they notice the black helicopter does not follow but instead banks back towards the crash site and the dark river valley below. Parks becomes uneasy. Doherty can see James in an outcropping of boulders, and he is frantically making his way down to help him with Parks once he sees the two approaching. Making it to James' defensive position, they automatically begin to reload their weapons and prepare for the inevitable onslaught from their aggressors.

"I fuckin wish I had grenades." Parks finally says out loud what has been on his mind since the first rounds started flying.

"Yeah, Sgt. Parks, I wish you had them too." James offers with a quick instinctive smile, knowing his old squad leader's penchant for employing flashbangs and grenades during firefights. "I got hold of my wife before I got engaged by that fuckin helo. I think I hit that fuckin door gunner, but I dropped the goddamn sat-phone on the ridge somewhere, hopefully it's still transmittin and not smashed to shit. I gave her the coordinates and said send the fuckin cavalry; we're under attack." He pauses and looks at his two friends. "It was her voicemail," James adds, looking down, deflated.

"Oh fuck." Doherty echoes the group's emotions of defeat.

"It's fuckin four in the mornin at home. Fuck." James discloses, trying to rationalize the missed call.

"Stop, Devil. It's okay." Parks says, putting a reassuring gloved hand on his troop's shoulder. "You got the message off and more importantly the coordinates. It's permanently recorded what's happening up here. Your wife's already a hero when she hears the voicemail." Parks trying to calm James, but more importantly calm himself. "Let's get ready for the assault." The squad leader surveys their surroundings, looking for the best attainable defensive positions for the three. James, Doherty, and Parks simultaneously watch in dread as the helicopter lands on the valley floor, picking up a team of the well-equipped enemy.

James stares on in dismay. "Here we fuckin go. Get some." His growl begins to fuel his rage.

Parks knows he and his men are about to be enveloped by a superior force. "We need to move, now." Parks snarls back to his two former troops, his rage growing along with Doherty and James. *Focused Rage* is the Marine Corps Infantry's secret ingredient that foreign armies will never duplicate.

Still looking about quickly, Parks desperately tries to plan their next move. He knows James and Doherty are counting on the *Sgt. Parks* from years gone. "Listen up, fellas, those fuckers are going to blast us with suppressive fire from below, drop that team down on the back side of the ridge and then they'll have us pinned in a crossfire. Alright, Devils, we need to disperse, and play talking guns with these fuckers as best we can until we run out of ammo." Parks tells the men without taking his gaze off the valley floor as the stealth helicopter rises farther into the darkness.

"Well, Sgt. Parks. I wish you luck, seein how I'm the better shot, you'll fuckin need it. Hey, but once I take care of my targets, I'll gladly help you with yours." James replies with a halfhearted smile, tapping his friend on the shoulder.

"You dick." Parks replies affectionately.

"Sgt. Parks, I want to thank you for everythin you did for us as our squad leader. It was an honor." James offering his old squad leader a sense of finality.

Parks exhales deeply. "Thank me for nothing. I owe everything to you men. It was my absolute honor to have served with the best." With that Parks puts both hands on his men's shoulders and nods his deep-felt appreciation. His worn, dirty face conveying understood emotions.

"Doherty, I love you, brother; we came up together at Bravo. I will see you in the afterlife." James gives his friend a wry smile across his dirt-soaked face, the two men then embrace quickly.

"I will see you soon, brother." Doherty forces past the emotional constriction in his throat and watches as James moves to take up the defensive position Parks assigned on the right flank.

"Hey, Sgt. Parks, thanks again for Iraq. I love ya, man." Doherty turns to Parks, adjusting his rifle across his chest and giving his old squad leader a look of heartfelt gratitude.

"There's no need for thanks, Devil. I owe you men my life. I love you and 1st Squad more than you men will ever know. In the afterlife I will take orders from you, brother." Parks replies, giving Doherty a quick embrace.

"In the afterlife, I'm done with war, Sgt. Parks. I better not see another fuckin weapon again." Doherty turns his focus down the ridge. He can see the advancing group beginning to move through the wreckage and disappear into the dark forest base below. "Man, our families are not goin to take this well." Doherty somberly states, trying to methodically find approaching targets in the darkness.

The Last Letter

"Yeah, I don't want to think about it. Let's get this done and go out on our shields, Devil." Parks, too, is looking for approaching targets to engage, he sees nothing yet. The helicopter has disappeared from view to his dismay. "And I hate to break it to you, brother, we die a warrior's death here, Valhalla awaits us in the afterlife, just more fuckin war."

Doherty smirks. "Fuck that, Sgt. Parks. I guess we're not dyin here today then."

"Errrr." Parks gives the customary Marine growl in response. Hoping to motivate his troop but more importantly motivate himself for the upcoming events. "Doherty, give 'em hell." Parks affectionately pats his friend on his Kevlar helmet.

"Aye, Aye, Sgt. Parks." Doherty snaps back with his trademark knowing smile. "It truly has been an honor." The men embrace once more, then Doherty heads off to his position in a rock outcropping on the left flank to sit and wait. The Marines are within sight and hearing of each other. They have formed a half circle with intersecting fields of fire, hoping to bottleneck the advancing enemy into a single avenue of approach. Parks knows the three are vulnerable to being flanked from their six o'clock position, he has no choice and must maximize their fields of fire where needed.

The men sit patiently waiting until the assault begins or Parks opens fires first. The black helicopter skirts behind the ridge and is now ascending on the opposite side. As Parks fears, he can hear the rotator wash of the dark helicopter's ascension. *We are fucked*, he sighs to himself.

James prepares himself the best he can and gives one last sentiment to God, he knows this is his ending. Flashes of his wife and daughters flood his conscious thoughts. Their faces, smiling, their laughter echoing, he hears them call him, *Dad*. A tear escapes his right eye, mustering one last emotional plea.

"Lord, watch over Doherty and Sgt. Parks, make my aim true, and please provide comfort for our families when the inevitable news arrives. Let my wife and kids know I thought of them until the very end, Amen." He closes his eyes one last time to immortalize a vision of his family in his mind. James opens his eyes; he stares straight ahead; he has now shut down all emotion, except rage and misery; the fuel for every Marine infantryman. James will become a machine until the end, everything will come from pure instinct and muscle memory. He is ready, a wicked smile emerges.

Doherty nestles himself into his outcropping and takes a deep breath. "God, please watch over James and Sgt. Parks. Please give comfort and solace to my wife and my expectant little one. Watch over them and provide my love to them. Amen." Doherty takes another deep breath, wiping his dirt-encrusted cheeks with his gloved hand. He then gives in to the rage and misery, becoming the warrior he once was.

Parks, staring up at the beautiful starry night sky utters the best prayer he can, tears dropping from his tired eyes down his mud-covered cheeks, "Whoever the fuck you are up there, God, I don't give a fuck, please get Doherty and James out of this, somehow, someway. This is my fuckin fault. The two deserve better. Just bring them home to their families, alive, I beg of you. I know I've cursed your existence many times, and you owe me no fuckin favors, but in the event, this does go south, give comfort and warmth to our loved ones, they don't deserve the pain that is to come, Amen." Parks looks to each of his flanks; Doherty and James are stoically at the ready. It is then Parks' guilt comes crashing down on him, *this truly is his fault*. His muscles tense, his anger becomes rage and like his men, Parks succumbs to that rage.

All three can hear the hovering helicopter over the top of the ridge they traversed that amazing morning, the engines barely audible. The old friends then hear the dreaded sound of the helicopter banking away, it has dropped the insurgent team on the backside of the ridge. Once that team is in position, the slaughter will begin. Parks knows they have mere moments left.

CH. 7
INEVITABLE

The actual "battle"' did not last longer than six minutes, but to the former Marines, in their final moments, it was an eternity. The men would make their last stand and it would be gallant. The opening salvo of fire does not in fact come from Parks, but from James. He sees movement of a silhouette that has somehow made it to his right flank without his noticing the aggressor skirt around his field of vision.

"Fuckin cocksucker, tryin to get me while I'm prayin. Well, fuck you," James utters to himself, sighting in on the dark silhouette. Lining up the green dot of his reflex sight on target, James fires. He knows, *headshot*. The silhouette drops in place. The ridge erupts in small-arms fire, tracers pour onto their defensive positions from below. James, Doherty, and Parks return as much fire as they possibly can, engaging multiple targets simultaneously. The three feel nothing but the calming effect of the adrenaline and the familiar sound of small-arms fire. Everything now is instinctual and guided by muscle memory.

"Fuck you!" Doherty yells, as he pops out from his covered position and fires, hitting another silhouette in the chest, the man does not make a sound dropping to the ground. Doherty quickly spots the silhouettes of a fire team and opens up in that direction hoping that he hits the advancing men anywhere trying to slow them down. He can hear Parks and James yelling their own profanities, returning their own fire as best they can.

"Motherfuckers!" Parks snarls, opening fire in the direction of the incoming rounds, he, too, hits a moving target in the leg. The target does not make a sound getting hit but instead rolls smoothly into a covered position to avoid taking further fire. The incoming rate of fire is soon going to overwhelm the combat Veterans, the team above them on the ridge will begin their assault at any moment, Parks knows the inevitable will fall upon he and his men soon.

The finale of James, Doherty, and Parks' gallant stand begins with a barrage of M-203 grenade fire peppering the friend's covered positions. With no grenades or support personnel, the former infantrymen are overcome with pure numbers and fire superiority.

The six man team that has been dropped into position atop the ridge, through their NVGs can see the battle unfolding below. The team leader halts his unit, and watches the action for a few precarious moments, amazed at the fight in these determined Marines below. To the team leader, this has been an excitement he has not known in many years. He will take a prideful pleasure in killing this stubborn enemy. They are worthy of what respect he can still muster for humanity. The team leader then signals for his men to begin their assault.

Parks can see the team above their position hesitate, by now all three are firing blindly within their lateral limits, in the direction of incoming enemy fire. "What the fuck are they waiting for?" Parks exhales, trying to catch his breath. On que the team above starts to make their advance, "Shit, on our six!" Parks warns the other two, unloading his magazine in the direction of the advancing enemy from above.

The six-man team from atop the ridge is caught off guard by the rate of fire in their direction from the targets below. Luckily, Parks hits one silhouette in the neck, he drops instantly. James, seeing where his squad leader has fired, turns and does the same, he, too, dropping another with a headshot. Doherty is about to follow suit, when he sees movement coming up directly to Parks' position from below. He reflexively fires, hitting his target in the back and the rear of the head with a double tap. This would be the extent of the men's brave hearted rally. The escalation of force that then rains down upon the three former Grunts, is like a tsunami of small-arms fire.

The leader of the team from atop the ridge, stunned by the actions of the foolhardy men below, witnesses two of his six drop in shocking fashion.

The Last Letter

He orders the return of fire from all angles; the team then methodically advances towards the former Marines, with small-arms fire and concussive grenades. The team leader wants at least one of the men alive. He wants retribution for his losses.

Concussive grenades begin to land around the beleaguered James, Doherty, and Parks; sending showers of rock fragments that slice into the men's flesh through their camouflage uniforms. The old friends at this point are overwhelmed, outnumbered, and outgunned.

"Motherfucker!" James screams out in pain as rock shrapnel peppers his position, tearing through his skin. Trying to adjust his position to avoid further damage, James is hit in the abdomen and chest with small-arms fire and drops, falling back against the massive boulder that provides his cover. He immediately puts pressure on his abdomen. The chest rig saves James from the round to the heart, but the impact broke a couple of ribs, his troubles breathing begin immediately. "So, this is what being shot feels like," he exhales dryly to himself, coughing up blood all over his flak. "You really do cough up blood. Fuckin movies." James then grabs his sidearm from his leg holster and waits under the barrage of small-arms fire and grenades for his chance to acquire more targets.

Parks witnesses James get hit and go down, he also sees his troop moving to cover and that means he is still alive. At that moment Parks is blown back by a concussive grenade, simultaneously being hit in the chest rig as well by small-arms fire. A couple of ribs fracture; he begins gasping, coughing and dry heaving trying to catch any amount of oxygen, to relieve the sledge hammer pressure in his chest. Another round goes clean through his left hand. "Fuck!" he groans. Parks has no more adrenaline, no more rage, he is spent.

Being the far-left flank, Doherty witnesses his two friends go down. He tries to rush towards them, but the aggressing team from above spots the former Marine moving to render aid and unleashes a barrage of suppressive fire and concussive grenades in his direction.

Doherty is hit right through the left kneecap and then another round through his left shoulder, shattering his collarbone. He immediately slumps back behind his cover. A concussive grenade lands at his feet and explodes. Doherty blacks out.

It is over; the old friends are then set upon by the insurgents. As Parks tries to stagger back up, he is met with a butt-stroke to the back of the head. The exhausted squad leader slumps to the ground with a grunt, two men begin kicking him in his injured ribs a few times, then flex cuff his hands behind his back. Parks loses consciousness.

James, with his back still leaning against the rock he uses as cover, tries to raise his sidearm in a futile attempt to engage the enemy standing over Parks but James' pistol is knocked from his grip. A team of men stand over the wounded Veteran, James mutters a defiant, "Fuck you." He smiles broadly, blood flows from his mouth down over his dirt-encrusted beard. The enemy personnel do not bother even kicking him; they flex cuff James' wrists behind his back, he moans in horrible agony from the abrupt movement.

Doherty still knocked unconscious from the grenade blast is flex cuffed in the same manner as the other two and a group of four assist Doherty to his feet. There is no abuse or harassment of their prisoner. On the contrary, one pulls a pack of smelling salts out of his side pouch to aid in regaining Doherty's consciousness. The salts work as expected and the Marine looks around frantically, realizing suddenly this is not a dream. "Fuck." Is all he can muster, watching James and Parks being dragged to their feet, gagged and escorted back down the ridge towards the crash site. Doherty is then gagged, and he, too, is escorted down the ridge in procession. What astonishes him is none of the enemy have yet to utter a word.

The light autumn rain once again begins to fall, offering a reprieve for everyone involved in the battle. The three captured friends and the enemy squad all seem to refocus with the cool of the cascading mist. After the former Marines are assisted down the rocky ridge by their enemy, gently, the captors then place the three against pieces of wreckage and have their ankles flex cuffed as well. The gags from the men's mouths are then removed.

"James, look at me, brother. How bad are you hit?" Parks worriedly asks the injured Marine with tears welling up in his eyes, not caring if the enemy kills him for talking. The group of silent combatants seem intent to let the conversation commence unfettered, staring blankly at the prisoners in their various states of misery. Their black masks under their helmets makes a menacing sight for the three old friends.

"I'm gut shot, Sgt. Parks, I don't think the outlook is particularly good." James offers exhaustedly, trying to raise his tired head towards his former squad leader. "I think one of these fuckers gave me some morphine. The movies are right, Sgt. Parks, you do spit up blood." James struggles, trying to manage a smile for his two captured friends, spitting out a massive pool of blood from his mouth into the mud below him. James hangs his head back finishing his statement, gasping desperately.

Doherty and Parks lock eyes and know it is over, their good friend does not have much longer and neither do they. Parks looks frantically about, looking for any sign of hope, but there is none, only a group of men, geared from head to toe, staring blankly back at the old *Grunt*.

"Doherty? You?" Parks asks, broken. The tears continue to silently run down his weathered cheeks, looking across over at his loyal troop.

"My head hurts, and I took two. One in the knee and one in the shoulder." Doherty emulates James's bravery, trying to keep his ahead aloft, while facing the dismal end. "You, Sgt. Parks?" he tiredly asks of his squad leader, the pain in his head is insurmountable.

"One in the chest and one in the hand. Chest rig stopped the round, my ribs are fucked up, I can't tell, everything hurts. Some of these fuckers are using 7.62." Parks gasps, breathing heavily, looking from expressionless aggressor to the next; referring to the size caliber round the enemy force employed. None of the imposing group seem too eager to end the conversation the prisoners are carrying on, more in fact, the group seem to be enjoying the exchange between these former squad mates.

"They gave me morphine and practically carried me down the fuckin mountain. What do you motherfuckers want?" Doherty asks with an exasperated and exhausted tone, looking around at the death squad surrounding them. He counts twelve heavily armed men standing about, muted. No response.

"Don't waste your breath. Save your energy. They're going to make examples of us or we'd be dead, already." Parks struggles to breathe. The pain from his ribs and hand, plus the shrapnel injury to his calf muscle earlier are sending shockwaves of misery circulating throughout his body, he groans as each wave of pain rolls over his tired muscles.

One of the group steps forward, removes his NVGs and then his hooded balaclava, exposing a chiseled, scarred face. He speaks with an obvious Russian accent; the Marines recognize that much. The scarred man's face is covered in camouflage paint, smeared on, no pattern. All three friends now realize their nightmare is beginning and there will be no support unit coming to the rescue.

"What the fuck are Russians doin in fuckin Idaho?" James mumbles, his Southern drawl becoming more labored, blood still leaks from his mouth pooling on the ground between his outstretched flex cuffed legs.

The Russian lets out a quiet chuckle at the statement of the dying man, crossing towards Parks and leans down close to the captive's muddied face. "Who do you fucking men think you are? *The A-team*? You killed four of my men and critically wounded two others. That is no good. There must be consequences. Who are you guys? DEA? CIA? FBI? SEALs? Which is it? Please pick one." the Russian asks of Parks cordially.

"Fuck him. Don't tell him shit, Sgt. Parks." Doherty tries to struggle, but the morphine keeps him too dreary to try anything substantial. All he can muster is a failed effort to stand with his ankles flex cuffed. He is immediately shoved back against the wreckage by one of the enemy assailants. Doherty groans in pain.

The Russian inches closer to Parks' right ear and hisses, "So, Sgt. Parks, is it? Who the fuck are you people?" He speaks fluid English, but he cannot hide his Russian accent or chooses not to. The rest of the aggressing squad stand emotionless, frozen, their unit has done this numerous times before.

"We're nobody. Just Veterans trying to enjoy the fuckin great outdoors, until you fucks showed up." Parks defiantly responds, turning to face this foreign squad leader. Their eyes lock. Parks can see in the Russian's stare an experienced coldness. Parks has seen this look before. It is a look of weathered detachment.

The Russian stands back up. "Nobody? Huh? Armed to the teeth with tactical weapons and rigs. I do not think so. So, Sgt. Parks, I will ask again, who the fuck are you three with?" There is no malice or menace to the man's tone; he is methodical.

"I fuckin told you; we're old Marines enjoying the fuckin outdoors. As far as our gear, this is America, most every swinging dick has this shit." Parks responds defiantly, looking over to James and Doherty, praying for some miracle that Parks knows will not arrive.

"It's fuckin true, asshole. We're here to have a reunion, fucktard." Doherty states, trying to wriggle his hands free of the flex cuffs to no avail.

Looking down at Doherty the Russian smiles broadly. "We will see." He then turns his attention back to Parks. "You know there is a reason we did not give you morphine, Sgt. Parks. We need someone coherent and lucid to extract information from. The subjects of my interrogations need to feel pain or what is the point of torture, am I right, Sgt. Parks?"

"Well, let's get on with it, then; the answers will not change. Or I could sit here and give you my fuckin name, rank, social over and over again. Either way, you'll get the same fuckin answer, dickhead." To Parks the inevitable has arrived on his doorstep. The three are going to die, horribly. *How could I have let this fuckin happen?"* Parks hangs his head with the crushing guilt.

The Russian moves towards the former squad leader, "Let us begin, shall we, Sgt. Parks?" In the dark with camouflage paint smeared across the Russian's face, his menacing smile looks like pure evil shining bright against the dark backdrop of the starry night sky.

"Stop calling me, Sgt. Parks. You're not one of my men or a friend. You're neither, fuckstick." The former Marine tries to provide a morale boost to James and Doherty before they are all in the grasp of *death*. She smiles her wicked smile; *Lady Death* has long awaited the arrival of Parks' tortured soul.

The Russian laughs slightly, his smile never wavering, "I like you three. You men put up an incredible fight, something we as a team have not seen in quite some time." He looks about the group of well-trained individuals, "I must admit, I was taken by surprise and that never happens. So, you three have earned a small amount of respect from myself and my men. I will make sure you die as warriors; but I need some information first."

The Russian pulls a serrated knife from his gear and smoothly strides behind Parks. He is terrified, all three of the men are. James and Doherty begin to shout obscenities at the advancing Russian circling behind their squad leader, but the insurgents quickly gag them once again. Their muffled screams and yells struggle to escape their muzzled restraints, pleading for the life of their old friend. The Russian is now standing directly over and behind Parks. Taking one last inhale, Parks prepares himself as best he can for the pain that is about to ensue.

The Russian proceeds to cut through Parks' flex-cuffs that are attached around his wrists, he then follows suit with the flex-cuffs around the squad leader's ankles. With a weary look, Parks eyes the man cutting him free, but he knows whatever is next, it will not end well for the three of them. The Russian instructs one of the men to administer aid to Parks' right calf and remove his chest rig. Every movement sends shockwaves of searing pain through his body. Parks looks to Doherty and James; he can see the absolute terror in their horror stricken eyes. James looking weaker by the second, but he is still struggling against his restraints and Doherty is still trying to hurl as many insults as he can, his profanities being muffled by the gag. The two Marines can register the absolute worry in Parks' tired eyes.

"I like knocking Americans down from their pedestals. Americans think you are so fucking tough and can kick anyone's ass. Well, we will see about that soon enough. Anytime my profession brings me across an American target, I get a sense of a rush I do not feel during other operations. These missions are an added bonus for myself and my men." The muscular Russian motions to his comrades standing about ready to engage. "And since you will not tell me what agency you are with, I will see what training you have. You can lie to my face, but your defensive and offensive actions in hand-to-hand will suggest your level of training." The Russian speaks, removing his own chest rig, laying it neatly on the ground.

Parks, exhaling deeply, tries again to convince his adversary one final time. "Listen, fuckin asshole, you have our IDs, and I'm sure with the amount of tech you have, you'll have an idea of who we are soon enough. We're Veterans who were just out having a reunion, nothing more." Parks responds, taking his gaze off his men and fixating his cold stare on his experienced adversary.

"We will see the truth soon enough." the Russian replies with a slight grin.

"Again, this is fuckin America, unfortunately every red-blooded man, woman, and child can buy this shit free and clear." Parks insists, realizing what is about to transpire, knowing he is going to lose. He has been in many a bar fight, and he is not on the winning side too often. Parks can see the hardness and coldness in the Russian's eyes, this is going to be a massacre. The foreign adversary means to dismantle Parks in front of his men, to break their will as much as his own, the former Marine is aware of this fact. Parks wants to try and buy enough time for hope, any hope, to appear over the ridgeline. "What's the plan? Hand-to-hand? Duel at ten paces, give me a fuckin break. Let's get this over with," Parks grimaces aloud, wanting to arrive at the inevitable sooner rather than later.

"Something like that, my friend. I promise, I will not use my legs, seeing you are down one. Are you ready, Sgt. Parks." the Russian asks coolly with a crooked, malicious smile.

Shit. Parks thinks to himself, "Yeah, let's get this over with." He looks over at Doherty and James and can see the absolute fear and desperation in their pleading eyes. "I am sorry." With that Parks turns his attention towards the smiling, advancing opponent.

James tries his best to keep his head up to watch his former squad leader, he knows deep down this will not end well. Regardless his main focus is trying to encourage his friend. He struggles to shout through his gag, tears streaming down his blood soaked bearded face. The pain in his gut, unbearable even with the morphine the tactical team kindly administered to him earlier.

Doherty, too, struggles to get words through his gag. Every time he shouts, the pain in his head seems as if his head will implode on itself. Doherty doubles over after each plea of desperation, his efforts are for not.

Parks waits patiently for the smiling opponent, looking for any opening to his advantage, but he clearly sees there is none. Parks decides enough games and begins the offensive. He rotates his shoulders to loosen them up, then he starts throwing fisticuffs. Both James and Doherty are surprised at the ferocity and combinations at which Parks launches on his advancing foreign aggressor, with the little amount of adrenaline he has left pumping through his veins. The pain in Parks' ribs is excruciating, he can only move in one direction, forward.

The Russian, too, is taken aback ever so slightly by the quickness left in this ageing Veteran, *Whoever he works for did put some basic training in, but it will be to no avail*, he ponders. None of Parks' combinations land but nonetheless it is an impressive display that is unexpected among the group of insurgents. Right then the Russian decides he will make these men's deaths quick and honorable, based off this profound surprise, continuing to smile violently, blocking the combinations from the former Marine effortlessly.

Parks is running out of energy, fast, he knows that his combinations are having no effect, his opponent is handily blocking everything he can muster. It is now the aggressor's turn after he decides enough is enough, the ensuing flurry of combinations that erupt from the Russian are a blur. The speed is unfathomable, Parks tries to dodge and counter, everything hurts but this man is another class of fighter and Parks is dropped in a matter of rapid, successive blows. It happens on a left hook that comes with blistering speed unnoticed as Parks is caught with a feint and a flurry of hand combinations from the foreign adversary.

The Marine crumples to ground and hunches over on all fours spitting blood from his mouth. He looks over at his men, James and Doherty; and can see the terror in their eyes. Parks gives them a wink and gets slowly, painfully to his feet, stubbornly advancing towards the Russian, who keeps his evil grin unchanged, and waits eagerly for the old squad leader. This time as Parks throws what little combinations he can, the Russian counters and drops him with a vicious right uppercut. The old Marine lay motionless on his back and for a moment, Parks looks to the beautiful stars above through his left eye, for his right has swollen shut, his jaw fractured. Parks rolls over slowly onto his stomach, refusing to look in his friends direction. He cannot bear to see their terror-stricken faces at the moment. *He has failed them, this is all my fault*, Parks accepts the blame, trying to push himself up to his hands and knees. A large amount of blood flows out of Parks' mouth, mixing with the mud and jet fuel underneath his body. *So, this is how it ends*, Parks thinks, coming to terms, trying in vain to again get up and face this unstoppable adversary.

The Last Letter

"Still, you try. I will ask again who you work for and what are you doing out here?" the Russian asks patiently waiting to see if Parks can make it back up to his feet. The muffled audible resistance of James and Doherty behind their gags grows ever louder, watching their former squad leader struggle.

Parks, on the verge of passing out, answers garbled but defiantly, "*'We're on vacation!'*" In a state of delirium, Parks quotes Eddie Murphy from *Beverly Hills Cop*. The Marine is rattled and trying to regain his faculties, his jaw not allowing him to speak properly.

James and Doherty both seem to register their squad leader's attempt at defiance with the movie reference. Both men look to each other, both want Parks to look their direction to know he is not alone, and that they are with him. It is a desperation that will go unanswered. Parks cannot bear to witness to the fear in his men's eyes.

"I admire that. That was funny. I am also starting to believe you. No matter, this ends badly for you three, but I made a promise to myself I would make your deaths quick and honorable. That is thanks to you, Sgt. Parks. I will make your death first," the Russian states, leaning down he grabs Parks by his camouflage blouse and begins to help the beaten Marine to his feet.

Parks rolls his head completely backwards, seemingly on the verge of losing consciousness, his head looking as if to roll off his body grotesquely, James and Doherty begin to fear Parks is dying. The old squad leader's movement is unnatural and confuses the emboldened Russian. The brief second the Russian takes to look over at his men, is when Parks launches his head forward as his opponent turns back to face him, smashing the aggressor's nose with a horrible *crunch*; blood spraying all over Parks' face, crumples to his knees when the Russian loses his grip on Parks' uniform to cover his broken nose.

"Didn't see that coming, cocksucker." Parks states, vomiting up more blood, heeled over on his hands and knees.

The Russian does not miss a beat, after dropping the dying squad leader, he immediately sets his nose, takes two strides and kicks Parks in the face, he is then at that moment knocked unconscious onto his back. The Russian straddles the unconscious Marine and unleashes a sickening onslaught; punch after punch, each making bone crushing impact to Parks' head. Ruthless ground and pound, fists and elbows. Both James and Doherty desperately, courageously fight to break their restraints, screaming through their gags pleas of mercy for their fallen squad leader. Blood erupts from their wrists and ankles as both men try to come to the aid of their friend, watching Parks being beaten to death in front of them. Doherty's and James pleas fall on deaf ears, the brutal assault continues unabated against the silence of the dark forested backdrop.

Two men break ranks and pull the Russian off the unconscious man, finally ending the onslaught. The Russian offers no resistance letting his men pull him off the beaten Veteran. One of the group immediately begins administering first aid to their team leader's nose and another tends to a badly mauled Parks, trying to ensure he remains alive. The enemy combatant administering first aid to the former Marine, begins with setting Parks' own nose, the medic notices it has been broken many times before, it sets easily. Parks' face is a bloody, broken mess; both his eyes are swollen shut, the medic does his best to clean up what he can and ensure the beaten Marine's airway remains clear.

"Is he alive?" the Russian asks calmly, snorting blood out of one of his nostrils. The medic responds with a nod. "Good, give him the salts. I want him awake for this." The man hesitates. "Give him the fucking salts!" the Russian commands again. The medic reluctantly breaks out the smelling salts from his aid bag and continues to bring the Marine to consciousness.

"What the fuck!" Parks groans upon coming to, he tries to open his eyes but fails. The blinding pain hits like a freight train, the badly beaten Marine lets out an inhuman moan. Doherty and James join in the agony, their woeful sounds echo throughout the depressed valley. The distant wolves answer the mournful sounds of the Marines with desperate howls of their own.

"Open his eyes," the Russian states flatly to the medic kneeling over Parks. The medic again holds for a second. "Open his fucking eyes!" the Russian commands of his subordinate.

A second man comes over and holds Parks head in a viselike grip. He tries frantically to struggle and his head free, but the enemy's hands are like steel clamps on the sides of his pounding, aching skull. The medic pulls forth a scalpel from his trauma kit,

The Last Letter

"Don't struggle, Devil," he whispers in Parks' ear. In a flash he cuts the swelling over Parks eyes so the old *Grunt* can raise his eyelids to see. The blood streams down the battered squad leader's face and onto his pepper grey beard. Parks pays no attention to the procedure or the pain; instead, the former infantryman is transfixed on what the medic whispered in his ears. It is not so much the message conveyed but the accent and sentiment in which the message is delivered to the battered Marine. The man tending to his wounds is American and Southern judging from the soft drawl.

"You're fuckin American!" Parks cries out, with the last of his fading life, blood streaming out of his mouth. He is crushed and slumps further into himself; they are doomed by their own.

The Russian pauses briefly, registering what the bloodied Veteran has groaned in agony. "What the fuck did he just say? Did you talk to him?", the team leader angrily demands, looking towards the man tending to Parks' wounds.

The medic does not have a chance to respond before Parks cuts him off. "You're fuckin Veterans!" Parks screams with utter despair and futility dropping his head into the mud before him, destroyed. James and Doherty still desperately struggle to be free of their restraints to come to his aid.

"You fucking idiot," the Russian scolds the medic, who is calmly wiping the blood from the former Marine's battered, beaten face. "You are lucky that you are good at what you do, and we have been through some shit together already. It matters not, you three heroes will be dead soon enough."

All Parks wants is a way out for his men, nothing else, his life does not matter. "Just let my men go. Make your fuckin point with me," the former Marine begs of his enemy, everything a blur through his swollen eyes.

"Go ahead and remove their gags, let them breathe peacefully their last breathes." the Russian commands his men to remove the gags from Doherty and James.

"How fuckin could you, cowardly motherfuckers?!" Doherty spits out to the American that tends to Parks' injuries. Doherty's rage is fueling another adrenaline dump and is keeping him conscious.

"Go ahead and tell them, Doc, since it is you that fucked up. You can tell these three battle-weary American Marines, why another Veteran would betray them. Tell them." The Russian motions for the tactical medic to speak.

Doc looks to Doherty and exhales deeply, "Listen, asshole, you know nothin. Fuck this country. What did they do for us when we came back? Fuck all. A *'go wait in line at the VA'*, for fuckin what? Pills? America gives two shits about us or what the fuck we've done. Most of us are homeless and if we do go the VA, they slap labels on us, preventin you from any real federal or governmental jobs. Fuck that." The outed corpsmen lowers his face to Doherty's and picks up the former Marine's chin to look him in the eye. "We are gettin what's owed to us and doin what the government trained us to do, while gettin paid like a professional athlete. The way it's supposed to be. What did you and your men make over there, twenty or thirty thousand, if that, for what? Not a fuckin thing. Fuck those bitch politicians who use us as pawns for elections and nothin more. Now do you see, Devil?" he genuinely asks of the former Marine.

Doherty only knows one thing to do, being restrained, he spits as much blood as he can in the corpsmen's face, "Fuck you, brother." He growls to the man. Doc drops Doherty's chin, calmly wipes the blood from his face, stands and moves back towards Parks.

"They have no honor or care about their oath. Don't waste your breath, brother." James slowly states, suddenly lifting his head towards his friend. Doherty can see James is not going to make it much longer, but to hear his old friend brings a smile to Doherty's face.

The medic turns to face the dying, James, "Oh, don't give me that honor and oath bullshit, dickhead. You know that shit went out the window when we got our DD214. Look at our politicians, they have no honor or care about their oath to this nation. Let this country burn, fuck them all."

James looks around with as much energy as he can muster, he is fading fast, and this betrayal is killing him faster, "So, you go work for drug dealers and kill other Veterans for money, nice, asshole. Does that come with college benefits or home loans?" James mumbles the best one-liner he can think of in the heat of the moment. He then slumps back against the wreckage, weakening by each precious second.

The Last Letter

The Russian then chimes in, "Drug dealers? Oh, my friend, do you think I would do this simply for drug money. No, no, no, no." He chuckles slightly. "No, this is about destroying America from within."

Parks suddenly reemerges from his rambling state and is back upright on his knees, he struggles in a final burst of energy and pain, "Fuckin traitors!" He looks around angrily, Parks' swollen eyes allowing only blurs of images.

"Oh, do not blame them, Sgt. Parks. Your fucking gluttonous country turned their backs on them long ago. Your politicians have driven this country right into the ground. I gave these men comradery, brotherhood and most important purpose once again." Some of the darkly clad men nod in agreement with the Russian, "Would you not want that sense of leadership, that sense of shared purpose once more?" he asks of Parks, genuinely interested in the old Marine's answer.

"My men and my brothers in arms call me Sgt. Parks, you're neither, fucktard. You're my executioner, so get on with it." Parks grumbles, blood pours down his face and flows from his mouth.

"Answer my question, Sgt. Parks," the Russian asks, smiling once again.

Doherty interrupts, hoping to draw the attention off his squad leader, "Leave the man alone. Let me guess, here comes the villain speech?" he glares angrily at his captor.

"Precisely, my friend. We are a media driven world, let these final moments play out like a clichéd movie," the Russian argues enjoying this banter with Doherty.

"Just fuckin kill me now. I don't have time for this shit. Valhalla awaits, asshole." James bursts into the conversation with a well-timed line. The former Marine knows each word is costing him precious life, the blood keeps flowing like a crimson river from his abdominal wound.

"In due course, my friend. But first my evil monologue." Smiling evermore the Russian begins his villainous dialogue, to the dismay of his three captives, all groan insubordinately as the speech commences. "The world wants to see America burn nothing there is new but for once it is within our grasp. Your country will soon learn what it is like to starve and be looked upon as third world. Are you listening, Sgt. Parks? Your former fat orange, corrupt elected leader has single-handedly destroyed your inflated country from the most coveted, powerful position in the world, the presidency, opening the door for a new America, a Russian America. Your own idiot compatriots are doing the work for us, we feed them bullshit conspiracies to spread like a virus amongst social media.

"You, Americans, are such gullible drones, repeating whatever we feed you. It is perfect. Your corrupt officials ignore Russia, and we have run rampant throughout your country. This is not about drug money; it is part of hundreds of billions in laundered cash for pay-offs of governmental officials, from the lowest to the highest offices in your country; all on that little hard drive," the Russian, motioning towards the black case attached to the dead man's wrist. "And when the storm comes—and it is coming, my friend—your country will be crippled from within by the very people you elected to defend democracy. We have hacked your infrastructure, and when the lights go out, we will watch your country tear itself apart from within. Then at your country's very weakest, *Mother Russia* and the *Great Republic of China*, will roll across your borders with the greatest coalition army this world has ever known. So, you see, you are but a grain on a coast of sand, Sgt. Parks. America's time as the leader of the free world is over. Your compatriots will tear each other apart and we will pick at the carcass of your beloved country."

Parks looks solemnly over at James and Doherty, through a blood-soaked blurred vision. They both stare back at their mutilated squad leader, acknowledging that they will not be able to protect their loved ones from the forthcoming carnage. "Good villain speech. What's truly scary is, I believe you."

Continuing the Russian strides closer to Parks, "Look around at this team, if you can." The battered Marine tries to focus his swollen eyes on the group surrounding them. "I have the best from America, Russia, Australia, England, Mexico, Israel, Middle East, Africa, and China. SEALs, MAR-SOC, Marine Raiders, Delta, Rangers, British SAS, Aussi Spec Ops; all them professional combat machines. We are but one team in many, using drug cartel pipelines to infiltrate your borders and help destabilize your country from within. It is your own CIA tactics we employ against you. You see, the rest of the world wants to see you burn and will stand idly by as your pathetic country falls.

The Last Letter

"By the time you Americans realize you were betrayed by your own greedy politicians, it will be too late. Sure, there will be some resistance, some *Red Dawn* rebel types, but it will be crushed, harshly. I know movies too, Sgt. Parks." The Russian stands back up, strides over to the case attached to the dead man's wrist, and with an electronic remote releases the restraint securing the case to the deceased. He then hands the case to one of his men in the group. A few of the enemy personnel gather up their dead and wounded, then head towards the clearing where the helicopter is preparing to land for the evacuation.

Two teams return carrying black duffel bags and begin tossing their contents about the wreckage. James, Doherty and Parks witness the telltale packages of wrapped drugs being tossed about by the group. The Russian is going to make this into a downed drug smuggling operation.

"Let me guess, there will be a story leaked that me and my men are part of some cartel as security or rival guns for hire or some bullshit like that." Parks mumbles, trying to look upon the Russian's blurry silhouette.

"Something like that. It does not take much in this country for you idiots to believe. A couple bullshit stories online, some dumbass conspiracy theorists and a few politicians to repeat the narrative and the problem will take care of itself. You and your men will be branded traitors, or worse a byproduct of a failed mental health system, *Crazies*." the Russian responds genuinely enjoying his triumphant moment over the three captive Americans.

One of the group quickly moves up to the Russian, "Mierda, tenemos un problema. El guardabosques local encontró un piloto de helicóptero y se está preparando para despegar. ETA 60 micros."

"Entendido." the Russian replies in return, looking about quickly to ensure everything is ready for EVAC[32].

"Sgt. Parks, the game warden…she's enroute," James slurs, struggling to lift his head towards his friend. "She found a helicopter pilot and is preparin to leave. Sixty mikes." Blood pouring through the dressing the medic applied to his gunshot wound to the abdomen, James is keenly aware his time is over.

The Russian whirls around to James, "Wow no estamos llenos de sorpresas, esta noche, estoy verdaderamente, verdaderamente impresionado."

---
[32] Evacuation

"Vete a la mierda. Me importa dos mierdas si estás impresionado." James defiantly answers. Doherty and Parks gaze at each other in exhaustive amazement at their old squad mate, not understanding the exchange between the two adversaries. Both absolutely petrified for James.

The Russian looks amusingly upon the dying Marine, "I like you because you surprised me, all of you did. You are not the mindless Americans I mistook you for." He turns to look at the other two injured captives, "But three Marines out for a reunion, happen to kill four of my best men and injure two others. And then one of you speaks fluid Spanish…. Now if I had time—no, no, I do not believe you. Normally I would torture you slowly, painfully but we are out of time. I will just threaten your families. I will find out who you are and then I will come for them or tell me now and I kill you here and be done with it. So, I will ask one last time who do you work for?", the Russian calmly asks the old friends.

"You fuckin asshole, we're just old war buddies out having a good time. We served together, that's it, dickhead. Just kill us and get it over with, motherfucker." James relays slowly, trying to keep his head up.

"Done." With that the Russian pulls his pistol from his leg holster and fires one round into James' head, killing him instantly.

"You motherfucker!" Parks tries to get to his feet but is butt stroked in the back and crumples onto the muddy forest floor.

Doherty lets out a primal scream of pain and tries to crawl, grief-stricken, over to James' body. The Russian lets Doherty get close and then he fires another round into the back of Doherty, he passes instantly.

A sound erupts from Parks' throat that is pure pain and the destruction of one's soul. It is wail of catastrophic loss and utter agony. Parks succumbs to the grief and falls on his back staring up at the blurry stars above in the soulless night sky. The rain starts once again, as if the heavens weep for the souls of the two lost warriors. Parks slips into a dreamlike state, but in reality, it is shock. He cannot move, *this is my fault*. He hears no sound. Not the sound of the insurgents scurrying about, moving bodies, cleaning up and staging evidence. Nor does he hear the helicopter in the clearing. He does not hear God. Parks hears nothing. The former Marine does not notice the Russian moving

The Last Letter

into a position above him. He does not hear the Russian ask him if he has anything final to say. Parks does not even notice the Russian point the sidearm at his head. He stares to the stars; *this is all my fault*. Parks witnesses a flash of lightning, *how peaceful*, but it is only the muzzle flash of the enemy's sidearm putting a round in Parks' beaten, swollen head. Doherty, James, and Parks are dead; forever immortalized on the forested floor, a *Band of Brothers*.

The Russian takes a moment, not to admire but to ensure everything around the crash site is staged to his satisfaction. Once satisfied with his team's operation albeit the slight hiccup with these Americans, the Russian strides over to Parks' bloodied body, takes a knee and places his hand on the dead Marine's chest, "Rest easy, my friend. You and your men will have your places in Valhalla." With that he leaps up and jogs out to the clearing towards the dark helicopter awaiting him to board.

As soon as he is on, the silent helicopter expertly ascends and tears off in the direction from which it came, flying *map of the Earth*[33], to avoid radar. Slipping silently into the darkness, leaving a wake of chaos and destruction behind. The dark forest falls eerily quiet once more, the sky openly weeps upon the final scene of this horrific tragedy.

---

[33] Hugging the Landscape

CH. 8
SPECIAL AGENT ALEXANDER

When Forestry Department Investigative Special Agent Lynda Alexander, gets the call on her government-issued cell phone; she is still up mindlessly watching a movie she has seen a dozen times before, trying to fall asleep. Alexander does not like taking the VA medications prescribed to her for insomnia. The medication leaves her groggy in the mornings and that is not conducive in her official investigative capacity for the northern region of Idaho.

Nicknamed affectionately the *game warden* by the locals, Alexander has come to love her posting in Idaho. Poachers and fugitives travel through her territory routinely and now with the rise of fentanyl, methamphetamines, and other opioids; Idaho forests have become a secret highway for cartels to smuggle up North into Canada. Her job is to stop the flow, but Special Agent Alexander lost the passion for the chase when her husband passed two years ago.

She replays the conversation in her mind quickly. The voice on the other end sounds winded and exhausted but not panicked or frightened. It is James, one of the nice Veterans that came to her office to request permission for their excursion. He is requesting assistance for a downed aircraft. Alexander relays to James she will scramble a helicopter pilot and will be out ASAP.

"Listen, I have to get back to my buddies. I'm calling the sheriff next; something doesn't feel right. You have the grid coordinates. Thank you, ma'am." With that, James ends the call on his sat-phone.

"James, wait, I need more info…," Special Agent Alexander asks of the Marine, but the call goes dead. He must be calling the sheriff, she quickly surmises. Alexander will not bother calling him back.

All James could give her was their grid coordinates, after stumbling upon the crash site. Alexander immediately springs into action and calls the local Sheriff's Office, "This is Forestry Special Agent Alexander, did an individual just report a downed plane to your office?"

The on-duty sheriff's deputy confirms she received the call from the former Marine regarding the downed aircraft. "Yes, ma'am. I called the sheriff at home and relayed the call from the individual you are claiming to have talked to. The sheriff told me, it was, and I quote, *'probably some dumbass militia callin in bullshit. If they call back, then get me up.'* I told him *roger that* and I hung up. I have not received another call from said individual about the aircraft."

"It's probably because they're dead by now, you fucking idiot! Get the sheriff's ass up now!" Special Agent Alexander yells into the phone, ending the call, sharing James' trepidation of something not feeling right about the situation. She then immediately calls her helicopter pilot she uses to search for poachers, smugglers, lost hikers, body recovery and to track animals. It takes Alexander a couple of tries, but she finally rouses him from bed with a groan.

The helicopter pilot tiredly answers, "What fuck, Xander? It's early."

"Bill, I don't have time to explain. Get the bird ready to go. I'm on my way to the airfield," she orders of her pilot.

"Roger that." With that Bill springs out of bed, throws on some clothes, grabs his jacket, AR-15, sidearm and bolts for the airfield.

Special Agent Alexander immediately jumps into her field uniform and boots, she keeps staged in her closet. She moves to her sixteen-year-old son's room and wakes him, "Honey, I have to go. Get your sister off to school, and I'll be back as soon as I can. Keep your phone next to you, I love you."

"Roger that, Mama. Love you too." With that, her son plops his head back down on his pillow. He has been through this routine many a time since his father passed two years earlier and understands the risks of her job. He is so very proud of his mom, he thinks, drifting off back to sleep. Alexander ducks her head into her fourteen-year-old daughter's room. She

The Last Letter

watches her sleep peacefully for a split second before mentally sending her love to her drooling daughter.

She stops by her weapons safe after leaving the daughter's room; using her fingerprints to unlock the heavy steel door, she grabs her chest rig already loaded with magazines, snatches her Smith & Wesson M&P AR-15, and her Springfield 1911 pistol, which she expertly places in her quick-release thigh holster. Darting out the front door of her cabin-like home, Special Agent Alexander hops into her governmental Chevy Silverado 4x4 and speeds down her dirt driveway into the black Idaho night. Dust from the dirt road aglow in the wash of the running lights of the vehicle.

Ten minutes later the special agent pulls into the tiny, one runway airfield, which houses mainly private hobby planes for the rich, when they vacation up in the Clear Creek area. Next to the runway is a small landing pad with the helicopter readying for takeoff. The pilot sees the forestry agent pull in, he quickly ducks out of the cockpit and heads to help her with her gear.

"What the fuck is this all about, Xander?" Bill asks surveying the gear she brought with her for this operation. To Bill it looks as if she was preparing to go into an ambush. Bill, also a former Marine and CH-53 helicopter pilot, remembers vividly the look of Marines he carried in and out of combat zones. It is a look of cool, resolved detachment, Special Agent Alexander displays the exact same look now, aggressive detachment.

"No, time. I'll explain once airborne," she cuts him off, handing Bill her rifle. He has been on many of these operations with the special agent, he has never seen her this determined. Bill recognizes his dear friend has an extremely dangerous job and deals with constant threats; especially now with the rise of gun-wielding untrained militias, cartel smugglers, poachers, and fugitives, but this operation feels different, rushed to the ageing helicopter pilot. The look on the agent's face, gives him the impression they are in for serious trouble, now he is glad he brought his own AR-15. In his helicopter he stows their rifles in specially designed brackets for quick retrieval. They both jump in the cockpit and throw on their headsets for communication. Bill instantly flipping switches, prepping for liftoff.

"Alright, let's go, Bill," Alexander anxiously orders through her headset.

"I'm going as fast as I can, Xander," Bill responds in typical military fashion by shortening her last name. It has been his name for her for years; of course, he asked her permission long ago. He notices a slight panic in her eyes, not the normal cold stare he is used to from her.

"I apologize, Bill, I know you are," the forestry agent responds patiently, blankly staring into the darkness of the early morning hours.

The helicopter ascends to Bill's desired cruising altitude, he then pushes the helicopter forward in the direction of the Clear Creek mountains. Bill asks impatiently, "Now, will you tell me what the fuck is going on?"

"Okay. You remember me telling you about those former Marines that came up here for their reunion?" Alexander recounts for her longtime friend. The helicopter strains as Bill pushes the machine to its' limits.

He looks about the darkness of the mountains, "Yes. I thought it was a pretty damn cool idea for a reunion. Don't tell me, are we enroute to engage a group of heavily armed former fellow Marines because I don't see that ending too well for either of us."

"Will you shut the fuck up and let me explain, damn it?" After unexpectedly snapping at her friend, Special Agent Alexander registers the hurt in Bill's demeanor. "Again, I apologize," she offers quickly. Bill waves off her apology. Alexander continues, "I got a distress call from one of the Marines on their sat-phone. They're at the crash site for a downed plane. I don't like this; I just hope we're not too late." Special Agent Alexander begins to worry, flashes of fallen Marines swarm her consciousness. She fights desperately to ignore her past's haunting images and their cries for help.

"What the fuck?" Bill suddenly scanning the dark skies ahead. "Over fucking Idaho." He thinks aloud to himself. His adrenaline begins to spike, he guiltily enjoys the forgotten rush. Bill instantly feels the hint of nostalgia from his days flying Marines in Afghanistan.

"Fucking Sheriff's Office got the same call. Dipshit deputy calls the sheriff at home, and I quote *'probably just some dumbass militia playing a prank'* and went back to bed. Can you believe that lazy prick?" she grumbles into the mic.

Bill nods his agreement. "Piece of shit," he says through the headset.

The Last Letter

"I ripped her a new ass; then I called the shithead on his personal cell enroute to the airfield and told him, *'To get his fucking ass out of bed this instant and get your helo up to these coordinates now or you will never fucking hunt in the United States again. I will ensure that"*, she recalls her conversation with the county Sheriff.

Bill chuckles slightly. "I bet that got his ass moving. How big a crash do you think judging from the call?"

"Not big. I have an uneasy feeling, Bill," she responds to his question. "You remember Afghanistan '08?"

The pilot suddenly looks to the forestry agent as she continues her surveillance out the right side of the cockpit. He knows exactly the incident she is referring to. "Of course," he answers solemnly. Bill happened to be one of the CH-53 CAS-EVAC helicopter pilots that responded to an IED ambush, on a supply convoy unescorted by infantry Marines, in the Kandahar region of Afghanistan. The ambush to the supply unit would leave six Marines dead, eight wounded and six left standing when the smoke cleared. Unknown count of enemy insurgents strewn about. Four of those surviving Marines would receive a *Bronze Star with Valor* for actions taken during combat operations to repel the enemy's assault. Of the four, one, a young Cpl. Lynda Alexander, for actions taken during hostile fire; running ammunition between gun trucks to help repel the hostile assault, administering aid to the wounded while firing her sidearm to engage the enemy, her award citation would eventually state. The two former Marines would not meet until Alexander was posted to Clear Creek as the Special Agent assigned to the region by United States Forestry Service. "That bad of a feeling, huh?" Bill exhales heavily. "Okay, let's get this done, Xander. ETA to grid coordinates forty mikes."

"Let's hope they can hold out that long. I sent a quick SITREP to my higher and they're in the process of contacting the DEA, FBI, and Homeland Security. I have a feeling we're going to need all hands-on deck." Special Agent Alexander deduces flatly, looking down at her rifle in its' bracket, ready to deploy.

They both keep silent scanning their sectors of responsibility, quietly hoping everything will be overblown but knowing they are about to step into something beyond their scope of operations. The night sky is warm and overcast with periodic drizzle but for Alexander the beautiful refreshing night air is making it hard for her and Bill to spot smoke or flames from any kind of crash site.

The cool engulfing breeze filters through the cabin of the helicopter, Bill flying map of the Earth, Special Agent Alexander cannot help but think of those Veterans and how they must have enjoyed this night before they were interrupted. Catching up on old times, rehashing their memories together as a squad in Iraq; she envies that camaraderie. Alexander and her unit have not spoken in decades, and none ever speak of the ambush. So, she occasionally has beers with Bill, and they will tell stories of their respective units, which is how she found out Bill was one of the CAS-EVAC pilots that day.

"Twenty mikes out." Bill gives an update on their ETA to the grid coordinates relayed to her by James.

"Roger that," she replies, still scanning the horizon for either another helicopter or signs of smoke. She is worried. Alexander does not like to feel worried… anxious, that is okay, but she hates worry. It is too emotional.

"What's our plan of attack?" Bill asks.

"Shit, Bill you were the attack helo pilot, you tell me?" she snaps back.

"I meant on the ground, asshole." Bill responds, chiding her through the headset. He can see she is worried and wanted to distract her. He, too, hates to see her nervous. He has seen it only once and it involved her husband.

"I will assess once overhead. How big is the crash? Is this cartel? Are hostiles there? Are the Marines holed up? Condition of the scene? What do I tell the families and friends if the worst happened? So many damn scenarios running through my head, Bill. I got it, though. I will make a tac decision once we see how your flyby goes." Special Agent Alexander responds.

Bill continues to skirt the treetops, pushing his helicopter as fast as his skills will allow without jeopardizing their safety. "Four mikes."

"Roger that." The forestry agent unlatches her AR-15 from its' bracket, keeping muzzle down as she was trained all those years ago.

"Do you want to get in the back and strap in by the door?" Bill asks her.

"No, I want to assess the situation, besides if you have to bank, I don't want to be tossed around latched the fuck up, bouncing all over the damn place," she responds, nestling her AR comfortably in the pocket of her shoulder still muzzle down.

"Makes sense," Bill shoots back.

"Okay, Bill, slow up. Let's hover for a sec. See if we see or hear anything before popping over the ridge into the clearing on the other side." They both keep scanning the horizon. The two see nothing. No movement, no muzzle flashes, no fire from the wreckage. They hear nothing as well, only the sound of their own rotor wash from the helicopter.

"I don't see or hear shit." Bill states, still scanning his lateral limits. "Me either. Okay proceed and God help us," she says, turning to Bill.

Bill throttles the helicopter up and over the ridge, hitting his flood light. It is then the scene of the battle is displayed out before the two. Their eyes widen at the first glimpse of the crash site, Bill hovers enough that both can make out the bodies of four men. Three men bound wearing tactical gear splayed out in various forms of execution. A fourth seems to be dressed in a pilot's uniform and is laying on his back by the wreckage. From their cockpit both stare in horror and pity at the individuals splayed out in the mud of the forest floor.

Before she can stop herself, a stunned gasp escapes as Alexander stares shockingly at the three Marines, she had met only days before. She turns to get in the back and latch in with her rifle, catching Bill rub his eyes in disbelief. She taps him affectionately on the shoulder, "We have a job to do. Let's get it done."

"Roger that. I'm going to take one more pass and I'll land in the clearing by the river." Bill answers. He is overwhelmed with the reminder of flying *Grunts* in and out of firefights and seeing the casualties splayed out waiting to be retrieved. *What the fuck? I thought I was done with this shit;* he thinks solemnly to himself.

"Hey, Bill, me too," Alexander expresses through the headset, as if reading his very thought. Bill knew he did not have to say anything back; she understood.

Bill takes the helicopter in a buzzing pattern to ensure no surprises when they land. He wished he had thermal sights (FLEER) but that was on a governmental requisition order. Neither one of them had NVGs, also on a requisition order, and neither one had the money for personal equipment like that. He puts the helicopter down expertly in the clearing and shuts it down.

"Well, if they were going to shoot at us, this would have been the time. Let's get to the men." Special Agent Alexander turns on her body camera, throws her weapon into the pocket of her shoulder as does Bill and they make their way across the clearing into the tree line. Once there, they see the in-depth horror that was not evident from the sky.

The wreckage is not as bad as Alexander expected, *the pilot must have been particularly good at his profession*, she surmises. What drops Special Agent Alexander to her knees is the bloody pulp that was, Parks. She kneels in terror; transfixed by the Marine's swollen, distorted, bloody, face. She cannot wrap her mind around, that this is the same reluctant, quiet man she saw days earlier.

"These two are unfortunately dead as well. No vitals." Bill takes a knee trying to keep his nerves from giving way. He wants to let his tears flow, trying to imagine these honorable warriors' last moments; Bill keeps moving, staying with the fallen Marines will mean certain grief. He checks the fuselage and sees a couple more bodies strewn about, obviously deceased, dressed in airline uniforms, same as the pilots in the cockpit. He exits the wreckage, looks upon the packages of drugs strewn about haphazardly, then makes his way over to the forestry agent, who is still slumped by the body of the unrecognizable squad leader.

Bill, as Alexander had done, slumps down to his knees next to the deceased Marine. Not only the trauma inflicted during his unrelenting beating at the hands of an unknown assailant but the trauma from the gunshot wound to the head has caused monumental additional swelling, resulting in a deformity of Park's bloodied head.

"Jesus, what the fuck?" Bill gasps, overcome with grief, letting out a sob.

Special Agent Alexander continues to stare blankly at the deceased Marine. She is trying to move to go check on the other two and to document as much of the scene before the world descends on Clear Creek, Idaho, but she cannot physically move her body from her position of horror at what she is witnessing. Parks' body torments her waking being, Alexander desperately wants to pull her gaze away from the battered Veteran, but past trauma will not let her remove her stare.

"Xander, look at me," Bill pleads, trying to break her gaze.

The Last Letter

"Roger that," Alexander answers, breaking her trance. Emotionless, she stands up and strides over to the other two Marines, quickly, double-checking their vitals to ensure the two have passed. She takes a knee next to the men lying close to one another, the two had been smiling and genuinely happy to be in each other's company only days prior in her office; *this cannot be*, Alexander's recycled thought. James, slumped before her, hands still bound behind him, gunshot wounds to the abdomen and head. Gone is the smile she witnessed when he would make fun of the others that day in her office, gone is his laugh at the expense of his old squad leader, Parks.

The special agent turns to Doherty and looks upon his peaceful thick bearded face laying on his side as if he were sleeping. He seemed so stoic and reserved when she met him, but she could tell he loved his fellow Marines, devotedly. With the loving hand of a watchful mother, she caresses his hair from his forehead, the light rain peacefully lands on his restful face. Doherty's death to her is especially heartbreaking, with his hands and feet still bound he tried gallantly to make his way to James, to comfort his fellow Marine. The scene is soul-crushing for the forestry agent. A flood of memories she dares not lose herself to, rage to the forefront looking upon the two friends: *not now, not here*. Alexander fights her dark demons; her right hand begins to quiver holding her weapon.

She looks to Bill, and he seems lost in his own distant memories, still slumped next to Parks. "Bill, come on, buddy, not now. We need to snap out of this shit. Get on the comms and get the ETA on the sheriff's bird. Also, relay we need a CAS-EVAC trauma helo, ASAP. I'm going to keep filming and take pictures of everything I can before this place becomes a clusterfuck. I'll contact my higher and get a SITREP from them," Special Agent Alexander explains to her old friend, retrieving the sat-phone from her gear.

"Copy that." Bill responds in the affirmative, moving quickly towards his helicopter in the clearing. He still has his weapon at the ready; he has no idea what is going on, but this is no time to be complacent rushing back to the aircraft.

Alexander dials up her superior and is informed that James got another call off to his wife and she is already in contact with the FBI and DEA. Both are sending the regional agents; their ETA is one hour. She is then ordered to secure the location with the local Sheriff's Office until the FBI, DEA, or Homeland security arrives. She will be the OIC[34] on the scene until then—no pictures or video; as of now this is sealed, she is told.

What the fuck, the forestry agent thinks to herself, continuing to take video and pictures regardless of orders. Alexander begins chronicling the scene with a digital camera that requires a memory card in case her body camera is seized; she will analyze the data when she gets back to her office, in Clear Creek. She painstakingly tries to keep steady filming James and Doherty. Alexander desperately wants to cut the Marines free of their restraints, putting them at a peaceful rest next to each other, but she must preserve the scene, though the light rain is causing evidence degradation rapidly.

Bill comes back from the clearing, breathing heavily, "Sheriff will be here in thirty. CAS-EVAC one hour. We have plenty of time to document everything." He, too, wants to cut the fallen men free from their restraints and put them to rest, but Bill follows Alexander's lead; she is a machine now.

"This is no way for a warrior to die. Not like this." Special Agent Alexander whispers softly to Bill, never taking her eyes off the camera screen, making sure she misses nothing of importance. The two head over to the body littered with AR-15 wounds from well-grouped fire. Alexander looks closely at the body in the airline uniform. She locates the man's sidearm and the shell casing next to his fallen body; to her it looks as if the deceased fired first then was subsequently dropped by the three Marines. She films the scene outside, then steps inside the fuselage and films that as well.

"What did higher say?" Bill asks Alexander upon her exiting the wreckage of the fuselage.

Alexander exhales, "FBI and DEA; ETA, one hour. We are also instructed no video or pictures and this matter is sealed until further notice." She responds to Bill's question, both locking eyes for a moment, dreading what is to come.

"Oh shit." Bill says, looking in the direction of the fallen Marines.

"Yeah, oh shit. There'll be some dumbass cover story, so that is why *'fuck them'*, I'm taking video evidence." Alexander angrily responds, continuing

---

[34] Officer In Charge

to digitally chronicle the catastrophic scene. "The families deserve to know the truth."

Bill surveys the crash site. "What truth? The only truth is that these fallen warriors were outnumbered and outgunned. That's the only truth I see." His jaw clenches with anger at the tragedy of the Veterans' final moments.

"I concur. Looks like they were set upon by whatever the fuck react force showed up following the downed aircraft and our men just didn't have the firepower to compete. I see frag shrapnel and impact craters. Grenades and 203s. Look at some these trees, all fucking splintered." Alexander motions to the scarred forest surrounding them. "Almost as if they were trying to drive the men back. Herding them. Let's go up the ridge and have a look around before the sheriff gets here." She sighs heavily, her thoughts traveling to what the three old friends endured in their final moments of life.

"Do you want to film the last Marine before we head up?" Bill asks her with solace in his voice, pointing to the body of Parks.

"Can you do it, Bill?" She turns to her friend and hands him the camera. "I just can't look at another dead Marine."

"Sure, no problem, Xander?" Bill affectionately responds, taking the camera gently from her hands. Alexander gives him a soft tap on the shoulder, then adjusts her rifle, making her way through the wreckage and up the ridge with her tac-light on the AR-15 illuminating the way.

The determined forestry agent makes her way up the ridge trying to follow the path the men took while withdrawing to a better tactical position. *Marine Grunts do not retreat; they regroup and counterattack. Or some shit like that…,*" she ponders to herself not quite remembering the Marine motto. Grudgingly traversing the ridge, Alexander can see the vast expenditure of ammunition used by the aggressing force towards the three Marine's defensive positions. Shell-casings are piled up in various positions where the enemy assumed their final assault positions before the final onslaught.

"Good for you, fellas. You gave these fucks hell for as long as you could." Special Agent Alexander moves silently, shining her tac-light about the ridge, making her way farther up the hill towards the Marine's defensive positions. She can hear Bill approaching from her six, she pauses briefly allowing him to catch up to her on the ridge.

"Fuck, I'm out of shape. I don't know how our boys did this while firing and maneuvering." Bill pauses to catch his breath. "I recorded the brass left behind by the opposing force at their initial positions."

"Our boys were determined. Only fucking *Grunts*. No way they were just going to roll over," Alexander states proudly, "and the last deceased Marine?" she asks, trying to avoid eye contact with Bill.

Bill responds solemnly, "It was rough, but he's recorded for evidence, may their loved ones never see these images, ever." He hands Alexander's camera back to her; she then quickly stows it in her chest rig.

Alexander looks up the ridge, the dark outline of the crest looms over the two, "James' wife is Border Patrol. She'll have access to the images. God be with her that day." She shudders, thinking upon the scene unfolding in her mind; images of her own husband's passing come to the forefront.

"Let's just get this over with and get back down to the clearing." Bill nods to her, prodding Alexander on, to keep her from dwelling on what is to come or what has been.

Special Agent Alexander without a word turns and leads the way up the ridge until she comes upon the final defensive positions of the former infantrymen. "They didn't have a chance. The firepower thrown at them was over- whelming even for a fully equipped infantry squad, let alone three ageing *Grunts*. Look at our boy's expenditure of ammo in both directions, twelve and six o'clock. Look at the concussive grenade fragments laying around their positions." She points out the used fragmented grenade bodies lying about the area. "The enemy wanted the Marines alive, if possible, to interrogate I assume. Jesus, what the fuck?" She provides her devastating theory to Bill, surveying all three final defensive positions of the former Bravo Co. Marines.

"Yep, and the brass is laying in two different directions. So, an enemy team had been dropped on top of them up on the ridge. I'm surprised the firefight lasted as long as it did," Bill imparts, still trying to catch his breath.

Alexander stares up the dark ridge. "Alright, let's go look at the advancing team's position up farther on and then we'll head back down to the helicopter. The sheriff should be here soon."

On the other side of the ridge, Bill judges the best place to insert a fast rope team and spots the landing point from the footprints in the mud. Judging from the treads in the wet soil, it was a six-man team by his calculations. "Six of them," he announces to Alexander. Bill is truly amazed the Marines lasted as long as they did. "Whoever these people are, they were expertly trained and organized." He shudders suddenly, an unease washes over him.

Alexander looks to him and replies, "Yes, they're very well trained and equipped. Cartels don't have this organization, do they?" She ponders aloud, more to herself than to Bill, looking about the remnants of the battle.

"Well, whatever the fuck's going on, it's above our pay grade. Let's get back to the helo." Bill turns to head back over the ridge and down to the crash site.

"Yep" Alexander replies, staring off into the black distance of the night sky. Suddenly another helicopter careens overhead, "Thank God, that idiot sheriff did something right and called in the state troopers." She states, watching the State Police helicopter go up and over the ridge to descend into the valley as Bill had done earlier. She grabs her radio from its' pouch, "I'll try to raise them on the handheld and let them know which direction we're coming from, so we don't have a friendly fire situation." The radios bounce grid coordinates from caller to receiver, provided the receiver has a GPS capable radio, which most agencies do around Idaho. It is a musthave for any wilderness rescue.

Both Bill and Alexander trek back the exact way they ascended, both mentally trying to block the images of the men's final moments, hoping to be clear of the scene soon. "Don't mention the camera," Alexander stresses to Bill over her shoulder, still moving towards the crash site.

"Roger that," he answers quietly. Bill receives a transmission on his radio and catches Alexander descending the ridge. "The State Troopers landed next to our bird and sent men to comb over the Marines' campsite. They have two men at the wreck site recording evidence as well. They know which direction we're coming."

"Okay, good. I would like to check the campsite as well when we get back. Less time around the fallen Marines, the better," she informs him of her plans upon arrival back at the wreckage.

Bill putting his radio away, looks to his friend, "Shit, I concur, Xander." As they are getting ready to break through the forest and onto the crash site, the sheriff's and the CAS-EVAC helicopters fly overhead, towards the clearing by the river. "Shit, can we squeeze any more birds into the valley?" Bill is getting anxious to leave.

"Let's just get our part done and get the fuck out of here." Special Agent Alexander states flatly to Bill. Her dark mindset beginning to take control, painful memories that are supposed to be locked way are resurfacing once again. *I need a fucking drink;* the thought drives her anger even more. Alexander's jaw clenches with rage at the senselessness of the tragedy, *why did it have to be Marines?*

CH. 9
THE SURVIVOR

"You colossal fat fucking asshole!" Special Agent Alexander screams at Sheriff Derek Cole as she and Bill emerge from the woods onto the crash site once more. Alexander wastes no time confronting the overweight sheriff surveying the wreckage.

"Oh, give me a fucking break, Alexander!" the sheriff retorts with an exasperated look on his face.

Alexander then moves aggressively closer, "You fucking shithead, Cole, you could have called this in immediately, instead of rolling your fatass over and going back to sleep!" She still advances towards the sheriff before Bill slings his rifle and steps between the two law enforcement officials.

"Fuck you, Alexander. How the fuck was I supposed to know? You, of all people, know we've had our trouble with dumbass militias around here lately. It's on the rise, asshole," the angry sheriff fires back at her.

Special Agent Alexander concedes that point, but the sheriff's lack of action may have cost these former Marines minutes they so crucially needed. That, Alexander cannot and will not let go of, "Look around, Cole, these Marines' deaths are on your fucking hands, and I'm going to make sure everyone knows of your lack of action, pussy." She snarls back at the sheriff, breaking free of Bill's grasp and heading towards their helicopter, in the clearing.

The sheriff yells after the forestry agent pointing his finger at her, "Don't you put that fucking shit on me, Special Agent. It looks like your boys got mixed up in something way over their heads. Fucking Marines, always think they're badasses!"

This time it is Bill who approaches the sheriff angrily, leaning down, inches from the sheriff's face, "Say that again, I goddamn dare ya'. You show some fucking respect for these men, or I'll bury you next to them." Bill breathes heavily in the sheriff's face, Alexander quickly intervenes, pulling her old Marine friend away.

A ranking state trooper interferes quickly, having had enough of the pissing contest between the local law enforcement. "Enough, everyone!", the trooper commands, all three pause to look his direction. "Special Agent Alexander, you and Bill go take a breather in the clearing. I am not asking." He orders the two away in their anger. "Sheriff, just stand there and do not contaminate my scene more than it already is." The State Trooper firmly instructs the group to move about their business. The three know Trooper Jon Soler, a Captain with the Idaho state police, respecting his authority and expertise; all comply without further argument.

The drizzle of rain that has been providing some relief from the unusually warm night air subsides as does the adrenaline that has been coursing through Alexander's bloodstream. Exhaustion is beginning to set into her aching body. She and Bill watch the flight rescue personnel exit their helicopter and rush to the crash site to tend to the fallen Marines, with the hope one or more may still be alive, Alexander knows the men are not.

Two state troopers, part of a team combing the Veterans' campsite, come across the river to report their findings to Trooper Soler, and are intercepted by the forestry agent, "Anything?" she asks them patiently.

Both troopers know Alexander well and have collaborated with her in the past on many cases involving poaching, the rise of domestic militias, and the drug traffic North, neither has any qualms about sharing their information with the forestry agent. Alexander is technically the OIC on the scene; due to the fact the crash and the ensuing firefight happened on federal land. Until the FBI arrives on site, she is the ranking federal officer.

"No, nothing really. Your run-of-the-mill outdoor enthusiasts. No militia shit or paraphernalia, no animal carcasses, no drugs. That's it. Nothing remarkable to explain all this, except, the camp was searched before us or should I say ransacked. I assume our assailants searched the camp prior to engaging the deceased." Trooper Neely responds to the special agent's inquiry.

"Thanks, Neely. Will you send me a copy of what you record?", she asks a favor of the grizzled veteran of the Idaho state police.

Neely nods in acknowledgment, "Yeah, no problem. Once Trooper Soler gives the go-ahead. I'm about to go report to him now. We're sending a forensics team to gather everything from the campsite and once it's processed, we will release it to the families. This, of course, if the *Feds* do not monkey fuck around." He answers encouragingly, trying to add some inter-governmental brevity to the scene. Like many in law enforcement, he, too, was a Marine, "Nothing hits home like the tragic death of one of ours." Neely stares off in the direction of the crash site.

"You're right about that, brother." Bill follows the trooper's gaze.

Neely begins to head towards the crash site, then stops, to look overhead as yet another arriving helicopter; this one emblazoned with the characteristic markings of the FBI in yellow across the belly of the aircraft. "Here come your boys, now!" He yells back to Special Agent Alexander and notices the eye roll she gives in response. He gives a quick nod to her and continues on his way to report to his superior. Alexander and Bill head in the direction of the landing FBI helicopter to meet the reporting agents.

Two field agents exit the helo and make their way to meet Alexander; the rest of the six agents exiting the aircraft split in two directions. One in the direction of the crash site and the other towards the Veterans' camp. Agent Alexander quickly briefs the two FBI special agents on the chronology of events that took place that evening, starting with the sat-phone call she received from James. "You said you saw the victims a few days prior to this incident?" Special Agent Lance asks Alexander. Lance, a stern-looking, physically imposing woman, not by size but by her aura of command.

Alexander eyes the FBI agent cautiously, "Yes. They voluntarily came to my office and relayed their intentions in the area over the next couple of days; former Marines having a small reunion, that's all. I took the pertinent information from the three men and ran background checks on all. Nothing to suggest this. Misdemeanors from over a decade ago for two of them. The other, James, was clean. Nothing. I'll send all information I have and my report over to your office, immediately."

"Thank you, Special Agent Alexander. Here is my card, please send all that you have. The FBI will take authority and command of the scene. You may stick around if you like or head back. The press has caught wind of this debacle, so be prepared upon your return. Refer all questions to my office. I will have Special Agent Kennedy, here, field all press related inquires." The FBI agent motions to her colleague. "Thank you again, Special Agent Alexander and Mr. White for your preliminary efforts on scene." With that Agent Lance brushes past both of them and heads towards the crash site to find Captain Soler.

Bill makes a shuddered movement with his shoulders, watching the agents disappear into chaos of the crash site, "Let's get the bird up in the air and head home. Your kids will be up soon, if not already and my wife will be starting to worry a bit."

"Yeah, okay," Alexander sighs. She is spent with exhaustion. Intense flashes of memories are starting to boil up, and she knows she needs to get her mind on something else and soon. The two start making their way back to Bill's helicopter, when both see the Med-Evac personnel come sprinting out of the tree-line with one of the men on a back board, IVs protruding from his arm. Rescue personnel frantically working on the patient, a four-man stretcher team carrying the critical patient to the awaiting rescue helicopter.

The whole scene takes mere moments, the Med-Evac helicopter ascends, throttling forward at a blistering pace disappearing into the vast night sky. "What the fuck is going on?" Bill asks Trooper Neely, who helped the litter team.

"One of the Marines is still alive. Barely. The vitals are not good." Neely replies. Alexander and Bill look to one another horror-stricken. "Don't look at yourselves that way, you're not the only ones who missed the Veteran's vitals. At least six of us checked, hoping one or all might be clinging to life. One of the medics said the swelling prevented us from feeling his pulse, and he barely has any respiration. So just don't go down that path." Neely offers, reading their expressions of guilt at having missed saving a man's life. He is stopping them from playing the *"only if I had"* game.

Alexander asks in disbelief, "Which one?"

"The one you two said the men called *'Parks.'*" The trooper answers her question with a bit of hesitation. "He's not conscious, and an FBI agent is with him for security. You two should go home. Call us tomorrow, Special Agent, we'll give you a full SITREP."

"Roger that." Alexander turns towards the helicopter she arrived in with Bill. She begins to load up and prepare for their departure, weapons and gear stowed properly. "Okay, Bill, let's go to the trauma center." Alexander defiantly tells her old friend.

"Roger that, Xander." Bill knows better than to argue with her. Besides, if he dropped her off at the airfield, she would end up driving to the trauma center on her own. He figures this way he will get Alexander home sooner to her family by obliging her command. Bill begins his ascent, hovers one last time over the scarred landscape of the crash site, for the two former Marines it is an all-too familiar scene. *The three friends were true warriors until the end,* Bill reckons to himself as he banks starboard, heading to the only trauma center in the state qualified to manage this level of injury.

"Bill?" Alexander starts to ask her old friend, never taking her gaze off the breaking dawn on the horizon.

"Yeah, Xander?" Bill responds, still lost in his own thoughts of his past, rekindled by the scene he witnessed.

"What the fuck do you think those men stumbled upon?" Special Agent Alexander asks more to herself than to Bill.

He replies with trepidation and concern in his voice, "I don't know, Xander. Whatever it is, it's big."

"That's what I'm afraid of, Bill." Alexander then seems to shut down; the weight of seeing the former Marines' tragic last stand proving too much. She leans her head against the cockpit glass and shuts her bloodshot eyes. She is not sleeping but giving in to her flashbacks she fought so desperately to keep at bay while on the ground. The clinging *memories* slam against her consciousness like breaking waves on shore. The *memories* show no mercy.

SSgt. Jacob Parkinson

. . .

The Life-Flight helicopter lands at Boise General, the nearest trauma center that has the minimum capabilities to manage the severity of the damage inflicted upon the Veteran. The trauma surgeon knows she has little time and resources to stabilize this man. The patient will need immediate Medevac to Denver Institute of Neurology (DIN), which specializes in traumatic brain injuries.

Trauma surgeon, Dr. Ellein Ripley, rattles off information at the cyclic rate; reciting years of knowledge and practical applications to her nurses, who frantically try to keep up. "Is OR 6 prepped and ready?", she asks calmly but firmly, getting her sense of urgency across to her team.

"Yes, Dr. Ripley. The OR has been prepped and on standby as soon as we received the call. We have Dr. Anand on video from the DIN, to assist.", the trauma nurse responds quickly.

"Thank you. I will prep and be ready in four minutes. Let's get this done, we have a patient to save." Dr. Ripley speaks authoritatively, beginning her own mental preparation for the procedure. The trauma surgeon adjusts the head-mounted camera, which will enable Dr. Anand, via remote viewing, to assist, their plan is to stabilize the Veteran enough for transport.

Dr. Ripley enters the OR and turns her masked face to the monitor displaying Dr. Anand's image, "The massive amount of trauma inflicted upon this man's cranium and facial structure is similar to a head-on collision. That amount of damage and swelling may have just saved this man's life. It seems to have cushioned the impact of the fired projectile. He is extremely lucky to be alive at this point. Dr. Anand, will you help ensure we keep him that way?"

"Yes Dr. Ripley. Proceed," Dr. Anand replies. Every doctor and nurse in the operating room, is nervous and doubting their own professional medical skills in the face of such a traumatic event; yet, as the procedure begins, their training is automatic, and they form a cohesive team to save a stranger's life.

Outside of the operating room, in a small bland waiting room sits Bill and an anxiously pacing back and forth Special Agent Alexander. Suddenly an assisting trauma surgeon pushes her way through the double doors, making a

The Last Letter

direct approach to the nervously waiting two. She instinctively puts her hand up to silence the incoming barrage of questions the doctor can see awaiting to spill from Alexander's mouth.

"Silence. Dr. Ripley has just begun the surgery. The Veteran is in a coma and there will be no information gained today or for the foreseeable future. We are trying to stabilize him enough for travel to DIN, in Colorado, where Dr. Anand, the head of neurology there will take over all treatment of the Veteran. The swelling from the assault the patient endured before he was shot may have ended up saving his life. Go home, Special Agent. There is nothing more you can do here." With that last statement the doctor turns on her heels, heads rapidly back in the direction of the OR and the double doors, purposely cutting off Alexander's ensuing questions.

The forestry agent exhales heavily, her uniform soaked through with sweat. "Well, fuck you, Doc," Alexander calls after the doctor who disappears behind the double doors. She is growing increasingly frustrated, but she knows there is absolutely nothing else she can do right now. The patient will be in surgery for hours and then be transported elsewhere.

"Come on, Xander. She's right. It's time to head home." Bill stares sympathetically at his old friend, rising from his uncomfortable hospital seat. The two make their way out of the hospital to the helipad where Bill had landed on the grass field adjacent to the Life-flight chopper. The helipad was only built for one, but Bill knew Alexander would not wait, so he landed anyway. Now, as they cross the parking lot on their way to the aircraft, their minds replay the horrible images at the scene they had witnessed. *Those poor Marines* is the only thought that keeps racing through their consciousness. Neither speak to one another climbing into the cockpit.

On their flight home, the two can hear the radio chatter from differing agencies responding to the incident. It has become chaos. Bill turns his radio off, Alexander follows suit. Again, silence fills the darkened cabin, each wanting to say something consoling to the other, but both are afraid of the floodgate of memories and emotions that will destroy their bearing and concentration. The scene of those Veterans splayed out in their gear, becoming too overwhelming for both, each desperately wanting to deal with it alone.

Bill gently sets the helicopter down on the tiny airfield after a muted transit back to Clear Creek. He quickly begins to go over his post-flight checklist, hoping not to make eye contact with Alexander; Bill cannot resist, out of the corner of his eye he spots her grabbing her gear and rifle, emotionless.

She catches his gaze and stares vacantly back at him. "Thank you, Bill, for everything," Alexander softly mutters, slinging her gear over her shoulders and heads to her truck, without looking back in his direction. Both fighting back the ghosts of Afghanistan , eye contact will only destroy them both.

Bill watches her pause, her shoulders drop a little more, continuing silently to her truck. "Don't go dark," Bill whispers after her, knowing she is out of earshot. He will text Alexander later to check in on her after he has a few glasses of Scotch and has cried himself into enough courage to do so.

Alexander climbs into the cab of her truck, finally giving into temptation, she looks back to Bill. She wishes she hadn't. Bill is crumpled on the ground next to his helicopter, his hands covering his weathered face to hide the tears pouring down. She wants to go to him, but that will not help either of them right now, they need to be alone. Special Agent Alexander turns the ignition, she briefly stares at the dawn creeping over the mountains, before slamming the truck into drive and speeding out of the airfield's dirt drive towards her sleeping children and home.

She fights back the images of this night events, which have become a blend with images from Afghanistan, Alexander having trouble separating the two. "Hold it together, asshole, you're almost home. One more mile, you can hold it together. Suck it the fuck up," she orders herself aloud, her grip on the truck's steering wheel becoming viselike, her knuckles turning white. "Motherfucker!" another outburst. Alexander knows that she is mere moments away from her mental dam breaking; she will be crumpled up like Bill, unable to hold back the wave of memories and emotions. She is running out of time. Her children will be up soon, and they do not need to see her when she crashes. They have seen it enough before and she vows never again.

The forestry agent quietly shuts the engine down, shifts into neutral, and coasts to a stop in her gravel driveway, trying not to wake her children. Her son, most of all, will know. She quietly shuts the door to her truck, withdrawing her rifle and gear. She heads to the back door, punches in the code to unlock it and stealthy enters the kitchen of her massive cabin. Alexander walks to the cold granite kitchen counter, gripping the edge angrily, breathing heavily but quietly. She opens the cabinet before her and grabs a *Johnnie Walker Blue Label* and cracks the seal. Alexander does not bother with a glass and slams several gulps of the succulent bourbon.

The warm liquid instantly calms her rage momentarily, as she is awash in the glow the bourbon provides. Alexander takes the bottle with her, heading down the hall; she stops to peek in on her children, her daughter is splayed across her bed. *Always the mover,* Alexander fondly recalls to herself. She crosses the hall and opens another door, her son would be getting up soon, to go workout and then get ready for school. She is so immensely proud of him, *so much like his father.* Alexander smiles down upon her son, then she quietly shuts his door and continues up the stairs to her own room. She gulps down more of the therapeutic bourbon, grabbing a photo of her husband in his blues from a Marine Corps ball they attended. Special Agent Alexander begins to sob, "I could really use you right now, Gunner." She stifles her sobs with a throw pillow from their bed, "I miss you so damn much, you bastard." She kisses the photo gently.

She stands reluctantly, quickly gets out of her uniform, scoops up the bottle of bourbon and jumps into a steaming hot shower. Alexander can no longer fight back the emotions and memories; they now have control. She slides to the floor of the shower, lifts the dark bottle to her lips, and lets go of the control.

CH. 10
WORD SPREADS

The house, in Northlake, Texas, is perfectly quiet as Jocelyn sleeps peacefully, after her fourteen-day tour at the border station of Laredo. She enjoys these moments when she has the whole king size bed to herself, when her husband is away. She did not have to listen to Ryan's incessant snoring or deal with his constant tossing and turning. She loves the former Marine with all her heart, but her alone time in their king size bed is a treasure.

Jocelyn is about to drift further into a deep beautiful sleep, when she groggily notices her cell phone displaying on the screen a missed call and voicemail from *James2*, signifying Ryan's satellite-phone. She bolts awake, fumbling for the phone on the nightstand trying to unlock the device. It falls on the floor. "Fuck!", she yells leaning over the edge of the king size bed, upside down, retrieving the cell phone from underneath. Jocelyn fears the worst, Ryan is not due to call until the morning, at the earliest. She immediately tries to call him on his sat-phone, hoping he answers, horrified there is not even a ring. The frightened spouse shakily taps play on the voicemail.

"Hey, babe, shit's going South. Those grid coordinates I gave you last night, I need you to report that me, Parks, and Doherty are securing a plane crash. I've called the local sheriff and game warden already, help is coming." Jocelyn's jaw begins to tighten in fear, the message continues, "Listen, a high-speed unit showed up too quickly and we're taking fire. Bring the calvary. Don't worry, we're fuckin big boys. I have to get back to the fellas. I love you and the girls so damn much."

Those last words break open the flood gate of tears, his voice seems so distant and final.

"Ryan!" Jocelyn lets out a primal scream, echoing throughout the cavernous ranch home. Her two children come tearing into the room and run to pick up their grief-stricken mother off the floor.

"Mama!", the girls shout, lifting their mother to the bed. Jocelyn looks from one girl to the other, tears flowing from their eyes. She can see the utter terror in her beautiful children's faces. She cannot tell them now. She has work to do first. Wiping the tears from her chiseled cheeks, Jocelyn stands up and looks at her innocent, loving daughters, knowing deeply their lives will be forever changed from this moment forward. She pushes that dread aside and begins to get to work; she has no choice.

Jocelyn looks down to her daughters. "I'm okay. You girls get to bed, right now. I'll fill you in on what's going on when I know more. Right now, I need you to go to your rooms or one another's and I'll brief you when I know more. Now go!" She orders her daughters with the tone of voice she uses for her men and women agents at the border station.

The girls know this tone all too well and dare not contradict their mother; their dad does not even stand in their mom's way when she uses that tone. The two quickly scurry to the eldest's room to console one another, for each of them fear the worst and are awaiting their mother's confirmation.

Jocelyn immediately dials Gunny Hoffman. Every infantry line company has a *"company guns,"* usually of gunnery sergeant rank; they are the final line between enlisted personnel and officers, Gunny Hoffman was Bravo Co's. Without an effective, respected, and admired company guns, the whole infantry line unit ceases to exist as an effective combat machine. Gunny Hoffman was known among the men of Bravo as a *"troops, troop,"* meaning any decision he made on a company level, he always considered the outcome and impact it would have on the men. The four crucial leadership billets of an infantry line unit are: squad leader, platoon commander, company guns, and company commander. The men of Bravo Co. 1/23 put a select few men on pedestals, Gunnery Sergeant Hoffman is on the top pedestal. Every man in Bravo Co. would lay down their life for Gunny Hoffman, and he the same; so, he is the logical first choice to call as Jocelyn prays he answers his phone at this hour.

"What the hell? If this is James drunk dialin me from his wife's phone, I am goin to have your ass!" Gunny Hoffman answers gruffly in a deep, hoarse Southern drawl.

"Gunny, it's Jocelyn." She struggles to keep it together, her voice quivering. She knows James and the others have mere moments to receive help—*if it's not too late already;* she stops the train of thought from progressing further.

Gunny Hoffman leans on his elbow, raising his ageing muscular frame from his bed, becoming more concerned, "What is it?" This time he asks with a rapid whisper, now awake and alert. Although he retired a Master Gunnery Sergeant after twenty-eight years of honorable Marine Corps service, he will always answer to his men from Bravo Co. as *Gunny Hoffman*, he is forever immortalized at that rank. He will always have a soft spot in his steel-clad heart for his Marines of Bravo Co 1/23. He would go on to command other Marine combat units, but Bravo Co. was his. Even the wives of his men have come to call him *Gunny*, which he and his own wife find especially endearing. He has been on the end of these calls at the wee hours of the morning, many a time, as members of Bravo Co. tragically pass over the years and is expecting the worst. Gunny Hoffman has no idea how catastrophic things are about to get for him and the rest of Bravo Co 1/23.

"Ryan, Parks and Doherty are in trouble!" Jocelyn blurts out the cold hard truth, as she knows it in her mind. She cannot hold back the flood of emotions that is now overwhelming her.

"Breathe, Jocelyn," Gunny Hoffman whispers softly, trying to calm James' distraught wife. "What's goin on?" He asks calmly, still not grasping the reality of what she has said to him. "What kind of trouble?"

Jocelyn tries in vain to calm her breathing, "Ryan called me from his sat-phone, said a plane went down, they are currently securing the crash site and some tac unit has shown up unexpectedly. Oh, Gunny, what the fuck are we going to do? I have tried all their phones, nothing. I'm so damn worried," she declares out of pure frustration, longing, and anguish into the phone.

"First, Agent James, we are both going to get our bearings. Real fast and in a hurry." Gunny Hoffman responds, appealing to her law enforcement side of emotion. He has worked in the past with her agency for joint operations alongside the Texas Highway Patrol, his agency.

Jocelyn replies exhaustedly into her phone, "Copy that." Her years of experience being a US Border Patrol Agent allows her to shut down her emotions effectively.

"Did you contact Doherty's fiancée yet?" He asks matter-of-factly, hoping Jocelyn had not, he would like to handle that call himself.

"No, not yet. I immediately called you. Ryan always said if the shit really hits the fan, to call you." Jocelyn says, determined to keep rational, but her control is begin to fade.

Gunny Hoffman sighs, hoping this is a misunderstanding, but he takes nothing for granted. "James was right. Listen, I'll make a call to the Idaho State Police and request they send help immediately. Secondly, I will contact Doherty's loved one and tell her exactly what you told me and any other information I receive; she may reach out, so be prepared for an emotional response, just keep her calm, the both of you, until you hear from me with a SITREP. Roger that?"

Jocelyn, appreciating the fact Gunny Hoffman is using military vernacular to keep her focused, replies, "Roger that."

He continues, laying out his next steps, not only for Jocelyn but to keep his mind grounded. "Good. Thirdly, I will contact Bgame and Attebery, to see if they can get ahold of anyone from Parks' family. That fucker keeps going dark on us. For now, Jocelyn, I want you to go to the girls and comfort them, do not watch the news, and believe only what you hear from me or your agency head. Copy?" Gunny Hoffman lists the steps he will take to relieve the stress and pressure that is suddenly leveled on James' wife at zero dark thirty.

"Copy that," Jocelyn replies, suddenly experiencing the crushing enormity that the situation has now escalated into. This is reality. Not a dream. *How can this be?* she wonders to herself; she pushes the button to end the call with Gunny Hoffman without saying goodbye. She stares out of her beautiful open-view master bedroom window, at the dawn beginning to show its' beautiful

The Last Letter

face across the East Texas landscape. *This is not going to be a beautiful day.* Jocelyn rises from the bed, then looks over at where James usually sleeps, tears streaming down her face. She begins her horrible trek to the girls' room. The hallway seems a mile long, her movements seemingly in slow motion.

Jocelyn pauses before entering the eldest, Amber's room. She can hear the two girls whispering and sobbing through the wooden door, Jocelyn opens the door gently, it is then the girls realize nothing good is going to be told to them by their mother. She looks down upon her beautiful daughters' tear streaked faces. *How am I going to get them through this,* her maternal instinct wonders. Both girls immediately run to her and begin sobbing uncontrollably. Jocelyn buckles, not from the weight of the girls but from the sheer amount of grief already weighing the three of them down. She has not told her two loving daughters anything yet, but the girls know the worst has yet come from their mother and they need their mother. The three remain huddled on the floor, holding one another, sharing an embrace of unknown, mysterious grief, fearing the worst.

. . .

Gunny Hoffman is in the study of his North Texas home and upon ending the call with Jocelyn, immediately Googles the Idaho State Troopers barracks that covers the Clear Creek area. He knew his three former Marines' location; James had briefed him of their plans beforehand. He was, of course, pleased to hear his men from Bravo Co. were still reuniting and ensuring that bond never fades, but now he fears that bond may have cost his Marines. He finds the number quickly and dials, hoping for an answer immediately. He is disappointed as he is met with a cadre of voice options before he is placed through to the attending Trooper.

"Trooper Neely," the voice answers firmly.

"Listen, Trooper Neely, this is Lt. Hoffman an agent with the Texas Highway Patrol's Criminal Investigative Division[35], ID 9888644," he rattles off without pause. Upon retiring from the Marines after twenty-eight honorable years, Gunny Hoffman became Trooper Hoffman for the Texas Highway Patrol. Many Marines from Bravo Co. would attend his graduation from the

---
[35] CID

academy, another example of the bond between the men of Bravo Co. and the former company guns. Now, Agent Hoffman, is an officer with the Texas Highway Patrol, part of an elite anti-gang unit, designed to combat the flow of military-grade weaponry that is reinforcing gangs on both sides of the Mexican/American border.

Trooper Neely, arriving back at the barracks from the crash site, looks at his phone confused as to why CID from the Texas Highway Patrol is giving him a ring. "How can I help you, Lt. Hoffman?"

"Have you received a distress call from three Marines originating from the forest outside of Clear Creek?" Gunny Hoffman asks, hoping for a positive answer from the trooper.

Astonished that this CID agent from Texas is asking about the scene he returned from, Neely proceeds curiously. He furiously types Gunny Hoffman's credentials into his database and is relieved to see the confirmation. "Actually, Lt. Hoffman, a US Forestry Agent received a distress call from one of three men on his satellite-phone…."

'James', Gunny Hoffman confirms the fear in his mind. He rubs his trademark bald head stressfully.

"Currently there is an ongoing incident outside the town of Clear Creek. I will confirm that for you. How do you know these individuals, Lt. Hoffman?" Neely asks, hoping to get some answers for his own investigation.

"They were my Marines in Iraq. What other information can you give me at this point, Trooper Neely?" Gunny Hoffman asks pointedly, trying to avoid the subject of Iraq.

"Nothing. I don't have enough; everything is pure speculation at this point. Call back in a couple hours, Captain Jon Soler is the OIC of the investigation for the Idaho State Police. Once he gives the okay for me to share information with your agency, I will, Lt. Hoffman." Trooper Neely replies helpfully as he searches his out-of-date desk in the rundown barracks building for a legal pad. "Goddammit. I haven't seen a new desk in sixteen years, yet the governor gets a new one every six months." The desk drawer pops open.

"Here we go. Give me your contact info and I'll email all the investigative contacts," the trooper offers.

The Last Letter

"I feel your pain, brother. My desk ain't much better from the sound of it." Gunny Hoffman sympathizing with his fellow law enforcement professional.

Neely rubs his eyes firmly, he is exhausted, "You might want to start with the Forestry Agent, she is under federal regulations and the incident is on federal land, she may be at liberty to divulge more information. She is good to go."

"Thank you, Trooper Neely, for the assistance. Stay safe, brother." The Gunny relays his gratitude to Neely.

"Lt. Hoffman, for what it's worth. You have some damn fine Marines. You should be proud." Neely replies heavily.

Gunny Hoffman can hear the exhaustion on the man's voice, he fears the coming reality, "I'm proud of all my Marines. Thank you, Trooper Neely." With that, he disconnects the call and stares at the screensaver of his wife and his grown kids in the background of his phone. *This is the beginning of a very long day*. He exhales heavily.

The retired Marine is now faced with the task of calling Doherty's fiancée and relaying inconclusive information, for that is all he has, inconclusive information, nothing to reassure a loved one. *Cassie must be made aware of the situation before it's all over the news*, is his only thought. The company guns tries constantly to keep current contacts on all his Marines, his concern never fading for his men of Bravo Co. He scrolls through his phone, finds Cassie's contact, and hits *Send*. The phone rings several times but goes to her voicemail. He notes how cheerful and full of joy her outgoing message sounds and how much that will soon change.

"Hello, Cassie, this is Gunny Hoffman, can you please give me a call immediately when you receive this message? Thank you." He leaves the only message he can muster.

He then scrolls through his contacts to find Todd Attebery's number. Attebery and Parks are close, have been since the two were squad leaders in Iraq, especially after Parks' incident outside Fallujah. Attebery should have Parks' family's contact information. "All you had to do was come down to a couple of functions, you fuckin asshole," the retired Marine curses Parks under his breath as he dials Attebery's number.

Attebery can hear his phone vibrating on the nightstand next to him but does not want to get up this early. He groans rolling over, with each passing year it becomes more exhausting to get up out of bed, *and this morning is off to a very rude start*, he contemplates miserably. Attebery tries to readjust his eyes, knocking the sleep from the corners so he can see who is calling him at this early hour of his precious morning. His screen displays, *Gunny. Oh, shit* is the only thought flashing in Attebery's mind, *this will not be good*. "Who's the bad news regarding, Gunny?" He asks heavy heartedly. It can be the only reason Gunny Hoffman would be calling him at this hour, someone from Bravo Co. has passed.

"Attebery, I'm going to tell you what I know, Devil. You know Parks, James, and Doherty are out on this reunion?" He directly asks.

"Yeah, Gunny. Parks called me a couple days ago, saying he's up in Idaho with the fellas. What the fuck happened? Just tell me, Guns." Todd requests, beginning to worry at this point, the uneasiness starting to set in.

Gunny Hoffman begins to explain the situation to his former Marine as he knows it, "James' wife called me frantic. She received a sat-phone call from James stating the men were securing a downed aircraft in the woods outside Clear Creek, James also mentioned the arrival of an unknown tactical unit on scene. I spoke with the Idaho State Police, they confirmed there is an ongoing incident involving our boys. No further details."

"What the fuck, Gunny?! Where's Parks now?" Todd quietly yells into the phone, trying not to wake his wife, Lacey. It does not work; she arises alarmed.

"What the fuck is goin on, honey?" Lacey asks, rising from the covers, her soft Southern drawl faltering under her growing concern.

Attebery shakes his head slowly, signaling bad news, "Something has happened to Parks, James, and Doherty on their reunion trip. Go back to bed, babe. I'll go in the other room. Sorry, I didn't mean to wake you," he apologizes, kisses Lacey on the forehead, and rises to head to another room to continue talking with Gunny Hoffman.

Lacey, too, has known Parks a long time and has heard the off-the-wall stories of Parks from her husband long before she even met the man. The two used to watch over Parks during his burgeoning alcoholic days when he lived in Texas, stumbling his way through life. Allowing him refuge in their home when he was a wreck. Lacey and Todd, never failing to extend assistance when needed, is a great dynamic of the couple that their friends find endearing still to this day. "Fuck that. I'm up now. I'll go get some hot tea going for us and then I'm going to smoke a damn cigarette. It's going to be a long day, babe." Lacey responds, gently hugging Todd and making her way out of the master bedroom and towards the spacious kitchen to start the water for tea and then head outside for a smoke.

"Shit, sorry, Gunny. I woke up Lacey." Attebery apologizes for the sidetrack conversation.

"That's okay, brother. I woke up my wife by accident as well. She's pacing in the next room as we speak," Gunny Hoffman replies candidly.

Attebery stands to close the door to the room, "Okay, what the hell is going on, Gunny?" He quickly gets back to the point of the early-morning-hours call from his old company guns.

Gunny Hoffman quickly relays all the information he has been able to ascertain up to his calling of Attebery. "This sounds like cartel, but for right now, Attebery, I need you to contact Parks' family if you have their info," he gruffly asks of his former Marine.

"Sure, Gunny. I have his mom's number and can contact his kid's mother, Sabrina, through social media. I will get on that right now. What do I brief them on, Guns?' Attebery asks of him.

The suddenly drained company guns sighs heavily, rotating his aching shoulders. "Fuck, this will be tough, brother. Tell the loved ones the truth and what we know as of yet. It's not much but let the families know that I have contacts and I'm on it. Please give them my number and I'll do my best to get what information I can. I'm going to call Bgame next, brief him of the situation and let him tell the rest of Parks' squad the news. This is goin to be a long fuckin day, Attebery." Gunny Hoffman concludes, opening the door to his office and seeing his beautiful wife standing there with a worried look of dread. He can only walk to his loved one and embrace her warmly. The day is beginning; he exhaustively looks out the massive office window at the arriving dawn.

Attebery rubs his eyes wearily, "Roger that, Gunny, I'll get on it. Good luck. I will call you in a couple of hours with a SITREP." He then ends the call. Attebery makes his way into the kitchen to pour himself some hot tea, knowing things were going to be rough this morning. He can see Lacey inhaling her cigarette at a rapid pace on their spacious back porch. *This must be her second already*, he reckons. She is scared and nervous; he can see that through the window. He, like, Gunny Hoffman, will have to explain to their wives what is happening and then that will make the situation reality, not some movie, but reality. Attebery immediately dials Parks' phone, nothing, voicemail. "Fuck," he blurts out. He grabs his mug of hot Earl Grey tea, and heads out to the back porch. It is a beautiful warm autumn morning in East Texas, it betrays the mood of dread that is encompassing Attebery's world now. Lacey turns as he opens the door to the back porch, she can tell by the look on his face, the news, whatever it is about Parks, is dreadful.

"Babe, what's goin on? What happened to Parks and the guys?" Lacey asks, trying her hardest to hold back the tears that want to erupt forth.

"I honestly don't know how to make sense of the information I just heard. So, I'm going to blurt it out to you and then maybe it will sound real." Attebery wants to tell her, but he stares off, somehow trying to find the words to explain the information he has received from Gunny Hoffman.

"Just say it, hon." Lacey pleads with him, putting out her cigarette and then wrapping her arms around his waist to hold him.

Attebery, still staring off, cannot bring himself to blurt out the words, it was all too surreal. Breaking his stare at the budding sun, he tells her, "Parks, James, and Doherty as we speak are involved in some incident involving a downed airplane in the woods of Idaho. It doesn't sound good. I tried Parks phone, nothing." Attebery states the facts as he knows them, swiftly.

"What the fuck did you just say?" Lacey asks, pulling back from her husband to look up into his eyes, hers still filling with tears. Lacey is a crier. It is a running joke among their friends. She can cry at a kitty litter commercial, but this early, warm, beautiful East Texas morning, there is nothing to joke about the tears that are starting to fall.

"Parks and the fellas apparently stumbled upon a downed plane, in the fucking woods of Idaho. Apparently after that, no one has heard from any them and Idaho State Police have nothing concrete to give Gunny," he says, repeating the facts again, more for his sake than for Lacey's. "Authorities are responding. James called his wife from a sat-phone, told her they witnessed a plane crash and are securing the crash site. Apparently, another unit showed up and now communication has ceased. This is all happenin in real time." Attebery takes a couple deep inhales of the crisp morning air. "I have to contact Parks' mom and Sabrina so she can tell his kids before the news gets ahold of the story," Attebery concludes never taking his eyes of the silhouettes of the mesquite trees littered across the Texas landscape.

"Oh shit, babe." Lacey begins to let the tears flow freely, sobbing uncontrollably into Attebery's chest.

Attebery begins to scroll through his contacts until he finds Parks' mother's information. He looks down at Lacey and wraps his free arm around her, "I have no fuckin clue what to say to his mom, kids, or anyone for that fact." He hits dial on the contact. Parks' mother lives in California, two hours behind Texas, *hopefully she does not hear her phone*, Attebery wishes silently. He needs more time to gather crucial information for Parks' mother before he can blurt out what he has told Lacey.

The voicemail begins to play its' message for would-be callers, Attebery breathes a sigh of momentary relief, "Ms. Parkinson, this is Todd, I have some news about Jake, and I want you to call me immediately as soon as you wake up at 716-262-9088. Please, Ms. Parkinson, call me immediately upon receiving this message; it is extremely urgent. Do not turn on the news. I'll try back in a bit, hopefully with more information. Take care." With that last bit of the message trailing off his voice, Attebery ends the call and puts the phone in his pocket. He is paralyzed by the coming dawn, realizing the enormity and reality of the situation. "This can't be happenin," Attebery states more to himself than for his wife. He now wraps both arms around Lacey.

Burying her head further into his chest, Lacey, tries to comfort, "It will be okay." Unfortunately, she does not feel this situation will be, a sudden chill runs the length of her body. A foreboding sign.

"Babe, will you contact Sabrina through direct messenger, give her our numbers and tell her to contact us immediately, and do not turn on the news but to call us first. We'll keep trying his mother and her until we can get ahold of one or both of them. That's all we can do, except wait for Gunny Hoffman to call me back. He has more contacts in law enforcement than I do," Attebery explains to his wife the busying steps they should take next.

"Sure." Lacey wipes her tears, thankful to have something to do. She grabs her phone and begins typing into direct messenger, but the tears keep falling as she is typing the words to express the urgency for Sabrina to call them. The tears are preventing Lacey from seeing her screen, clouding her vision, "I'm a fuckin wreck, Todd."

"I know babe, me too." Attebery grabs the end of his shirt to wipe the tears from Lacey's eyes and face so she can type again. She finishes typing the request as fast as she can, then collapses into their nearby spacious padded patio chair, lights a cigarette, and begins to quietly sob.

Attebery walks to the end of his property line, never breaking his gaze from the horizon. His thoughts immediately flash to a sandy rooftop in Iraq and a smiling Parks hilariously begging him to share his box of *Whoppers* candy. Attebery defiantly resisting the urge to eat or share the candy until the final day of the operation, telling his friend it would be appreciated more at the end. It was. Attebery smiles broadly at the reflection of a smiling Parks enjoying the shared *Whoppers* on that dirty, sandy, hot rooftop after eight long days. *1st Squad is not goin to like this*, Todd thinks, rubbing his eyes and not looking forward to the news breaking of the troubled Bravo Co. Marines.

. . .

Gunny Hoffman sits at his large oak desk in his office looking down at his black cup of coffee, memories of James, Doherty, and Parks flooding his conscious thoughts. He shakes his head, trying in vain to shake away the flashes of images he remembers of the men. His lovely wife, Tina, wraps her arms around his neck, trying to comfort him, but she knows it will be of no use. Soon her husband will gather his steely composure and start doing a million things at once, accomplishing all with a determination and grace, that she has seen in no other man. It is one of the reasons she loves him so.

The Last Letter

He is preparing to call Bgame, short for Burlingame, and break the news to him. Both Parks and Bgame served in the same platoon together, both in the fleet and with Bravo Co. in Iraq. Parks was even Bgame's squad leader for a time until Bgame was promoted, replacing a dysfunctional squad leader in that same platoon. He does not know how Bgame is going to react; the Marine is always the wild card of the Bravo Co., and he lives by that philosophy as well, the *wild card*.

"Take a deep breath. Exhale. *'Clear the mechanism,'*" Tina quotes one of Gunny Hoffman's favorite movies, Kevin Costner's *For the Love of the Game*.

The salty Marine gives her a kiss on the forearm and looks up to give her a wink, she could not have said a more suitable thing to break his trance and get him back to work. "Thank you, hon. That was perfect." He then finds Burlingame's contact in his phone, hits Send, hoping Bgame answers.

He does, "Fuck, Gunny, what fuckin time is it?" Bgame groans with his deep raspy voice.

"Too fuckin early, brother. Listen, Devil; James, Parks, and Doherty are in some kind of bind out in Idaho for their squad reunion…" Gunny Hoffman tries to quickly relay the information to his former Marine.

Interrupting his former Company Gunnery Sergeant (which is a no-no in the Marine Corps) unintentionally, "What kind of fuckin bind, Gunny?" Bgame asks, realizing his mistake. "Shit sorry, Guns."

"It's okay, brother. Here are the facts, James called his wife left a voicemail; they're securing a downed aircraft, and some unknown tac unit has arrived on scene and opened fire. I have confirmed with the Idaho State Troopers an ongoing incident with our Devils, in the forest outside the town of Clear Creek. No further information at this time."

Bgame groans loudly. "I know the place. Fuck, Gunny, I was supposed to be there." His body comes awake with a sudden wave of guilt.

"Don't start that shit," Gunny Hoffman orders his former Marine. "You and the rest of 1st Squad don't need that extra shit now. Focus on what we can control, alright, Devil?" he growls authoritatively.

Bgame hangs his head low and heavily breathes his frustrations, "Roger that, Gunny. What do you need me to do?" he whispers, trying not to wake his wife, but it is too late, Roca is beginning to arise from the commotion.

"I need you to jump on the horn, try and contact the rest of Parks' squad, tell them to contact myself or you for information and no fuckin news. Unless it comes from me, it is not fact. Copy that?" Gunny Hoffman instructs Burlingame on what to do next, directing him as if they were both back in the Marines with Bravo Co.

"Roger that, Gunny. I'm on the next fuckin flight to Idaho," Bgame states in the affirmative to Gunny Hoffman's direction

The old company guns sighs heavily, rubbing his temples, "I would actually appreciate that, Devil. I need trusted eyes and ears on the ground up there, to see what the fuck is goin on. As soon as you touch down in Boise give me a call and I'll give you another SITREP. Send me your flight itinerary once you have it. You be careful, Bgame, and keep your cool, brother." Gunny Hoffman says, voice starting to soften into a low rumble. The thought of his men in need of assistance at this very moment weighs heavily.

"Eeerrrr. You got it Gunny. I am fuckin on it," Bgame snarls the customary Grunt response to his former company guns. "Hey, Gunny, let's hope it's nothin."

"Keep me posted, Bgame. Love you, brother. Take care of yourself up there, in Idaho." The old Marine responds, his feeling of unease beginning to rise.

"Yut." Bgame responds, ending the call. He pauses for a split second to gather all that has transpired. He immediately dials all three missing Marines, nothing. *What the fuck is this bullshit?* Bgame thinks to himself, standing up to pull on his jeans that are laying crumpled on the floor next to the bed.

Burlingame's mind quickly flashes to an ambush on his platoon in 2004, outside of Fallujah. His and Parks' squad taking contact simultaneously from the left and right flanks of a main supply route. *What a fuckin shitshow*, he reflects involuntarily. Bgame remembers that day would end in infamy for Parks and the men of 1st Squad. Snapping out of his trance, Bgame throws on an old T-shirt. He knows he needs to keep moving or he will be caught in the memories, and right now he needs to focus on booking the next flight out of *Dallas/Fort Worth International* to Idaho.

"Babe, what is it?" Roca asks, turning on the light next to their bed. That's when she notices the look in his eyes; black and cold. She has seen it numerous times, during Burlingame's struggles with alcohol. His time in the Marines always being a catalyst, like so many other struggling *Grunts*, but that was the past and until now she has not seen that look in years. "Please, tell me what it is?", she pleads with him as she crosses the bed to grab his hand in both of hers. Roca loves the feel of his callused hands from his time as an underwater welder for the off-shore oil companies. His hands, as rough as they were, reassure her and give her an inner comfort.

"Parks, Doherty, and James are in some sort of trouble. I have to get to Idaho, now." Bgame responds coldly.

Roca studying her husband carefully, softly states, "Oh fuck." She knows this is much more than some stupid drunken brawl or some Marine needing to be bailed out of jail. Roca knows what this could mean for the men of Bravo Co. She has been to many Bravo Co. functions with Bgame and seen firsthand the inspiring bond these men share with one another. Being an Army Veteran herself, Roca has seen camaraderie among military units before but nothing on the scale of what she has seen with the Marines of Bravo Co 1/23.

"I have to go," Bgame responds without ever breaking his stare into the blackness of the hallway leading to the rest of his expansive house. The darkness beckons him. He becomes lost in his own metaphor, seemingly not responding to his environment, not even hearing Roca barking orders at him.

Roca finally comes into view, and he hears her commands as he begins to regain his focus. "Babe, can you hear me? Get your ass in gear and get packed. I'm online looking at flights to get you up to Idaho. Let's get moving. Come on!" she orders to snap him out of doldrum, simultaneously scrolling on her phone, scanning flight itineraries.

Bgame, finally registering his wife's urgency, snaps out of his trance "Right, right. I'm fuckin on it." He hurries to his cavernous closet, grabs a quick carry-on bag, stuffs it with a couple T-shirts, socks, underwear and an extra couple pair of jeans. He then heads to the master bath, grabs his toiletries from his side of the bathroom and slams them into his carry-on.

By the time Bgame's exiting the master bath, Roca has already booked him on a flight and a rental car upon his landing in Boise. "You're good to go, hon. Your flight leaves in two hours, first class. I figured you wouldn't want to be around too many other people and just want to focus."

"Thank you, babe. You are a life-saver." He finally makes eye contact with her and kisses her forehead gently. Bgame heads out of their master bedroom, down the dark cavernous hallway, makes a left and enters the foyer, where he stages his gear. He heads to the kitchen to make them both some hot tea, hoping to calm his nerves. Bgame upon retiring from underwater welding, medically, due to too much time spent at depth, made his fortune in offshore oil consulting.

Roca joins him the kitchen, but she can see that Bgame is lost in flashbacks of the three Marines from his unit. He stares vacantly out their beautiful kitchen window towards the pre-dawn East Texas horizon. She strides over to his side, says nothing, rests her head against his right arm and grabs his hand with both of hers. The two stare out the window together, neither saying a word. The water Bgame put on for tea begins to boil, that is the only sound that can be heard in the lonely silence. They both know the real storm that is hanging over Bgame. He is supposed to be on that trip with Doherty, James, and Parks.

"Do not even go there," Roca warns him, reading his mind.

"I'm not… yet. I'm sure I will on the flight." Bgame stares blankly at the counter. Since the United States opened more off shore oil leases recently, and due to this expansive growth, he could not make the trip to Idaho for the 1st Squad reunion as an honorary guest. Bgame was originally Park's 1st team leader but due to failing leadership and incompetence in 3rd squad; Bgame was promoted to that squad leader, thus leaving 1st.

Roca rubs his back as she puts her teacup in the sink, "Come on let's get you on mission, hon."

"Roger that," Bgame softly replies, placing his own cup in the sink as well and walks over to his luggage, scoops up his carry-on and ruck, heads out the door, setting the alarm behind him. Roca is already in the driver's seat setting the GPS for the airport, she is not going to let him drive. Bgame knows better than to argue and throws his luggage in the cab of the black Dodge truck.

Roca pulls out of the driveway and points the truck towards the DFW International Airport. It will take them approximately twenty-eight minutes to get there and Bgame cannot help but think James, Doherty, and Parks do not have twenty-eight minutes. He rips his eyes away from the truck's GPS only to be met with the beckoning darkness out the truck's window. The cab of the truck is engulfed in an eerie silence, a cloud of doom resides inside the vehicle. Bgame cannot take the silence anymore, grabs his phone and finds Attebery's info, hits the *Call* button, hoping Attebery will pick up.

Attebery, still sitting at his dining room table with Lacey, both in silence staring at their cups of hot tea, feels his phone vibrate and sees the ID as *Burlingame*. "It's Bgame, Gunny must have called him as well," Attebery tells Lacey, leaving the table to head outside to talk to his old friend. He does not want to take the chance of waking up his still-sleeping kids, in case he receives news that will overwhelm him. "I heard. Gunny already called me. I have contacted Park's mom and left a message. I also reached out to his sister and his ex-wife on social media, to contact me immediately upon gettin my message." Attebery rattles off before Bgame can get in a word edgewise.

"That's good, Devil. Thank you. I'm fuckin at a loss, man," Bgame groans solemnly in his raspy gruff voice.

"Me too, brother. I don't know what else to do. I'm hopin this is all just a big fuckin misunderstanding. What're you doing now?" Attebery asks, pacing on his back patio, wanting to go back to bed, hoping this is only a bad dream.

Bgame sips some water to clear his dry throat, "I'm heading to the airport as we speak. I'm flyin up to Boise and then driving a rental to Clear Creek. I'm goin to see for myself what the fuck is goin on. Gunny asked me to keep him posted. I'm about to contact the rest of Parks' squad and let them know what I'm doin." Bgame grumbles into the phone.

"Easy killer. This is probably nothin and Parks will have just another damn story to add," Attebery responds, trying to calm Bgame and hoping a bit of levity will work.

"We will see, brother…." Bgame's voice trails off, contemplating what he is going to find up in Idaho, staring into the dark abyss outside his truck window.

Attebery once again tries to be the voice of reason, "Brother, we handle any news as a unit. Just focus on the task at hand. We can't have some *Grunt* Marine blowing through Clear Creek, Idaho like some damned tornado." He can tell Bgame is upset and so is he, but he needs his friend to be calm, enabling him to get as much information in Idaho as he can.

"Roger that," Bgame replies with a defeated flat tone.

"I know, man, I even tried calling Parks, hoping he'd answer and ask me *'What the fuck are you carryin on about?'* You travel safe and keep me posted once you land. Godspeed, brother." Attebery says still in disbelief.

Bgame answers reflexively, "Thanks, brother. Will do." Bgame hits *End* on his phone and stares out at the passing streetlamps, capturing his gaze. He fears nothing good is going to come of this trip to Idaho. Bgame does know one thing for sure, Bravo Co. is about to be forever changed.

"Babe, you need to keep your cool when you land, okay?" Roca tells him, glancing towards him, witnessing the stress in his eyes.

He smiles halfheartedly at his wife. "I will, I promise," he responds, continuing to focus on the fleeting lights passing by the rushing vehicle. His mind drifts to Parks pinning his sergeant chevrons on him at *29 Palms* with Major Miller. He looks back on when James came to his squad after the Fallujah incident. Bgame's mind flashes to the last time he saw Doherty at a Bravo Co. reunion, smiling his joyous smile. "This is going to be an absolute crushing nightmare, if this goes South." Bgame seems to sink lower into his seat, wanting it to swallow him whole. He can feel his own dark thoughts creeping in and he wants no part of their haunting images. Roca looks over and gently pushes his thick red hair back but speaks not a word.

Roca brings the big Dodge to a stop in front of the United terminal, Bgame quickly hops out, grabs his pack and carry-on out of the cab of the truck. She runs around the back of the truck, jumps into his tired arms and grips him as hard as she can. "Please be careful, dickhead." She kisses him forcibly, tears streaming down her cheeks.

"I will, babe. Thank you for everythin, I love you." He kisses her on the lips and grabs his stuff, turning to leave before she can see the worry forming in his grizzled, bearded face. It would only upset her more.

"I love you too," she calls after him, watching him disappear through the automatic double glass doors. *Nothing after this will ever be the same for anyone in Bravo Co. or their families*, her only dreaded thought.

Bgame checks his bags at the kiosk and hands his checked bag to the attendant behind the counter. He heads towards the TSA security checkpoint, the line is not long, the last thing he needs right now is to be stuck in a slowly moving checkpoint. All the Marine wants is to get on the plane and stare out his window into the *nothingness* of 36,000 feet and be left in silence.

The old squad leader makes his way through the security checkpoint without trouble and is slipping his boots back on, when he notices a young boy looking at him. Bgame gives the child a quick wave and half smile as he grabs the handle of his carry-on. *To be that young again, full of innocence and hope. No fuckin worries,* he thinks to himself. The weight of what is to come suddenly drags his shoulders back down, he is suddenly tired and exhausted. An unknown awaits Bgame, and he is not prepared. The tired former Marine finds a chair in the waiting area to board, shuts his eyes and loses himself to memories of Iraq and Bravo Co.

CH. 11
MORNING REPORT

Special Agent Alexander springs awake from her bed, as if an unforeseen enemy is mortaring her position. She instantly jumps into her uniform, grabs her sidearm, a cup of coffee, and is out the front door to her truck. Alexander already knows her loving responsible son has gotten himself and her daughter off to school. She did not know how long she was asleep for, but it was not near enough. Every joint aches, every muscle screaming with agony, and her head is still in a state of fog, but she needs to get to the office and facilitate the investigation in any way she can.

She also wants a clear space to go over the footage and pictures she shot of the crash site. The memories from the night before with Bill at the tragic last stand of the former Marines, still flash before her consciousness. She floors the accelerator on her ugly beige government truck, heading to her office in Clear Creek, when her work cell phone begins to ring. She does not recognize the number but does recognize the area code, one of many in Texas. "Who is this?" Special Agent Alexander grumbles.

The voice on the other end seems to be caught off guard by the abruptness but gathers their composure rather quickly, "Special Agent Alexander, I am Texas State Trooper Lt. Hoffman, more importantly right now, I'm known as *Gunny Hoffman* to the men that were in your AO last night and in trouble."

Alexander looks at her phone curiously, still blistering towards her office. "I apologize Trooper Hoffman for my shortness, it has been a long night. I will assist in any way I can," she responds, her tone easing back.

"Thank you, Special Agent, I talked with your Idaho State Police, and they passed along your number as point of contact and said you might have further information?", he replies cordially.

"Lt. Hoffman—", Alexander tries to begin.

"Gunny, please…," He offers a less formal approach to the conversation.

"Sounds weird for me to use again," the forestry agent returns matter-of-factly.

Gunny Hoffman huffs slightly between sips of his cold coffee, "Yes, I was informed you did a tour as a Marine in Afghanistan drivin for EOD and supply, went straight into law enforcement after. Motivatin shit." He knows of her unit's ambush while she was a driver, as well as the combat decoration she holds; it is heroically tragic and depressing at the same time. He has done his due diligence before his call to the special agent.

"Sure, Gunny?" she replies with a slightly warmer tone in her voice.

"Roger that, Special Agent." He replies, using her formal title currently. She has more years in law enforcement than he currently has, out of respect he refers to her rank.

Alexander stares down the lonely highway heading into Clear Creek, still in disbelief. "What can I do you for, Gunny? I'm currently enroute to my office to piece together my fucking report from last night. I assume that's why you're calling; they're your men, correct?" she rattles off quickly.

"That's correct, Special Agent, they're mine; from an incredibly special unit I hold dear to my heart. What can you tell me, unofficially?" Gunny Hoffman asks sincerely, memories flash of his time as company guns of Bravo Co. 1/23, the smiling tired, dirt-encrusted, miserable faces of all his Marines bear down on him hauntingly.

Alexander relaxes her breathing, she feels her pulse slow, "I stayed up, researched the men and your unit, impressive. Gunny, I'll give you the basics because I'm sure the scuttlebutt will spread, and families will come to you for answers. I want you to be able to give them something for now, without all the bullshit." The forestry agent gets straight to the point. She was a Marine and knows the pain the families suffer being left to guess.

"Thank you. Do you mind if I record this for my own recall later, this is between you and me, Special Agent Alexander," Gunny Hoffman replies sincerely.

The Last Letter

Alexander is cautious but something in the Marine's voice makes her feel at ease, "Shit, Gunny, I don't give a fuck, to be honest. I'll even do you one better and send you what I have, I could use a more involved tactical outside perspective." She quickly seizes on the opportunity for a trusted outside resource. Special Agent Alexander fears this incident is going to be more involved than some ridiculous wanna-be national guard reject military militia.

"Send whatever you got when you get to your office. I will text you my secure email." He, too, knows this is going to be nothing but horrible news for Bravo Co. Gunny Hoffman's shoulders sink farther into his plush, leather office chair. *What the fuck?* is the only thought that comes to mind.

Alexander relieved to finally release some of this information, begins, "First Gunny, your men put up one hell of a fucking fight. It was crushing to be the first on scene, absolutely devastating. Bill, my pilot who was a 53 pilot in the Marines, and I had to take a moment when we first came upon the crash site. It was too fucking much. You were over, you know what the remnants of a firefight look like, I will not go into the details. You'll see it on the video I send you." She pauses for a brief second to gather what she wants to say

next to the former company guns.

"All three men are down. Two are KIA and one was Medevac'd to the nearest trauma center in Boise, he is now enroute to Denver. Gunny, I cannot divulge the survivor's identity until higher gives the *'okay'* and proper notifications to next of kin." Alexander waits patiently for his reply, she knows the shock he is facing.

It is Gunny Hoffman's turn to exhale heavily, "Roger that, Special Agent. I understand. Is there anything else you can tell me that might stick out to you," he asks.

"Listen, Gunny, I'm going to reveal something to you and it's only because the men are yours…" Alexander pauses, wondering if she should proceed but decides she must. "I videoed the scene and you will see the extreme amount of effort the assailants poured into stopping your men. That's why I'm glad you called, Lt. Hoffman of the Texas Highway Patrol, you can view the video and pick apart the tactics used by the aggressors, this was not some fucking dumbass militia; I need some combat experienced eyes to look over the evidence."

Alexander explains, guiding her truck down the desolate highway, closing in on Clear Creek, the tiny lights of the town on the horizon.

Gunny Hoffman rubs his eyes, the soreness does not dissipate, the finality of the situation beginning to set in, his fears being realized. "Definitely, send me what you got. I'm goin to have a bunch of fuckin old crusty Marines itchin for revenge very soon," The old company guns grumbles into the phone, not wanting to believe the scenario playing out before him.

"Now, listen Gunny, you need to keep your men on a short leash. The last thing Clear Creek needs is a bunch of hellbent Marine *Grunts* running around up here looking for vengeance. Roger that?" Alexander requests firmly.

She is right, of course, and he nods in agreement, subconsciously, "Roger that, Special Agent. I have a troop headin up your way to get eyes on for us Bravo Co. bubbas, is it okay if I give him your point of contact info to touch base with you?" Gunny Hoffman inquires respectfully.

"Gunny, I don't have a problem with your man inquiring about the incident, I will be glad to share with him what I have, within reason. Copy that?" Alexander shoots back, hoping there will not be a tidal wave of former Marine infantrymen flooding her small town looking for payback.

"Yes, ma'am, not a problem. His name is Sgt. Steven Burlingame, and he is already enroute to Idaho. He will be my eyes and ears up there until I can go through proper channels with your Idaho State Police. You will have all my contact info, so you can send what you have. Special Agent Alexander, I want to sincerely thank you for your help and for taking care of my Marines." Gunny Hoffman concludes exhaustedly.

Alexander can hear the weariness in the man's voice, "I want these motherfuckers to pay, just as you do. Good Marines do not deserve this end, I will help any which way I can. The Idaho State Police are keeping the name of the surviving Marine under wraps as much as possible for the protection of him and his family, for now anyway. Nothing stays hidden for long in this day and age. I will send what I have, and I will take care of your Marines," Alexander affectionately offers.

"I will be in contact after I view the files. Again, thank you, Special Agent." With that, Gunny Hoffman hits *End* on the phone and slowly takes a sip of the cold, stale coffee. He ponders on the good fortune of having a former Marine on scene to look after his fallen men; he knew of Alexander's heroics when she was a Marine. A then Corporal Alexander was assigned as a driver for EOD, after the commanding officer lost his driver due to shrapnel and was sent home with a Purple Heart. He has never met Corporal Alexander but her bravery, not only when her supply unit got hit but to stay in Afghanistan after the attack and finish her tour after injury shows the grit and fortitude that young woman has, nothing short of astonishing.

. . .

Special Forestry Agent Alexander kicks open her office door after unlocking it, hurrying to set the hot cup of coffee down on her desk and fire up her computer. She frantically slams her fingers across the standard issued keyboard, each key echoing the veracity of the pressure, her angry fingers forming words at the cyclic rate. She quickly pours over her emails, spots the sheriff's request for her to turn over all evidence and a written statement as soon as possible. *Go fuck yourself, Sheriff. I will get right on that*, she thinks angrily to herself with a slight smile, and types exactly that in her response email… and *Send*. Alexander nods approvingly.

She spots an email from the Idaho State Trooper's Command HQ in Boise, probably requesting a debrief and to turn over all related evidence, which she of course will comply with in her own way and fashion. The email is exactly what she predicts with a rub of her tired eyes. Alexander's mind wanders to the events of last night as she stares out the window of her office, located in shabby run-down vacant strip mall.

The sun is rising on this unusually warm fall morning, Alexander decides to grab her cup of coffee from the desk, stopping to pour some bourbon in the cup from a bottle in her desk drawer, and goes to stand outside of her office to soak in the crisp, clean morning air and breathe for a solitary, uninterrupted moment. She allows her mind to drift to the survivor, her heart aches at the thought of those men's last desperate moments, knowing there was no REACT force going to arrive in time. Her anger begins to rise. Alexander takes a large drink of the coffee, shakes her head and looks back to her office, back to work. *It's time to find those fucks* is Special Agent Alexander's only thought.

. . .

Attebery looks down at his phone; *Carp*, another Bravo Co. Marine, is trying to reach him. Carpenter, good friends with both Doherty and Parks, must have heard the news. Attebery sighs, not at having to talk with Carpenter but knowing this is going to be an exhaustingly long day of communications for everyone, Bravo Co. will come to a stop today. He knows this is the beginning of a marathon of grief and pain for all involved. "Hey, Paul, " Attebery answers the phone, sipping his tea that Lacey had prepared for him.

"What the fuck is goin on?! I have Devils callin me askin me all sorts of questions about Parks, Doherty, and James up in Idaho. I have no fuckin clue. I can't get through to Hoffman. Everyone is passin bullshit scuttlebutt—" Carpenter rattles off into the phone, in his customary frantic Southern drawl that Attebery has become accustomed to over the years.

"Hold the fuck on, Paul! Fuck, Sergeant Major, let me get a word in, ass," Attebery replies in a somewhat combative tone.

Carpenter huffs back, "It's Master Guns, dick," correcting Attebery to his correct rank, he is used to his old friend purposely incorrectly addressing him. "Okay, what's happenin right now as we speak, enlighten me?" Paul asks calmly. He, too, reaches for a cup of hot tea.

Attebery begins with what he knows, "Man, here is what was told to me from Gunny Hoffman. At fuckin zero dark thirty James, Doherty, and Parks secured a downed aircraft. An unknown armed unit arrived on scene, opened fire and that's fuckin it. We don't know if it's armed militia, drug dealers, fuckin Bigfoot, I have no damn clue; neither does Gunny at this point. No comms with any of them. Not Doherty. Not James. Not Parks. Nothing. Bgame is already in enroute to Idaho to run point for Gunny. Basically, that's all I know, brother." Todd quickly rattles off the bullet points of the facts so far.

"Get the fuck out of here," Carpenter fires back in disbelief.

The Last Letter

"To be honest Carp, if this goes South, I hope Parks doesn't survive," Attebery cuts himself off, staring blankly at his cup of cooling tea. "He won't make it if he survives, and his men didn't." He trails off, trying to hold back his anger and grief. Flashes of times spent annoying Parks in Ramadi, constantly to his old friend's frustrations. Incessantly interrupting Parks with, *"what movie are you watchin?"* during the downtime and, of course, Parks would purposefully ignore him, giving Attebery rise to escalate his annoyance of his old friend using his dirty feet. Attebery can't help but smile faintly at the fond memory.

"No, he won't." Paul agrees in a depressed tone, the gravity of the situation beginning to take hold. "So, this is real? No bullshit, real?" Paul quickly reflects on the first time he met Parks at Bravo Co's first ball weekend upon returning from Iraq, he had heard the stories, of course. Carpenter had the opportunity to head to Iraq with Bravo Co., but he chose to stay and take care of his young family. He deployed with Bravo Co. to Guantanamo Bay in '01 and having returned from Kuwait in '03; where he and other infantry Marines were on standby as body fillers for different Marine combat units in case those units took overwhelming casualties during the invasion of Iraq.

A then Sergeant Carpenter, would sit in the hot Kuwaiti desert with other disgruntled Marines, having to be relegated to the bench and do nothing while war raged around him; he hated every minute of it. Upon his return, while the crowds cheered, he felt hollow and somewhat disgusted with the Marines for leaving him on the sidelines. Now, Master Gunnery Sergeant Carpenter, always somewhat regrets not going with Bravo Co. He would eventually deploy to Iraq in '07 with Doherty, but it ended up being a peaceful combat tour much to the relief of loved ones back home. Now bombarded with images of his time spent with Doherty and Parks, he rubs his sore eyes.

"Yeah, it's real," Attebery responds lost in his own thoughts of Parks smiling, goofily on the rooftops of Iraq, arguing over a box *Whoppers*, whether giving oneself oral is a homosexual act or not, Parks believing it is, Christianity versus Islam, and of course the age old favorite, *Six Degrees of Kevin Bacon*[36].

---

[36] Common game linking the famous actor with others in six moves.

Carpenter continues rubbing his strained eyes, "Fuck," he utters, again lost in his own thoughts. "We are going to have some very angry Devils on our hands very fuckin soon," he says in his deep Texan accent.

"Have you told Kat?" Attebery asks, referencing Carpenter's wife.

"No, she's still sleepin. I wanted to know more. I saw my phone lightin up, I thought we were being attacked by the look of the urgent texts: *call me ASAP*, *have you heard*, shit like that," Paul responds quickly.

"Hopefully, Gunny or Bgame gets some real news before the media picks up this story. I'm flippin among all the national news channels and fuck all has been reported," Todd answers, using the remote to scan the channels on his TV.

Carpenter suddenly spits out some of the tea, "This is about to get a shit ton worse…. Hold the fuck on, Todd." He stops on a channel blaring breaking news. "I see something on CRN, yep here we go. Flip to CRN quick. Hurry, fucker!" He urges, getting nervous about the forthcoming news report.

"Give me a second, fuckface, I'm tryin." Attebery scrolls through the guide to the channel. "Got it. You happy, Sgt. Major. God?" he shoots back at Carpenter.

"It's Master Guns, dick, and yeah I am, now shut up so I can hear the news," Carpenter immediately fires back. A typical exchange between the two that always made their wives roll their eyes and ignore the two friends when they got going.

CRN's trademark breaking news soundtrack blares from both sets of televisions. Both men have their speaker phones turned on and are staring at their TVs, dumbfounded. Attebery frantically begins fumbling with his phone to send out a mass text to all his Bravo Co. contacts (90% of them are awake and have been texting him consistently) to turn on CRN. Attebery nervously sipping his fresh cup of hot tea. *This is going to suck*, he exhales deeply. He is soon joined by Lacey as she comes in from yet another nervous smoke. He gives her a quick look, she can see the worry on Attebery's tired, stubbled face.

"Another?" Attebery concerned with Lacey's uptick in smoking this still morning. He instantly regrets the remark.

"Hey, don't you give me shit, not this mornin, ass." Lacey shoots him a quick fiery glance that he has seen one too many times. Attebery nods his apology to his strong wife. Lacey then settles in next to her distraught husband,

The Last Letter

with a fresh cup of hot Earl Grey, both are desperately dreading the upcoming news. Todd and Lacey suddenly hold each other's hand, preparing for the worst possible outcome. The devoted couple have no idea the extent of traumatic damage that is still to come.

Carpenter sits down on one of the bar stools tucked under his massive, speckled granite countertop. He hears his bedroom door open and knows his ever-loving wife is about to enter their kitchen. She has yet to receive the horrible news, for Carpenter did not want to wake her yet.

"Hey babe, you're up early. What's up?" Kat asks, pouring herself a cup of hot tea out of her morning routine, not quite registering the shock on her husband's face. Known as *"Kat,"* Katherine Carpenter is a decorated Major in the United States Marine Corps Reserve. To Paul's dismay he is constantly chided by his fellow infantry Marines, that she outranks him and therefore he must salute her in the mornings, or that she has seen more combat than he did while in Iraq, which is untrue, but the men of Bravo Co. find a great delight in chiding their old Marine friend, especially now that he outranks them all.

Carpenter looks to his beloved, "Have a seat next to me, please. We need to watch this news report. No words, I will brief you with everythin I have after the report, Major," Carpenter responds downtrodden.

He has never called her *"Major"* at home, ever. Carpenter is speaking to her as a Marine. *This can't be good*, is Kat's only thought. "Paul, how bad?"

"Bad...." Carpenter trails off, his eyes slowly move from her to the TV.

. . .

At that very moment, Jocelyn, back in the home she made into a loving nest with James, is currently fixated on the same news broadcast from CRN that Attebery and Carpenter are watching. Her two girls circling around their stoic mother, they, too, see the breaking headline, and all settle onto the large couch. Jocelyn wraps her arms around each of them tightly, both girls notice their mom's tactical gear is staged by the garage entryway. The girl's faces turn to dread, tears start to form; whatever is to come will be horrific.

None of the three say a word as the CRN correspondent begins his report:

"Yes, thank you Sarah…To be honest, what we have here is a bit of a hornet's nest. Law enforcement agencies from all over have descended into the woods of this idyllic quaint little town of Clear Creek, Idaho. The reason: a major gun battle took place just outside of this silent little town in the National Forest that surrounds this dreamlike area in a beautiful green. Now that is marred by a gun battle and tragedy." The journalist initially reports in the universal trademark monotone voice they teach at all TV journalism schools.

"For those just joining us, CRN field reporter Preston Smith, is on scene of a breaking tragedy in the American heartland. Now, Preston, if I may interject, what law enforcement agencies are currently on station? What do they seem to be saying about a gun battle between two armed groups?" Sarah asks quickly.

"Currently on station, Sarah," Preston silently accepting the prodding to move his story along, *"are the FBI, ATF, DEA, Homeland Security, Idaho State Police, and the local Sheriff's Office. I am also hearing that a US Forestry Agent may have been the actual first responder on scene but that is yet confirmed, Sarah."* Preston concludes in the traditional monotone narrative.

"As far as who might be the participants in this traumatic event, the authorities are not speculating, but Sarah there are rumored armed militias training clandestinely in these woods to the dismay of the local populace. What we do know and are being told to us by law enforcement, is that two heavily armed groups of men did in fact engage one another in a small-arms gun battle, a firefight, if you will. As to the identities and number of deceased we are not being told at this time pending notification to the families. Sarah?"

"Preston, do we know of any survivors?" the news anchor fires back a quick question to keep the information flowing.

"Now, Sarah, this is unconfirmed but from one of my local sources, I am being told that there is one survivor and that he is listed in life-threatening condition and not expected to survive. According to my source he was air-lifted by Life-Flight to Boise Trauma Center and from there transported elsewhere, as far as any identity; that is being withheld at this time." Preston answers quickly to the satisfaction of the news anchor.

Sarah presses on, *"Preston, has there been any kind of formal statement? If not, who or what agency will be giving that briefing subsequently?"*

"*As of now, Sarah, the FBI is taking the lead on this incident and will be releasing a statement either themselves or through the Idaho State Police.*" The field reporter again quick with the answer.

"*Thank you, Preston Smith, our local CRN correspondent on the scene of this unfolding tragedy in America's Heartland.*" Sarah thanks her coworker for his report, graciously.

"*You are welcome, Sarah.*" As the camera shuts down and takes its focus off of Preston, he momentarily looks behind at the scene of the different law enforcement agencies scurrying about this crisp fall Idaho morning. Makeshift tables and tents propped across the parking lot of the local Walmart; the only place big enough to accommodate the influx of network traffic. The sun is starting to make its daily rise, to signify a new day. Preston has a feeling this day is the beginning of something momentous but does not quite know how to place his feeling. Is it dread, intrigue, fear, or worry? Something will be born of this travesty; *from every tragedy is born an opportunity*. He shrugs smugly, packing his gear away in the network van.

"*Thank you, Preston. Preston Smith with the up-to-the-minute information on the tragedy seemingly unfolding in Idaho. We, here at CRN, will certainly keep you up to date with any breaking news and, of course, will be going live to the FBI's press briefing when it becomes available. Again, for those of you just tuning in: A large gun battle erupted between two sets of heavily armed men in the Idaho National Forest, just outside of Clear Creek earlier this morning. We do not know the number involved or the number of deceased, we are also trying to confirm the story of a survivor. As soon as we, here at CRN, know any further details, we will interrupt programing to bring you live coverage of this developing tragedy.*" Sarah nods towards the camera as it fades to commercial.

. . .

Lacey picks up the remote from their granite countertop and taps the mute button. "Fuck", is all she can produce. Attebery sits motionless, silent, and stares coldly, vacant out of their bay windows at the rising sun, knowing everything changes today. *This can't be*, his only thought, resting his aching head in the palms of his hands. Lacey then wraps her comforting arms around her defeated husband.

. . .

Simultaneously, a few miles away sitting at their own kitchen countertop, watching the news coverage conclude, Carpenter and Kat sit in silence. Kat eventually does the same as Lacey and silences the TV with the remote. He looks up at her from the stool, she can see the fear welling up in Carpenter's eyes. Not the fear of fright but the fear of the rage that will soon come from the men of Bravo Co. Like Attebery, he stares out the massive back windows of his own home and into the expanse of the awakening East Texas horizon. Today, Carpenter wants more than anything not to have his phone.

. . .

Jocelyn, still holding her daughters under each arm, let's go of the eldest and turns the television off after the news coverage. "You motherfuckers…. I'm coming for you." Her grief is filled with rage, letting go of her youngest and starts to scroll through her extensive contacts within the Border Patrol and other law enforcement agencies; she is going to get answers. Jocelyn stills hears her husband's last words to her on the voicemail, tears welling up and flowing over her bottom eyelid. "I fuckin told him not to go," she grumbles, tears falling onto her phone, preventing her from dialing her command.

James' two girls quietly hold each other; their mother is not ready to grieve or console. They have seen her in this type of rageful state only a couple of times, and that is with the loss of one of her fellow Border Patrol Agents. The girls know they are on their own for the time being in their shared grief of what is to come. Jocelyn looks down at her beautiful daughters huddled on the couch, the youngest looking so much like her father, the rage flows freely now, her only thought, *Fuck you Sgt. Parks, this is your fuckin fault.*

CH. 12
THE MACHINE BREAKS

Dr. Rahandar Anand has concluded the single most difficult surgery of his exemplary and distinguished career as head of neurosurgery at the world respected Denver's Institute for Neurology. Outside of Walter Reed Veteran's Hospital, Dr. Anand's department is regarded as the premier traumatic cranial surgical and research center in the world. The respected doctor sits behind his massive oak desk in his beautiful office and collapses his head into his hands; the patient is stable, but he knows any number of things can undo the number of hours and emotion he and his team put into saving the man on their table.

His team has been in surgery for what seemed an eternity of nerves, was in fact four intense hours that ran the gambit of neurological surgery. Dr. Anand sent his surgical team home and promised to keep them apprised of any changes in their patient. "Bless my team," Dr. Anand exhales aloud into the deafening emptiness that is his office. He begins to lay his head down upon his crossed arms on the well-crafted desk; the surgeon wants to rest, *for a second*, he pleads mentally to the ever-present ghosts of those he could not save but especially to one ghost in particular. "No, please do not let my mind wander to those memories, not now."

Dr. Anand's pleas with his soul are in vain; his exhausted mental state has left the door open for his trauma to come flooding back in a torrential downpour of emotions. His trauma begins; he has no fight left. He was at work, as usual, his wife calling in hysterics… their son was dead. Suicide. Their world ended that day. Dr. Anand's son lost his beloved wife to COVID-19 in turn losing their unborn child as well, his son could not continue without her, the note would further explain the pain of loss. The beautiful sound of grandchildren never to come, their home now, a shell of vacant memories. The tears begin to stream down Dr. Anand's face and fall silently to his large desk in a tiny puddle of despair.

The good doctor gradually picks his head up to ingest the view of the city from his office's large pane windows on the twelfth floor; when he notices his phone has been ringing nonstop. He must have turned off the sound/vibrate settings after the surgery. The calls are from within the hospital, simultaneously his hospital pager begins to alert him of an emergency that requires the doctor's immediate action.

Quickly he hits the contact for his nurse, she immediately answers without pause, "Dr. Anand you need to please come down to ICU regarding our patient, he is stable and still in a coma, but there is a man here trying to gain access to our patient and his medical records. Please, Dr. Anand, we require your immediate presence, the police detail are getting quite nervous as well as our own hospital security and staff," his ICU nurse states calmly but firmly that he should make haste before the situation escalates.

"I will be there urgently. Allow no one access to that patient. Thank you, Nurse Bennett," Dr. Anand states registering the senior nurse's calm urgency. He stands up, wipes away his tears, and heads towards the elevators on the other side of his double office doors.

Dr. Anand exits the elevator, heads down the corridor to the isolation wing of the ICU, where he is met by Nurse Bennett, almost slamming into the doctor as she rounds the corner, "Thank Christ you're here, Doctor. Security is getting very antsy, and the police detail has already called into their watch commander," Nurse Bennett nervously rattles off, following in-step.

"What is the urgency? Who is this man and is he threatening?" Dr. Anand asks his head ICU nurse.

Nurse Bennett, keeping pace with the frantic doctor, answers, "He displayed credentials I have never seen before, so I don't know who the hell he is, and he's not really threatening per say; it's just the coolness of his demeanor. He is patiently waiting against the wall for you to arrive, Doctor," she replies, still confused as to the whole situation. "Who the hell do we have in there recovering? Did we save the life of a real nasty individual? No one has a fucking clue, Doctor. Pardon my language, but this whole situation has us all on edge."

He looks to her reassuringly. "That is fine, Nurse Bennett. Who the fuck knows? But I will find out." Dr. Anand fires back with his own profanity to lighten the mood between them. It works, Nurse Bennett smiles at his humor and puts her faith in the man she has worked alongside for the last sixteen years. Dr. Anand quickly makes the turn around the corner of the sterile blue and white corridor; upon rounding the corner he quickly ascertains why everyone seems on edge, everyone except the gentleman that the commotion is centered around. No, that gentleman seems perfectly at ease.

The gentleman is equal height to Dr. Anand, probably 5'8", he would guess. The man is dressed in a form-fitting blue polo, tailored grey slacks, and impeccably crafted loafers. He smiles as Dr. Anand approaches, keeping his hands clasped in front of him. The highly astute doctor notes all of these details, drawing closer to the individual, who seems to be chiseled of granite. The outline of the man's muscles plainly seen through the shirt, and the ripple effect of the muscles on his forearm as he prepares to extend his identification once again, display the mysterious man's subtle power.

"Dr. Anand, I presume? I am Supervisory Special Agent Victor Medina. I would like to see your patient, please," the gentleman immediately requests without a pause waiting for the neurosurgeon to peruse his identification.

"Your ID says Department of Homeland Security, who is that man?" Dr. Anand motions to the room next to the two men, guarded by two of Denver's finest. "And furthermore, I am not going to allow you to see my patient without proper authorization from the board of directors or from local authorities with a court order in hand. So, Mr. Medina, you might as well come back when you have those two things. Until then, my patient is just that, *my* patient." Dr. Anand calmly states to the mysterious gentleman.

The doctor then feels a vibration in his coat pocket, it is his intra-hospital pager directing him to call the board's private line. Dr. Anand immediately looks up at the stern-looking gentleman in front of him, bewildered. The man does not take his glance off the doctor but simply waits patiently. Simultaneously the nurse's center phone begins to ring as well, as do the cell phones of the two uniformed police officers standing post on the patient's door.

"That call will be for you as well as those of the officers, instructing all to let me see the patient. I am not trying to make trouble for you or your staff. I mean no difficulty to anyone here," Supervisory Special Agent Medina calmly but loudly explains so all can hear him.

The gentleman is correct. After hanging up the phone, Dr. Anand hands the gentleman his identification back angrily, "You must be very powerful. The board convened and a court order was signed all within a matter of a half hour. I have never seen such a thing. You may go in. I am told to wait outside and answer all questions you may have. I do not like this at all Mr. Medina, not one damn bit." The doctor defiantly refuses to address the intruding agent by his title.

"Thank you, Dr. Anand. Please know that no harm will come to your patient. Have the police officers and your hospital security stand post until I arrange for a proper detail, thank you, Doctor." With that, the mysterious gentleman slips into the ICU with the survivor.

"Dr. Anand, I do not like this, is my shift done yet?" Nurse Bennett tries to bring some brevity into a cloud of tension. The head nurse is echoing what every staff member is feeling in that ICU corridor, even the police officers.

The doctor huffs in frustration, watching the mysterious stranger through the glass windows facing the corridor. "I have never seen our authority cower to an outside agency so quickly. What danger is the hospital and staff in? That is my only concern." He looks about at his nervous team, "Sooner we get our mystery patient stable enough he can be transported to a more secure facility the better. For now, I expect the board is convening and all of us are about to receive a non-disclosure agreement within minutes." Dr. Anand states, continuing his watchful vigil from the patient's window.

The room is dark. There are no exterior windows as was prearranged; the constant beep of the machines keeping the patient alive chirping their presence about the gloomy room, the only sound heard. The tubes down his throat and in his arms gives the veteran agent paus, the patient's head is swollen to the point of seemingly bursting like a bubble. It is a tragic sight to behold for the experienced agent. Medina draws closer to the patient, staring down for a moment, pondering how it came to this, how of all places this would be the place he sees this man again. The agent is overcome with a warmth of memories from simpler days gone, and a slight affectionate smile creeps into the corner of his mouth at one particularly fond memory of the man lying before him.

"How is this possible, old friend?" The agent looks down upon the man and rests his hand gently on the patient's right shoulder. The sounds of the machines keeping him alive continue their chorus in the dreary background, as there is no response from the patient. Medina gives one last look at his old friend, the anger boiling in his chest, "I will see you soon, my friend."

He gives one last gentle pat on the patient's shoulder and heads for the door, to find an anxious crowd of first responders gathered about the corridor outside of the room. "Dr. Anand, here is my number; you will keep me posted as to any changes in the patient's condition. You will call me before you call the board for any decisions regarding the safety of this patient, do you understand, sir?" Agent Medina speaks urgently and swiftly.

"Excuse me, Mr. Medina, if that is even your real name." Dr. Anand begins to question the man's directives.

"Good one." Agent Medina quips at the doctor's quick wit and sarcastic tone.

Dr. Anand grows angry with the flippant agent, "You do not have the authority to illicit such demands, definitely not in my ward under my authority, I decide what is the absolute best course of action for my patient without having to seek permission from some outside entity. Now, do you understand, Mr. Medina," the doctor declares, defiantly objecting to the demands from this stranger at his hospital.

The agent calmy raises his hand to assure the gathered crowd, "Dr. Anand I am not here to crush your toes or undermine your authority in any way in front of your staff. I, too, am looking out for the safety and security of this patient. I must take my leave, but you will find all the authorization paperwork on your desk by the time you reach your office. I thank you and your team, truly, for the lifesaving measures you have taken to ensure the survival of this patient. I will be in touch." With that Agent Medina briskly pushes past the bewildered hospital staff heading towards the elevator, when two very imposing men, with extreme intensity in their demeanor, dressed head to toe all in black make their way towards Agent Medina from the opposite end.

Agent Medina stops and turns back towards Dr. Anand and the now frightened crowd of hospital staff. The police officers and hospital security instinctively place their hands upon their sidearms, preparing for the worst to come but Agent Medina holds up his hand as if to tell them to relax. "These men here are the new security for that patient, I expect all authorization should be forthcoming at any moment." As if on que the phones of the nurse's station, police officers, and Dr. Anand's hospital pagers all begin to chime in unison once again.

"You are fucking something else, Mr. Medin.," Dr. Anand states, growing furious over the whole mess that is this situation he finds him and his staff a part of; he does not like it.

"Thank you, Doctor." Agent Medina replies as the two hulking men move into position to relieve the police officers by the door. Medina returns to his brisk exit to the elevators and disappears around the sterile blue and white corridor of the ICU wing.

Nurse Bennett joins Dr. Anand in his heated stare down the corridor at the exiting agent, "Doctor, I think we're fucked."

"I agree. The sooner this patient is well enough to be transported to wherever this agency wants to take him, the better. Which I am assuming will be Walter Reed. To be honest judging from the latest results I have reviewed, I do not see our patient waking from his coma within in any reasonable amount of time or if he ever wakes at all." He looks into the survivor's solitary room. "But we will comply and ensure that our very best efforts are rendered to ensure the survival of our patient like we always do. Understood, everyone?" Dr. Anand bellows the last sentence so that all in attendance understand that nothing will take away from their professionalism to their craft or the hospital's premier reputation.

"Yes, Doctor!" All in attendance repeat in unison, even the police officers who were relieved of their post, understood the necessity of the situation.

Dr. Anand begins his journey back to his office, quickly realizing any adrenaline he had coursing through his body the past four plus hours, has quickly dissipated. His encounter with Agent Medina and his men, has sapped the doctor of any remaining fortitude. Dr. Rahandar Anand is mentally and physically spent, and his day has only begun. He will get to his office and get some rest on his plush couch; a place where he spends most of his life since his son's tragic passing. Anything to avoid the deafening, hollow silence that has engulfed his marriage and once bright home.

He swipes his keycard to unlock his office door and heads immediately to his desk. Dr. Anand's face grows tighter, his jaw clenches in rage at the sight of a large manilla envelope, with his name written in black sharpie across the front. Growing exceedingly frustrated with the invasion into his office, the doctor slices through the lip of the sealed envelope; the contents falling upon his beautiful desk that his wife spent so much time meticulously picking out for the office, the hours spent pursuing the landscape with her for the ornate furniture. He misses their love. He sighs at the distant memory, surveying the contents of the envelope. True to his word, Agent Medina followed through with the proper authorizations from the board, the local and federal district judges. Also attached is a blank card with: AGENT MEDINA 668-464-8408, nothing else. No insignia, no department crest, no title, only: AGENT MEDINA.

"This is bullshit," Dr. Anand grumbles to himself, sitting down in his leather chair, welcoming the relief to be off of his feet. He checks his messages which are transcribed and sent to his email. There are two messages from the board which he skips, undoubtedly ordering him to comply with the government officials regarding their mysterious head trauma survivor. The doctor has no time for hospital bureaucracy, he wants to spend his few precious solitary moments thinking upon his lost beautiful boy.

...

Jean is hurriedly scurrying around her living room throwing things into her suitcase haphazardly, letting things fall at will into the luggage. She had received two phone calls, and both were horrific. The woman of her 70's stops and grabs the edge of the nightstand to steel herself. She is supposed to be enjoying her golden years, living in a beautiful home nestled in wine country of

Napa Valley. Jean is not supposed to be dragged to this depth of hell. Not now, not at this point in her life. How can she move forward after this? *No parent should outlive their child, this cannot be.* The thought reaching out of the depths of her sorrow to take grip on her reality. She knows she must re-focus, her twenty-two years in the military has left her with an unwavering sense of bearing and fortitude. The aged woman pushes forward, her son needs her and so do her grandchildren.

Jean analyzes the first call she received; it was from Attebery waking her around 4:00 a.m., her time. Her phone buzzing on the nightstand next to her bed, she sees it is his name. He had tried earlier, but she was asleep and did not answer. This could only be an emergency; they have not talked since her son's failed suicide attempt over a decade ago and Attebery went out to try and help him pick up the pieces. Her panic sets in as she answers the phone, "How bad is it?"

Attebery is not at all surprised by the straightforwardness of Parks' mother. He has met her on a few occasions, and she always seemed a stern and professional Veteran. He knows from his past experiences of being a patrol officer, to be straightforward with relatives of devastating news, "Ms. Parkinson it's bad. I will tell you all that I know." Attebery hoping to get through the facts as he knows them without faltering, this is personal for him as well, "Parks and his men were apparently involved in a tragic incident while on their reunion trip in the woods out in Idaho. From the preliminary reports I have received and the early news, there appears to be a survivor. I wanted to call you as soon as I could piece together the information I have just absorbed and processed, Ms. Parkinson?" Attebery states the basic information of the dire situation that has engulfed this small community of Veterans and their families. He is worried, his tone does not belay his emotions, but he is worried.

"Yes, I am here. Is that all the information you have at this moment?" Jean's serious and emotionless response takes Todd aback a moment.

"Yes, ma'am. Bgame is on his way to Clear Creek as we speak to gather more information and will debrief everyone on *Facebook Live* at 1800, with what he can discover. Ms. Parkinson, are you okay? Do you need me to call anyone?" Attebery is genuinely concerned about her well-being and needs Jean to respond to alleviate his own concerns.

The Last Letter

She has always feared for her son from the day he joined the Marines, requesting infantry, "I'll be fine, Todd. Thank you. I'll be leaving immediately for Clear Creek. Please keep me posted with any new developments," Jean responds in a detached tone. She has reverted to her "*machine*" persona; it is an affectionate nickname Parks' first wife, Sabrina, uses to describe his mother. "*She is an emotionless machine, Jean the Machine,*" his first wife would always say. His second, Katie, thought she had ice in her veins. Parks never noticed his mother's "*machine*" persona. To him it was normal, for Jean it meant survival for her and her two children as she raised them as a struggling single mother, no child support, left to fend on her own in West Texas upon departure from active duty in the United States Air Force.

"I will, ma'am. Ms. Parkinson, I'm so damn sorry. I told him I thought it was good idea to see the fellas again," Todd acknowledges for the first time, he championed his old friend's novel idea for a reunion. A lump forming in his esophagus starts threatening to constrict his air flow. He quickly takes a huge gulp of his hot tea, the warmth instantly relaxing his throat.

"Do not start down that road, Todd. Jake would not want any of that. Please, keep me informed of any new developments," Jean responds plainly.

Attebery begins to focus on the next task., "I will. I'm making arrangements to head up to Clear Creek and join Bgame as soon as I clear my schedule at work," he adds, hoping that will add some comfort to Jean's current state of mind.

"Thank you, Todd." Jean hits *End* on her phone and then she falls to the floor, catching herself on the edge of the bed. The tears start flowing as images of her smiling little boy dance through her head. To Jean, her son will always be that naked little child running around the backyard at four, laughing and smiling. That is until he fell headfirst into some cactus, and she spent the afternoon pulling cactus quills out of a crying little rambunctious boy's forehead. The tears flow heavier now, she lets out a muffled scream into her bed's comforter, wiping the tears away.

"Get the fuck up, Tech Sgt!" Jean urges, by commanding herself up off the carpeted floor, reverting to her rank. "Suck it up." Again, she is pleading with her seventy-four-year old body to move. It is then her phone begins to ring again; she moves quickly, like a cat being startled and closes the distance in a flash to her phone. It is not Todd or any number she recognizes. "Yes." She is back in *"machine"* mode. Emotionless.

A soft-spoken voice on the other end asks, "Yes, ma'am. Jean Parkinson?" "Yes. Who is this?" the Machine responds coarsely.

The gentle voice continues, "I apologize ma'am. I am a Supervisory Special Agent with Department of Homeland Security, my name is Victor Medina. Please allow me to speak before any questions, can you allow me that, ma'am?" Agent Medina asks still in a very humbling and soft-spoken tone.

An awkward silence falls over the conversation, ever so briefly, "Yes, proceed." The Machine answers emotionless. But something in the back her mind is telling her, she has heard this man's name before.

"I am going to tell you all that may be allowed under my current directives, but I will also allow myself to add personal thoughts and information on the subject," SSA[37] Medina begins to speak but is abruptly cut off by Jean.

"Agent Medina, please, get to the fucking point," the Machine sternly says, the phone speaker picking up the anger in her tone of voice. *Why does she recognize this man's name?* The thought persists in her mind.

Medina is sympathetic and understands the anger. "Yes, ma'am. I am sure by now you have been told as to the situation regarding your son and his fellow Marines?" The agent directs the statement as more of a question, trying to gauge Jean's response, so as to see how he should proceed.

The Machine slows her frantic pace of packing and is hit with the pain of suffering once again, "Yes, Agent Medina, I am aware of a situation involving my son and his friends. I am on my way out the door, so please, Agent Medina, the point?" Jean's armor of resistance to emotion exposing a slight chink as she lets her thoughts drift to her son and his beloved squad members. She begins to buckle again but steadies herself quickly with the nightstand.

Special Agent Medina continues, "Yes, of course. Your son survived the incident and has been relocated to Denver's Institute of Neurology. He is in critical condition. A Dr. Rahandar Anand, chief of neurosurgery, performed the emergency procedure. Your son is in a non-medically induced coma. Please change your itinerary to Denver, there will be a car waiting for you at

---

[37] Supervisory Special Agent

the airport to take you to the trauma center. Ms. Parkinson do you understand the facts as I have relayed them to you?" Agent Medina explains truthfully.

Jean sits calmly on the bed's edge, stunned. The constant swing in emotional states has left her depleted of all power to stand. The Machine is slowing, and the emotions are overwhelming the mechanism of avoidance. "Yes, Special Agent Medina, I will make arrangements for Denver."

"Your son is under twenty-four-hour security, and no one is allowed access without my authorization. You are cleared upon arrival to the hospital to see him. Present your identification to my men at the checkpoint and one of them will escort you to your son's room. The car will bring you directly to the hospital from the airport," Agent Medina begins to rattle off his mental checklist but is quickly interrupted by the Machine.

Jean's anger beginning to flare, "With all due respect, Special Agent, I do not know you and I will check into this by calling this Dr. Anand and then I will find my own means to the hospital." The Machine's defiance is not to be trifled with. "Answer me a couple of questions, Agent Medina, one, what does this have to do with Department of Homeland Security and two, why does your name sound familiar to me, Agent Medina?" The Machine, back in control of her emotions, cross-examines the agent.

The Special Agent cannot help but admire this woman on the phone, "Fair, enough ma'am. I understand completely. I will let Dr. Anand know to expect your call. He does not like me very much, so he may be skeptical, but he is one of the foremost neurological trauma experts in the country. Your son and his men were at the wrong place at the wrong time, ma'am. They did nothing illegal or wrong. They were trying to render aid. Do not listen to the press, I will give you my direct number through text upon termination of this call. Feel free to call or text that number regardless of the hour. I will respond directly. I happened to recognize Parks' name as it came across my radar and I have the resources to aid your son," Medina responds, this time with a touch of remorse in his voice.

The recollection hits the Machine like a freight train, she remembers how she knows this man's name—"The tarantula!"

Supervisory Special Agent Medina almost chokes on the sixth cup of coffee he has had in the past hour. The hours have dragged, and he has been very busy doing all he can for the survivor. The absolute shock of Jean's statement has him spitting the warm, dark beverage onto the hideous governmental desk he is currently commandeering. He places the cup down quickly and races to grab some paper towels from the absolute bore that is called a break room.

"Special Agent Medina?" the Machine asks, thinking the line cutoff.

"Yes, ma'am, I'm fine," Medina responds with a lighter tone to his voice.

"It has been over two decades since I've thought about that. Yes, I served with your son at India 3/5 before the Osprey crash in 2000."

The Machine softening her harsh tone in the slightest, "You put the tarantula on his chest while he was sleeping or was it in his Kevlar if I remember the story correctly?" The brevity of the dialogue has given her some sense of warmth and slight relief that her son is in good hands.

"*Allegedly*, ma'am. Allegedly put the tarantula on his chest and in his Kevlar." The Machine can almost hear the smile stretch across Special Agent Medina's face as he recollects the hilarity of the memory.

Jean keeps pushing for more, to assure her son will be in familiar company. "Wasn't another accomplice with you? I cannot remember his name," the Machine asks.

"Yes, his name is Mitchell." The special agent cannot help but chuckle slightly at the memory almost thirty years ago, when he was a young infantry Marine. The incident of which they speak, would become a running joke for decades between the three men of India Co. Parks always promising to give the guilty one an *ass whippin* once the guilty party finally admitted to the placement of the tarantula. Medina and Mitchell, both blaming the other over the years; all in keeping the legendary joke alive for decades.

The Machine is beginning to let her mental wall waver, "My son always speaks fondly of you; his face always lights up when he reenacts that story to our family. It is magical to see him smile; it's such a rarity now. Okay, Supervisory Special Agent Medina, I place my trust in you. I will see you in Colorado," she solemnly states, trying to focus on the next step.

Medina grateful he is able to place her mind at a slight ease, replies, "Thank you, ma'am. Please, allow me to have someone waiting at Denver International and have you brought directly to the hospital if you accept. There is an open ticket to Denver already waiting for you in San Francisco."

Rubbing her pounding temples, Jean relents, "Thank you, I do accept. How does he look, Agent Medina?" The Machine instantly regrets asking the question. She did not want to know or to think on her son's state on the trip there. No, the Machine wants to remember the crying four-year-old little boy, pulling cactus needles out of his tiny head. *"Oh, the poor baby, there, there"* she would repeat to him, laughing lovingly.

"Ma'am, I think it best you focus on your trip at hand, I will make sure he is safe here. Please call me Vic or Medina, your son always did." He did not want Park's mother focusing on the hideousness of the situation. Agent Medina wants to be there for her when Jean sees her son for the first time. "I will call Dr. Anand and have the hospital expecting you."

"Thank you, Medina." The Machine tries to take control again but is having trouble putting the emotional wall back up into position. She feels suddenly incapable of moving.

Agent Medina can feel the deflation of Parks' mother, "Ms. Parkinson, I will find the motherfuckers that did this to your son and his men. I assure you of that. These next few moments take in small phases: pack, get to the airport, board the plane. Small steps, ma'am. Would you like me to arrange for someone to pick you up at your residence?" Medina reassures Jean, hoping to ease the next few minutes for her.

The Machine takes a deep cleansing inhale of the cool California ocean breeze coming off the bay through her bedroom window. "Again, thank you, Agent Medina but I will manage. Goodbye." She appreciates his efforts at reassurance, and she relays that affection in her tone as she hits *End*. She hurries about the bedroom grabbing clothes, toiletries and tossing them into her carryon. Anything else she needed she would buy when she got there. The Machine is moving once again. She quickly orders an Uber with her app—ETA twenty minutes. Jean quickly locates her passport, mask, wallet, and shoves them in her fanny pack.

Then it hits her, the silence of the predawn northern California morning. The second hand ticking away on her enormous living room wall clock. She never noticed the sound before; now it is excruciating. *Tick, tick, tick, tick, tick….* The Machine quickly rises and heads to her kitchen; she starts to prepare some hot tea while she waits for the Uber. The Machine is weakening, and she feels herself grip the kitchen granite tighter. "Dear Lord, be with the families of the fallen and watch over my son as he fights for his life, Amen." It is all the prayer she can muster for now. If she dwells on a lengthy prayer, Jean may not recover. She checks her phone: ten minutes until *Dave the Uber driver* arrives.

She is debating whether to call her daughter and pass along the horrible news, but she decides quickly against it, not while he daughter is still with that waste of a man. The Machine will call her daughter with news on her big brother from the hospital in Denver. "Oh, son, what happened to your men?" her voice quakes, trying to sip the fresh cup of hot Earl Grey. Jean again, must steel herself against the cold granite countertop. She wishes the Uber driver would arrive immediately but even then, she will be forced into awkward silence and must confront her images of her dear boy flashing before her tightly closed eyes, a collage of beautiful smiles of her radiant son. *The families, the pain the other families are going through, Lord, please, please give them your strength.* The prayer flashes across her mind as the gravity of the situation finally is taking hold of her ageing self. She knows those families are in *Hell* at this moment. Jean can no longer stand and rushes to her living room couch before her legs give way, collapsing onto the comfortable sofa.

The fresh ocean breeze comes sweeping in from her open patio door. The breeze rejuvenating her lungs as she exhales the negative air she feels at this moment. Her phone vibrates from an incoming text, the Uber is waiting in the driveway. The Machine is relieved to be moving forward and for the moment pushing her rampant thoughts back into the recesses of her mind. She hurriedly grabs her fanny pack, pulls the handle on the carry-on, arms the security system, and heads out the front door to the awaiting Uber. The Machine once again in control, slides into the backseat of the Ford Bronco Sport.

"Heading to the airport, correct?" Dave the Uber driver asks politely from behind his mask.

"Yes, thank you, San Francisco International." The Machine replies flatly.

The Last Letter

The driver was expecting a more courteous, soft tone coming from this seemingly frail woman, but then he notices her gaze in his rearview mirror, her steel grey eyes seem dead... vacant. It sends a chill down his spine. "Yes, ma'am." Dave the Uber driver responds softly, politely.

The Machine does not notice his reaction as she becomes again haunted by images of her son dancing across her consciousness. Jean shuts her eyes tightly, her phone buzzes again with another text, Agent Medina has sent his contact information:

Supervisory Special Agent Victor Medina
614-426-8886

It comes as a great relief to Jean; fortunes worked in favor of her son and with it comes great trepidation. Only her son's friend would know the tarantula story but on the other hand the *Department of Homeland Security* regardless of friendship brings only more mounting questions for her to consider, and at this point she has no energy to direct towards these questions. The Machine continues to stare blankly out the window of the Uber's Bronco Sport; the darkness of the ocean, the vastness of its reach into the expansive silent horizon hypnotizes Jean, paralyzing her thoughts for a brief meditative moment. But it is only a moment: *What happened? I just talked to him. Why? What were they doing? Is he in pain? Please, Lord, don't take him. The other poor mothers, Oh God....*

Jean cannot stop the onslaught of torturous thoughts on her protective emotional wall, the Machine is fading quickly. She feels so very tired, she has about six more hours of this mental torture until she touches down at Denver International Airport. She slowly lowers her face into her aching, tired hands and finally begins to release her grief, he woeful sobs echo throughout the small vehicle. Dave the Uber driver is a reluctant witness to a rarity as *The Machine* breaks.

CH. 13
1ST SQUAD HEARS THE NEWS

The news is starting to spread rapidly throughout the rest of the Bravo Co. community. Rory Perry, a 6' natural rock of a man, is stepping out of his silver 2020 Dodge Ram 2500 truck, onto his gravel drive. He is out here in the middle of nowhere Louisiana building his dream house himself, and it is coming along tediously. Perry, returning from a rotation of underwater welding for an oil platform out in the Gulf of Mexico, looks about his property with pride and exhaustion.

"Fuck, I have a shit ton more to go," he complains audibly to himself, getting his dive rig out of the back of his truck. Perry is building this house as a surprise for his young daughter, to provide a better place for her when she visits him on his weekends. Perry knows his past troubles have led him to this point in his life and he acknowledges he now must endeavor on a new path for his daughter. He has destroyed enough in his life. *No more*, he would promise himself. Perry, a once-promising young undercover narcotics officer allowed his baggage from Iraq to interfere and so Perry fell victim to the job. Drugs and alcohol would send his life into darkness. He needed change. Doherty, who would also struggle, reached out and together they helped Perry get back to moving in the right direction. Bgame would also step in and help Perry secure his position as an underwater welder, exactly the direction he needed. It's grueling but Perry enjoys his work.

The former Marine slings his gear bag and helmet over his shoulder with a grunt, missing the weightlessness of the gear in the water, and heads to the double-wide trailer he has on the property he uses as his residence until he is finished with the house. He unlocks the front door as he gets to the top step and immediately unloads the weight of the gear on the little, tiny linoleum entryway. Perry walks over to the oak dining room table and drops all his tired weight into an unforgiving wooden dining room chair. The place is meticulously clean; it is something Perry ensures after a long rotation; to relax in a clean, calm environment is a must for the experienced welder.

He turns the television to JKL NEWS to have the incessant chatter in the background as he prepares himself some coffee with his Keurig K-cup brewer to unwind before he jumps in the shower and turns in for a few hours before his daughter arrives for her visit. *"To our viewers; we are receiving preliminary reports from our affiliate station out of Boise, Idaho; KTCY. I now go to Chuck Knowles reporting live from outside of Clear Creek, Idaho. Chuck, what is the situation?"* the anchorwoman asks with a feigned interest, not expecting much out of Idaho.

"Well, Jane, apparently I am getting reports from multiple law enforcement sources that there was an apparent shootout in the early morning hours up in the thick forested mountains that you can see behind me." Chuck initially responds after a couple seconds delay in the live feed. Perry, oblivious to the report, continues to make his coffee, utterly exhausted from his most recent rotation underwater. His mind focused on the hot shower that lay ahead after he finishes with his warm cup of coffee.

"Do you mean a shootout with law enforcement, Chuck?" Jane responds, her interest beginning to pique.

The field reporter, resenting the softball response from his colleague, responds, *"No, Jane, I believe what I am learning is that it was more than just a shootout but a firefight with hundreds of rounds being exchanged; some are speculating this maybe drug related."*

Perry turns his gaze towards the television at the mention of the word *firefight*. *Grunts* know this term well and Perry will always be a Marine *Grunt*. He quickly grabs the remote off the kitchen counter and turns up the volume and strides over to the couch. *Please no, Oh God please no,* the silent prayer flashing across his mind.

The Last Letter

"*Are there any fatalities, Chuck?*" Jane quickly throws in the question before Chuck can continue.

"*Yes, Jane, I am being told three men are dead and their names are being withheld due to the ongoing investigation and the notification to next of kin. I am also being told the deceased were very heavily armed at the time of their deaths; adding even more speculation as to why they were out there in the middle of night,*" Chuck relays, seemingly disturbed by the incident he is reporting. *Too close to home; this shit doesn't happen in Idaho*; he thinks to himself quickly.

"Please, fuck no. Fuck no!" Perry bellows, smashing the coffee cup on the end table next to his couch. He is reading the ticker at the bottom of the screen and realizes the crucial detail that solidified his fears. The location flashes across the banner and the color drains from his face: *Clear Creek, Idaho*.

Perry frantically digs his phone from his work trousers, immediately finds Doherty's contact and hits *Send*, it goes to voicemail. "Fuck!" *James… voicemail. Sgt. Parks… voicemail.* "Fuck, Fuck, Fuck, Fuck!" Perry, slamming his feet heavily on the thickly carpeted floor, frantically moving about, his bare feet begin to ache from the constant thudding as he grips on to the kitchen counter to steady himself.

He tries Bgame, nothing. "What the fuck?!" Perry checks his Facebook and then he sees the Bravo Co. Community page bombarded with messages and postings. The posts are coming in at the cyclic rate and he cannot keep up. Perry sees Bgame's post about a debriefing at 1800, he is on the way to Clear Creek and not answering the phone. What catches Perry's eyes are the final words of Bgame's post: BE PREPARED FOR THE WORST.

Perry quickly checks his phone for the invitation to the trip from Sgt. Parks, the first line: *Perry, please join 1st Squad in beautiful Clear Creek, Idaho.* He grabs a small wooden framed 4x6 photo that proudly sits atop his counter and stares at the young faces gazing back at him. *We had no fuckin clue, did we, fellas*, The Marine reflects, dropping the framed timeless image to the counter and slamming his heavy fist through his wooden cupboard. "I should have fuckin been there!"

SSgt. Jacob Parkinson

. . .

Angelo, known to old friends simply as Del Vecchio, is in his office, staring at his monitor going over the interest rates for the day. He is always the first one in the office of his mortgage company and unless it is a meeting with lenders or something of importance, he is the last to leave. He does not do this to chase the dollar or make riches; he has the wealth; no, Del Vecchio does this because he truly believes it sets a prime example for his employees to follow. He is not above sacrifice, and his employees respect him for the selflessness. Though considered young to be in such a position, Del Vecchio earned every bit of his success.

It is early, but out of the corner of his eye he sees his personal phone light up with Facebook notifications consistently. He scoops up his phone and checks his profile page; he immediately sees the Bravo Co. community page being slammed with messages from guys around the country.

Parks, James, Doherty have been hit… WTF!

Any survivors?

Bgame is going live at 1800. This can't be happening!

I just talked to Doherty… please don't be true. What the fuck is going on?

Repeated messages of disbelief. Del Vecchio types in the search bar, *Clear Creek*. He stares in horror at the first link: *Firefight in the Foothills … 3 presumed dead. Clear Creek.*

"No, no, no. no," Del Vecchio mutters to himself incoherently. He stands to take a few deep breaths, his form-fitting suit suddenly feeling as if it is going to cut off circulation to his sculpted arms and legs from years of playing rugby; are suddenly weak and unbalanced. Del Vecchio quickly loosens his tie, sitting back down at his desk and begins to devour the headlines related to the incident in Idaho. He cannot find names of the victims anywhere; he is dreading what is next. Del Vecchio picks up his phone and calls:

James…nothing.

Doherty…nothing. Sgt. Parks…nothing.

"Fuck, please no. Fuck." Del Vecchio looks at his phone and scans the invitation: *Del Vecchio, please come join 1st Squad in beautiful Clear Creek, Idaho.* He puts his head in his palms and breathes heavily. Del Vecchio scans the messages again and sees Bgame's post about being prepared for the worst. *1800, okay? I need to make arrangements to get up there,* he begins planning to himself, not fully believing in the circumstances of this cruel morning.

The office suddenly feels hollow and empty. Del Vecchio's fingers begin slamming into his keyboard scouring flights to Idaho and the quickest route to Clear Creek. The former Marine immediately starts making arrangements and reservations at lightning speed. He will be in Clear Creek by 2000 hours that evening. He pushes himself back from his ornate wooden desk that his dear wife designed herself from her own collection. Del Vecchio runs his hand along the smooth surface; he looks over at his beautiful wife's picture on his desk and begins to feel the guilt of having realized Doherty, James, and Sgt. Parks' loved ones are waking to a catastrophic day, and yet her radiant smile beaming from the picture engulfs him with a sense of strength.

The employees of the firm are starting to trickle in, and he must brief his associates as to his immediate departure, but he knows he cannot tell them why. They do not know much about that part of his life, except a Marine photo here and there. His honorable discharge displayed proudly on the wall next to his two degrees. Del Vecchio likes to keep that part of his life to himself. He looks at a tiny 4x6 framed photo from 2004, a bunch of young ragtag Marine *Grunts* posing for a squad photo before rolling into a major combat operation. *Those young men,* he muses, looking at the picture fondly, *had no idea what lifetime of experience was in store for them, all because of that man in the middle, Sgt. Parks.*

Del Vecchio grabs the photo, he has not seen any of the guys from the squad in over twenty years; he never tried making any of the reunions, as most didn't after a while. Del Vecchio gets lost in the memory, his stare goes blank, he then scans the email's opening line again. *I should have been there,* he leans back in his leather chair, closes his eyes, and deflates allowing the chair to swallow his guilt.

• • •

Pierce Cooper is already at the office getting together his day's agenda. He scans over potential clients files and possible violations of agreements. Cooper runs a successful chain of bail bonds outlets across the state of Louisiana. His business is known throughout as honorable, fair, and willing to work with their clients provided they uphold the law. It is this integrity and openness to those in need of help that has made Cooper a very successful man at a very young age. He leans back in his leather desk chair and rubs his face with the palm of his manicured hands, it is already going to be one of those days. The vibrations come in quick hits, Cooper quickly looks down at his iPhone and notices the Bravo Co. community page is getting bombed with numerous messages.

"Jesus." He picks up his phone and resumes his leaned-back posture in the comfortable leather chair. Cooper bolts upright at the first message he sees:

What the fuck happened to James, Doherty, and Parks?!!

Hundreds of messages and threads going back and forth. His own messenger is filled with unanswered responses. Everything is coming in too fast. Cooper quickly smashes the keys into the Google search bar for *Clear*, but he did not need to finish to see the page fill with headlines. He begins quickly scanning the news feeds and articles. Each one mentioning: *three presumed dead, massive firefight, drugs, cartels, hired guns*. "What the fuck is going on?!" he screams at his computer. "No, no, no, no." he repeats to himself. Cooper quickly dials Bgame, straight to voicemail. "Fuck!"

Cooper keeps reading the headlines and knows the inevitable will become true. He then dials Jackson, who he has not talked to in over a decade, except the occasional comment or like of a post; it, too, goes to voicemail. He then shoots off a quick text: *hey brother call me ASAP!!* He quickly checks his email for the invite from Sgt. Parks, and the first line seals their fate.

Cooper,

Please come join 1st Squad in beautiful Clear Creek, Idaho.

Sinking further into his chair, this time for Cooper, the leather offers no comfort. He scrolls through the messages on the Bravo Co. page, no one seems to know what is happening, but the consensus is that the three; James, Doherty, and Parks are gone. He checks his messenger; it's filled with worry from fellow

The Last Letter

Marines of Bravo Co. reaching out to him, he does not feel like responding; he knows it is coming—the guilt.

His gaze begins to lift to his bookcase, in the middle of a shelf with other Marine memorabilia, is a tiny 4x6 picture in an ornate wooden frame. The shelf of memorabilia is centered around that lone tiny picture. Cooper reluctantly gets up and strides over to the bookcase. Every Marine has one, especially *Grunts*, they tend to call it a *Wall of Shame*[38], but it consists of their individual and unit accomplishments displayed not for anyone else but the Marine to reflect upon; a constant reminder from the peak of their youth, the absolute best they will ever be.

Cooper swiftly grabs the photo and studies those young, naïve men, completely oblivious as to what was to come. He sees himself kneeling in front of Jackson and James, the three SAW gunners of 1st Squad; their faces hardened already, awaiting another test of their bravery. He sees Jackson's arm on Doherty. Cooper feels a lump start to form in his throat, a constriction of emotion; his eyes move towards the middle, and he sees Sgt. Parks, his stoic squad leader. Cooper's memory starts to drift back to Iraq over twenty years earlier; it is crushing to reflect upon. He places the photo gently back to its' resting place on the shelf. Those men had no idea what was to come the following days, especially that day; *that was a long fucking day*, his body suddenly seems to feel the weight of his grief.

Scrambling back to his desk, he starts making plans to fly out to Idaho. Clicking frantically, booking flights and reserving rental vehicles. Completing this task, he begins to call his office manager, apprise her that he must leave immediately, and she will be in charge of day-to-day operations. He has the utmost confidence her; Alice is overly qualified, and he is lucky to have her expertise. Cooper knows this and he compensates her handsomely.

Why the fuck didn't I go? I didn't even attempt to clear my schedule, you motherfucker, I should have been there; and so, begins Cooper's guilt. Unfortunately like the other members of 1st Squad coming to terms with the "*should haves*," Cooper feels drained before the sun has risen. He sits his short,

---
[38] Wall used to display accolades and awards

stocky, muscular frame down in his now-uncomfortable leather chair, leans back, and shuts his eyes, hoping the specter of guilt will stay at bay until he has a moment of clarity.

. . .

Morales rolls over and stares at his beautiful wife snoring loudly, never believing him when he tells her she snores. It is a never-ending back-and-forth that he finds endearing. Known by his civilian friends as Erick, he quickly sits up, rubs the sleep from his eyes, and stretches his upper body. Everything aches. Morales heads to the master bath to make his morning ritual urination, much to his relief. After flushing, he heads to the sink to wash his hands, brush his teeth, and shave—another ritual absorbed from his time as a Marine.

Heading back out of the master bath, he passes by his beautiful snoring wife. *I need to record that shit.* He pauses. *No, she would kill me*, Morales quickly dismisses the idea. He exits the bedroom silently, heads to the kitchen to fix a bowl of Honey Nut Cheerios, the familiar hard sound of the cereal hitting the bowl is oddly comforting to him. Morales turns on the small flat screen television that is mounted underneath a kitchen cabinet, to catch the morning national news. Moving to the fridge to retrieve the milk, he barely catches the morning news report:

"Yes, Samantha the FBI, DEA, and Department of Homeland Security are reportedly on scene."

"For those of you just tuning in, we are reporting what is being called a 'massive firefight' in the forest outside of Clear Creek, Idaho. Three heavily armed men presumed dead, drugs were found on scene and apparently there may be a plane crash involved as well, is that correct, Jason?"

"That is correct, Samantha. I am hearing from multiple sources that there was indeed a plane crash in the same vicinity as the gun battle. I believe the FAA is in enroute to also aid in the investigation."

"Jason, can you tell us more on the heavily armed men that are presumed dead and apparently found on scene?"

The Last Letter

Behind the field reporter is a scrum of news crews and varying agencies of law enforcement; each trying to control the other. *"What I have gathered so far, is that the identities of the men are being withheld due to notification of the families, but I am also told that all had identification on them. We should know more in the coming hours. Samantha."*

The anchor woman nods understandingly into the camera. *"Thank you, Jason. For those just tuning in, a massive shootout in the woods outside of Clear Creek, Idaho, three heavily armed men presumed killed on scene. We will have more live from Clear Creek as the story unfolds.*

Morales stops cold, the milk jug begins to tremble in his hands. *Clear Creek?* He races to his phone and opens his email app, scrolling frantically looking for Sgt. Parks' message. Morales finds the email but cannot bring himself to open the invitation, he knows if he opens this email and it confirms the rising fear in his gut, the guilt will be relentless. The mouse moves as if controlled by another entity and clicks on the message:

Morales,

Please come join 1st Squad in beautiful Clear Creek, Idaho.

The first line is unmistakable. Morales knows James and Doherty were the only ones that made the trip to Idaho to join Sgt. Parks. The two posted several photos and messages pertaining to the trip upon arrival in Clear Creek. It was endearing to see the three squad members reconnecting. He wishes he had made time to join his squad, but he did not even attempt to. Work at the ICU post-pandemic is still unrelenting, he is overworked as is all in his profession, too many open shifts and not enough medics. The guilt is creeping up the back of his neck, the hairs standing on their ends; like a ghost blowing its sorrow across his back.

"Fuck!" he bellows, opening the Bravo Co. community page and grasps the enormity of the situation. There are too many messages and posts to keep track of and the flow is not stopping as more of Bravo are waking up to the news that three of their own are gone tragically. His messenger is filled with fellow *Grunts* reaching out to him about 1st Squad and if he has heard from the three.

He did not have the contact numbers for any of the squad but frantically messengers who he can from 1st Squad through Facebook. He knew Sgt. Parks did not have social media, but James and Doherty did; Morales scrolls through their page, both of their last posts are from yesterday before they set out on the hump into the woods of Northern Idaho.

Morales quickly scrolls through the current headlines on the tragedy. The same key words are used in almost all articles and news reports: *three presumed dead, massive firefight, plane crash, heavily armed men, drugs, cartels, hired security.* "This is fucking bullshit; none of this is accurate. It was a fucking reunion!" Morales cursing at his laptop screen. He stops himself to listen and make sure he did not wake his snoring wife and their six-year-old son. Nothing, they are still asleep. He scrolls to Bgame's page and sees the post about 1800 and that he is already in enroute to Clear Creek.

"What the hell? How did he get up there already? When did he find out? What the fuck is happening?" Morales moans to himself, rubbing his aching neck. He stands up from the table and stretches his compact, slender frame, trying to garner some relief in his suddenly sore, aching body. He quickly strides through the living room to the den, stares at the wall his wife dictated to be his *"Wall of Shame,"* and quickly finding what he is looking for—a 4x6 photo of 1st Squad taken hours before *Operation Phantom Fury*. Morales scans the photo; he spots his younger self looking back at him with not an ounce of fear in the stare. He locates James and Doherty, standing proud and ready for anything. Morales then stares at Sgt. Parks standing center of the squad with his hand on Delta's shoulder. Sgt. Parks would lead their squad through much but none more so than what the squad would encounter days after the photo.

None of them knew what was to come, Morales lifts the photo off the wall, sits down on the sofa and stares intently at the picture, hoping with all his might that what is to unfold will be a bad dream and none of this is real. "I should have fucking been there," he tells the timeless photograph.

・・・

Rolling over in his bed, laying there staring at the ceiling, Colby reluctantly looks over to the spot that his wife had occupied for eight years, rubbing his hand slowly along her spot, he then begins to shed a tear. A drunk driver had

The Last Letter

killed her a year and half earlier in a midday crash, his wife coming home early from work that day for his birthday. Thomas cannot bear the thought of acknowledging her passing, her memory haunts him. The life he envisioned for them both tragically taken away from them in flash. Lorraine did not deserve to be taken from this world so soon, *not like that*. Thomas inhales deeply, hoping to retrieve a trace of her scent, but he finds none. He rubs her side of the bed one more time, then sadly rolls off his side of the queen mattress. Thomas still cannot sleep using the whole bed; she is still there, her presence felt always.

His dog waits patiently for Thomas to get up and let him out into the backyard to do his morning business. Thomas scuffles the dog's ears affectionately, "Okay you, let's get you outside." He walks down the hall to the back door of the single-story ranch; opening the door for the dog and watches as the animal sprints around the yard looking for the perfect place to take a crap. Thomas smiles, turning from the back door and heads to make a cup of coffee. Waiting patiently for the cup to fill, he begins to look at his phone; his face tightens, jaw muscles clenching. He frantically fumbles to his email app:

Thomas,

Please come join 1st Squad in beautiful Clear Creek, Idaho.

"Goddamnit, no, no, no," He repeats to himself barely audible in the ghostly cavern that is his house since his wife's passing. The posts throughout the Bravo Co. community page confirm his fears—James, Doherty, and Sgt. Parks are feared dead. His dog begins to impatiently scratch at the back door, desperately wanting to come in and receive his morning belly itch, Thomas blocks out the animal's whines for entrance.

"Shit, what the fuck?" the pit of his stomach dropping lower and lower by each headline he reads. Thomas does not keep in regular contact with any of the Marines of Bravo Co., nor has he heard anything from 1st Squad except the occasional post on Facebook. Sgt. Parks did attend the funeral after his wife passed but before that he had not seen or heard from the squad in years. Thomas quickly moves to his office, still ignoring the dog's pleas for entry, pushes the blueprints of the latest steel project his company is working on, off the desk and slams his Marine album down.

SSgt. Jacob Parkinson

Flipping through the pages of pictures, he finds the photo he is looking for—a 4x6 of 1st Squad hours before rolling into the Fallujah Peninsula. James, Doherty off to the left side standing with Cooper, Jackson and Del Vecchio; all stone-faced. He finds himself standing behind Sgt. Parks and next to that *fucking AT 4*[39]. He smiles slightly to himself; he hated that thing. If Sgt. Parks had it his way, Thomas would have been the first and only member of Bravo Co. to use an AT-4 in combat. He reflects on Sgt. Parks' order, *"Thomas get ready to use that fuckin AT-4!"* but their cowardly platoon commander put a stop to that beautiful course of action. Thomas stares at Sgt. Parks standing behind Delta, both *warriors*, he reflects. Sgt. Parks used to constantly yell at him, constantly; Thomas, still reflecting on ghosts of the past, smiles a bit broader.

He pulls the picture from the album and begins scanning his computer for the news headlines. *Massive firefight, hired professional security, plane crash, cartels, drugs*; Thomas reading off the keywords of the breaking stories. He begins watching several news feeds, trying to follow the most current up-to-date information. There is such a vast amount of coverage, his head begins to ache. Thomas finds the post from Bgame about a live stream at 1800; *damn that is a long time from now*, he thinks, looking at his Apple watch. Thomas quickly begins to check flights, knowing they are going to need Marines to escort the bodies home and he wants to be one of them, regardless of the years gone. *The rest of 1st Squad, I'm sure are booking flights as I sit here*, pondering his next course of action. Thomas quickly looks at his schedule for the day, "Okay, just a steel fab bid on a high school stadium and field house; shit won't take long and then I can head out."

The former infantryman brings the picture back with him to his desk chair, stepping on the blueprints he had thrown to the floor. He sits and stares at the 4x6 image blankly. Their young faces haunt him with their gaze. None of them knew what was to come. He looks to Sgt. Parks, then to James, and finally to Doherty, *I should have been there*, the only thought flashing through his mind.

---

[39] Anti tank weapon for infantry Marines

The Last Letter

. . .

Bradley Culpepper stands and stretches his tall, thick muscular frame, hardened by years spent in the oilfields. He runs his rough, massive hands along his long brown wavy hair and puts it up in a ponytail and scratches at his greying wooly beard. Culpepper is preparing for a thirty-day rotation on an offshore oil rig as site foreman. He knows his family will miss him and he is crushed every time he leaves them, but Culpepper provides substantially well for his family despite his rocky start since returning from Iraq decades ago.

Lumbering into the kitchen, Culpepper heads grudgingly to the coffeepot, pours day-old coffee into a mug and throws the cup into the microwave to heat up. He towers over the kitchen island, finds the remote to the TV and turns on the morning news. Culpepper wants the background noise, while he makes himself some bacon and eggs. The big man almost misses the mention of *Clear Creek*, he turns slowly towards the island and grasps the remote to turn the volume up to an audible level:

"*Yes, Samantha, the FBI, DEA, and Department of Homeland Security are reportedly on scene.*"

"*For those of you just tuning in, we are reporting what is being called a 'massive firefight' in the forest outside of Clear Creek, Idaho. Three heavily armed men presumed dead, drugs were found on scene and apparently there may be a plane crash involved as well, is that correct, Jason?*"

"*That is correct, Samantha. I am hearing from multiple sources that there was a plane crash in the same vicinity as the gun battle. I believe the FAA is in enroute to also aid in the investigation.*"

"*Jason, can you tell us more on the heavily armed men that are presumed dead that were apparently found on scene?*"

"*What I have gathered so far, is that the identities of the men are being withheld due to notification of the family, but I am told that all had identification on them. We should know more in the coming hours, Samantha.*"

He mutes the television before the report is finished, and stares as the reporter's mouth moves incessantly; *how the fuck can this be?* Culpepper moves purposely to his laptop and finds his email.

SSgt. Jacob Parkinson

How the fuck Sgt. Parks found my email or even began to know where to look is astonishing or fuckin scary, the Marine thinks to himself, opening the email:

Culpepper,

Please come join 1st Squad in beautiful Clear Creek, Idaho.

"This is not right man. Fuck!" He looks back at the television. Culpepper does not have social media of any kind and does not have any contact with anyone from Bravo Co., by his design. The only correspondence he has received over the years is the invitation from Sgt. Parks and he still does not know how Sgt. Parks found his email. "Fuck!" his deep gravelly voice booms throughout the cavernous kitchen.

Culpepper quickly grabs his laptop and does something he vowed he would never do. It takes him less than two minutes to create a Facebook profile and find the Bravo Co. community page. His fears are confirmed by the posts: James, Doherty, and Sgt. Parks are presumed dead. Looking through the mountains of threads, he stumbles upon Bgame's post about 1800 livestream. He will make sure he is watching. Culpepper continues to read the alarming posts but not wanting to believe any of them.

He heads to his family room, which at one point was his *"man cave"* with his *Wall of Shame* proudly displayed, the wall is no more after three boisterous daughters. Culpepper's *Wall of Shame* is now relegated to a mere corner of the family room, surround by pictures of his girls, his beautiful wife, slowly pushing his Marine memorabilia into an ever-decreasing space; he does not mind at all. The Marines for him was a complicated relationship that he is happy to have put behind him.

The big man finds the picture he is looking for, a simply framed 4x6 photograph. It is of 1st Squad hours before they rolled on *Operation Phantom Fury* in 2004. He is on the extreme right flank, the lone one that he was. Culpepper marvels at how young they were and not knowing what lay ahead. He stares at James, moves his gaze to Doherty, and then finally to Sgt. Parks in the center. Himself, James, and Sgt. Parks always together; Culpepper, Sgt. Parks' RO[40], and James was the three's security with the SAW. *Team OFP (On Fucking Point)*, James would eventually dub the three, Culpepper grins, a tad. Sgt. Parks

---
[40] Radio operator

would be the one to push for Culpepper's combat decoration that is displayed proudly in his ever-shrinking *Wall of Shame*.

I should have fuckin been there, the big Marine sighs heavily.

. . .

Standing in front the massive mirror, Aubrey Jackson wipes away the steam and stares at himself. "What the fuck?" he says to himself in the mirror, as he has done thousands of times before. He is still in great shape, lean, sculpted and, of course, he is tall. *It could be worse*, he thinks, admiring his 6'4" frame. *I could look like those sad sacks on Facebook*. Jackson smirks at himself in the mirror, rubbing his face with lotion.

Then his mood shifts, knowing he will be stuck in his office dealing with mountains of master's theses awaiting his scrutiny. Jackson, an esteemed tenured psychology professor at Louisiana State University, hates the neverending babble of his master's students, semester after semester. "What the fuck?" he moans. He begins to brush his teeth, as he has every morning since Marine boot camp, spits and rinses with mouthwash. The same routine day in and day out. Jackson then heads to his closet to begin laying out his tailormade suit for the day, when he notices his phone notifications have been pinging nonstop.

All seem to be from the Bravo Co. community Facebook page. He sits down on the edge of the enormous California king. *What the fuck*, his only thought. Immediately his mind wanders to the impending doom that will await him as Jackson opens the Bravo Co. page; he is not disappointed. The doom is being reiterated with every message scrolling past before his very eyes. Jackson scrambles to find his contacts on his phone:

Doherty…nothing. James…nothing.

Sgt. Parks…nothing.

He calls the only other contact he has of 1st Squad and that is *"Delta."* Jackson frantically hits the *Send* button on the contact's name. It's ringing, *Thank God*, looking up to the ceiling, as if he is giving a silent *thank you* to his savior. "Come on—shit voicemail!" Jackson bellows helplessly. *What time is it at Sgt. Heis'*, he can't remember. "This is Chief Heisinger of the Sedona

Fire Department, please leave me your name, number, and type of call and I will get back to you. If this is a life-threatening emergency, please hang up and dial 9-1-1 immediately and help is on the way."

The audible annoyance of the beep can be heard, "Sgt. Heis, it's Jackson, man give me a call as soon as you get this. Shit is fucked up, brother. I know you don't have social media but give me a call ASAP, please." Jackson hits *End* and continues to scroll through comments on the Bravo Co. page, he comes across Bgame's post about 1800 and a live stream. *Okay, I'll set a reminder.* The messages are pouring in from the other Bravo Co. Marines, all reaching out to members of 1st Squad ensuring they are okay or need assistance.

Jackson sprints down his expansive hallway, grabs his laptop from the kitchen table and flings it open to begin his search. The machine cannot boot up fast enough for him, so he begins scrolling through his phone at the news headlines. It is horrific, Jackson's eyes widen. No names being released, only descriptions. Words being thrown around in the media: *firefight, drugs, armed men, cartels.* Jackson could not keep up with all the narratives online but one thing for certain, the incident is in Clear Creek, Idaho.

The pain of guilt is already beginning to creep into the recesses of his mind, and he knows he cannot go down that road. *Focus.* Scrolling through his messages, he finds his invitation and reads the first line: Jackson, *Please come join 1st Squad in beautiful Clear Creek, Idaho.* It was from Sgt. Parks, and he declined to join the trip due to his blistering work schedule. Here it comes, *the guilt.* Jackson recalls James and Doherty were the only two members of 1st Squad that could make the reunion trip. He quickly strides to his office; proudly displayed on one of the walls is Jackson's Marine memorabilia. He scans the pictures in frames and quickly finds the one he is looking for, removing it from the wall.

It is a 4x6 photo in a nondescript wooden frame, Jackson stares quietly at the young Marines staring back at him. The Marines were so young and naïve, having no idea a lifelong bond would soon be formed. *To the man, we were changed forever*, Jackson ponders to himself. He stares intently at James, a fellow SAW gunner: he looks upon Sgt. Parks standing in the middle, ready to do his consummate part and then he finds Doherty's image, a solitary tear starts to fall down his right cheek, *my brother.*

The Last Letter

Jackson does not stop the tear, but instead lets the teardrop follow the lines in his face down to his meticulously manicured beard from where it falls to the floor. There are more to follow as he is fixates on the timeless image, his arm resting calmly on Doherty's shoulders; everyone in the picture willing to die for one another without fail. *I fuckin should have been there;* thus, begins Jackson's self-torment.

. . .

The man stumbles out of bed at the sound of the baby crying; it is his turn to care for his newborn bundle of joy while his wife gets her much-deserved rest. This is their third and the routine is second nature to him. The bottles are prepared and need to be heated in the bottle warmer, then the rocking chair in the nursery beckons him. He quickly puts the bottle on the warmer, heads to the nursery and scoops up his little bundle of joy.

"Oh shit! That is ripe, buddy." The proud man suddenly is stopped cold by the smell of his baby boy's awakening predicament. He smoothly scoops up his son and transports him to the changing table. The baby boy is smiling, as his father tickles his belly and begins to expertly change his son's diaper.

"Don't you piss on me, don't you do it, don't you do it," the man repeats over and over in his soft baby voice, tickling his son's belly. He receives the expected response from the infant, smiles and laughter. Retrieving the bottle from the warmer, he heads back to the rocking chair to feed his son and rock him back to sleep when he is full. The tired father looks at his phone and sees a voicemail is left by a Louisiana caller. He knows only a handful of people have his number from that area, a sense of gloom begins to creep up the back of his neck, his arms begin to prickle with goose bumps. He plays the message with trepidation: *"Sgt. Heis, it's Jackson, man give me a call as soon as you get this. Shit is fucked up, brother. I know you don't have social media but give me a call ASAP, please."* That is the end of the message.

"Fucking Jackson," Brian Heisinger, known as Sgt. Heis or more affectionately nicknamed by his squad leader as *Delta*, blurts aloud causing his son to bobble the bottle a bit in his tiny little hands. He frantically texts Jackson:

Can't talk w/baby…wtf?

Oh shit, sorry man, shit is fucked up.

What the fuck happened?

Man, I think Parks, James, and Doherty got hit.

What the fuck do you mean, got hit?

I mean I think they're dead! Check your news feed: Clear Creek, Idaho!

Wait one

Roger that, Sgt. Heis

Heisinger starts smashing his fingers across his phone's enormous screen, googles *Clear*, and before he could finish typing in *Creek*, news reports of a firefight in the woods outside Clear Creek, Idaho are listed. Numerous headlines: *firefight, drugs, 3 presumed dead, armed security, cartels, hired ex-military*, the news is spreading like wildfire.

What the fuck is happening? His thoughts are beginning to race through his mind at a frantic rate. His son begins to squirm at his father's sudden change in body posture. Heisinger's muscles are beginning to tighten in anxious anger as he tries to follow headline to headline. *It doesn't make any sense*; searching for any name of the deceased but cannot find any. Searching his contacts, he finds Parks' number, "Please, please, please. Come on, fucker answer." Nothing. "Fuck!" the baby begins to get more agitated as Heisinger is foaming through clenched teeth. Scrolling through his emails he finds his personalized invitation from Parks:

Delta,

Please come join 1st Squad in beautiful Clear Creek, Idaho.

The eye-opening first line. "No, no, no, no. This is not fucking happening." Delta is no longer able to deny the reality. He knows that Parks, James, and Doherty are going to be the presumed dead. He knows the pain the families will feel; he knows the pain this will cause Bravo Co; he knows the pain this will cause 1st Squad; and he knows the pain this will cause him. He quickly puts his new bundle of joy expertly back in his crib so as not to disturb one wink of his son's beautiful slumber.

Heisinger strides to his closet that he keeps for his military gear and unlocks the door. He scans the loadout that Parks had put into the email for the trip, surveying their chances in a firefight. Heisinger has now flipped a mental switch from Chief of Sedona Fire Department to Delta, the *Grunt* team leader, expertly weighing his options going forward. Every decision will have a purpose moving forward, beginning with traveling to Clear Creek, immediately. Delta quickly finds his laptop, flings the screen open and begins searching flights from Phoenix International Airport to as close as he can get to Clear Creek. *Boise*. His fingers deftly punching the keyboard as he books, confirms several itineraries, shuts the laptop, and begins to tremble standing in kitchen, leaning over the island. The overwhelming sense of guilt is starting to come from the recesses of his soul, Delta knows he does not have much time before he will succumb to that guilt. *Not now, not here*, he begs himself. Delta lets go of his grip on the marble countertop of the island and heads to his office. He knows exactly what he is looking for, takes it off the wall and vacantly stares.

A 4x6 photo from over twenty years ago; young eager men staring back at him, their faces hardened beyond their years.

Fuck we had no idea what was to come after, no idea, Delta thinks, transfixed by the haunting images. He finds Doherty with Jackson's arm draped over his shoulder; it is crushing they were his team along with Perry. He finds James, bandana on his head standing behind Cooper, looking dangerous with the SAW, which he was. The guilt forming a lump in his throat. Then finds Sgt. Parks standing directly behind his kneeling self, Parks' gloved hand resting on his right shoulder at the center of the photograph. Both staring back at him, that *stare*. The stare unleashes the lump in his throat, Delta collapses onto a bar stool, suddenly exhausted.

"What the fuck happened out there, Parks?" Delta asks the ghost in the picture; he stares despondently at the photo, wishing this not to be true. He knows he must wake his beautiful, slumbering wife soon and relay the tragic news. Janet knows extensively of her husband's time in the Marines as a *Grunt*. He has held back nothing from her, and they are one as a couple because of that openness. His wife knows every anecdote and tall tale of 1st Squad. Parks the *Jackrabbit*, Delta smiles at the moniker given to the squad leader, but name never stuck because everyone in the squad enjoyed calling him *Sgt. Parks*. 1st

Squad would adorn the nickname to a plaque they presented their squad leader upon returning stateside, much to Parks' humbled chagrin.

Delta's sorrow quickly begins to turn to unbridled anxiety; the thought he feared the most creeps into the forefront, *I should have been there.*

CH. 14
THE PLAYBACK

Burlingame, known as "*Bgame*" by his fellow Marines, disembarks from the United Airlines 737 and heads straight to baggage claim. He catches people gawking at his appearance, making his way through the airport, he is accustomed to the stares; Bgame looks every bit the old crusty war Veteran. People tend to leave him alone and never make small talk; he revels in the aura. Not today. Bgame is every bit warrior, and his demeanor has sent anyone near him to scurry out of his way. Today is not going to be one of Bgame's finest.

He grabs his rental keys from the attendant looking cautiously at him, the tired Marine ignores it this time. Normally, he would have sassed the man for gawking. With both pieces of luggage in tow, Bgame moves briskly towards the brand-new Ford F-150 he reserved. He remote unlocks the truck and tosses his luggage in the crew cab. Bgame whips out his iPhone, which he purposely left off until he was secure in his rental and away from nosy civilians. "Turn on, motherfucker," Bgame angrily growls at his phone as it powers on, and as he expected, there were texts messages and missed calls from all sorts of Marines wondering what happened to Parks, James, and Doherty. *So, the news has broken? Fuck*, he thinks to himself. He didn't have the time to deal with that now. He is looking for only one text and that is Gunny Hoffman's: giving him the point of contact at the US Forestry Service.

"Special Agent Lynda Alexander, 44 Main St., Clear Creek. Roger that," Bgame mutters to himself, punching the address into his Google directions. "Two hours, ten minutes. Fuck that's a long time to be answerin fuckin phone calls. Call the old lady, first and foremost," grumbling to himself. Bgame knows once the rest of Bravo Co. finds out about the tragedy unfolding in Idaho, there will be a nonstop stream of texts and calls he will be forced to answer.

It is too late. The texts start flowing in as he finishes his thought. "Ah fuck, Park's squad knows," Bgame exhales through clenched jaws. He looks at the simultaneous texts flowing in from Cooper, Del Vecchio, Delta, Perry, Jackson, Morales, Thomas and even the never found Culpepper; all texting wanting to know *"what the fuck is going on?"* in some form of the expression or another.

Bgame decided to group them in a text conversation with all his Bravo Co. contacts. He replies simply: "Heading to meet POC. Will send out SITREP @1800 with all pertinent info. Please just stand by, Devils, allow me some fuckin time."

With that group text sent, he asks Siri to call Roca. She answers in a very exhausted but concerned tone, turning to nestle into his side of their king bed, "Hey, babe. You, okay? I know it's a stupid fucking question, but are you?"

"I'm okay. The men have started to find out about the tragedy. I told them I will brief 'em all at 1800. I'm just fuckin beat."

She sighs supportively, "I bet you are, hon." Roca smells his pillow and wishes she could be there for her ageing Marine.

"I'm on my way to meet Gunny's point of contact, some Forestry Agent, she was supposedly first on scene. She's also a former Marine and so was the helicopter pilot that took them to the scene; I believe they both served in Afghanistan, according to Gunny. She apparently was a badass in the military, just like you, hon." Bgame tries to bring some levity into the conversation while also flattering his lovely wife.

"Shut the fuck up," she coyly replies. Then solemnly adds, "Will you facetime me after you brief everyone at 1800. I want to hear from you after, I want to see the enormity of it all on your face. Listen, babe, I know the men were special to you, but don't you go dark on me," Roca requests, demanding Bgame stay in the now and not head down the destructive path of grief and guilt.

"I won't. Thank you, hon. I love you," Bgame responds tiredly, suddenly drained of the energy to focus directly on the circumstance at hand, everything happening at a blistering pace.

"I love you too," Roca whispers softly into her phone as she ends the call. She did not want Bgame to hear her break down and cry. She is crying for the fallen men, Bgame's pain, the pain that is about to sweep over Bravo Co., for the families' terrible torment to come. It has only begun.

. . .

Bgame pulls into a very nondescript plaza with a tax office, shabby defense lawyer's practice, a Subway, and the United States Forestry Service. "A fuckin Subway, even out here," he grumbles to himself, shutting the truck door and heading towards the US Forestry Service regional office, hoping to find Special Agent Alexander, his point of contact.

It is early, and he does not expect to find anyone present, but to his relief, he finds the lights on, but the door locked, so he lightly taps on the glass. Suddenly a head pops from an entryway, as an officer makes her way towards the door with her hand on her sidearm. The officer then stops about eight meters from the doorway, "Who the fuck are you and what's your business here?" Special Agent Alexander plainly states, still with her pull hand casually on her sidearm, surveying this Viking of a man before her door, with his fiery red beard and hair reflecting the morning sun.

Taken by surprise by the intense agent before him, Bgame immediately but slowly puts both hands slightly in the air to show he is not armed but understands the situation he has put himself him, "My name is Steven Burlingame, I believe you spoke to a Gunny Hoffman, shit, Texas State Trooper Hoffman. I was told to contact you regarding our Devils that were attacked in your AO last night," he states in his deep raspy voice, which makes him sound even more menacing to the forestry agent.

"Shit sorry, I'm exhausted," Alexander apologizes, still cautious of the stranger outside her office door. "Right, I did talk with your Gunny. Let me open this up," she states, relaxing her pull hand and heading to the door.

"Would you like some coffee? I'm making a fresh pot in the break room," Alexander asks, propping open the door.

Bgame feeling a slight sense of relief and welcoming the offer of a warm cup of coffee, responds politely, "Thank you, I would. It was a long damn flight and drive; I need to wake the fuck up." His eyes widen at his own slip of profanity, "Sorry, pardon the language."

"Your Gunny told you I was a Marine, right? I give two shits," Alexander fires back with a slight hint of a smile. "Come in, please." She waves the tired former Marine into her office.

"Thank you," Bgame replies, entering the small, quaint, shabby, three-room space with a bathroom, office space, and break room; one he would expect to find from an out-of-sight small-town governmental office. Bgame follows her to the break room and graciously accepts the cup of coffee that the forestry agent hands him. "Thank you again, much needed."

She nods slightly in response. "Well, all the stuff you need is right there cream, sugar, Splenda. Help yourself before we sit down and I answer what questions you may have, and I have some questions of my own if I may ask?" Alexander extends her hand towards the powdered creamer and bowl full of packets of sugar and the substitute.

Bgame scans the nondescript break room. *Boring* is his only thought. "Of course. I will answer anything I can for you," the rough looking Marine humbly responds, grabbing a couple packets of sugar and relinquishes the contents of the packets into his cup. He grabs a plastic coffee stir and swirls it around in his paper cup and takes a sip of the fresh coffee. The warmth of the liquid immediately gives Bgame a jolt of energy and calmness after his long, fraught travels.

Alexander nods slightly, "Please come with me and sit. Get off your feet." She leads the Viking to her desk in the main office, strolls around the vacant desk opposite hers, grabs the leather roller office chair, and brings it to the front of her desk, replacing the horrible government-issued secondary desk chair. "This will be more suitable after a long trip."

"Thank you, I hope your partner won't mind." Bgame instantly feels the weight of his rushed long trip suddenly drop off his shoulders as he sits and feels the padded leather engulf his aching back muscles.

The Last Letter

Alexander almost laughs at the former Marine's statement. "Oh no, Bill, he won't mind. That desk is more an honorary station for him to stop in and bullshit. He's also a fellow Marine. A captain. CAS-EVAC pilot. 53s. I call him in on emergencies," she replies, waving off his concerns.

Bgame, not needing explanation, understood everything the forestry agent rattled off, "Shit, it's good to know that I'm talking to fellow Devils. I'll get to the point then. Who's the survivor, please?" Bgame fires off the question quickly before he takes another drink of his coffee.

Special Agent Alexander stares coldly at Bgame, debating whether to divulge the information to this Viking before her, she decides to trust her intuition, "I believe you know him as *'Parks'* or *'Sgt. Parks'* as the other two kept calling him, giving him shit and laughing. It was actually quite endearing to witness." Alexander replies honestly and without hesitation. "Listen, Mr. Burlingame—"

"Bgame, please," he offers the forestry agent.

Alexander nods, "Bgame, we are under a strict gag order, but I don't give a fuck. The one, James, got off three calls from his sat-phone: the Sheriffs Office, me, and his wife. I suppose that's how the word spread so quickly to you and your company, I'm not going to bullshit you, Bgame—"

"Please, Special Agent, just tell me straight. What did James say to you?" Bgame asks, trying to soak in the information he is receiving at this moment.

"It was late, zero dark thirty. He called, I answered. I recognized the satphone number, when all three stopped by my office to fully discuss their intentions in the forest. James offered his number due to the fact there is no service in the forest outside of Clear Creek. He relayed that a plane went down near their campsite, the three of them went to recon the crash site for survivors. They encountered an armed man and had to put him down. He gave me their grid coordinates. I told him I will be heading up ASAP, to stay put and not touch a damn thing. I asked how the others were, he answered, *fine*, and I told him I would get on the horn to the State Troopers and Sheriffs Office. I immediately called my second, Bill, to get the helo warmed up and ready to fly," Alexander steadily states the facts of the phone interaction with James.

Pausing to understand the scenario properly, he asks politely, "May I have those grid coordinates?" Bgame hopes to grab the location of the site from the forestry agent, hoping to mount his own reconnaissance of the crash site, or in his mind the battlefield.

Alexander's look turns cold once again, shaking the old Grunt's posture, "Now, Bgame, I know where you're heading with this. It's an active crime scene and you will not be permitted access to the site, even if you were to get close. The Feds are crawling all over the area along with local law enforcement. Shit, I don't think they'll even allow me access back up there," she responds, eyeing Bgame's reaction to her warning of trespassing on an active crime scene.

She knew Marines well; her beloved husband was a Chief Warrant Officer in EOD for the Marines but there is something about *Grunts* and their undying loyalty to one another through shared misery that sets them apart from the rest of the Marine Corps. Although she never worked with infantry units personally, she being a driver for EOD and supply while in the service, Alexander would find herself along with others, staring at the *Grunts* as they came in and out of friendly lines to and from patrols. Their demeanor so stoic and determined; never any emotion in their faces as they exited and re-entered friendly lines. You would never see an infantryman's emotion unless he was with his other shared combat Marines. Then and only then did you get a glimpse of a *Grunt's* frailty and vulnerability.

Everyone in camp usually kept their distance from the infantry Marines, there were the running jokes from the others about how the dirt and shit smell from the landscape would be encrusted into their uniforms, of course these jokes were passed in silence, *Grunts* were a different breed of animal. Those dirty, shit-encrusted, smell like swamp water men were the epitome of what it is to be called a Marine. She finds it beautiful.

"Roger that. Were you first on scene?" Bgame asks, desperately hoping to find any details he can on the situation. He knows Bravo Co. will want answers soon and he wants to be the one to deliver the news to them, good or bad.

"Bgame, we are treading very close of what I am allowed to divulge at this point," Alexander sternly states, letting Bgame know that she is a law enforcement officer first and a former Marine second.

The Last Letter

Nodding his head reluctantly, Bgame recognizes the precarious situation the agent has put herself in, "I apologize, please any information you can give me will be priceless. I have a company full of former *Grunts* wakin up to news of this fuckin catastrophe and they're goin to want blood. I need to give the brothers some sort of information or otherwise you will have a bunch of fuckin former Devils up here tryin to find their own answers. Please, Special Agent Alexander, anything you can tell me?" Bgame's naturally harsh, raspy voice gives way to a soft audible plea.

The forestry agent can feel the sadness in Bgame's soul, the weight he must be carrying for a collective of individuals plus his own inner turmoil. She wants very much to tell him everything, but she is bound by her oath. She personally hates to see leaked information in the news citing, *"sources within law enforcement;"* it goes against her morale code as a law enforcement officer. "Listen, Bgame. Let me ask you a few questions first about the men and I'll be putting this on the record for my own investigative report, agreed?" Alexander begins to set up the video app on her phone, "our *interrogation room,*" she adds, noticing Bgame's look of sarcastic confusion.

The Marine is caught off guard but complies, "Sure, ask me anything," settling into the office chair the agent had swiped from her second desk.

"These questions will be blunt and uncomfortable, but I need your best recollection of information you can muster. Understood?" Alexander hits *Record* on her phone.

"Roger that," Bgame nods, tiredly rubbing his coarse fiery beard.

Agent Alexander then begins her line of questions, "Do the ones you know as James, Doherty, and Parks, belong to any far-right extremist groups, militias, or any organization supporting crazy conspiracy theories?"

A flash of anger crosses Bgame's cold eyes, "Get the fuck out of here. No!" He answers, getting slightly annoyed.

"Did the ones you know as James, Doherty, and Parks belong to any known drug organizations, running armed security for any known contractors, anything that might have any link to some sort of paramilitary style organization?" Alexander continues her rough line of questioning, noticing Bgame's agitated state.

"No, no, and no. Listen, Special Agent, James is a fuckin history professor, Doherty is a Veteran treatment counselor and advocate, and Parks, that motherfucker is installing solar panels and fixing wind-turbines last I talked with him or any of them," Bgame growls slightly with frustration.

Alexander continues, "When was the last time you spoke with your friends?"

Bgame's jaws clench ever tighter, not liking the direction the conversation has turned. "Look, I am sure they came armed to the teeth; I know the loadout they were going to carry. Originally there were supposed to be about ten more of us that were supposed to make this goddamn trip and now we are fucked to be haunted by our decision *not to show* for fuckin eternity. Special Agent, we will be left with the eternal fuckin words, *'I should've been there.'* Do you know what that hell is goin to be like? I am tired and it has only just begun. Please anything you can give me," Bgame once again pleads with the forestry agent.

Exhaling heavily, Alexander sympathizes with the distraught former Marine before her, "Bgame, I never once suspected any of this to apply to your friends; I'm just doing my due diligence. I also want to make sure that no bullshit narrative gets leaked to the press and that such is the case, already. I will be able to bring forth to the press evidence to counter such claims being the first law enforcement officer on scene. So, please understand I ask these questions to ensure that nothing tarnishes the images of these Marines," Alexander explains to the former Marine, whose shoulders seemingly shrink farther into his body, she can see the toll the situation is taking on the man.

"I do understand. " he responds, grabbing his coffee cup for another sip, hoping to garner some energy from the warm liquid. He does not.

Alexander stops the video recording on her phone and leans back in her own chair, looking for relief in the faux-leather governmentbought office chair. She finds none. She is exhausted from the activities of the past sixteen non-stop hours. "Okay, Bgame your turn, ask me some questions and I will try and reveal as much as I can to alleviate some of that weight on your shoulders."

He raises slightly in his chair. "Thank you. Please walk me through what you can," Bgame asks softly. He, too, begins to bring his phone out to audio record but Alexander waves him off, so he puts his phone back down on the desk.

The Last Letter

The forestry agent begins cautiously, "Bill and I arrived about an hour after receiving the sat-phone transmission from James. We were the first on scene. Bgame, I'm going to show you something and you will only see it once, I will not show you again, but I need a combat perspective. This is the video of the crash site I recorded. Now, listen, the images will be fucking hard for you, I'm not joking. You were all in the same unit in Iraq?" Alexander asks, digging for her thumb drive in her pocket with the saved footage.

Bgame again takes a sip of his coffee and then begins to rub his weary eyes for relief with his hand, "Yes, same platoon actually. Parks and I also served in the same platoon for a bit in the fleet together at India 3/5. You wouldn't know it, but Parks and his buddy lost half-their squads in the first infantry loaded Osprey crash back in 2000. Now this?" Bgame looks down wearily at his worn Red-Wing boots, wishing to be anywhere but in this horrible little office.

"Shit," Alexander replies, vaguely remembering the Osprey crash of 2000. She was still in junior high school when the accident occurred. The tragedy becoming part of Marine Corps lore.

Sipping his lukewarm coffee, Bgame looks back at the agent, "Yeah, that's usually what people say."

"Well, it gets a fuck ton worse. I am sorry." The forestry agent turns her computer monitor towards Bgame so that he can observe the video she shot the night before of the crash site. "Okay, I'm going to let you watch, but I want your honest opinion as to what you think may have happened and how your friends got caught up in this, to a horrific end."

"Roger that." Bgame steels himself, for fear of what is to be displayed.

As she is about to hit *Play*, Alexander pauses, "Bgame, this is going to be horrific, absolutely and utterly fucking horrific. You will not be able to recognize your friends, I honestly don't know if I should show you. I have my reservations. It will haunt you, Mr. Burlingame. Forever."

Before she can continue, the former infantryman softly raises his hand, as if to halt her explanation politely. "Please." His soft raspy voice begs of her to continue. The special agent hits *Play*, and she readies herself for what is to come from this war-torn *Grunt* before her.

Special Agent Alexander watches Bgame intently as he continues to watch the video; his face is tense with anticipation for she knows they have not reached the point in the video playback of the crash site. His face suddenly grows stern, Bgame witnesses the scarred landscape of the crash site, recognizing markings from small-arms fire on the video playback; he listens intently to the commentary Alexander and Bill exchange. She sees Bgame begin to stroke his beard nervously as the video comes upon the crash site and then it happens; the video comes upon James.

Bgame leaps up from his seat, heads out the front door of her office in two quick strides and immediately climbs into the cab of his rental truck. Putting his head into his hands, hoping his coarse hands will muffle the gut-wrenching moan that is bellowing up from within, trying to be released like a volcano on the precipice of eruption. Bgame knows he cannot hold back the eruption of pain that is flowing upwards through his throat, willing itself to be released. The Marine, fighting the onslaught of pain no longer, erupts with a woeful moan deep into the palms of his expecting hands. His palms cannot successfully muffle the eruption of agony, for Alexander hears the guilt ridden wail from her desk. She does not chase or pursue Bgame to offer condolences, she was a Marine, she knows this is his pain to bear alone without interference. The agent calmly grabs a bottle of whiskey from the bottom desk drawer and pours some into her coffee. Alexander will wait patiently for Bgame's return, no matter the time.

The Viking slowly lifts his head from his palms; he is spent. The weight of it all since he received the news, has come crashing down upon him at this very moment. "Get your fuckin ass back in there, pussy. Fuck. Fuck. Fuck. Fuck. Fuck." Bgame slams his fist into the side door panel, he then smashes the heads-up display in the rental Ford F-150. Blood starts to trickle from a couple of knuckles and with that Bgame seems satisfied with the inflicted pain to snap him out of his remorse. He knows he needs to get back into the Forestry Office and watch the rest of the video; all of Bravo Co. and its family members are anxiously awaiting news from the tired Marine. Bgame reluctantly opens the door and climbs out of the truck, feeling as if he is carrying the weight of his combat loaded flak all over again. Heavy. Stifling. Draining.

He strides exhaustedly back into the forestry agent's office and sits again in Bill's faux leather chair and steadies himself for the rest of the playback.

"Would you like some?" Alexander offering Bgame some of the whiskey she pulled out of the drawer of her desk.

"No, thank you. I stopped. This will put that to the test," Bgame replies respectfully, pointing to the computer screen.

The forestry agent scoffs affectionately, "That's exactly what your buddies Doherty and Parks said, but James jumped on the offer and said '*Shit, I didn't stop,*' thanked me politely, and slammed his shot, a double, I might add." Alexander states, trying to give Bgame a positive to hold on to as he begins to witness the rest of the video playback.

Bgame gives a slight sigh and smile, "That sounds like James." He lifts his head and nods for the Alexander to continue. She desperately wants to save Bgame from the ongoing onslaught of emotion, but he needs to witness the playback and his sorrow will only continue to get worse, there will be no stopping the damage.

Bgame watches the playback, listening to the forestry agent and Bill converse about what they are tragically witnessing. He hears Alexander expertly diagnosis the situation as she progresses through the crash site. The camera then suddenly pans on a body lying face down in the mud; Bgame knows it is Doherty, he recognizes the familiar silhouette. He grips the armrest of the chair; his massive knuckles turn pearl white watching the video of Bill slowly roll Doherty over so Alexander can assess vitals. The camera moves in for a closer look, as she moves quickly to ascertain Doherty's vitals, her hands frantically searching for a pulse. She finds none, as the GoPro attached to her helmet shakes in the negative and tells Bill he is gone.

Bgame's knuckles, now ghost white from the intense grip he has on the armrests of his chair, desperately seeking relief from the bellowing moan trying to erupt from his chest, wanting to rabbit out of the office at the sight of Doherty on the screen, but he is frozen. Alexander steels herself from rushing over and putting her hand on his shoulder, but all she can offer is, "It gets worse."

From that Bgame slowly looks towards the forestry agent and sees the dread in her face for what he is about to witness. He can see the pain in her eyes, not the pain for what she witnessed last night, but a pain of futility. She cannot protect the former Marine from what is to come; the camera progresses forward; she and Bill make their way to the final body. Bgame knows it's Parks, so that shock will be benign. He believes he is ready. That is a mistake.

"Doherty, we believe was trying to crawl to aid the one you call James," Alexander narrates as the playback continues; she hits *Pause* before arriving at Parks' body. "Please be ready."

The camera pans upon the body of Parks as Alexander desperately feels for a pulse, purposely angling her head to try and not look directly at what was once Parks' face and head. Finding no pulse, she slowly stands and the camera pans directly at Bill's horror-stricken expression, "What am I looking at Xander, what the fuck am I witnessing?" The camera pans back down on the face and head of what was once Sgt. Parks. His face swollen and distorted, as if he had been beaten with a baseball bat, the gunshot wound to the head has made one side of the head disproportionality larger than the other.

Bgame bolts from his chair, whisks himself from the forestry office, slams the truck door, throws the vehicle into reverse, jumps on the accelerator, the tires scorch the pavement leaving burnt rubber; he is down the main road heading out of Clear Creek in a flash. He does not care where he goes; Bgame wants only to be away from the world. The bellowing cloud of pressure in his chest is finally going to get its' sweet relief of eruption. Bgame cannot hold back the flood any longer; the gut-wrenching moan bellows forth from his throat and erupts with a grief-stricken sound in the cab of his truck. The Viking is mortally wounded.

Alexander does not pursue Bgame when he bolts from her office, nor does she try and call him either, she is transfixed on the last image Bgame witnessed on the playback, Parks brutally mangled and deformed head. She pours more whiskey into her coffee. They were both Marines, Bgame a *Grunt* at that, she knows he wants to be left to his own cruel agony, as Alexander did hers and still does. No, she will wait patiently for Bgame to make contact again, she will make no mention of his presence in town to the Sheriff's Office either. She absolutely knows, the Viking needs to be left alone. It is the exact reason why she took this position in Clear Creek, due to the affordability of loneliness.

The Last Letter

Her world only needs to encompass her children and her career. The exhausted agent quietly gets up with her coffee, walks out the glass office door, takes a sip of her drowned-in-whiskey beverage and stares off at the direction Bgame has traveled in a painful rage.

He has no clue what to do or where to go. Bgame has the accelerator floored, the speedometer approaching 98. The former Marine is hoping to get pulled over, something to end the madness racing through his staggered mind. He sees a road heading up to the mountains and quickly veers the truck right while slamming on the brakes, leaving a trail of gravel spewing everywhere. *Just get to the woods. Just get to the woods.* This is the only thought racing through his mind. To his astonishment he is quickly engulfed by forest on both sides of the upward winding road. It is a relief. Bgame veers off the road and slams the rented F-150 into park. Springing from the cab of the truck, leaving the driver's door ajar, Bgame sprints up the embankment into the forest, breathing heavily almost immediately, his chest feels as if it is going to burst, the taste of blood forms in his throat from the lack of oxygen to his lungs, the Marine drops to his knees. Panting. Then it comes. The blood curdling moan that has been building since he first saw the image of James on the video. He cannot hold back the moan any longer and he unleashes.

"AAAAAAAHHHHHHH! MOOOOOTTTTTHHHHHEERRRRFF-FUUUCCKKKERRR!" The sound of guilt and rage. "AAAAAHHHHH!" Bgame falls to his side on the forest floor and stares up at the beautiful pine canopy above him. He wants to move but cannot. All he can do is breathe; his body is numb and unresponsive. Then the dark idea creeps into his mind, an idea that will haunt many—*I should have been here. I should have fuckin been here, it would have been different.*

The sun peeks around a cloud, breaking through the forest canopy and shines on Bgame's closed eyes. He can feel the warmth on his eyelids, "Get the fuck up," he mutters to himself. The old squad leader slowly rolls to his side and up to his knees. Bgame takes a deep long inhale of the forest's crisp pure air and then he opens his weary, tired eyes; they were burning with uncontrollable intensity. He stands, looks back down the embankment at his rental truck and begins the trek back to the driver's seat. He needs to call Special Agent Alexander and reassure her that he will be there shortly.

Bgame climbs into the driver's seat and releases one final time, "FFFUUUCCCKKK!" and then slams his head into the driver's side window, cracking it into a spider's web. Blood instantly begins to trickle down the side of his head from the impact on the shatterproof glass, Bgame welcomes the pain and the sight of his own blood. He shifts the truck into drive and begins to head back towards Clear Creek and the forestry agent's office to finish the dreaded task at hand: completing the video playback.

Bgame cranks the volume up on the truck's speakers, blasting his playlist from his phone, starting with *Let Bodies Hit the Floor*. His head beginning to throb both from his self-inflicted wound and the volume of the music pushing the truck's factory speakers to their limits. He does not care. He wants the headache, anything but the reality of the present and the haunting memories of the past. Bgame wants desperately to call his wife, Roca, but he cannot find the words to tell her what has happened. *How do I explain this to the men of Bravo Co? 1st Squad? What happens next? Where do I place my rage and at who?* These questions, plus thousands more race through his consciousness, as he pushes the accelerator farther down to the floor of the cab, passing 88 on the speedometer, heading into Clear Creek.

Battling the onslaught of unrelenting questions racing through his mind, the music blaring, his vehicle speed increasing, Bgame does not notice the red light at the intersection telling him to stop. Another truck comes racing through the intersection as the driver has the green, the former squad leader notices reflexively at the last second, slams on his brakes and careens off to the side of the intersection, narrowly missing the oncoming truck. He quickly brings the truck to a halt and grips the steering wheel as tight as he can, his heart feeling as if it is going to pound a hole through his chest, trying to escape the confinements of his sternum.

"What the fuck is your motherfucking problem!" the driver of the other truck shouts, exiting his vehicle, heading towards the cab of the rental F-150. Bgame, of course, sees him coming up the side of the truck in his driver's side mirror. *Time to place this rage*, the only thought going through his head as the Viking opens the door.

The Last Letter

Exiting the rental truck, with blood flowing from his head wound caking his full red beard on the left side of his face; Bgame says nothing but efficiently closes the distance towards the other driver. Stopping dead cold in his tracks at the sight of the blood soaked Marine emerging from the cab of the truck, the other driver's face contorts into fear. Bgame is a visage of pure rage. The blood covering the side of his face and red beard, staining both a dark crimson, makes for a formidable war paint but that is not what has the man backpedaling for the safety of his own vehicle. It is the maniacal smile stretching from ear to ear across Bgame's face. It is a look of carnage.

The man turns to run back to the safety of his truck, but Bgame closes the distance in a flash, snatching the other driver by the hood of his flannel overshirt and spins the man around towards him.

"I'm sorry! I'm fucking sorry!" the driver pleads desperately. Bgame badly desires to cave the man's petrified face in with his concrete-like fist. He breathes heavily through his clenched teeth into the man's recoiled face as blood trickles down his beard and begins landing on the pleading driver's flannel overshirt. Bgame does not even see the man, but rather he is looking through him and into his uncertain future. He lets go of the other driver.

"Get the fuck out here!" Bgame roars, trying to slow his breathing, noticing a couple of onlookers filming with their phones, hoping for something to post to social media, to feel important for a few seconds. *Fuckin' cannibals of humanity*, races across his violent mind. Bgame needs to quickly refocus.

He commands the rental F-150 back on course towards the US Forestry Office. Bgame grips the wheel as tightly as he can, his knuckles turn white from the strain of his grip, a constant color for the knuckles. "Get your shit together, fucktard! Fuckin, fuck, fuck, fuck!" he barks at himself in the cab of the truck. Hoping the weasel of the other driver does not run off and alert the authorities to his presence here, Bgame does not want to compromise the intelligence he is receiving from Special Agent Alexander.

He pulls back into the run-down strip plaza housing the Forestry Office. Alexander is leaning against the front of her office, drinking her spiked cup of coffee. Bgame is suddenly flush with embarrassment upon exiting the rental truck. "I apologize. I—" Bgame is suddenly cut off by Alexander's hand waving him off as she finishes her drink of coffee.

"Stop. No need. I would have reacted the exact same. Would you like to continue?" the forestry agent asks sympathetically.

"Yes, thank you," Bgame replies graciously in his gruff voice, still feeling slightly embarrassed by his reaction but more than anything, he feels the uncontrollable anger not subsiding.

Alexander looks curiously at the wound on Bgame's forehead, "But first let's get that cleaned up. I don't think Bill would appreciate blood all over his upgraded leather chair. I will never hear the end of his shit," the forestry agent offers, trying to add some slight levity to ease Bgame's tensions a bit. She guides him towards the break room and has him sit on one of the hideous beige folding metal chairs. Alexander then grabs the trauma kit; she has stashed in the cabinets.

The former *Grunt* moans, sitting in the horribly uncomfortable chair, leaning upright with his back against the wall. She grabs some rubbing alcohol, douses a sterile trauma pad and begins to clean Bgame's head wound. He does not flinch as the alcohol seeps into his wound, Bgame welcomes the momentary sting of pain. It is a most welcome distraction.

"Are all *Grunts* like this?" she asks Bgame while wiping the blood from around his wound to get a better look at the damage.

"Like what?" he replies without looking up, so as not to interfere with the agent's triage.

Alexander continues to clean the wound. "Reserved, quiet, hardened, distant?" she asks, genuinely interested in the response he may provide.

Bgame chuckles a little bit. "I don't know. Why do you ask?"

"No real particular reason. Your friends: James, Doherty, and Parks all have the same demeanor, at least that's what I observed."

Well, except for maybe James. He is definitely the livelier one of the three, when they stopped by." The forestry agent says, searching for the butterfly strips to help close the wound on the side her patient's head.

"Yeah, James has a quick wit. He will give a smartass quip to just about anythin," Bgame replies after a brief pause to readjust his sore body in the uncomfortable metal folding chair. He notices the forestry agent did not use past tense when talking about his dear friends, and he appreciates the sentiment. "I don't know. Maybe it's age or just our shared experiences. Who the fuck knows, but we were not like this when we were actual *Grunts*. That's why we were always kept separated from the POGs," Bgame states. "POGe is a—"

"'*Person Other than Grunt*, I know. I'm familiar with the term," Alexander quickly interjects with the correct meaning of the acronym, to Bgame's astonished face. This time he does look up.

"I was a POGe, remember?" she says to Bgame's puzzled and surprised look.

He shakes his head in slight embarrassment. "Shit. Everything is a haze after receiving the news up until this actual point right now. I apologize," Bgame offers respectfully.

"No, fucking need. I was a POGe, and you're right; they did keep you *Grunts* separated from the rest of the Marines as much as possible. James even joked to me, that the Marines were like a sanctuary, and *Grunts* were the rabid animals; caged and separated until you need to release them back into the wild." Alexander continues to dress Bgame's self-inflicted wound.

"That sounds exactly like James, all balls." Bgame stands, the gravity and weight of the situation is finally catching up to his body. Every part of his ageing body aches and screams for a hot shower, but he needs to push forward; Bravo is counting on him to find answers whether they know of the situation yet or not. He needs those answers, desperately and that means finishing up with the forestry agent. "Thank you for everything you're doing for the men and for aiding me in this FUBAR[41] situation."

The special agent taps the tired Marine lightly on the shoulder. "No need for the gratitude, your friends made an impression and not because they were Marines. I want justice, as do you. No one deserves what happened out there let alone three honorable combat Veterans," she offers while leading him back to her desk.

Bgame takes his seat in Bill's leather chair once more, a much needed relief from the metal chair in the break room. He adjusts to try and get a little more settled before gaining the courage to look up at the agent and give her the nod to continue.

---

[41] Fucked Up Beyond All Recognition

Alexander internally debates whether to continue, she does need his valued expertise but offers one final reprieve, "Are you sure you want to continue; I can simply brief you as to the facts," she states, concerned for the Marine.

"I'm sure. Please continue," Bgame replies dryly. Rubbing his worn hands across his eyes one last time before the video plays.

The video immediately picks up on Parks' body and his grotesque, disfigured head; Bgame wants to bolt again for the door but locks his grip into the chair's armrests to anchor himself stationary. His jaw clenches tighter as he watches Alexander check the vitals of Parks on the playback. Again, Bgame wants to inflict pain on himself as he hears Bill explain to the forestry agent, he can find no signs of life from Parks.

Alexander stops the video, "That's all I can show you and I'm not even supposed to do that but once a Marine always a Marine," She placates to Bgame's espirit de corps.

Bgame, looking out the front of the office, simply exhales a soft, "Yut."

Staring at this ageing warrior before her, Alexander cannot help but feel remorse for the situation this man finds himself in. "Please, Bgame, is there anything you can tell me about them, anything? I'm afraid our dumbass sheriff is going to go with the narrative of drugs and that your war buddies were either, one, involved as some sort of armed escort for hire or security for drug cartels; or two, your men are part of some dumbass wanna-be weekend warrior bullshit militia group and took it upon themselves to be vigilantes against the cartels."

He shoots her an angered look, "That's fuckin bullshit."

"I know it is. Here's what I believe is the likely scenario—your friends stumbled upon the crash site trying to be good Samaritans, uncovering something that was way over their heads, tried to do the right thing by calling it in, and got caught by some very highly trained, very well-equipped individuals. But the third scenario leaves too many questions nor brings the case to a close, and that does not look good for a sheriff up for re-election. So, the fucktard is going to pass the buck to the Feds, claiming it is a federal problem and not related to the area at all, everything is safe. Isolated incident. Which is of course, is bullshit. Anything will help, Bgame. I want these fucks to pay and judging by the destroyed armrests on Bill's chair, you do as well."

The Last Letter

Bgame leans back and rubs his weary eyes once more. *You should have been there*—there it is again, that *fuckin* thought. The thought is beginning to take hold in his psyche and Bgame knows he cannot let that happen, he must remain determined. "Do you mind if I take a moment? I just need some of this clean mountain air you have up here."

"Of course, take all the time you need. You sure you don't want some?" she asks, again offering Bgame a Dixie cup with a double of whiskey filling the bottom of the container.

He moves quickly and softly takes the cup from her tiny hand; the whiskey is smooth, comforting, and warm. "That's fuckin good, thank you." Bgame replies, savoring the liquid flowing smoothly down his throat. It is a calming relief for a split second. He politely nods his head to the forestry agent and lumbers out the front glass door of the office. *You should have been there*. Bgame exhales and sighs heavily in defeat for he knows he and 1st Squad will be forever haunted by those five little words.

CH. 15
KHARKOV

The helicopter silently, effortlessly careens down for a soft landing on the well-established helicopter landing zone at the back of a sprawling fortified compound. Groups of medics are standing by with aid for the wounded and body bags for the four dead operators and disguised flight crew. The doors of the helicopter careen open and the well-armed men come slowly pouring out, the awaiting groups of medical personnel hurriedly scurry about like rats tending to their tasks. The uninjured men dump their gear at the edge of the helo pad to take an assessment and have a quick team debrief before they head to their own bungalows to decompress from the previous night's operation.

"Alright, get the fuck in formation so we can get this over with and tend to our fallen. Questions? Problems? Complaints? Speak up, I do not have all morning or day, for that matter. I have my own debriefing to administer." The Russian's thick accent exhausted as he puts a finger up to one nostril, closing it off so he can blow blood out of the other. "That old fucking cunt. Tricky fuck, he was," the Russian mumbles, smiling fondly at the memory of the dead warrior that got one by him.

One of the men quickly looks down in disgust, it is reflex, but the Russian does not miss the gesture out of his peripheral vision. "Something to add, Doc?"

The man quickly looks up, unafraid and snaps back, "I didn't sign on, to smoke check old war horses. I signed on, to help you with the cause and make money. Nowhere did it say smokin old war Vets, fucktard militias and drug hit squads, absolutely. We crossed a line tonight, sir."

Wiping the blood with his uniform sleeve, the Russian looks patiently at the speaking individual. "Need I remind you, Doc. They planted four of our own, the other two barely clinging to life! Men you are friends with and fought beside numerous times we went out! Do I need remind you of what is at stake here! All of you!" the Russian roars, growing ever irate at the lack of composure of his team. He gets within inches of the man known as Doc, "Need I remind you, there is no quitting until this is done and everyone is wealthy beyond means. No one leaves, except in a body bag or when the mission is accomplished. Each one of you I personally hand selected and recruited. You are each needed and valued. But I will classify you *'expendable'* if I sense hesitation." The Russian gets even closer to the corpsman, and he can smell the blood on the Russian's nose. "Do you copy, Doc?"

Doc knows he has no chance in a confrontation with the Russian, and looking back into those dead black eyes, the man is soulless. The former SEAL grits his teeth under his mask, "Copy that, sir."

"Good. Now go drop your gear in your haciendas, get showered and meet in the courtyard at 1400 to pay our respects to our fallen comrades, who died for the greater purpose, the absolute dismantling of that gluttonous pig of a country, the United States. It will be reshaped in his vision. We watch America what?!" the Russian ends the impromptu speech.

The group of elite tactical men, all respond in unison, "Burn, burn, burn!" All except the one they call *Doc*. He merely mutters the words, defiantly.

The group of highly experienced men disperse to their own private villas, to drop their gear and shower. The Russian grabbing his gear, heads up to the main compound to speak to his higher command. One, a pig of a drug cartel overlord that he must placate to use the cartel's established political networks and pipelines in the United States. The second he must report to, and where his true allegiance belongs, is the orchestrator of the greatest revenge plot ever conceived, one that will reshape the world. This man, the Russian genuinely enjoys carrying out his orders for without question or hesitation; for the cause is above any one man and he is but an instrument that will go down in history as the *"hammer"* that drove the final nail into the United States's oversized coffin. The Russian revels in this vision of destruction.

The Last Letter

He makes his way up the beautiful, lavish, lush walkway that stretches a quarter mile to the main compound. The Russian always enjoys this moment of brief solitude under the beautiful colors of the foliage that line the walk. He never saw colors like this in his homeland and the only other times he was in such lush vegetation, it was always for some military or hostile action. *Soon, this will all be over. I will enjoy my spoils and finally rest.* The Russian allows himself a moment of tranquil thought.

Quickly approaching the team leader from the direction of the compound is the cartel head's chief of staff. *Sniveling fucking asshole. I will enjoy killing you.* The Russian makes a mental note to self, to enjoy killing the approaching man. The chief of staff, is dressed in an impeccable hand-tailored suit, not suited for the morning heat or humidity; the short run from the compound to meet the Russian has the rat of a man sweating profusely and in absolute misery. The Russian finds this perpetually amusing. He drops his gear and waits for the pathetic man to run the rest of the way; the man knows the Russian has stopped at his position on purpose.

The little sweaty individual has never trusted the foreigner and has reservations about keeping his employ, but his boss loves the results the Russian and his team achieve. They are without question, favorable. Still his senses perceive the foreigner as a threat, and he will likewise treat the team leader as such. He stops a few paces from the devilishly imposing Russian to try and compose himself a bit. This he notices amuses the Russian as well. *Piece of shit.* The two both think to themselves of the other in unison. The sweaty, pudgy, little man finally is within conversation distance of the cold-eyed Russian and that is all he wants to be, "Kharkov, you are urgently needed by him in his study."

"I am aware it is urgent, otherwise your little shit stain ass would not be impeding my progress through this, my most precious of walks." The Russian motions to the beautiful foliage surrounding the two men. "One of the few pleasures I enjoy in this fuckhole. What is so urgent, Bernard?" He answers, hating the fact this organization knows his real name. Kharkov knows he will kill them all eventually, but the fact they have that little, tiny sliver of information over him, causes him anxiety or some form of it.

With an angry look the little man retorts, "You know my name is Benjamin."

"I do," Kharkov replies, not particularly wanting to continue this conversation. He reaches down and grabs his gear and brushes past the sweaty assistant.

Undeterred by the Russian's disrespect, wiping sweat from his pudgy clean shaven, red face, Benjamin gloats, "You left one alive…. Does that matter to you?" he calls after the team leader.

Kharkov stops immediately in his tracks and grits his teeth, "Which one?"

The pig of a man basks in his diluted superiority. "We do not know yet. Our contacts in law enforcement are working on the specifics. Should be only a matter of time," Benjamin answers, cherishing this moment of triumph.

Kharkov can detect the tone of jubilance in the little assistant's voice. He now realizes the exact method of which he will kill this man when the time is upon them. It will be pleasurable, with this thought, he smiles, cruelly. "If he survives, they will put him into protective custody. Get me the details, ASAP." With that, the Russian continues on his way to see the cartel head.

Benjamin knows there is nothing left to gloat about, for Kharkov will surely kill him if he continues to poke the bear. He scurries along to the compound's operations center to get the required information on the sole surviving witness, Benjamin knows his boss will need the information to properly chastise the Russian for the mistake.

Kharkov stops before the entrance to the mansion that serves as the cartel head's personal villa. Everything about the place is state of the art and heavily fortified, except the decorative main gate made of some imported wood, which escapes the Russian's recall at the moment; although it is manned by four armed personnel at all times, specially trained by Kharkov himself. The Russian must place his gear and all weaponry in a locker, before stepping through an x-ray machine. He then must place his hand on a fingerprint reader, in conjunction with a retinal scan. This, of course, is done under constant surveillance and at gunpoint, all of which he implemented.

After the security checkpoint and through a large atrium foyer; Kharkov is then escorted up a magnificent cascading marble staircase with gold inlaid railing, that stretches up three flights to the office. To Kharkov, next to the walk up to the compound under the breathtaking foliage, the walk up the staircase

The Last Letter

is second on his list of peaceful beauty. The art that the cartel leader has '*acquired*' is unparalleled to anything the Russian has ever seen; *Rembrandt, Picasso, Pollock, Koontz, DaVinci*, etc. Even the stolen artwork from the *Boston Gardener Heist* sits on display somewhere along the walk up the staircase. The guards that accompany Kharkov up to the office suite are taught patience for the guests are supposed to marvel at the collection on their way up to a meeting with the head of the number one drug empire across the Americas. The Russian is no exception. He always takes his time to appreciate the pieces of decadence as if he were in a museum on a private tour. Kharkov seems to discover something new and fascinating each time he must report upstairs.

Upon arriving on the top floor and turning to his right to head down the massive corridor to the cartel head's office, which sits behind two massive mahogany doors, each standing about twelve feet in height. The Russian must pass through another x-ray machine manned by an additional four men, all, of course, trained and implemented by himself years ago. He does not mind the procedures because he knew complacency meant death and his procedures prevented such a thing, Kharkov needed the cartel leader to stay alive until all his resources were exhausted for the benefit of the cause.

After proceeding through the security procedures, the Russian waits for one of two security guards to press a security code into a keypad, then both mammoth mahogany doors began to open. To Kharkov it always seemed like he was entering a vault rather than a lavish office, he smiles to himself at the analogy because it seems fitting under the circumstances.

As the Russian enters, the head of the organization is residing behind his massive overly unnecessary desk, rises to greet his foreign friend. "Kharkov, I am glad you made it back. I am sorry for the loss of your men, quite unexpected. I have never known you to lose a man, now four, the injured may die as well and we have a survivor, what a shame. Explanation please?"

Clenching his chiseled jaw due to the condescending tone of this exquisitely dressed man standing eye level before him, the Russian begins his debrief. "We got complacent, and my men paid the price, or should I say I got complacent. I was not expecting three heavily armed old men to be trapsing across the crash site. Only in America. Fucking Americans. Do you have that tiny rodent getting the required information I seek, Daniel?" Kharkov asks, gritting his teeth, using the cartel figurehead's real name.

The cartel leader loathes when the Russian uses his first name, but he tolerates the inconvenience because Kharkov and his team have made Daniel the most feared and respected cartel ruler in the Americas. The organization known as *El Soberano[42] Cartel*, is the world's leader in the making and distribution of Fentanyl; none more profitable than the United States, in which Daniel retains with a ruthless iron grip. His rivals have all submitted to his organization, absorbing their resources and personnel; it was a hostile takeover, with his Russian friend administering that hostility with surgical precision. "Yes, Benjamin is almost certainly done retrieving the required information on our little survivor. He should be finished shortly. Por favor continúa con los hechos," Daniel asks patiently, sitting on his massive desk, motioning for the Russian to sit down in one of the beautiful leather chairs.

Kharkov understands the cartel head still persisting to know further facts from the night's operation, "We located the wreckage. Enroute we were notified there were men camping in the vicinity and had discovered the crash site. My men swept the area, and we engaged the three combatants at the crash site and adjacent ridgeline. They were challenging but succumbed. I learned through subsequent interrogation that they are just old war veterans, no affiliation to any rivals or any American governmental agencies. I am sure the rodent will discover this as well from our contacts in law enforcement. The drive was recovered, and decoy drugs, i.e., meth, fentanyl, and heroin, were thrown in its place. Brought back the dead, both my men and our disguised flight crew. Now it is time for you to use your pawns in the American government to spin this into *'drug cartels trying to poison America from south of the border and good American heroes are paying the price.'* Understood?" Kharkov states firmly, giving the cartel leader an order.

Daniel of course knows Kharkov is right, it will be the next item on his agenda as soon as he is finished with the Russian. "And what of the survivor, any strategy for that circumstance; seeing as he surprised you once already in Idaho," Daniel asks, offering a crooked little smile.

---
[42] The Sovereign

Kharkov for a millisecond almost loses his control again in a matter of twenty-four hours, but he steadies himself. Daniel's time is near, this lone thought keeps the Russian from killing the cartel head with satisfyingly with his legs. A simple snap of the neck, and then it is Kharkov who returns the crooked smile. "If he survives, I have a plan ready to enact."

"Por favor, por favor dime esta obra maestra?" Daniel asks, irritated by the Russian's return of a cruel smile, knowing the team leader probably thought of a way to kill him in a split second, hence Kharkov must go and soon. Daniel must begin planning his next move against the Russian and his *puppet master*.

Leaning back calmy in the leather chair, Kharkov stares directly back at the cartel head. "I think once your rodent, returns with the required information we both seek, I will then advise and execute a plan that you would consider a masterpiece," Kharkov responds flatly.

"And what of witness protection by the US Marshals, DEA, FBI, Department of Homeland Security or any other fucking government agency you may have brought down on our fucking heads!" Daniel bellows from the massive desk, his patience running thin with the smug Russian.

Kharkov knows he can only push Daniel so far. He still needs the drug kingpin, the Russian relents. "You are right, we were sloppy. It was unexpected. We did retrieve the flight recorder, at least we can figure out what the fuck happened inflight. Daniel, we need to spin this as drug cartels, and I left appropriate evidence to suggest your young up and coming rival *La Parca* cartel is the responsible party. The American agencies will then turn their extensive resources, with the backing of the stupid American public, all seeking revenge for their *'fallen heroes'*. *La Parca* gets hammered, and I do not have to endanger my men wiping them out for you. Of course, we need your extensive connections in the Justice Department and other federal agencies, especially the DEA, to handle the direction this incident will take in our favor."

Daniel, calming himself after seeing the Russian withdraw, knows Kharkov is correct; the narrative is solid and easily passed. Kharkov surprises Daniel every day, and that is what makes him uneasy about the mysterious Russian. At Daniel's direction, all Benjamin could find on the foreigner, was his military service record, which was filled with awards, medals of valor, almost all of it redacted; but listed in his record of service was a list of training, Kharkov has trained all over the world including with the FBI's counterterrorism team, the most highly trained advanced SWAT team in the world. Daniel prides himself on having information and he is lacking crucial information pertaining to the Russian and that makes the cartel head extremely nervous.

It is always a chess match with Kharkov when they have these little strategy meetings, playing against one another with the pawns of information. Daniel hates chess. "That is a sound plan. We will see what Benjamin will bring along shortly. Please, let us go out on the balcony, we will take in the scenery." Daniel stands from the beautifully crafted desk and motions Kharkov to join him. "Besides, you smell awful." And there appears that crooked smile again.

This time Kharkov does not mind the slight. The Russian stands and makes his way around the desk, looking upon the wall, still amazed by the degrees Daniel has earned at various prestigious colleges across the United States. Kharkov would have loved to have studied at any one of the schools, especially MIT. This is why the Russian's superior chose this struggling cartel head six years ago; a young, cruel, ruthless drug lord trying to survive and about to be wiped out by the now extinct, *Aya Cartel.*

Daniel enjoys the fact the Russian always pauses at the degrees on his wall, as he is extremely proud to display them. Certified genius at age six, discovered by a Mexican government official. It was Daniel's only way out of the slums of Mexico City; immediately sponsored into the most prestigious schools Mexico had to offer but soon he exceeded their capacity to provide knowledge and was immediately sent to schools across the United States, on a joint program with the US government. Doctorates in pharmacology, chemistry, engineering, business, communications, and forensic accounting soon followed. Instead of going to work for the Mexican government as originally intended by all who sponsored his education, Daniel wanted far greater power and wealth than a governmental position provides.

The drug kingpin's financial portfolio and his understanding of the international market funded his upstart fledgling cartel. Being ruthless or cruel was never a problem for Daniel in the beginning. The difficult part was gaining the loyal manpower and fear necessary to establish a foothold in the Mexican drug market. It was then, the Russian found him and offered his expertise in all matters of tactical importance. The partnership has been lucrative ever since, Daniel does not press the Russian for his agenda and in return Kharkov and his highly trained team of scalpels, destroys all in their path with precision violence; it is glorious.

The two men step out on to the expansive balcony of Daniel's office, the view is, of course, breathtaking, overlooking beautiful, lush landscape, straight to the edge of the property and the cliffs that plunge to the Gulf of Mexico below. "Would you like one?" Daniel asks, offering the Russian a cannabis pre-roll, knowing the Russian will refuse. Kharkov predictably refuses with a wave of his hand. "You partake in nothing. Drink, smoke, drugs, whores, even regular women. Nothing. You train and you train your men. They do the same," Daniel ponders aloud, lighting the cannabis pre-roll of his own stock. It is delicious; he truly enjoys growing and selling cannabis, but his primary source of income is the distribution of methamphetamine, opioids and fentanyl into the United States. Daniel does so enjoy the dismantling of the American way of life from within using his beautiful poison.

"My men and I will celebrate enough when the mission is accomplished. All that poison only distracts from our purpose. I let my men celebrate when they go home for leave, and only then. What you do here is fucking low and beneath me, but we need each other," Kharkov replies without taking his eyes off the horizon.

Exhaling a large waft of smoke, Daniel cringes, "Ouch, my friend." The cartel head leans on the marble balcony railing, "What of the four operators we lost last night?" Daniel inquires, not really caring about the lives lost. He feels no empathy, but the cost of the setback and the amount of money that went into and will go into each one of Kharkov's men's accounts is quite an investment. Each lost life costs Daniel in excess of an eight million dollar investment. It is all numbers for the young cartel head.

"Their families will have their bodies returned, fed some lies about a classified mission and *'insurance'* will reward the men's families generously per our agreement." It is an order Kharkov is giving to Daniel, not a request.

The young handsome cartel head nods, "Agreed and what of replacements? Would you like in-house you have trained here? Loyal as dogs, less risk, and cheaper," Daniel mentions, slightly annoyed at the Russian's tone.

"Yes, loyal to you, less risk for you, cheaper for you. None of which I want in an operator. No, there are numerous former special forces out there from around the world that I have profiles on; with real-world combat experience, not this bullshit your hit squads partake in. I'll begin recruiting the dead's replacements within the week." Kharkov states, never taking his gaze off the sunny horizon.

"Well, too bad you did not have the men from the battle last night on your list, looks like we could have used them," Daniel makes a stinging rebuke to the Russian's condescending tone.

Kharkov does not flinch at Daniel's snide remark but internally he visualizes the charismatic drug lord having his throat ripped out and drowning on his own blood, while the Russian smokes his cannabis and smiles. "Yes, those men were an anomaly. Fucking Americans, every one of them is always armed. Yet, they complain about their homicide rate. We do not have this problem in Russia."

"You do not have free will either," the drug kingpin counters. "Please send the possible replacement's profiles and I will have Benjamin comb through their lives with a microscope." Another exhale of smoke, "Your men are hammers and you train them as such, but even your hammers need the company of someone to release that energy," Daniel inhaling, chides the Russian. "You know the women in the compound are clean and safe, or men if you prefer." Daniel smiles, leaning against his beautifully crafted marble stone railing of the balcony.

The Russian keeps his gaze out to the sea, "These are not women, they are hostages. You send out hit squads to capture young women, some still girls, in the neighboring towns and force them into slavery to satisfy the depravity of your men. No, my team will not partake in such vulgarities." Kharkov states emotionless. "I see your cockroach, Benjamin, running across the walkway, sweating like the pig he is, must have the information we seek on my survivor."

"Kharkov, you say such hurtful things, but let us see what our '*cockroach*' brings us." Daniel replies with another exhale.

The Last Letter

The two sit quietly, staring out at the serenity of the landscape, listening to the waves crash on the private beach below the cliffs. Neither one wanting to interrupt the peace. The double doors to the office push inwards, the guards escort Benjamin into Daniel's office. Benjamin quickly makes his way out on to the veranda and joins the two men, Kharkov looking ever so pleased at the sweaty disheveled appearance of the little chief of staff.

"What of our survivor, Benjamin?" Daniel beckons him over and takes the iPad from the assistant's outstretched hand. The young cartel head pours over the information on the screen and slightly begins to smile to himself, knowing the Russian is analyzing every aspect of his reaction.

Kharkov notices the inadvertent smile Daniel is cracking at the corner of his smug little face, but what is troubling the Russian, is the fact they hold information that he does not possess and that makes Kharkov a very agitated man. Benjamin sweating profusely from his scurrying about retrieving the required information, seems to have that same inadvertent smile even though he is surely in misery, and this, too, is giving the Russian pause. Kharkov's mind begins to plan, how to kill them quietly, circumvent his own highly trained guards, get his team and the helicopter out without bringing the cartel's personal army down on he and his men? *Done*.

"Would you care to look over the information?" Daniel hands the iPad to the Russian, still with that slight mischievous smile.

Kharkov retrieves the iPad from Daniel's grasp and surveys the information on the screen, he absorbs all, remembers all and hands the iPad back to Daniel.

"And?" the cartel head asks calmly of the Russian.

"Who is taking charge of his security?" Kharkov turns his question to Benjamin. Benjamin wants very much to chide the Russian about his ineptitude but thinks otherwise, Kharkov would surely kill him in front of Daniel and the two of them would go on and recruit another intelligence analyst out of the CIA. So, Benjamin keeps his tongue in cheek and answers directly, "It is too early to tell. It depends on if the authorities buy in to the *'drug cartels are responsible'* narrative unless our little survivor knows a little more than that; so that either means the DEA will take point or the very competent Department of Homeland security will take over. Either one, we have contacts."

"And what does our survivor know?" Daniel asks still going over the contents of the iPad, not bothering to look up at the Russian.

The Russian's gaze becomes transfixed on the sweating little rodent, Benjamin. "He knows America is about to burn from the inside, that is all." Kharkov's grip tightens on the railing, calmly responding to the cartel head's question.

"Pray tell what was that conversation like? Cordial?" Daniel raises his head to gauge the Russian's response.

Kharkov turns and faces the educated cartel leader, "It was cordial to a degree."

Daniel, frustrated that he is not getting clear answers from the Russian, tries a different approach, "Was this cordial conversation before or after the survivor broke your nose? I have never seen you actually take punishment on these raids we orchestrate… shocking." Daniel receives the desired effect from the Russian, Kharkov takes a step towards the drug kingpin.

Instinctively, Benjamin moves to intercede on behalf of his employer. The Russian immediately then turns towards the slimy assistant. Benjamin stops cold, noticing a glint of pleasure in the Russian's eyes, as if Kharkov had already killed him in a fraction of a second in his mind.

Daniel is not concerned with the advancing Russian, fearful, yes but not concerned. The cartel head is highly trained in all various forms of fighting styles, some even taught to him by Kharkov himself. Daniel is not concerned because the Russian still needs his resources for the final objective, and he needs to figure out when the endgame is and kill the Russian beforehand.

Kharkov has no intention of killing either man at this point in time, if the Russian is honest with himself, he is impressed with the little cockroach for even moving to intercede. "I will handle the survivor with my team. We have a small window before the governmental agencies get their heads out of their asses and decide who is going to protect him."

"Handle it? You and your men got handled by a bunch of regular Marine infantry. Just three of them, how is this possible? I was expecting a group of former Navy SEALs, MARSOC, or even Delta Force but fucking former reserve Marines." Daniel begins to chuckle, exhaling his smoke in the Russian's direction.

The Last Letter

"No, Benjamin here will get the required information on the families and friends of the deceased and the survivor. From there we will survey the landscape of the situation and decide the best course of action going forward," the cartel head explains, finalizing their progression forward to finding a resolution to a problem Daniel deems only he can fix. "This will take finesse, not an assault."

Kharkov shakes his head disapprovingly, "These men had actual combat experience, knew tactics, and employed them expertly. They did not freeze or hesitate. Under the circumstances and odds, I would have employed the very same counter measures. The deceased and the survivor are going to be made national heroes regardless of the narrative released to the public. We do not have the time for that. The survivor is in a coma, let us strike now. Once he is moved to a secure location by whatever agency takes point, our efforts to locate and destroy the witness will take ten times the amount of effort. The confusion among US agencies is the perfect time to end this permanently. We will not be able to reach them or their families without drawing unwanted attention to our cause and organization," the Russian counters.

"You are fucking impressed by them now!" Daniel declares, getting angry with the Russian for his praise of the fallen Marines.

"Yes," Kharkov smoothly answers the bellowing drug kingpin.

Benjamin quickly interjects before the Russian is pushed too far, "Sir, if I may, Kharkov is right. We must strike now during the confusion, while the survivor is in a soft target, such as the hospital. Guards posted can either be bought or eliminated and we do have a pool of highly skilled eliminators from which we can pull," Benjamin says, offering his humble agreement to the Russian's plan, hoping to diffuse the brewing anger of his boss.

Daniel reluctantly calms himself "We wait." He inhales deeply, "What do we know of the survivor and his band of merry Marines that got the best of your men?" The drug lord eyes his Russian counterpart, but his gaze is not returned.

"They were loyal to each other." Kharkov respectfully states. He then turns to Daniel, his cold stare unrelenting, "This is a bad plan. It shows weakness." The Russian returns his gaze to the distant Gulf of Mexico. *I will end the survivor on my own*, Kharkov decides with satisfaction.

CH. 16
PARKS SCORES A TOUCHDOWN

Supervisory Special Agent Medina enters the hospital room of the survivor, the machines giving off their audible beeps keeping the patient alive, echo throughout the cavernous, dark room. He has always wondered what became of Parks after he saw him at Camp Lejeune all those years ago and now this. Medina, then a gunnery sergeant at the time with MARSOC, happened to cross paths with Parks as he was attending Infantry Unit Leader's Course as a staff sergeant at Camp Lejeune. *What an absolute fucking wreck you were the whole goddamn course*, Medina reflects, looking down upon his disfigured friend laying before him on the verge of death.

"What the fuck happened to you, brother?" the supervisory special agent silently asks the patient as the machines keeping their life-saving beeps in rhythm, echo throughout the silence of the dreary, dark room. Medina slumps into the uncomfortable hospital chair and stretches out his legs, hoping for a couple minutes of uninterrupted sleep. It was not to be, Dr. Anand enters the room looking as sleepless as Agent Medina himself. *Fuck!* Medina shouts in his mind, "Yes, Dr. Anand?"

"I am here to check on our survivor and register any changes post-Op," Dr. Anand quips annoyed with Agent Medina's tone and question.

"Continue by all means," Medina responds, ignoring Dr. Anand's annoyance and frustration.

"Why, thank you, my liege," Dr. Anand sarcastically fires back, still annoyed with the situation.

Agent Medina cracks a slight smile, leaning back again watching the doctor perform his tasks at hand. "That was funny, Doctor."

The exhausted doctor pauses a moment, "What is your interest with this patient besides the obvious incident this poor man found himself in?" Dr. Anand asks, assessing the patient's vitals.

"Your meaning, Doctor?" Medina inquires, still coolly watching Dr. Anand, his gaze never portraying intent or malice.

"Besides the classified jargon I am sure you are going to regurgitate to me and the rest of my staff, but you sit in here not as protection but to me as a friend. So, who is he to you?" Dr. Anand questions the agent.

There is a momentary pause, the agent seems to contemplate how much to tell this good doctor. "That is classified." Agent Medina smiles slightly back at the doctor.

"I figured as much." Annoyed once again, Dr. Anand finishes his check on the patient and begins to exit the dark and irritating room. "I am assuming as soon as he is in stable enough condition, he will be transported to Walter Reed?"

"That is classified," Agent Medina responds, beginning to shut his eyes, watching the doctor open the door to exit.

"You my friend, are an asshole," Dr. Anand fires back at Agent Medina.

A smile spreads across the special agent's face, "Duly noted, doctor." Medina then shuts his eyes; he knows his reprieve will not last.

The supervisory agent disturbingly receives a notification that the driver has secured Ms. Parkinson, and they are currently enroute to the hospital. He looks to his watch and then to the patient. He has time for a quick few minutes of sleep, he hopes. Agent Medina is about to drift into that perfect stage of drowsiness, when a nurse flings open the door and heads directly over to the patient, ignoring the sleepy agent. Medina quickly recognizes her as one of the nurse's cleared for entrance into the room, his men outside would not have let her pass otherwise. *Shit*, Medina contemplates; he knows there will be no rest for him at the moment.

"Didn't Dr. Anand just come in and perform his evaluation?" Medina asks, slightly annoyed that his much-needed sleep is not going to happen.

"Yes, Agent he did, but I am here to administer the doctor's specified treatment for the patient and then check his bed pan. He insisted it be now. Would you like to take over?" Nurse Bennett quickly snips, putting Agent Medina on notice she will not tolerate his rudeness.

Medina scoffs slightly, "He insisted, did he? Dick. No, please, Nurse Bennett carry on. I apologize for my curtness." Agent Medina responds, as he stands to leave behind the discomfort of the horrible hospital chair. Nurse Bennett performs her duties expertly and flawlessly. Before preparing to leave the room, she walks over to the patient, gently puts her hand on his head, and whispers a silent prayer: *God, please bless and watch over this man, Amen.*

"Thank you for that Nurse Bennett, he will appreciate knowing you said a prayer for him." Agent Medina consoles the well-intentioned nurse. There are no exterior windows in the patient's room, at the agent's insistence, which makes the room ominous with the shadow of death lingering in the corner, waiting patiently for the survivor to expire.

"It's nothing," she replies with a warm smile, that Medina genuinely appreciates. She closes the door gently behind her.

Medina strides over to the side of the bed and stares down at his wounded friend. He begins to reflect on all the fun they had together while in the Marines at Camp Pendleton and Camp Lejeune. Parks was out of control when he was at Lejeune, but no one really knew what was happening to the returning infantry Marines back then and why some seemed to be lost, and some moved on. Medina threw himself into the Marines further, while others like Parks, drank or others found opioids to bury that failure or loss of purpose away deep in their subconscious.

"What happened to you, old friend?" Medina asks again of a comatose Parks; he lays there with the incessant beeping of the machines keeping him alive. There is no response, only the rise and fall of the patient's chest.

The special agent's face becomes tightened, reflecting on his own men, their faces covered in sand and grime looking to him. *That was back when warfare was simple*, Medina thinks to himself. Kick in doors and engage the enemy but once he moved over to MARSOC; warfare became a political weapon and so had Special Forces from all branches of the military. He grips the railing of the hospital bed, stares down at the swollen, deformed, grotesque head of what used to be his friend. "There will be vengeance, my friend," Medina whispers to Parks through gritted teeth.

The door to the room opens and one of his men posted outside peeks his head in, "Sir, she has arrived."

"Thank you, please have them escort her to Dr. Anand's office, I will be there momentarily," Medina responds sullenly, without looking up.

"Yes, sir," the agent responds.

Agent Medina walks to the bathroom sink and splashes water on his chiseled face; he does not recognize the reflection staring back at him. "What the fuck?" is all he can muster of an explanation to give the unrecognizable reflection in the mirror. Medina has been alone a long time; his job has kept any meaningful relationship at bay, and he is tired. Of it all. *Soon it will be our time*, he swears, looking to the patient.

. . .

Jean, nervous as she is, seems to have reached her patience with not being able to see her son. The agents say nothing to her, instead they stand there like Dobermans towering over her, ready to snap at anything perceived as dangerous. She hates the attention. "Where the fuck is my son?" she asks in a stern voice to one of the agents.

"Ma'am, please if you could just be patient. Our silence is not meant as disrespect," the agent politely replies to the concerned mother.

She is about to respond angrily when the elevators open at the end of the hall; Special Agent Medina and Dr. Anand both step out into the sterile corridor. Jean notices they do not seem too relaxed to see her arrival, both making pitying eye contact with her. *This will not be good*; she knows that now. Tears begin to form in the corners of her eyes, but she quickly dismisses them with a slight of her hand.

"Ms. Parkinson, I am Dr. Anand, please come into my office," the good doctor cordially greets Parks' mother and gently escorts her into his spacious office. Agent Medina follows closely behind the two as they step into Dr. Anand's quarters.

Medina softly introduces himself to Parks' mother, "Ms. Parkinson, Special Agent Medina, we spoke on the phone."

The stern woman extends her frail hand to the special agent, "Call me Jean. Now please explain to me what is happening with my son," the concerned mother sternly delivers to the two men.

"Yes, ma'am. Your son suffered traumatic brain injuries, along with other bodily injuries. He endured a significant amount of trauma. Your son is in a coma, and it is not medically induced. I performed emergency neurological surgery to reduce the swelling of the brain and to remove the bullet lodged in his skull. He is stable but in an extremely critical stage of recovery. Ms. Parkinson, your son is very lucky, any less swelling or a millimeter either direction and the round penetrates your son's skull, and he would have expired at the scene of the tragedy. That is in laymen's terms of the scenario. I do not want to get into the specifics of intercranial bleeding and how these next forty-eight to seventy-two hours will decide what fate your son will have. We just do not know enough at this juncture to speculate on what type of recovery he will undergo in the future. I know that is not a lot of information. I am sorry. Do you have any questions for me, Jean?"

Jean fixes her steel blue eyes coldly on the doctor, "When can I see my son?" she coolly asks.

"Right now, ma'am," Special Agent Medina quickly, softly responds to Jean's question. He rises from Dr. Anand's leather sofa to help escort her to the patient's room.

The three make the silent, uncomfortable trip to the elevator as they wait, the silence grows ever more depressing for all three. Jean is steadfast in her gaze upon the steel outer doors of the elevator; Medina desperately wants to tell her he will get vengeance for her and the other families. Dr. Anand nervously awaits the elevator, hoping he has done enough to save this poor woman's son, his own son's death reverberating in his consciousness, screaming for his attention. *Not now*, he begs of himself.

As the tension and unease become palpable, the elevator suddenly pings, the doors open and the three step slowly inside, "Agent Medina, what happened to my son and his men?" Jean directly asks. For Dr. Anand, it is a question he, too, wants answered and he enjoys the fact that Special Agent Medina seems for once uncomfortable in his presence.

Shit! Agent Medina screams in his head. "Ma'am I am not at liberty to discuss the ongoing investigation." He wants to tell her so much more. *Asshole*, flashes across his mind, he sees the effect those words have on Parks' mother.

Jean's shoulders depress. "I see," she quietly replies, her small frame, seemingly buckling under the weight of the situation.

Asshole, Medina tells himself again. In time his plan will come to fruition.

"And his men?" Jean turns and looks at him with her steel-blue grieving eyes. Feeling the guilt of not being able to answer the concerned mother's queries, Agent Medina concedes, "Again, I cannot discuss the investigation."

He feels worse by the second.

Dr. Anand scoffs at the agent's response, "Sounds about accurate."

"What can you discuss, special agent? You told me you and my son served together and were friends once. What can you tell me of comfort?" Jean hammers away at Medina. Dr. Anand witnesses how uncomfortable the special agent is becoming, *The agent is human after all*, the doctor thinks to himself.

Touching her arm slightly, the doctor interjects, "Please, Jean. Let us discuss what can be of use to you. Your son seems to have the inner fortitude to recover but as I said the next forty-eight to seventy-two hours are critical. We are the foremost experts on traumatic brain injuries in the world, next only to Walter Reed. Your son is in expert care. We will exhaust all avenues to ensure his recovery. His coma is completely on him and so is his recovery. The best thing for him is to have you by his side, talking to him." Dr. Anand warmly comes to Agent Medina's rescue, who in turn gives the neurosurgeon a gracious nod of appreciation.

"Thank you, Dr. Anand." Jean feels the sincerity of the good doctor.

The elevator doors open to the hospital wing housing the intensive care unit. Jean is escorted to the secure room that houses her son; the two men standing post hold the door open to the dark room. Jean is hesitant to go in. She does not want to see her son in this state. She forges ahead into the darkness of the room, her eyes trying to adjust from the bright hospital corridor.

The Last Letter

She can see the glow of the machines monitoring her son as her tired eyes come into focus. Jean moves slowly forward, her eyes adjusting rapidly, her gaze finally falling upon her beloved son. The deformity that was his beautiful head, looms massive in her field of vision. She drops from the shock but Medina moves swiftly and catches her with his decades-trained reflexes and steadies the somber mother.

Jean says nothing but reaches out and grabs the railing of the hospital bed. Mournful tears stream down her weathered face, but she makes not a noise, not a sob. Medina marvels at her strength and composure, as does Dr. Anand. She slowly retrieves her son's uninjured hand, no longer able to stare at his horrifying injuries; the doting mother clasps his hand in both hers, she shuts her eyes and whispers, but it is so faint the two men cannot make out her words.

The three stand in silence after Jean finishes her recitation. She then asks softly, "Dr. Anand, how long will his coma last in your opinion?" Jean does not turn to look at him, keeping her gaze upon her son's hand.

There is no definitive answer to be given to the worried mother. "Ma'am, it is not as simple as that. His coma can last hours or years. It is all dependent on the individual person. He is strong, and we did everything within our expertise. All we can do now is monitor him and ensure his best possible care while here at our facility."

"What do you mean *'while here at your facility'*?" Jean asks sternly, still without taking her gaze off her son's hand. Tears littering his hospital blanket.

"Ma'am, I just assumed with him being a Veteran that he would surely be transported to Walter Reed," Dr. Anand says, trying his best to conceal his uneasiness. He did not like this level of attention at his hospital, nor did he want the potential risk to his staff.

Defiantly Parks' mother coldly states, "And if I so chose to keep my son here at your facility, would there be an issue with that? Supervisory Special Agent Medina, any problems? You say you know my son and were friends, so you know he calls Colorado home now. So, I ask, is there a problem that my son, the decorated combat Marine receive the finest care at this hospital?" Jean commands from the men.

"No, ma'am. I will make all the arrangements," Medina answers without hesitation.

Embarrassed for upsetting this grief-stricken frail woman, Dr. Anand tries to backpedal, "Of course not, Ms. Parkinson. I did not mean to imply anything—"

With a slight wave of her hand, she waves off the doctor's attempts. "It's fine, Doctor. I would just as soon not move my son, and if he is to die, I want him to do it here, in Colorado. He longed for this place; he loves it here." Jean smoothly rubs the back of her son's hand.

"Of course. I assure you my staff and I are going to use the extent of our collective knowledge to aid your son in any fashion necessary," Dr. Anand offers humbly.

Jean nods appreciatively, "Thank you, Doctor." She never wavers from her post hovering like a watchful guardian over their charge.

"Well, if you two have no further questions for me, I will see to the preparations of his stay and I will find a more accommodating room for our purposes," Dr. Anand nervously vouches, heading for the door of the dimly lit room.

Medina calls after Dr. Anand, "Thank you, Doctor. I will be along momentarily to discuss the logistics of our situation."

"Looking forward to it, agent." Dr. Anand shoots back over his shoulder with a heavy coat of sarcasm.

I am beginning to like him; Medina flashes the thought to himself. He turns his attention back to the destroyed woman in front of him, wishing he could give her some comforting information or solace.

"Agent Medina, tell me, have the other mothers been notified that their sons have been taken from them?" Jean solemnly asks the former Marine standing behind her.

Exhaling, Medina grimly responds, "Yes, ma'am., I believe next of kin are being notified as we speak."

"Those poor mothers. We shared our fears that our sons would come home from Iraq in a box and now all these years later their sons are coming home in a box. How is this just, Special Agent Medina?" Jean allows her tears to flow freely now. "Those poor mothers." This time she drops to her knees

The Last Letter

before Medina can make it to her. "I'm fine, agent," she directs, steadying herself once again with the use of the hospital bed's rails.

Agent Medina hurriedly grabs the horrible excuse for a chair and places it alongside the bed so Jean can still grasp her son's hand in hers. The stricken mother nods appreciatively as Medina makes his way around to the opposite side of the stale hospital bed and stands dutifully next to his old friend, as if awaiting orders from Jean. The two both wait in silence; it is not uncomfortable; neither one wanting to break the tranquility of the moment.

The worried mother finally breaks the rhythm of beeps emanating from the machines providing lifesaving support for her son. "Agent Medina?"

"Yes, ma'am?" Medina responds politely, still staring at the damage done to Parks. His rage boiling internally, externally the supervisory agent portrays no emotion, to his detriment.

Still not bearing to look past her son's hand, Jean softly asks of the agent, "Tell me something of my son, when you two served together, please?" She asks politely, maternally grasping her son's hand, refusing to look past his waist.

Looking towards the grief-stricken mother, Medina contemplates. "Besides the tarantula story? Let me see…," the special agent begins to reply with a slight smile. "He was fast, Ms. Parkinson. I don't mean long distance fast, he could run in the 18s for the 3 miles, that was common; what I'm talking about was on the football field; he had moves and speed." Medina chuckles slightly. "We were in Okinawa '98, playing the island champs in flag football. They, of course, were from the Air Force base at Kadena. They had the time to put together a championship team; practice, uniforms, and designed plays, whereas us *Grunts* trained constantly, especially since your son and I were boat company, always training."

Jean smiles, lowering her head, "He was always so proud of being in boat company. Even though he liked to bitch about the cold. Please continue, Agent Medina, I find this helpful," she quietly asks of him.

The machines still beeping their chorus of life-giving noise in chaotic rhythm, Medina is transfixed between the sounds of the machines and his memory of Okinawa, "Yes, of course, ma'am. Your son was the fastest on the team and I hate to admit that because I am pretty damn fast." Medina says with a slight smile upon the momentary reflection. "Your son was our running back, so the quarterback pitches the ball to Parks on a sweep; I was out as a receiver, and I came and threw a nasty block on two guys, leveling them, springing Parks to the outside. Parks has three men in the open closing the angle, he jukes two and outsprints the angle down the sideline on the third. I think that was an eighty-yard run. It was a beautiful sight to watch from the ground after the block."

"So, you guys won the game?" Jean asks with genuine curiosity, enthralled with the tale of her son.

"Oh, good Lord, no, ma'am. They were good and their speed was unmatched. Your son and I were the only ones that could keep up. They torched us 55–7, his being the only touchdown. Air Force had all the time in the world to practice. But the remarkable thing was, after that run the whole opposing team came over to Parks in the endzone and they were the ones cheering him, before we could get to him, all of them saying they never seen anyone like him move like that. It truly was the ultimate compliment," Medina offers, reveling in the memories of that sunny day in Okinawa.

Jean sighs heavily at the memory shared of her son. "Thank you, Agent Medina. That was touching and needed," the exhausted mother replies thankfully, adjusting her position in the uncomfortable chair. "You know he talks about you often. He would always tell me *'Medina, did the Marine Corps the right way.'* He wanted so much to correct the wrong and follow your path. He idolized you and your accomplishments. Anytime the family mentions his service, he will always find a way to bring your name into the conversation."

"That means a lot. Thank you, ma'am." Medina still gazes upon the damage inflicted upon his old friend. The silence once again falls upon the dark, cold room.

After some time spent listening to the incessant machines beep, Parks' mother opens up in a barely audible voice, "Medina, he was really struggling lately. I thought this trip would be good for him. The past year all he focused on were his failures, constantly. He would breakdown and wish he could change things, never forgiving himself for his past…." Jean trails off, still grasping her son's hand tightly.

"I am sorry, ma'am," Medina responds kindly. "The past haunts us all, even myself, there's no running from it."

She wipes the silent tears from her aged cheeks. "What happens next for my son?" The concerned mother inquires, finally taking her gaze away from her son's hand to look across to the special agent.

"He will be under twenty-four-hour protection by my men. Once he wakes, we will see what he remembers about the incident, and any aid Parks can give, we will use to get these motherfuckers, ma'am." Medina recites without emotion.

"I'm afraid you may have competition once his men become involved. They will want vengeance for their fallen." She closes her eyes to relieve them from the strain of the constant production of tears.

The supervisory agent nods in acknowledgment, "I'm sure they will, ma'am. That's what I'm counting on." Medina contemplates his next course of action, trying to always stay a strategic step ahead of his adversary, and he knows exactly who is responsible for the attack. Proving it to his superiors and the corrupt political machine is another matter Medina has become tired of doing during his career. Supervisory Special Agent Medina will play the game, but his endgame will be his and his alone; this incident may have given him the final ammunition he needs to achieve his goal. Parks and his men are the vengeful key.

CH. 17
IT'S NOT GOOD

Bgame does not want to turn his phone back on, but he knows Roca is waiting to hear from him soon. He is reluctant to push the *Power* button because as soon as he does, his phone will ping nonstop with fellow Marines from Bravo Co. trying to get answers. The Viking is not disappointed, his phone immediately starts pinging with notifications: voicemail, Messenger, posts, Instagram, as soon as it comes alive.

"Fuck me," he groans aloud in his business-class suite at the local Holiday Inn. He does not want to answer anybody's line of questioning, not after his meeting with the forestry agent; Bgame lays back on the basic, shabby hotel comforter and shuts his eyes. *You were supposed to be here*, the only thought racing through his mind. He rubs his closed eyes, hoping to rub this nightmare scenario away but upon opening his eyes, Bgame is bathed in this new reality. The ageing Marine needs to call Attebery; he promised he would. Parks and Attebery were close, especially after the incident outside of Fallujah. Bgame owes Attebery a heads-up; he dials his old friend's number, still hoping for voicemail; he has no such luck.

A soft, shaky voice answers Attebery's phone. "Hey, Bgame. Todd's in the shower. He'll be out in just a sec." Lacey heads to the back porch, sits in a beautiful wooden rocker, and immediately pops a cigarette in her mouth. *Todd be damned*, flashes across her mind in defiance, not today. "How bad is it?"

Bgame is relieved to be talking with Attebery's wife. It makes delivering the news easier for him. "It's not good, Lacey. James and Doherty are gone.

Parks has been CAS-EVACd, I don't know where, his condition unknown." Bgame rushes it out of his mouth as fast as he can, hoping the speed will make the news less traumatic for Lacey.

"Oh fuck." Lacey is suddenly glad she answered the phone instead of her husband, to absorb some of the detrimental news. She exhales the smoke heavily. "What do you need from us, Bgame?"

Staring up at the hideous ceiling of the hotel room, Bgame is at a loss for words. "To be honest, Lacey, I don't know what the fuck I need right now."

She sympathizes with the distraught former Marine, as she sympathizes with all of Bravo Co. during this time of tragedy and confusion. "Shit, I'm sorry Bgame. Here comes Todd, hold one."

"Thank you, Lacey," Bgame answers with a heavy, raspy sigh.

Handing the phone to Attebery, Lacey shakes her head towards her husband, her tears welling up in her sorrow-stricken eyes, "It's not good, babe," she says, trying to prepare her husband as best she can.

Taking the phone from his endearing wife, Attebery hesitantly answers, "Alright, Bgame just fuckin tell me."

Having no desire to repeat himself but knowing he must, "Doherty and James are gone, and Parks is in bad shape somewhere. I don't know where yet. That's fuckin basically it, brother." The reality becoming more apparent with each time Bgame has to summarize the events surrounding the three fallen Marines.

"Copy that. What do you need from me?" Attebery asks of his old friend.

"Aww, Devil, nothin right now. Maybe get with Gunny and Frazier, some of the other Bravo Marines and start locking on funeral details. "About all we can do," Bgame gruffly answers Attebery.

Attebery is having a tough time believing any of this has happened, but denial is not an option for him right now, "Fuck. Roger that. I'll talk to Gunny next. You still givin your debrief at 1800?"

"Yeah, brother. It'll be basically what I told you. I won't be answerin fuckin questions," Bgame groans as he rises to an upright position on the hotel bed.

"I don't blame you. Alright, man, you call me when you need somethin. I'll try and find out where Parks is located. Take care of yourself up there, brother." Attebery offers sympathetically to the ageing Marine.

The Last Letter

After a brief pause, he gives a confirmation, "Roger that." Ending the conversation, Bgame heads to the bathroom, turns on the shower and sits on the toilet cover. He again rubs his eyes with his calloused hands; He, too, was an underwater welder for the offshore oil rigs but too many dives had given him life-altering side effects that he could no longer dive. His head is pounding, a searing pain forming in the corner of his right eye, one of many side effects from the numerous dives. He undresses quickly and jumps in the scalding hot shower. Bgame notices nothing and feels nothing. He lets the water engulf his aching muscles with a warm embrace. He could almost fall asleep standing up. An agonizing groan from his feeling of guilt hits him in the chest like a freight train; the groan echoes through the cheap walls of the hotel, startling guests unlucky enough to pass by in the halls.

The Marine shuts off the shower after about twenty scalding hot minutes, his skin reddened to match his Viking beard. He quickly grabs an uncomfortable hotel towel and begins to dry off, the mirror covered in steam; Bgame is thankful for that fact, for he does not want to see his reflection at this particular moment. He quickly dresses in some desert brown khakis and throws on a T-shirt. Bgame leaves his socks off, he wants to scrunch his toes in the old carpet, a little trick he picked up from the great John McClaine in *Die Hard. The only fucking good one*, Bgame thinks to himself about the franchise, scrunching his toes in the horrible carpet of the hotel room.

He gingerly strides over to the nightstand on the right side of the queen bed, looks at his phone, he emits another customary audible Bgame groan, like a hurt, angry grizzly bear, known only to the men that served with the ageing Marine. He notices the notifications on his phone, the home screen is covered in various notifications from different apps. "Fuck!" He ignores them all except one, Gunny Hoffman's text: *Call me, Fucker!* Even Bgame knows better than to ignore him. Every man in Bravo Co. owes their successful deployment to the company guns, he was instrumental in the company not losing a single Marine; sustained several casualties but no killed in action and Bravo Co. saw its fair share of action. Bgame is not ready to talk to anyone, but he knows he must, he reluctantly dials Gunny Hoffman's phone.

"Hey. Fucker, what the fuck? You shut your phone off?" The retired Marine scolds Bgame.

"Fuck, sorry Master Guns. It's been rough." Bgame suddenly feels like a young sergeant again.

"I take it Special Agent Alexander showed you the video?" Gunny Hoffman asks in his gruff voice.

The deathly images of James, Doherty, and Parks come flooding back to the forefront of his thoughts. "Yeah, Master Guns, she did," Bgame replies flatly, detached from the conversation.

"Those motherfuckers will pay, is that understood, Bgame?" Gunny Hoffman growls into the phone. The Bravo Company Gunny loves every one of his men, he knew James and Doherty as good young upstanding and perfect Marines. Sgt. Parks was part of a dump of prior active duty squad leaders to Bravo Co., each one: competent, eager, and respected at the time. The experienced squad leaders were crucial, ensuring the sustained success of the company during its' combat rotation to Iraq.

"Yut, Master Guns. What do you want me to tell the men?" Bgame asks hesitantly not wanting to go through with the live stream.

Gunny Hoffman softens his voice to a low rumble, "Just state the facts as you know them. Do not mention the video. Special Agent Alexander stuck her neck on the line allowing us to view the fuckin thing."

"Master Guns, you able to find anythin else out?" Bgame asks, hoping Gunny Hoffman can provide him with more details.

The old company guns huffs futilely, "I'm lookin into the situation, but my hands are tied due to this now belonging to the FEDs and is out of my jurisdiction, but I'm still trackin down contacts both in the federal and local agencies. I'll find out more, Devil," Gunny Hoffman reassures his former troop. "Stay the course, brother. We need you up there on point."

"Thanks, Master Guns." With that, Bgame hangs up and lays his upper body back on the bed with his lower half hanging off. He turns his head to the generic hotel clock; the red lights display 1742; time for him to get ready; he quickly fires off a post on Facebook to let everyone know not to ask questions during the live stream and he will answer all through messenger as soon as he can. Bgame stares at his laptop screen sitting on the wooden hotel desk/table. He wants more than anything not to be the one doing this, but he is aware

The Last Letter

that Bravo Co. has always looked to him as a point man all things pertaining to the Marines of the company these past few years, especially after he settled his life down. Now the men see him as the old warrior trying to keep the Marines of Bravo Co. together and helping the ones in distress, however he can. "Fuckin, Parks, you had to pick the one place you've been to before. Couldn't just do this in Colorado. Fuck!" His mind suddenly racing to images of him and James meeting out for beers, reminiscing about Bravo's tour and the lasting memories that will forever haunt them both—the good and bad. Bgame watches as the clock on his computer strikes 1800. He logs into his Facebook account to begin the live stream. *Holy shit.* He sees the amount of people logging in to the feed. Bgame knows he must be careful with what he says next; he begins:

"Listen, Devils, I'm going to state the facts as I know them. Brace yourself. Do not fuckin interrupt me." Bgame's tone broadcasts his anger. "James, Doherty, and Parks did in fact get hit while out on the reunion trip. By who or what, I do not know. James and Doherty are gone. Their bodies are here in Clear Creek pending autopsy and notifications to next of kin. I need Marines to escort our boy's home. I'm sure you, 1st Squad bubbas, watchin are already making arrangements to be here, so please email me your itineraries. Parks is in critical condition somewhere and the authorities have deemed that classified." Bgame exhales, rubbing his red beard, the stress weighing heavily on his features.

"We all know these men, served with them, drank beers and swapped stories with these men. Don't believe shit in the news, unless it comes from Gunny Hoffman or myself, don't believe fuck all. If you're on your way to Clear Creek, be advised I don't know how welcomin the local law enforcement will be to a bunch hardasses showin up all pissed off, so be on alert upon landin and try not to scare the locals because we don't need that shit. I'm goin to sign off and will try and answer as many emails and messages as I can. I know this is fucked up news and we all will grieve differently but please reach out to the 1st Squad bubbas and others. Bravo takes care of one another, yut."

Bgame shuts down his laptop before the questions from Bravo Co. begin, goes over to the bed, and flops back down on his back. He shuts his eyes for a brief second, the moment of peace is much desired.

SSgt. Jacob Parkinson

The former Marine scrolls through his various apps looking for a response from the members of 1st Squad, they will take priority. He sees that Jackson, Cooper, Del Vecchio, Delta, Morales, Thomas, and Perry, all left him various forms of messages and itineraries. What shocks him most of all is seeing Culpepper's name in his email. "What the fuck?" he mutters to himself, no one has heard from Culpepper in over two decades. The big man leaves a quick message:

Sgt. Bgame, I will be in Clear Creek in the morning. I would like to aid in escorting James home. Contact you in the AM -Culpepper.

"Holy shit. That big motherfucker is on his way." Much to Bgame's relief. He knows the worst is yet to come, planning and attending the services of the two fallen warriors. Having every member of 1st Squad coming to Clear Creek will help Bgame manage tremendously. He will not be alone. The questions that race through his mind are too numerous to answer. The one thought that he knows will haunt all of those who are enroute: *I should have been there*; Bgame understands that this will be an undying thought for the rest of their lives. Every reunion, every anniversary of the tragedy, every post with the fallen's pictures, that same thought will accompany each event: *I should have been there.*

Bgame sets his alarm on his phone, to wake him; he then shuts his eyes to the vision of James, Doherty, and Parks screaming for help and he not being there to answer that call. This will become a tortuous, sleepless night.

. . .

Delta gets into the driver seat of his rental car, a nondescript Toyota sedan. He plugs in the destination of the Holiday Inn in Clear Creek; he looks at the ETA: 0238, about two and a half hours, long time to be left to his thoughts. Delta is not looking forward to the solitude of the drive, the trip up to Idaho was filled with flashbacks and memories. The *'I should have been there'* thought constantly beating his head in with guilt.

"Why the fuck did I not go? Fuck!", he slams his fist into the steering wheel. Doherty was a rifleman in his team and the memories of his smiling

The Last Letter

dirty face haunts him in every window or mirror reflection he comes across; even now as he stares out the window of the rental, he sees the three men smiling back at him.

Delta puts the car into drive, beginning his trek up to Clear Creek, never to be at peace the entire trip. He does not want to communicate with anyone until he gets to the hotel, he connects his phone to the radio to listen to his own music, to drown out the incessant lies about those who he knew told on every news network. The former Marine needs peace on this drive down; he lost a fellow firefighter and friend in the line of duty earlier this year and now this. To hear every news network, berate and diminish the men he knew becomes rageful to Delta, but he cannot succumb to that rage, not yet.

"It going to be a long drive," he mutters to himself, turning on the classic rock of his playlist for the drive. Delta gets outside of Boise and his mind begins to drift to that day back in Iraq outside of Fallujah. *Fuck that was a long fucking day*, his mind racing back to the inevitable words Parks spoke over the radio at zero dark thirty: *"Negative Gunny, I will not give that order to my men."* This would become the catalyst of a bond never spoken of in the middle of combat, Anbar Province, Iraq 2004. Delta knows to this day the importance of that moment and subsequent events that transpired after, it was in that moment in time that cemented 1st Squad's status as a legend never to be told or whispered about.

"Fuck, fuck, fuck, fuck!" he screams, the classic rock melody does nothing to calm the sorrow brewing in his chest. Delta does not want to remember, but it comes flooding back. *How could it end like this? Why?* He tries desperately to block out the memory before it takes hold. Delta never hesitated that night. He immediately backed his squad leader and to the men of 1st Squad it was a beautiful moment in the middle of hell in a land forgotten by the rest of world. Delta's phone begins to ring. He doesn't recognize the number; there is no choice but to answer, "Yes?"

The voice on the other end softly speaks into the phone with his Louisiana drawl, "Sgt. Heisinger? It's Jackson, man."

Delta feels a sudden relief at the familiar voice of his team member, "Oh shit, hey Jackson. Where are you?" Delta responds with a subdued, drained voice.

"Man, I'm at the Holiday Inn here in Clear Creek. Room 234. I just wanted to see if you were comin up," Jackson asks his old team leader.

"Good. I'm enroute to your location. How've you been holding up?" Delta asks with concern and sincerity in his wavering voice.

There is a pause before the former Marine answers., "Shit is fucked up, Sgt. Heis. I can't believe the shit they say on the news. It was a fuckin reunion of buddies, and they are makin it out like James, Doherty and Sgt. Parks were part of some international drug ring. It was supposed to be a fucking reunion!" Jackson declares, upset at the headlines flashing across the television in his room.

"I know, Devil. Don't listen to that shit. Concentrate on getting our boys home and then we will worry about defending their names." Delta tries to calm his former team member. He knows it will be of no use for anyone; as more members of 1st Squad descend on Clear Creek, he knows their anger will become a blanket that comforts them all.

"This fuckin asshole Kevin Karlson on JaKL News keeps bashing our boys and the Marines, fuckin saying they don't have this problem with Russian veterans and military personnel. Motherfucker!" Jackson continues on his anger-fueled tirade, knowing he needs to calm down but cannot find the restraint to do so; he has been bottling up his anger since he left this morning after receiving the news about his squad mates.

Delta still tries to calm Jackson, "Fuck that guy. Focus on the task at hand. Our revenge will come in time, hopefully. Just breathe. Anyone else there or headed this way that you know of?"

"Man, Sgt. Heis, I think all of 1st is on the way. Even the ghost, Culpepper. In fact, I think I saw that big motherfucker checking in; I couldn't be too sure. No one has seen him in over twenty years," Jackson explains, calming his temper.

"Will you stop with the Sgt. Heis shit. Fuck, call me Brian or just Heis." Delta tries to lighten the mood for the two friends.

Jackson lightly chuckles, which he could feel ease his tension, "Fuckin Brian? Heis? Nope I don't like that at all. You will always be Sgt. Heis to me."

"Whatever the fuck you want, then, brother." Delta sighs to himself. "Fucking Culpepper, that's crazy. I know we all disappeared after we got back, but Culpepper took it to another level. It'll be good to see him again. Him, James, and Parks always in that little three-man fucking element that Parks always put up on point," he continues half-heartedly.

"That fucker did lead from the front, literally. Not very tactically sound," Jackson notes about their squad leader and the patrols they embarked on. He leans back on the cheap hotel bed, trying not think about the nastiness of the sheets he must be laying on.

"Yeah, he fucking did, much to my dismay sometimes." Delta starts to smile slightly at the memory. So it begins, *the memories*, he curses to himself. Jackson gives a huff of humor. "Remember that patrol with HET team, when Sgt. Parks was on point and fell in the shit canal. Goddamn he was not happy."

Delta reflects solemnly, awash in the interior glow of the instrument panel of the rental vehicle. "No, Parks sure the fuck was not."

A pause of silence, both men remembering that night for the first time in decades. "Hey, Sgt. Heis, it'll be good to see you. I fuckin wish it was under different circumstances. Does the thought haunt you yet?" Jackson suddenly dreading that he asked the question; he knows his former team leader understood exactly what he was asking.

"Every fucking minute, brother," Delta responds flatly.

Jackson suddenly feels very tired, the guilt beginning to weaken his mental fortitude. "Hey, Sgt. Heis, I'll see you in the mornin for breakfast?"

"Yeah, brother. Hey, Jackson, thank you for being here. You were always the levity of our squad; it will mean a lot to the guys you're here." Delta graciously thanks his old team member.

Jackson sighs a long exhaustive sigh, "No problem. It's goin to be fuckin brutal these next couple weeks for us. See you in the mornin."

"Yes, it is. See you soon, brother." Delta hits *End* on the touchscreen, the music suddenly coming back to life on the car speakers. He does not notice. Delta stares into the blackness ahead, knowing there is no light coming for him or the men of the 1st squad anytime soon.

CH. 18
1ST SQUAD COMES TO TOWN

Cooper wakes abruptly at the sound of the dreaded alarm on his phone, 0530. He groans, as all do this early, painfully moving his body to the edge of the bed, rubs his eyes and stretches his upper torso. He struggles to the bathroom, trying to get his muscles to wake up and follow his commands. Cooper does not recognize the man in the mirror. He had gotten slow by his standards, but he still tries to maintain a workout regime when his business allows. "What the fuck, move." he grumbles to the old man staring back, still muscular but not as fast he remembers. He turns on the shower, dreading what is in store for him and the rest of 1st Squad.

First, Cooper knows it will generally be awkward seeing all the guys again, some had not seen each other since the day Bravo Co. returned from Iraq. Second, the tragedy they must deal with lays before them and shows no end in sight. Cooper witnessed the news vans all over the city as he came in and is thankful Bgame had the foresight to reserve a block of rooms in the hotel for the Marines to use if they so choose. After the shower, Cooper quickly dresses in a black polo shirt, a pair of black slacks and black dress shoes. He adorns his tiny red and gold rank insignia on one of his collars and stares at himself in the mirror one more time, trying to garner the strength to head down to the lobby. Cooper does not know what to expect, but he knows the consensus in thought being a collective, *I should have been there.*

. . .

Culpepper, posted once on the Bravo Co. community page, *I will be there by morning*. He answered no messages or posts directed towards him. He knew everyone would ask where he has been and about his life. Culpepper disappeared for a reason and does not need to dig up his complicated past relationship with the Marines; he wants no friends; he wants his simple life and his family. That is all. He sits alone at a small table in the breakfast lobby of the hotel sipping coffee he had made himself from the free continental breakfast bar. Culpepper's massive frame dwarfing the small wooden table. The large Marine sees Copper exit the elevator; he smiles to himself a little bit. Cooper looks the same, a bit older, to the big man. He watches Cooper slowly make his way to the coffee vats and pour himself a cup. Culpepper stands, strides over to the vats in two quick steps and is immediately behind his friend.

Sensing a giant looming presence, Cooper quickly turns on his heels and finds himself staring at the huge chest of a mountain of a man. Cooper looks up, sees a wiry dark beard, long dark hair pulled into a ponytail surrounding the granite face of someone he knows he should recognize but does not; trying his hardest to remember this Sasquatch in front of him, he finally spits out, "Fuckin Culpepper?!"

"Yeah, man." Culpepper responds softly in his deep Louisiana drawl.

"Holy fuckin shit!" Cooper tries to hold his voice and excitement down.

He grabs hold of Culpepper in a big hug, trying to get both arms around the mountain, the big man gives Cooper a reluctant hug in return. Culpepper has not had an emotion for anyone except his family in two decades, but seeing Cooper brings that quiet brotherhood storming back. Never missing a beat, the squad will always be connected by their shared experience from that fateful night, no matter how much time passes.

They both release each other, head over to a table to sit and talk about what has brought them here all these years later. "How many others from the squad are here?" Culpepper asks Cooper quietly.

"Shit, brother, I'm pretty damn sure all of us are here from 1st. I think we all filtered in at various points throughout the night. I know Bgame has the final tally of who's here. Doherty's mom and James' wife are also here in the hotel somewhere. This is goin to be rough, man," Cooper explains, staring into his coffee cup and realizing how fast he is drinking the caffeinated beverage.

"Fuck." Culpepper rumbles, drinking his coffee as well, noticing he needs another refill already.

"Hey, brother, nothin we ain't used to." Cooper looks Culpepper in the eye and they both know what Cooper is speaking of.

Culpepper finishes his bland cup of coffee and asks, "Any word on Sgt. Parks?"

Looking about as if in a spy movie, Cooper tries to keep his voice down in the early morning hours of the lobby, and whispers, "Nothin yet. I've been checkin online and still nothin. All I know is he survived and was transported some-fuckin-where. Media still doesn't know his name yet but that will change soon and then the shitstorm will begin. Of course, there's all this bullshit about drugs, hired security, cartels; it was a fuckin reunion. That's all."

"I know, brother. A storm is comin." Culpepper growls, staring into his empty cup and then looking about the lobby.

Drinking the last bit of his cup, Cooper leans back in the uncomfortable plain dining chair. "You know the thought racin through my fuckin head, the same thought that kept me up last night."

"Don't fuckin say it," The large Marine pleads with Cooper quietly.

Cooper understands and pursues the conversation no further; they both sit in silence; it is only a silence the two men can appreciate. Cooper sees Perry exit the elevator; he lightly taps Culpepper on the arm; Culpepper follows Cooper's gaze. The two both stand, head towards Perry, who, upon seeing the two of them begins to tear up. Perry quickly closes the distance and wraps his powerful arms around them both and lets out an agonizing wail. The hotel clerk becomes alarmed immediately by the appearance of the three. Cooper looks in her direction to wave a hand of reassurance to calm her. The three former Marines embrace as Perry sobs into Culpepper's massive chest and then down onto Cooper's shoulder. Yet the two men do not push Perry away or feel uncomfortable, despite differing backgrounds. The experience of serving together has provided that bond, which will never be uncomfortable or go unrecognized.

Culpepper and Cooper support their fellow brother in arms as he grieves.

Perry gathers himself and breaks the embrace, wiping away the tears streaming down his face with his rough hands. "Culpepper what the fuck, Devil? You can't give me a call or email in all these years. I love you, brother." Perry hugs Culpepper again. He turns and grabs Cooper, hugging him once more as well. "I love ya, brother." Perry tears up some more.

Cooper is astonished at the man before him. This Perry before him looks tired but still has that same fire and passion that he remembers. "I love you too, Devil," he replies softly.

"I can't believe this. I just can't," Perry continues with a hand on each of their shoulders for stability. "I should have been—"

"I'm goin to fuckin stop you right there, brother." Culpepper puts his large, calloused hand on Perry's chest affectionately. "None of us are goin down that road, you hear me? Or I will walk. That shit will do us no goddamn good right now."

Perry, understanding the coldness in Culpepper's eyes, relents and agrees. "You're right, big fella, that shit does us no good. I fuckin couldn't sleep a wink. You two?"

Culpepper shakes his head, looking back towards the coffee maker. "Nah man, not at all. I keep rememberin fuckin Iraq and all of us. That's all that flashed before my mind all fuckin night, brother."

"Fuck, me too, Devil. I just fuckin talked to Doherty too, right before he came up here. He was excited man, he fuckin was…." Perry breaks down again. Doherty and Perry had their struggles upon returning, not unlike thousands of other Marine infantrymen, but they had their struggles together. Drugs, alcohol, loss of everything, the shame of loved ones; they did most of it together. Tragically the two of them lost a close friend and a fellow *Grunt* with 2nd Platoon, Cpl. William Lensing, dramatically too soon. All of Bravo Co. loved Lensing, he could make anyone laugh by being his normal common-sense self. Lensing's shock passing was the first of Bravo's and soul-crushing for all the Marines, especially Doherty. Doherty gathered the strength to become a better human being, to find that purpose in life again, to find that love, and Perry knew he lost the one person who could guide him through his own personal hell. The tears keep falling.

The Last Letter

All three stand in comfortable silence. No words need be said, all are reflecting on various images of their time in 1st Squad together. "Alright, brother, let's get you some coffee." Cooper guides Perry over to the coffee vats.

"Thanks, Devil. I fuckin need some, had a few drinks to try and sleep but of course, that didn't work, so I stopped that shit. But I still get a fuckin hangover. Must be from the fuckin years of hammerin away at the bottle. Shit, none of us are sleepin for a while." Perry gently pours himself a coffee as he rambles on, trying to avoid the reason all of 1st is in Clear Creek.

"I reckon we won't be," Culpepper offers, staring out the window towards the parking lot, noticing the news vans he did not see the night before. He lets out an audible groan. The large Marine does not want the attention. Culpepper came to escort his fallen brothers home, as a warrior should be. He did not have the time to deal with the coverage or the negativity.

The massive Marine is starting to get agitated, and Cooper, sensing the big man's unease, puts his hands up on Culpepper's large shoulder. "Easy big fella, none of us want to deal with that shit. Don't worry, we're here to get our fallen and take them home. Fuck the rest of the world."

"Thanks, Cooper," Culpepper responds, looking back over his shoulder and watches as Jackson exits the elevator and heads in their direction with a somber look about him.

Jackson's usually beaming smile is vacant from his smooth face. He immediately runs up to Culpepper and gives him a huge embrace, not letting go. Almost the same height, Culpepper is in no rush to break the embrace.

"Man, fuckin Culpepper. Holy shit, it's so good to see you here. It will mean everythin to the guys you came out of the shadows, shithead." Jackson states, his pronounced Southern drawl adding to his outward charisma.

Culpepper responds with an affectionate rumble of his deep voice. "Nothin would have kept me, brother."

The hotel clerk is getting more nervous as more grizzled Grunts start to fill the breakfast lobby. Cooper again sensing her unease, waves and smiles to reassure her again that everything is fine.

Jackson following Cooper's gaze. "Any more of us come down here and the cops will be here."

"Shit ain't nothing we ain't used to, brother." Cooper walks up to Jackson and gives him a heartfelt hug.

"Yeah well, a bunch of old hardasses beating the shit out of local PD for harassin us, will not make for good headlines alongside our fallen brothers," Jackson wearily eyeing the hotel clerk but politely waving. His tailored black suit adorned with mini-ribbons from his service in the Marines, decorates his left jacket breast pocket.

"Fuck all that craziness. Damn you look good, Devil." Cooper tries his best to get Jackson back on point. Jackson relents and makes his way to Perry. Jackson, twenty years ago, only tolerated Perry, but the two have grown close over the subsequent years. They were perfect teammates under Delta, and they formed an undeniable bond by being a part of 1st team, along with the ever-smiling Doherty.

Perry turns to Jackson, immediately the tears form, and he grabs hold of Jackson and buries his face in the taller Marine's chest. "I'm so fuckin glad to see you, brother." Perry tightens his arms around Jackson in painful remorse.

Jackson tries to remember quickly if Perry and he ever had an argument. They did not. The two performed together in the most extreme of conditions and they performed beautifully as part of a fire team. True Marine rifle squads are a destructive machine if employed and led properly; this is why the Marine Infantry are regarded as the true sledgehammers of every major American war. Not one combat Veteran will deny Marine infantry are a different breed. The unheralded dirty, miserable, angry *Grunts* of battle. "You here to escort Doherty home?" Jackson asks, already knowing the answer.

"Of course. I'm so glad to see ya here, man. Thank you for comin. I didn't want to be the only one. I knew that wouldn't fuckin happen," Perry rattles off. sipping his coffee and then steps aside so the nervous early morning guests can make their own cup. They are news crewmembers from what he can tell, judging from the identification badges hanging from lanyards around their necks. "Fuckin hyenas," he grumbles audibly for the gathering civilians to hear.

"Sgt. Heis is here as well. So, we have our fire team to escort Doherty home; Doherty will be honored," Jackson gloomily replies, taking a sip of the water bottle he picked up next to the coffee.

Perry nods up to Jackson with somber acknowledgment, "Fuck, I've not seen Sgt. Heisinger since we got back or... shit, even talked to him. I know he doesn't have social media, but fuck, I don't even have his email."

"You hear any word on Sgt. Parks?" Jackson asks quickly, regretting the question immediately.

Perry begins to feel that emotional constriction in his throat, "No, the news doesn't know who survived. I don't even know where the fuck he is. I hate this shit." Perry starts to feel agitated, grabs a whiskey shooter from his pocket and dumps it into his coffee.

Jackson nods to Perry cautiously, "Fuck, you got another one of those?" he asks, pointing to Perry's whiskey bottle.

"Sure, Devil." He pulls another from his vest pocket, handing it to Jackson.

Jackson grabs the whiskey, opens the tiny cap, and downs the tiny bottle in a gulp. "Thank you. I needed that shit." Jackson closes his eyes, relishing the warmth of the dark liquid.

The elevator doors open once again, Cooper looks up from his conversation with Culpepper and recognizes his fire team leader, Morales and his fellow team member, Thomas, step from behind the elevator doors. Both men have slight smiles from their reunion from the short ride down. Cooper walks over to meet his fellow brothers in arms.

"Oh shit, Devil!" Thomas whispers as he sees Cooper walk over to greet them. They embrace, again Cooper being the shorter man puts his head into Thomas's chest and both let out an exhale of burdened air.

Cooper turns to Morales and embraces him as well. "Fuck it's good to see you, brother. Morales, you look as pretty as ever. Is Del Vecchio here?" he asks, referring to the final member of their fire team.

Morales scoffs at Cooper's playful remark, "Fuck you. You look good too, brother. Yeah, he's still in his room getting ready. How you been with this shit?" he asks his old troop, genuinely concerned.

"Man, not good. Fuck after all the shit we been through for this to fuckin happen. I just fuckin can't comprehend it, you know?" Cooper looks up at Morales as the two step back to head to the breakfast area.

SSgt. Jacob Parkinson

The three continue to walk towards the coffee nook. "I know, man. Shit is terrible. The guilt... that's eating me up," Morales shares with the other two members of his old fire team.

"I didn't sleep at all. Thomas?" Cooper asks, making another cup of coffee.

"No, not much. Just a fucked-up situation all around. None of us know what to do." Thomas tries to make sense of the tragedy for his own sanity. He stops suddenly, a shocked expression plasters his stubbled face. "Holy shit, is that Culpepper?" Thomas asks excitedly, not believing what he is sees.

Cooper lets out a slight chuckle, "Yeah, man. It's Culpepper. Big-ass motherfucker that he still is." Like the rest of the squad, Thomas thought Culpepper disappeared and became a ghost of Bravo Co. only to be talked about in whispers. The members of 1st Squad always tried to locate him but to no avail, as Culpepper had done by design.

The Marines meet up with Culpepper by the fireplace in the center of the lobby. Each takes their turn smiling and embracing, turning back time twenty years. "You look great Culpepper. It's damn good to see you finally after all these years. You still considered UA?" Thomas chides the large Marine about his disappearance upon returning from Iraq.

Culpepper, never one for a sense of humor does not crack a smile at his former squad mate's attempt at comedy. "No, squared away. Thomas, it's hard to recognize you without Sgt. Parks on your ass, screaming at you for some absent-minded bullshit." He counters, taking his own shot at his old squad mate.

"Touché. Nice one," Thomas replies with a slight sheepish grin. The men pause at the memory of one instance or another of Sgt. Parks yelling at Thomas for something, each wanting to bring up an instance but afraid of the emotion it carries; they fear the guilt of laughing.

Cooper, breaking the still silence of the group, starts to smile, recalling, "Fuck, you remember that time during the company VCP our squad was REACT[43] and Thomas lost his AT-4."

The group freezes, afraid to smile or laugh at the hilarity of the memory. "Oh shit, I thought Sgt. Parks was going to kill Thomas and me. That was the only time I really saw Sgt. Parks lose his shit to the point of actual rage."

---
[43] Reactionary Force

Morales looks down, trying to hide the smile. "Thanks a lot, dickhead, way to fuck over your team leader." Morales turns to Thomas to chide him, slapping him on the shoulder.

"How the fuck do you lose an AT-4?" Culpepper continues the dry humor at Thomas's expense.

Thomas instantly regrets giving Culpepper a hard time, earlier, "Hey, man, I put the damn thing in the hummer; then we rolled out *zero dark thirty* for base and I fuckin forgot it, okay? You happy, assholes?"

"What if that AT-4 had been used against us a few days later when our squad got ambushed and we find a discarded tube like we did that SA-7 Grail launcher? How would you feel then?" Cooper joins in on the humor of his former team member's mistake.

"I know, I know, I know. I fucked up," Thomas admits, giving up in the battle of unrelenting humor at his peril.

Morales offers a saving grace for the former rifleman, "You two leave my troop alone. We found the fucking thing." Morales comes to Thomas's defense in a condescending tone. "Shit that night, Sgt. Parks unloaded on Sgt. Heis and me; Heis for not listening accurately to his command covering the exfil of Bravo back to base and myself for not having accountability for Thomas's ass… again. Thank you for that, dick." He gives Thomas another light slap on the back.

Culpepper notices the elevator open and out steps Sgt. Heis; his demeanor portrays the nickname he was given, *Delta* bestowed the name by Parks, due to the fact Sgt. Heisinger would attach all the high-speed gear to his flak jacket and legs as he could. The box of gear Parks received from a tactical supply company from the US he had written a complaint letter to about defective magazine pouches. Parks let Heisinger have it all, once attached he looked like a *Delta Force* operator during his tour in Iraq. The "*Delta*" moniker stuck ever since.

Delta standing about 5'9" is the average height of a Marine, but he carries himself with a quiet stoicism that never portrays the consummate warrior within. He recognizes the group, even the mysterious Culpepper; he spots Perry and Jackson off by the fireplace, both notice him, and start making their way over. All three converge, give each other hugs, and try to keep Perry from crying too much.

"What the fuck are we goin to do, Sgt. Heis?" Perry blurts out, suddenly counting on his team leader once again.

"First, we're going to escort Doherty; our teammate, our friend and our brother, home." Delta replies steadfastly.

Perry, gathering his bearings and resolve answers, "Roger that, Sgt. Heis."

"Fuck, it's good to see you both but not like this. Jackson, what're you thinking, brother?" Delta asks concerned for his team once again, almost as if twenty years never went by.

The taller Marine shakes his head in defeat, "Man, Sgt. Heis, shit is fucked up. I don't know what to think. I'm in shock, I guess, we all are. I just know it will get worse and not better any time soon. If you fellas need to talk and get this shit out, come talk to me. I'm fuckin serious." Jackson states, scanning the room, getting agitated at the amount of people flooding the breakfast lobby, most with name placards hanging from their necks.

"Thanks, man. I know you're a doctor of psych now. You would probably be the only damn doctor I talk to, brother. I'm just glad you two made it up here to help. I couldn't do this alone, no fucking way," Delta replies. He, too, surveys the increasing amount of people gathering in the lobby as daylight starts to break on the horizon.

Jackson looks down at his former team leader, his eyes flashing with intensity. "No fuckin way we were goin to let that happen, Sgt. Heis."

"Delta or Brian, please." Delta tries to get his two fellow warriors to drop his rank.

"Brian!?" Perry exclaims. "Fuck that. No, you will always be Sgt. Heis to us two." Perry puts his arm up on Jackson's shoulder. "And *Delta* is what Sgt. Parks called you. That was his name for you."

Delta reflects on what led to his nickname in the first place. "Fucking Parks."

"Fuckin Sgt. Parks," Jackson echoes; he then notices the stairwell doors open, and a short, compact, stone-faced individual exits through the steel door. He is dressed in all custom fit black attire. Jackson instantly recognizes him as the shortest and youngest member of their squad, but what astonishes Jackson is the appearance of Del Vecchio, he still looks nineteen years old.

The Last Letter

"Oh shit, look who it is, *Mr. IED* himself."

The other two follow Jackson's gaze towards the individual making his way to the group surrounding Culpepper. The former Marines begin to embrace each other and exchange greetings once again. Jackson quickly grabs his phone and takes a picture of the rarity of them all together. Delta immediately sees what Jackson's attention is drawn to: Culpepper, the ox of a Marine and Del Vecchio the small honey badger of a Marine, have embraced. Del Vecchio standing well below Culpepper's chest, made for a comical sight.

The smaller Marine, sensing he is the subject of Jackson's laughter, gives him the middle finger with a slight smile, making his way to Jackson. The two embrace, same comical situation due to Jackson's height as well. More pictures ensue from the rest of 1st Squad. "How the fuck are you?" Del Vecchio asks.

"Shit could be better. Glad you're here, brother." Jackson bounces back to the gloom of the situation.

Del Vecchio quickly offers, realizing it too late., "It was a stupid question. I have no clue what to say in this situation. It's all just a complete shock, brother."

Jackson nods in agreement, "Why the fuck did you come down the stairs?" he asks, pointing to the stairwell.

"Fucking elevators are packed with news crews. I'm not dealing with that shit," Del Vecchio states, coldly, looking about the now-crowded lobby.

Following the gaze of the other two, Delta, too, starts to become uneasy.

"I don't blame you. It's getting packed in here. I think it's time we move our gathering to a different POS[44]." Delta offers, giving Del Vecchio a hug. The rest of the squad naturally gather around Delta, per instinct. Perry hugs everyone he has not yet, in the only way Perry knows how to hug—big. The men smile at various points and embrace one another.

The gathering of placard wearing strangers in the lobby begin to take notice of the rough group of men, all dressed in some form of black, some adorned with miniature medals, others with rank insignia. But to all gathered in the lobby, the men were Marines and that meant news. One of the men from a group of placard-wearers makes his way towards the broken, embracing, men of 1st Squad.

---
[44] Position

Culpepper spots the knit-vest-wearing weasel gather his courage to approach the group. The massive Marine moves quickly to confront the shorter man, lowers his clenched iron jaw to be eye level with the placard-wearer, "Walk away," Culpepper snarls, his menacing tone calm but filled with approaching violence, his eyes flashing impending doom. The once self-thought courageous news crew stumbles backward, the coffee and the smile he is holding disappearing into his knit vest. "We definitely need to move," Culpepper continues angrily, rejoining the group, watching the buzzards of the news gather ever closer.

"I think we just need Bgame to join us, and he'll explain what's next from what we communicated last night. I know that Viking motherfucker has been goin nonstop since he got here." Cooper anxiously eyes the crowd after Culpepper's interaction with the news member. More will get the courage to ask questions, which will not go well at all, for civilian and Veteran alike.

Bgame steps out of the elevator; he is instantly recognizable to the squad. The Viking knew all these Marines of 1st Squad and loved every damn one of them as if they were his own squad; James eventually became one of his SAW gunners after the night outside of Fallujah. Bgame hurriedly walks over to the group and puts up his hand to silence them.

"Stop. No questions. Everyone follow me outside, and then we're going somewhere to talk," he growls unhappily, pushing past the group. Bgame does not want to get caught up in the emotions of the moment seeing everyone here, together, one squad again. He begins to choke up at the thought of Doherty, James and Parks. This right here was the only moment Sgt. Parks wanted, 1st Squad together one final time. *Motherfucker!* He screams internally.

The group of bygone warriors follows the red-bearded *Viking* to his rental truck outside the hotel. All anxious for any news that he may have regarding their fallen brothers. To the men gathered around him, Bgame looks destroyed, the mood is set for the impending conversation. "Okay, listen up. No hugs and bullshit until we get where we're goin. Pile into as few vehicles as possible and I want you to follow me. I can fit two more, but we will not be talking the whole trip. It won't be fuckin fair to anyone else. Right now, we are headin to see someone who will fill you in on the facts better than I can,

The Last Letter

and not the bullshit reported in the news. I mean all news, not one fuckin station is reportin shit right. She was a Marine, and she served a tour in Afghanistan. Has a combat action ribbon and a bronze star; she has seen some shit, so we will listen. Yut?"

"Yut," all respond in unison softly. Which piqued the interest of some gathering news crews outside the hotel.

Del Vecchio spots the onlookers. "Bgame, I think it's time we head out."

"I concur. Y'all divvy up and follow me. "We roll in four mikes," Bgame responds, looking past the group at the vulturing onlookers, some already taking photos in case it is a newsworthy moment. 1st Squad's anger becomes a collective wave.

The group split systematically. Perry and Jackson ride with Delta in his rental sedan. Thomas, Del Vecchio, go with Morales in his rental truck. Cooper and Culpepper join Bgame in his F-150 rental. Immediately the three vehicles are moving as one unit, a maneuver that is second nature from countless convoy operations and mounted patrols they spent together in Iraq. Delta's vehicle brings up the rear of the formation, constantly checking if they are being followed by the vultures of news crews from the hotel. He sees they are not, yet Perry and Jackson both keep constant watch of their six. No one says a word in any of the vehicles. It is an understood stillness as they navigate the Idaho landscape. The lush scenery passing them by, the *I should have been there*, echoes through the minds of the Marines as the silence remains unbroken.

...

It is a crisp, warm, fall Idaho morning. Forestry Special Agent Alexander grabs her coffee, dropping a splash of Jack Daniels into mix with the Irish cream. The forestry agent wants nothing more than to go back to bed, with her kids off to school and wake in a couple of hours. She knows that is an impossibility. They are coming, and she expects all of them will want true answers. They are going to be angry and want justice, and she sympathizes with their plight. Her job is to reassure them, she will do everything in her authority to see that justice is rendered. What she does not want is a bunch of *Grunts* running around her crime scene looking for their own answers and payback.

They will be here soon; she heads back inside from her porch overlooking the expansive meadow running off her gravel drive before disappearing into the forest a half a mile away. She can picture no better place to be or raise her children, although they do not see it that way. Her son accuses her of hiding, and her daughter is tired of paying for her mother's demons that they will never know anything about. Alexander does not blame her beautiful children because they are right. She is hiding since the passing of her love; she hates the world without their father. The forestry agent's phone buzzes with a notification that someone is at her front gate, she quickly checks the app and turns on the video feed. She recognizes the Viking staring back at her through the camera. "The two cars behind you?" Alexander asks pointedly.

"Yes, ma'am, they're 1st Squad, all of them." Bgame responds respectfully. "Roger that," Alexander replies as she finishes putting on her uniform and sidearm. She pushes the *open* button on her phone app to allow 1st Squad entrance to her property. Grabbing her mug of coffee, she heads back out onto her expansive porch and watches as the vehicles make their way up the dirt road of her drive. The three vehicles park side by side and the men all start to clamor out of the rentals. The former Marines groan upon exiting the vehicles and look quizzically at the cabin of Agent Alexander. It is an exquisitely large log cabin, which all the men find suitable for a forestry agent. She notices their expressions grief, anger; she hopes she can bring some comfort to these exhausted men.

Alexander begins to head down the steps of her large wood porch, noticing the size and height of most of the men, with exception of the two tall ones, most of the men were shorter than she expected. She quickly goes to greet the remnants of 1st Squad as they congregate on the gravel drive.

"Fellas, this is Forestry Special Agent Alexander, she is also Cpl. Alexander with a combat tour. Yut?" Bgame introduces Alexander to the group.

"Yut," all reply in a soft respectful unison.

"Thank you, gentlemen, and Bgame for the introduction. Please come inside and have some coffee, whiskey, or beer. Yeah, I know it's fucking early, but you men look like shit," Alexander offers with quiet humor.

Again, a humbled reply in unison from 1st, "Thank you, ma'am."

"Listen, if you need to smoke, feel free. Just leave no butts behind or I will have your ass," the forestry agent offers with a tender smile. A couple of men look at each other and peel off to go smoke their cigars. The rest head inside with the forestry agent as she holds the door open for the men to gather in the massive cabin's living room.

"This is beautiful," Morales offers, entering the beautifully rustic living space.

"Thank you. Coffee's here. Hot water if you want tea; beer is in the fridge and whiskey is next to the coffee," Alexander offers while putting out the rest of the beverages for the group. "Would you like some?" she turns, asking Del Vecchio as he walks over to the hot water and tea supplies that the agent has graciously laid out upon her large oak table.

Del Vecchio smiles shyly, "What is it? Del Vecchio, by the way." He extends his hand graciously to his host.

"'I thought you would be bigger,'" Alexander responds with a smile, quoting the movie *Roadhouse* with Patrick Swayze, shaking Del Vecchio's hand. Her quick wit sharpened once she married a Marine EOD specialist and his off-the-wall, beloved humor.

"'*Gee, I never heard that before,*'" Del Vecchio responds sheepishly with the appropriate quote from the same movie in return. It is a joke Del Vecchio has heard a million times before, yet today he does not mind. He needs some levity at the moment.

Special Agent Alexander smiles at the former Marine's response and answers his previous question, "Earl Grey or Green Tea. It will help relax the nerves."

"Absolutely. Thank you." Del Vecchio offers up his cup to the forestry agent.

Morales approaches the both of them and puts his arm on Del Vecchio's steel-like shoulders. "I see you've met, *Mr. IED*. "May I try some of that, ma'am?" Morales asks politely of the special agent.

"Of course. *Mr. IED*?" Alexander asks of Del Vecchio's nickname, handing Morales a honey packet for his hot tea. Bgame joins the group as he, too, tries a hot cup of tea to calm his nerves after nonstop pain, guilt, and remorse.

Del Vecchio begins to feel on the spot, futilely tries to steer the conversation in another direction, "It's nothing, and Sgt. Parks made that shit up for me later on after we got back and never told me."

"What do you mean fuckin nothin? Shit, you got combat decorated for that day." Bgame makes sure to keep the topic of conversation on Del Vecchio's achievements, the agent now very much intrigued with the story.

"I only got decorated because Sgt. Parks kept fighting to get some of the squad decorated upon our return. Our *Dickless* platoon commander burned the original recommendations Sgt. Parks wrote up for us after the Fallujah offensive, right in front of all of us. You remember that shit, Cooper?" Del Vecchio tries again to steer the conversation away from himself.

"Yeah, man, shit was fucked up. Burned the recommendations in a firepit and made all of 1st Squad watch. He had that evil fuckin grin on his face. I hate that motherfucker. Remember that fucking horrible evil childlike grin? Fuckin *Chucky*." Cooper responds angrily, gritting his teeth, comparing his platoon commander to the evil doll of the horror films. "Pardon my language, ma'am."

Alexander almost spits out her coffee, "I don't give a fuck." The agent smiles to ease Cooper's worry at offending her.

"We all hate that motherfucker," Bgame snarls, taking another sip of the hot tea.

"I would love to hear the story on *Mr. IED* here, before we begin my debrief," Alexander asks while pointing her coffee cup in the direction of Del Vecchio.

"Shit," Del Vecchio mutters under his breath knowing he cannot escape the past this time. "It really is nothing." Again, he tries to downplay his decoration adorned to his left breast suit pocket.

Morales begins with a little too much excitement, it has been ages since he has told one of his Iraq tales. "Okay, I'll keep it short because the extended story is an epic tale. Bgame was there for this, but his squad was on the right flank."

"Yep. Having our own troubles." The Viking stares out the bay window, spotting to the men gathered smoking cigars, they seem to be smiling at the same shared memories.

The Last Letter

Morales continues. "1st Squad had just got hit with an ambush and were clearing houses down this block. Sgt. Parks gets a bullshit command to withdraw and to his anger, is ordered back to the road. I won't get into all of what 1st Squad found clearing those fucking houses—"

"Crazy shit," Bgame jumps in to add credence to Morales's tale of action. "We kept hearing Parks on the piece of shit radios, *'we found this, we found that.'*"

"It was fucking crazy shit. So, Sgt. Parks has 1st Squad get online on the left flank of *MSR Michigan*, I believe it's called." Morales looks to Del Vecchio, who does not answer, trying not to encourage the tale.

Cooper answers for the shy Marine, "Yeah, man, it was *Michigan*." Referring the main supply route that ran through the Anbar province of Iraq.

Morales drinks more of the tea and trying to remember, "We start sweeping for IEDs and it seemed like every other step we took Del Vecchio would halt the squad, find some wires or the trigger source amongst the brush and buildings. Sgt. Parks would verify, trace the wires to the buried IEDs on the road and call it in. Since EOD was scarce, Sgt. Parks cleared the area of all the men, and then the fucker cut the wires. Crazy shit."

Jackson approaches with a mischievous smile, sipping his coffee with a bit of *Captain's* splashed in the warm beverage. "No shit we cleared the area each time he cut those damn wires. I was fuckin right there on the road every time Mr. IED here, found another set of wires or trigger source, I had to pick up that fuckin SAW and run my ass to safety each damn time, fuckers. Remember that, Sgt. Heis?" He pats Del Vecchio on the shoulder towering over the former Marine, looking past his shorter friend to his team leader entering the room.

Delta comes in from outside, after taking a lone walk along the beautiful property. He catches the end of the conversation and not missing a beat, adds, "I do remember you bitching every time, *'Y'all runnin a motherfucker to death today.'*"

The group break out into a slight relief of laughter, even Del Vecchio, who is the subject of the tale, smiles a bit. "Shit, how many IEDs did 1st find that day? Twenty?" Jackson reminiscing on grabbing the SAW every time they moved to perceived safety.

"Fuck, I don't know. It was a lot. What did your award say Del Vecchio?" Morales putting the smaller Marine on the spot again.

"I don't remember," Del Vecchio avoids shyly.

Bgame drinks some more of the hot tea, not feelin the relaxation he usually feels. "James always said it was something like sixteen IEDs that day, whenever we went out and had a few."

"I don't think it was that many," Delta says with a slight chuckle. "Sgt. Parks always said he stopped counting at ten, so he stuck with that number. Fucking nuts. So, you see, Special Agent, this is but one experience of many we have shared."

"Yut. That was a long fuckin day for sure. Man, fuck *Dickless*." Jackson angrily states.

Delta puts his hand up on Jackson's shoulder, "Easy Devil, we do not say his name, not today."

"Well, the moral of the story is, Del Vecchio can find an IED anywhere. We will call it twelve for our purposes today. Justly awarded and damn proud of him." Morales proudly wraps up the story of his young troop.

"I love it." Alexander flashes a genuine smile. It has been a long time since she felt comfortable in a group, this being a special moment.

"They definitely were not bright thick red wires like in the fucking movies, which is for sure. So, for Del Vecchio to spot them, truly amazing," Delta points out candidly.

"No, they were not red. Copper, very thin." Del Vecchio quietly adds sipping his tea rapidly.

Delta nods. "Comm wire."

Bgame scoffs in a raspy half cough, "Yeah, Parks would always get pissed when he was drinkin and bring up *The Hurt Locker* and their stupid thick red wires. *'Where the fuck were those wires for me!'* he would yell all fucked up."

The mood of the group starts to shift back to the grim situation that is at hand. "Special Agent, you served a tour in Afghanistan with the Marines?" Jackson asks, refilling his coffee with another splash of rum the forestry agent provided the former Marines.

Alexander's smile fades, hit with the sudden reminder of her own combat tour. Bgame, noticing the tension shift, slightly shakes his head towards Jackson, silently telling him, *man, not a good question*.

"Yes. Motor T. I drove for both supply and EOD runs." Her distance beginning to grow, the mental wall she has built starting to go back to its guarded position.

Delta tries to steer the conversation in a lighter direction, "No wall of shame, Special Agent, like the rest of us have?"

"Nope, no wall of shame. All my Marine shit is in boxes." Alexander suddenly feels distant again.

Bgame notices the shift in the forestry agent's demeanor and tries to refocus the group. "Special Agent, shall I gather everyone for your SITREP?" He asks, using Marine terminology to get the group in the right mindset for the upcoming brief.

"Yes, thank you," Alexander replies, snapping out of her fog. She powerfully pushes back on those emerging images into the dark recesses of her mind by grinding her teeth forcibly. *One day, but today is not that day*, she thinks to herself. "Gather the troops in the living room and I'll be along momentarily." She heads towards her kitchen, knowing exactly what she needs. In the kitchen she grabs the vodka from the freezer, opens the bottle and gulps down four huge swallows of the ice-cold liquid. The burning cold followed by the warm feeling in her bloodstream, provides instant relief from the torment that was sure to engulf her, had Bgame not changed the subject. Alexander collects her thoughts, wipes the splash of vodka from her cheek and readies herself for the briefing to follow.

The men file in from outside, the rest come over from the coffee area set up in the dining room. All eager to hear the details from the forestry agent's SITREP. "Please have a seat wherever you can get comfortable; the news will not be good," Alexander suggests as she enters her living room to stand before the massive fireplace, the mantel littered with photographs of her husband in his blues and from his various combat tours. The men shuffle past, eyeing the collection of framed images, trying to find room to ready themselves.

"Listen, I am going to share what I can. Sgt. Bgame has been briefed of this when we met yesterday. It will be discomforting. There will be no solace here. I'm sorry, men." Alexander begins carefully, trying not reveal more than she should. "At zero dark thirty, forty-eight hours ago from the one you call, James, I received a distress call about a crashed plane and the subsequent death of a crew member. I responded for them not touch anything and to stay put, I will be there as soon as I can with a helo. He gave me a *'roger that'* and said he would call the sheriff as well. He did, call records confirm. My pilot and I reached the destination almost an hour after that initial phone call."

To the special agent's surprise, every Marine in the room has a notepad of some sort and all are frantically writing the details she has relayed. Alexander continues, "We were the first on scene, no sheriff. We encountered no resistance or combatants. My partner and I found your men and immediately checked for vitals. There were none, initially. Sgt. Parks was eventually to be discovered with a pulse by a medic later; he was immediately CAS-EVACd[45] out of the area. His known location, classified. I do not know. If I find out, I'll contact Bgame; he's authorized, and he can disseminate the information as he sees fit."

"Ma'am, if I may, can you also share all info with Delta, here? He is Sgt. Parks' 2nd." Bgame politely asks of the forestry agent, not wanting to carry this burden alone, knowing Sgt. Heisinger should be involved in all phases going forward. Delta standing in the back looks up from his notepad, with a distant stare as if he is figuring out the squads next two moves, nods with gratitude towards the agent.

"Of course. Roger that." Alexander perfectly understands the chain of command in a Marine unit. "Here are the facts as I know them, to put this in order for you men. Your friends witnessed a small plane crash, went to investigate, encountered a lone gunman, the gunman opened fire, your Marines put him down." To the man in the room, all subconsciously want to growl in unison or shout, *yut*, but all refrain. The forestry agent continues, adjusting her leg holster, due to her constant pacing, "They then encountered an armed unit apparently following the flight path of the crashed aircraft. A firefight ensued. James, Doherty, and Parks all fought like true infantry Marines. Everyone here

---

[45] Casualty Evacuation

should hold that in regard. James and Doherty were spared the physical damage; Sgt. Parks took major physical trauma before he was eventually executed like the other two."

Every Marine in the room shudders at the harshness of her last statement; Alexander finishes her coffee, now wanting more of the spiked beverage, but she continues on, "James and Doherty's bodies will be released from the coroner's office at 1000 today. James' wife Jocelyn is here and at the medical examiners office already. Doherty's mother has been notified; Bgame and Delta, I will meet with you after this to discuss those arrangements for Doherty's release."

"Roger that, Special Agent." Both Delta and Bgame give her the proper respect in their unified response.

Alexander cracks a slight appreciative smile, "Do not listen to the *Crying River Network* or *JaKL News*, your friends are not involved with drugs, cartels, or hired security. You already know this. Drugs were found on scene, not with your men. This is something else and the FEDs are taking the investigation over from this point. I do not know who—DEA, FBI, Homeland Security. I am not in the need to know. I'm a uniformed witness at this point. If you have questions, I will try and answer as much as I can. Understood?" she offers sympathetically.

All nod slowly, the gravity of the crisis now trying to crush the very last of their resolve, no one wants to be the one to ask the first question. Delta breaks his angered silence, "How many aggressors, do you think there were, Special Agent?" Delta's mind immediately goes to the tactics of the situation.

"Alexander, please," she adds, hoping to make the room less formal. "I did not get a chance to walk the entire scene before I was asked to politely leave, but by my initial examination, more than a Marine rifle squad worth of men. I will not be allowed back to the crime scene so that is all I can offer." Alexander tells the men, a collective groan from the group at the number of armed assailants Doherty, James, and Parks may have faced.

"What type of weapons did the enemy have, Agent?" Perry asks, gripping the back of the couch directly behind Cooper, his knuckles cracking the calloused dry skin.

Alexander debates quickly but decides to proceed, "Small arms, judging from shell casings I found. 5.56, 7.62 automatic weapons, 203s, concussive grenades. They were well prepared and well equipped." She appreciates the respect the men show by the continued use of her title. It brings back emotions she did not realize she still had regarding her hesitant past in the Marines.

"Special Agent, you said drugs. What does that mean and how does that impact our cause going forward?" Cooper asks, feeling the tension from Perry behind him, gripping the couch.

"Yes, we found large quantities of fentanyl, methamphetamines, opioids strewn about the scene. This is all information that I can tell you. That amount of drugs does not warrant the response in nature by the armed team that engaged your fellow Marines. It does not make any sense. We have our problems of armed militiamen running drugs through the woods here but nothing of this nature of armament. Again, I will disseminate all relevant information through Delta and Bgame here." She motions to the two ageing Marines, frantically taking notes. "I'm here to help you men receive the justice that is warranted, do not, and I repeat do not go looking for it on your own. I don't need you trapsing around my woods on some vengeance tour, understood?" Special Agent Alexander orders through gritted teeth, hoping to make her point land.

The remnants of 1st Squad understand perfectly and respond in kind, with a sense of finality, "Yut."

Culpepper speaks up from the shadow of a bookcase against the back wall opposite the fireplace. "Justice is on its' way, Special Agent, of that you can be assured." The room gets tense, Culpepper's eyes go cold, his body flexes under his black suit, straining the very fabric ensemble.

She compassionately but sternly pleads with the group, "I know you men want retribution but let law enforcement handle everything. We do not need vigilante *Grunts* running around up here getting the local populace in a panic. They're on edge as it is, and they, too, want justice. These are good, quiet people up here. It's why the fuck we moved here in first place, so please just everyone breathe. Copy that?"

"Yut," all say in soft, detached unison.

The Last Letter

"I will coordinate with the coroner and Sheriff's Office on your behalf in regard to the escort of your fallen back home." Alexander resumes her post in front of the fireplace directing her question at Bgame.

"I have spoken with Doherty's mother. I will coordinate with Delta, as I assume your team will be escorting his body home?" Bgame asks of Doherty's former team leader.

Delta is suddenly flooded with remorse; the gravity of the situation becomes ever heavier. "Roger that. My team will be taking our fallen brother home. Along with any others from 1st that would like to join the escort."

Perry grabs hold of both Cooper's shoulders and begins to tense up. "Let's go outside, brother.", Cooper offers, tapping Perry on his hand to offer support.

"No, I'm okay. I need to push through this." Perry quickly wipes away a couple of tears falling down his cracked, dry, stubbled face. "What is the plan from here, Sgt. Heis?"

Delta, stunned by the suddenness of the question, quickly responds as the leader he is, "First off, since we know when James and Doherty are being released at 1000, we coordinate with the airlines about our escort status, then get our own flight arrangements made on the same flights. Bgame, I'm sure will contact Gunny Hoffman who will in turn coordinate with Bravo Co. and the families to lock on services. Right, Bgame?"

"Roger that, Devil." Bgame still carrying the images of the video in his mind, answers in a distant, forlorn tone.

Still thinking two steps ahead, Delta rattles off orders, "Jackson, Perry, Del Vecchio, and I will escort Doherty home to his mother and fiancée. Del Vecchio, making you a fourth with our team." Del Vecchio nods affirmatively. "Bgame, Morales, Cooper, Thomas and, of course, Culpepper will escort James home with his wife. Sound like a plan?" Delta tries to get things moving so the men will not dwell on the events past or future.

None of them gathered are ready for what lies ahead, but begrudgingly answer, "Roger that."

Thomas sits up in one of the living room chairs and asks the dreaded, "Sgt. Heis, man, we need to talk about the ghost that still lingers in this room. What about Sgt. Parks?"

The room goes eerily quiet as all realize that they did not want to acknowledge the situation of their old squad leader; James and Doherty's passing has them at the mental edge.

"Special Agent Alexander, what do you know of Sgt. Parks condition?" Jackson breaks the silence after what seemed an eternity.

"All I can tell you is that he survived the initial trauma, CASEVACd to Boise Medical, and from there airlifted to an undisclosed trauma center for now. I would assume if your squad leader would end up anywhere due to his Veteran status, it would be Walter Reed. I don't have that information for you or know his current medical status or prognosis. I'm sorry, Marines." Alexander offers, sensing the worry filling the room.

Bgame stands and heads over to the hot water carafe that Alexander has offered the men, begins to pour another cup, adds some bourbon, gulps down the beverage, and in a low subdued voice asks, "Special Agent, unfortunately you know what a firefight looks like, and you know this area. Please in your honest opinion what the fuck do you think happened up there?"

The men in the room begin to stare in respectful awe of the special agent's past accomplishments. They now have a deeper appreciation for this forestry agent taking her time to help a bunch of ageing *Grunts*. Alexander suddenly on the spot, feels a rush of embarrassment hearing her past rattled off, but she understands why Bgame mentioned her time in the Marines.

"Fine. My theory is simple. Your men found the crash site, were fired upon by a surviving crew member. Your men put him down. They were then engaged with some sort of REACT force following the flight path. Overcome by superior numbers and fire power, your men succumbed. This is a highly trained unit, even more experienced than normal cartel hit squads or dumbass militiamen. These men were something different. My feeling is your friends were mistaken for a threat and engaged. This seems more than just cartel traffic but again, I am now a glorified uniformed witness. I will help you Marines anyway that I can, until this case is resolved."

"Thank you, Special Agent," Delta responds graciously. "The rest of us, let's head back to the hotel and regroup into the escort teams. One in my room, the other Bgame's and let's coordinate our flights and escort status. No fucking

The Last Letter

media. We will handle Sgt. Parks once we receive his location and status; we cannot do anything for him at the moment. Copy that."

"Yut," the men give a beleaguered response, rising from their seats.

Bgame nods in agreement with Delta. "I concur, that's a fuckin good plan of attack. All of us will meet in my room at 0920 and by then we should have everythin coordinated. Gives us just a little over two hours."

"We do need to talk about Sgt. Parks at some point. If Sgt. Parks is alive and he is finding out about James and Doherty as we speak, someone better be watching him, fuckin 24/7. That motherfucker is not going to take this well," Jackson trying desperately to bring some attention to the inevitable.

Delta turns to his former troop, walks over, and puts his hand up on Jackson's shoulder supportively. "Devil, we'll get to Parks, trust me. First let's get our fallen home. I promise once that's done, you and I will figure out our next step for Parks, deal?"

Jackson, looking down at his former team leader, nods his head in reluctance. "Roger that, Sgt. Heis."

"Men, if there are no further questions, please feel free to have some more coffee, smoke outside, or my liquor cabinet is open to all. Bgame, Delta, could you come with me to finish the logistics after you dismiss your men." Alexander states, ending her SITREP.

"Thank you, ma'am," all again say in unison. One by one the men move to shake the foretry agent's hand and express their individual gratitude for her assistance. Once again Alexander is overcome with the overwhelming comradery and sadness shared by these men of 1st Squad, she wants desperately to leave this situation and the presence of the Marine Corps but knows she is vital in helping these men get their deceased brothers home.

After each give her thanks, she moves towards Bgame and Delta, standing by her huge glass door leading to her expanse of wilderness behind the cabin.

"It's gorgeous. I can see why Parks wanted to come back up here." Delta points to the scenery as Alexander approaches.

"Yes, it is. Your friend told me why he chose this place; his other unit came here for a month to fight the wildfires. The Clear Creek Fire of 2000, I searched it. He wanted to show you men what it looks like now, compared to then.", she relays what Parks had mentioned to her.

"Yeah, we all should have been here, I fuckin get it." Bgame states angrily, staring into the dark heart of the forest.

Alexander steps in to dispute the wounded Marine, "Do not fucking do that to yourselves, and I know it means jack shit but don't go down that road, at least not at the moment, any of you. You two have too much responsibility right now to these men and number one is getting Doherty and James home."

"Roger that. I need to get in touch with Jocelyn at her location and then go meet her ASAP," Bgame answers robotically.

"I'll take you to her as soon as we disperse here. I am pushing the coroner to release the men as soon as possible. Plan your trips accordingly, of course, at the family's discretion, hopefully without much hassle. Delta, would you like to accompany Mr. Burlingame and me to visit James' wife?" Alexander asks cordially of the former team leader.

"I'm sure she has enough to deal with rather than seeing another fucking Marine, constant reminder of James. I'll be in attendance at the service. Besides, I'm needed back at the hotel to get these men locked on," Delta states turning away from the expansive view and looks at the men gathering outside, the morning sun breaking through the canopy of the forest, offering glimmers of warmth and solace, Delta feels neither, only cold.

Alexander turns to look at the beleaguered men. "Are you going to be alright? I know it's a stupid question."

"No, I don't think any of us are going to be for a long while. Are we going to tear up this town in some drunken chaos? No. We'll attend to the mission at hand, as Marines," Delta reassures her. "Thank you again for all that you've done for us. I won't say those fuckin five words, *'thank you for your service,'* but I will say: my hat's off to you; you're a *Grunt* in my book, Corporal." Delta hands her his card and shakes Alexander's hand.

She feels that instant pain in her stomach, she needs to leave the room but knows she must stay. All Alexander wants is to bury her time in the Marines, deep down, never to be reflected upon. It is not to be, she knows after the men leave; she will fall apart. A tear starts to form from Delta's sentiment and gratitude, but she quickly turns away.

"Thank you, Delta." Alexander notices the men have naturally gathered around Delta in her gravel drive once he makes his way outside, all of them listening as if in the Marines again, with unabated attention. the group disperses quickly, climbing back in their vehicles, and begin to depart as if dismissed on command.

"Bgame, how bad is this going to be for your friend Parks when he finds out?" she asks gently.

Bgame looks at the dispersing group of 1st Squad, grips her hand in his and looks back at Alexander with fear in his eyes. "Bad."

CH. 19
ESCORT HOME

Dr. Anand moves swiftly around the patient's bed ensuring all vitals are in the acceptable ranges for his professional liking for the fourth time on the early rounds of the day. The machines make their constant orchestra of chimes and beeps. He looks over and sees Ms. Parkinson asleep in the next bed over from her son, Agent Medina asleep in the chair or pretending to be, "You look like shit, Doc."

"Thank you, Agent Medina, I was going to convey that very sentiment to you as well," Dr. Anand quietly quips back. The agent is right, the doctor has not had much sleep, now that he reflects, he has not had much sleep since his son took his own life a few years prior. He feels his weariness every time he moves, the doctor spends his days and nights at the hospital to avoid going home to the cold that has become his failing marriage; both seeking their own paths to grieve their family's loss. The consummate doctor continues his checks, every so often glancing in Agent Medina's direction to see if he is watching him perform his rounds. He is.

"What is it, Doctor?" Medina asks, rubbing his face with his palms. It is early and neither have slept much in the last forty-eight hours.

"If I may be blunt with you, Agent. I do not like this scenario in my hospital. Is my staff or any patient here at risk because of this man here lying in a coma?" Dr. Anand quietly asks, looking over at Agent Medina seated in the uncomfortable hospital chair.

Medina stands, "Listen, Doc, your hospital and patients are being well protected and there is no immediate threat to this establishment. Do not believe the news reports, Doctor, any of them. They're full of shit."

Dr. Anand, wanting answers, keeps at the agent, "Then why the protection?"

"He is a friend from a bygone life. This came to my attention. The rest is need-to-know, Doctor." Medina calmly walks by the doctor and looks over at the resting the mother. "Now if you would like to speak more on this, we can go to your office."

"I do not. I am tired, but my duty is to this patient and that is what I will uphold to the extent of my abilities." Dr. Anand musters up enough conviction in his voice to convince himself of his vow.

Medina registers the turmoil within the doctor. He knows everything about the good doctor's tragic loss. "Dr. Anand, I will not put any undue risk to you, the patients, or the personnel at this hospital. You have my word."

"Thank you, Agent Medina," Dr. Anand replies sincerely, tiredly.

Medina then moves to the side of the hospital bed, staring down at Parks' disfigured swollen head. He cannot find one recognizable feature. "Dr. Anand, what are his chances of amnesia at this point?"

"That is a difficult question to answer, agent. In my experience with a trauma such as this, I would estimate his chances of amnesia at 90%. The mind is such a fragile and powerful tool but has little in the way of protection. Your friend, although strong and fighting for his life, has sustained damage that far exceeds that protection for the mind. It is a very real possibility your friend never wakes up, or if he does will most likely have suffered irreparable brain damage." The doctor responds to the questions as he would to any family member in this terrible situation, with direct, honest, to-the-point answers.

Jean rising from here tumultuous slumber, hears the tail end of the disruptive conversation. "Let us hope my son remembers nothing upon waking, Doctor." She throws off the nondescript hospital blanket and stands gingerly, trying to get her legs to find the strength. Agent Medina rushes to steady her, but she waves him off with a gesture of her hand. "I'm fine," Jean scolds the special agent.

"Yes, ma'am. Didn't mean to wake you." Agent Medina apologizes to the exhausted, steadfast mother.

Jean moves to her son's side, still trying to not to look past his chest, grabs his hand in hers. "I was never asleep. Sleep does not come to the grieving."

"Yes, ma'am. Do you need anything?" Medina asks, responding to Jean's solemn statement.

She looks over at the battle-hardened agent, knowing he genuinely wants to aid her, "No thank you, Agent Medina. I will go to the cafeteria in a moment and grab some hot tea."

"Roger that, ma'am." Medina shyly replies with a softness for the ageing woman.

Jean looks to the kind agent, "Any word on my son's squad, Agent Medina?"

The special agent knows the exact location of 1st squad, he had their names flagged for travel and has been kept abreast of each member's itinerary. "Yes, ma'am. They're currently in Idaho awaiting the release of James and Doherty's bodies to be escorted home."

She sighs heavily, worrying about the poor loved ones of the fallen Marines, "How many showed to escort?"

"All of them, ma'am," Medina offers with a small amount of pride at the actions of Parks' former squad.

Still not being able to look past her son's chest, she tucks his blankets in around his waist. "That's good. They won't be alone. Marines will be with them heading home, as it should be."

"Ms. Parkinson, your son is in stable condition. Again, I cannot stress the importance of the next forty-eight to seventy-two hours. He is in excellent physical condition for his age and is a fighter, we can only hope for the best at this juncture," Dr. Anand explains, trying to reassure the loving mother.

Jean looks towards the doctor and sees that he is sincere in his sentiment. "Thank you, Dr. Anand."

Dr. Anand begins to put notes into his medical tablet and starts to head for the door, "If you two need me, I'll be in my office, the door is always open for you both."

"Do you not go home, Doctor?" Jean asks, noticing the doctor has never left the hospital since she has been with her son.

He pauses at the door for a brief second, "I wish I could, Ms. Parkinson." The doctor then quietly slips into the cold hospital hallway. The memories of his son and daughter-in-law come crashing against his strong, determined will; he is losing his battle against the past. His shoulders slump under the weight, the walk will be long to his dark empty office. The staff watch as Dr. Anand slowly, defeatedly walks by their station; the staff have seen this walk before.

. . .

Delta, Perry, Jackson, and Del Vecchio stand outside the Clear Creek Coroner's Office; it is attached to the police station, not a very large building for a new law enforcement complex with hopes of keeping up with the number of rising illegal marijuana growers and drug flow that has permeated the area. Jackson and Del Vecchio changed into their Marine dress blue uniforms, they being two of the four escorts for Doherty still able to fit perfectly in their uniform. It is a respectful sight to behold. Delta and Perry still dressed in black with miniature medals adorned. All wear dark sunglasses to hide the detached gaze that accompanies their solemn duty today. The men patiently wait for the body of Marine Ian Doherty to be released to their escort, so they can begin the guilt-ridden journey back to Louisiana and his patiently awaiting loved ones.

"What time is James being released to Bgame's escort?" Jackson asks Delta. It has been a frantic past thirty-six hours. The release of the bodies were delayed by a day, allowing everyone to change flights and destinations. Delta and Bgame dealing with the logistics of getting escort status for the men. Cooper keeping contact with the rest of Bravo Co. to help the families plan for the military burial.

"James should be released in about another hour," he answers, distracted by the throng of news crews waiting outside the perimeter chain-link fence. "Fucking cocksuckers," Delta rumbles at the contingent of media personnel gathered filming the group.

The Last Letter

Perry looks over at the scrum news crews, "Fuck 'em." He then moves over towards the side of the hearse that will be taking Doherty's coffin to the Boise International Airport, looking upon the vehicle, giving a final inspection. There must be a Marine escort with the body twenty-four hours a day until turned over to family, the fallen are never left unguarded during transport.

"Hey, Sgt. Heis, you remember that patrol Sgt. Parks took us on after Schick got hit with that Russian anti-tank IED at Dulaab?" Jackson asks, solemnly reflecting on the past exploits of 1st Squad.

"Which one, Devil?" Delta responds, slightly paying attention.

Jackson keeps focused on the news crews taking video and photos of the waiting Marines, "The one where they kept denying us re-entry and Sgt. Parks decided to go off-script?"

"Oh, that fucking patrol," Delta acknowledges. "What about it, brother?"

"I was rememberin when Sgt. Parks had us stop outside that shit village and we were all just lounging around the hummers," Jackson continues, still staring at the reporters milling about. "That little fuckin shepherd boy whippin the shit out the goats he was herdin, havin a good ol time. What the fuck did Doherty say?"

Del Vecchio chimes in from behind Jackson, "*That fuckin boy won't be laughin when that goat turns around and bites his little tallywacker off.*" The Marines quietly laugh amongst each other, for they are the only ones who would understand the humor in the story.

Jackson ponders aloud, "All of us stuck in the middle of shithole Anbar Province, Iraq laughin our ass off at this little cruel shithead goat herder." He rubs his face as the flashback comes to him. "Goddamn, *tallywacker*."

"You think any of those fucks would understand any of that! The brotherhood! No. Those fucks just sit back and report bullshit about warriors who signed on the dotted line, stood on those yellow fuckin footprints, put it all on the line for this country. Worthless fucks," Perry bellows, unleashing an emotional tirade and gesturing towards the gathering media, who are starting to gain in numbers.

Delta spies the gathering storm of news crews, thinking instinctively about the two-and-a-half hour escort to the Boise International Airport. His mind running through various scenarios, where these news vans impede their mission. He is getting anxious, but his calm demeanor portrays no emotion. "Easy, brother. Calm down. We'll be enroute soon enough." Delta makes eye contact with Perry, reassuring the distraught Marine that everything is under control.

"Roger that, Sgt. Heis. It's damn good to have you here. Fuck, we should have been here, Sergeant." Perry wraps his arms around Delta in a monstrous hug, Perry's natural strength crushing Delta.

"You stow that shit right now, Perry. Let's get this done for Doherty and James. Yut?" Delta eases Perry upright to look at him.

Del Vecchio joins the two and taps Perry on the shoulder for support. "Yeah man, *Rangers lead the way, all the way. Whoohoa.*" Del Vecchio says, mocking the Army Ranger motto. It is a running joke Marine Corps wide amongst infantry; anytime a situation arises a *Grunt* will mockingly say *"Rangers lead the way, all the way,"* another will answer sarcastically, *"Whoohoa,"* and the unit will erupt in laughter. *"Where the fuck are they now?"* is another common response from infantry Marines to any mention of the Rangers.

"Whoohoa," Peery responds in the appropriate mocking tone.

Jackson turns upon hearing the back double steel doors of the complex open and Doherty's body in the protective enclosure begins to be wheeled out towards the back of the open hearse. The men quickly move into position on either side of the crate. It is an intimidating scene. The news crews cameras roaring to life.

"Present arms!" Delta commands, the men slowly render a hand salute as Doherty comes to rest before them. "Ready two." A second command from the former team leader. The men slowly lower the same salute in memorial fashion as required by Marine ceremony. They then grab the sides of the protective crate and gently slide their fallen brother into the back of the hearse. Everyone relinquishes a tear down their gritty, aged, hardened cheeks. Perry a few more. It matters not the men have not seen each other in over twenty years; the bond 1st Squad made in the short time they were together spans a lifetime.

Delta secures the back of the hearse. Jackson slowly climbs into the front seat of the vehicle. The men know the plan, no outside vehicles will jump the escort. The fire team is now focused and angry, it is time to get their brother

The Last Letter

home, and nothing will stand in their way. The vehicles begin pull out of the compound, and to the Marines' surprise an Idaho State Police cruiser arrives as the convoy is beginning its trek to Boise.

"Follow us, and we will have a vehicle bring up tail end Charlie, behind your men." The tall, intimidating state trooper speaks to Delta.

Suddenly at ease for the first time in days, relieved he no longer has to worry about the security for the trip, the team leader exhales heavily, "Yes, sir, thank you." Delta replies respectfully.

The state trooper turns back to look at Delta, "Anything for a fallen Marine, let's get him home." With that the trooper gets in his vehicle, turns on his lights and begins the proud escort

. . .

Bgame, Thomas, Morales, Cooper, and Culpepper wait anxiously outside the same law enforcement complex as the others had an hour earlier. Jocelyn, wife of the fallen Marine Ryan James is inside the complex signing the release and sitting with her husband one more time. It was crushing for them to see her in so much grief. The Marines take up their posts outside waiting for their fallen friend. The news crews have not diminished, adding to the agitation of the group of ageing infantrymen. They, too, in the appropriate all black attire with their ranks affixed to lapel or collar, Morales and Cooper opting to change into their Marine dress blues, looking imposing with medals adorned and sunglasses affixed. The Idaho State Troopers have extended the barrier outward to keep the press at bay and have an escort on standby as the troopers provided for the earlier Marines.

"This is not how they were supposed to go. Not on our soil. No way for a *Grunt* to go," Morales comments, trying to avoid the silence. The anger and sorrow is palpable amongst the group; their forged bond allows for comfort from that anger and sorrow, they were a Marine rifle squad, nothing further need to be said amongst themselves. There are no publicized stories, tales of glory, or acknowledgment for the Marine infantryman. No, those miserable men are the dirty unheralded warriors that change the course of war. Training

SSgt. Jacob Parkinson

and misery are all a *Grunt* knows until it is time for them to do their job, then it is guided rage.

"Payback is comin," Culpepper, growls. His massive frame convulses, stretching the fabric of his black suit. Even he adorns his left breast pocket with miniature medals, none more proudly displayed than his Navy Achievement Medal with Combat Device.

Thomas, moving to Culpepper's side reaches up and pats him on the back. "Easy, big fella." Giving him a slight smile. "We'll get to that. Nice medal, you got there."

Culpepper exhales a gust of air from his large lungs, "Fuck you."

"Don't worry, big man, 1st Squad will get theirs," Cooper replies, staring at the gaggle of reporters waving in his direction. "Look at these fuckin assholes. Not a one can report the fuckin truth." Cooper glares towards the awaiting media, insistent on exploiting the moment for ratings.

Bgame turns and coldly stares at the reporters. His imposing red beard and hair, looking like a mad Viking ready to go to war, his shades hiding the fire burning in his eyes, "At ease, Devil. Culpepper's right, payback is comin. Just need to know who."

"Well, shit, while we wait, Bgame tells us the *'Hot Nurse Day'* story. That's legend. Put us in a better mood, brother." Morales urges, trying to distract the group from thinking about the vengeance they want to inflict upon an unnamed adversary or the trespassing news crews.

Bgame is immediately distracted by Morales request for the story, he looks down, too tired for stories, though he can see the men need some sort of distraction, "That's a good one. I haven't told that story in years."

"Is that one with the hemorrhoids and BAS[46] with the Navy docs at *29 Stumps*?" Thomas referring to Bgame's legendary case of hemorrhoids while training at 29 Palms, California.

Cooper tries to remember the details of the story but is having trouble. "We never got the full fuckin SITREP from that, I just heard the scuttlebutt from the fellas."

Almost cracking a smile, the Viking puts his head down in reflection at the pain of his ordeal. "Not today, Devils. That's a story that must be told

---
[46] Battalion Aid Station

when Sgt. Parks is around. He tells the opening sequence with fuckin comedic genius; besides Parks was my roommate in the barracks, and he was the first one I asked to push them back in. You should've seen that fucker's face."

"Fuckin gross," Culpepper huffs with a disgusted curl of his mouth.

Bgame does actually smile at Culpepper's repulsion. "Remind me when Parks is around, roger that?" He promises the men, his smile starts to fade at the long-ago memory.

"Fuck, Culpepper tell us the story of how you came up with our platoon slogan for Iraq." Morales turns and looks up at Culpepper. "We need some levity during this moment."

Culpepper takes a deep breath. He does not want to remember; this is the reason he disappeared when he got back from Iraq. Culpepper went down the rabbit hole, like so many frontline warriors upon their return. He does not want these memories resurfacing, not now.

"Man, which is another Sgt. Parks story. He opened that up; I was tired, and it came out. Didn't know Sgt. Parks was goin to fuckin run with it." Culpepper almost breaks a smile recalling the memory of that long day of training.

"Oh shit, was that almost a smile." Thomas points to Culpepper, trying to make the bigger man smile even more. Culpepper gives Thomas the middle finger."

"Shit, I haven't heard the story how the platoon got its' slogan," Bgame says, happy to have the spotlight off of him.

"I remember it perfectly fine." Cooper turns to Bgame with a quick smile. "Remember when we were at Victorville for MOUT[47] trainin?"

Bgame nods slightly and gruffly adds, "Yep. I was in Mabe's squad at the time." He scoffs at the memory of his defunct squad leader.

Cooper continues quickly, "Glad, I wasn't in his squad." He glances at the steel double doors where James will exit, Cooper loses some of his zeal for the story but carries on. "We get a break in trainin; 1st Squad had just finished attacking some stupid shit and Sgt. Parks took the squad off away from the platoon to give us a break from *Dickless*. We're all just flopped around in our gear, as only we can do, like a bunch of beached whales. All of

---
[47] Military Operations Urban Terrain

us, fuckin miserable. Full gear, summer heat in SoCal. Not an inch of me was dry from fuckin sweat."

"Fuck ain't that the truth. Shit sucked ass." Thomas grimaces at the memory of the discomfort from all that gear plus the summer heat.

Again, the group seems to collectively shudder at the memory of discomfort. "Sgt. Parks is sittin on a concrete block and has Culpepper right next to him, like always." Cooper smiles and winks up at the massive Marine.

"Fuck you, I was the RO," Culpepper flatly states, referring to his having to always be by Parks' side due to the fact he was the squad's radio operator.

Cooper fires back, "Hey, man, it could have been worse you could have been stuck with that fuckin SAW."

"Oh, this fuckin shit again. Every damn SAW gunner." Culpepper knew he could not win that argument; infantryman hated the SAW. It was a horrible rite of passage to carry the weapon but if you did not, you were extremely fortunate, especially Culpepper as big as he is, always a candidate to carry a machine gun.

Cooper continues his tale of times gone, "The rest of us were just loungin around with our flaks open soaking in the sun. I forgot who asked Sgt. Parks some dumbass question about us kickin in doors when we get in-country. Probably fuckin Thomas, here." He turns to smile at Thomas.

Thomas nods in agreement, "Shit, probably."

"Sgt. Parks goes into detail about how when we kick in doors, the hajis will start screamin and cryin as we haul their bomb-makin men away at zero dark thirty." Cooper then asks almost to himself, "What the fuck did you say?" Cooper, then on que moves his gaze up to Culpepper, hoping Culpepper would finish the statement.

The mountain of a Marine looks down and answers in a flat tone, "They can get over it or die pissed."

The men erupt in subdued laughter, the news crews snapping their photos of the warriors reminiscing. "Fuckin the squad dies laughin except for Culpepper of course. Sgt. Parks goes nuts, sayin that's our new fuckin motto. And the rest is history." Cooper smacks Culpepper on his large granite back.

Bgame still smiling from the story, "I remember hearin that come down the pipe and thought it was fuckin perfect but never knew the whole origin."

The Last Letter

"Didn't Sgt. Parks tells us *Dickless* tried to claim that slogan as his own or some shit?" Morales looks over to Bgame.

"Fuckin wouldn't surprise me. Fucker used Potter's nut protector to demonstrate it would stop a 9mm round, which it didn't. Piece of shit *Dickless*, couldn't even use his own nut protector had to use a troop's," Bgame snarls at the thought of his cowardly platoon commander.

Morales reflects on the combined hatred the men had for their platoon commander. "I remember that. 1st Squad had just come back from either the front post of Dulaab or some fucking out the box patrol Sgt. Parks took us on. He was pissed too."

"I think I was the one that told Parks when y'all came back from patrol. His first response was *'why didn't that fucker use his own nut protector?'*" Bgame states, beginning to get agitated with the length of time it is taking to release James. "Definitely no love lost between those two."

Culpepper turns to the reporters still vulturing for pictures of the men, "Why do you think Sgt. Parks never stayed with you squad leaders and *Dickless* at the CP. He always stayed on the line with the squad or taking us off on some fuckin patrol to get away from that chickenshit. I had the radio, remember? I heard every bullshit cowardly command that fucker gave Sgt. Parks, and he disregarded every damn one until that night after the ambush. Sgt. Parks finally had enough of his bullshit, no fuckin more. It wasn't just one fuckin night, goddamn culmination of chickenshit orders," Culpepper says to Bgame, staring out past the mob of photographers; his eyes transfixed on the forested horizon, his anger growing, his peripherals becoming blurred, caught in that distant *nothingness*.

Cooper looks over shocked, "Fuck, Culpepper I think that's the most I have ever heard you say, ever." A slight chuckle from the group, except for Culpepper, of course. He wants to get on with task at hand.

"Yeah, I wondered that at first, why Parks was never around the CP with *Dickless* Daisy but once I became squad leader, I understood. That fuckin coward never shuts up talking about himself or some dumbass story from when he was a boot POGe reservist or some stupid shit bicycle cop story from his job with the Fort Worth police in the *Stockyards*. I tried to do the same, but *Dickless* wouldn't fuckin let me, Stockwell, McDonald, Delacruz, or SSgt. Ruiz leave the him , kept us all there; but he never once tried to make Parks stay, those two hated each other from the fuckin get-go." Bgame explains, bristling at the thought of having to listen to another one of his boring platoon commander's prolonged stories.

"Now you know why the bond is so strong with 1st Squad. It was more than just that night outside of Fallujah. Sgt. Parks had been protecting us from that asshole's fucked commands since we arrived in-country," Culpepper adds, his gaze still locked on the blurred nothing.

"*Fuckin A right, Cotton,*" Thomas chimes in with a quote from the movie *Dodgeball* that all in the group recognize.

Bgame nods in agreement, following Culpepper's gaze, looking past the distracting mob of the media, "I know you men have this bond, fuckin James would always talk about 1st Squad stories when we go out drinkin. Fuckin miss that Devil, already." The deep exhales become more frequent as the reality becomes more concrete—*they are gone*.

The steel double back doors to the new law enforcement complex begin to slowly open simultaneously, the coroner's staff wheel out the gurney with James in the protective crate. The men quickly get into position on either side of the crate as it approaches the back of the hearse. "Present Arms," Bgame quietly commands, he hears the roar of clicks from the news gallery. The men slowly raise their hand salutes. "Ready two." The former Marines slowly lower their hand salutes and then each grabs a handle and loads James into the hearse to the sound of cameras and reporters bustling about to get the best angle on the procession.

Jocelyn begins to cry at the presentation from the men James served with, gripping tightly to Bgame. "Why, Bgame? Why the fuck did Parks pick this place? Why did this happen to Ryan? Why him? Why the fuck did Parks bring them here?!!" Jocelyn erupts and grabs hold of Bgame around the neck and begins to cry. The others can only look on in pained silence.

"I am so fuckin sorry", is all Bgame can manage to get out of his mouth. He has no other words of comfort for her. He dare not say *"everything will be alright,"* for he knows nothing will ever be the same and those that utter those patronizing clichés in times of grief have never experienced true emotional pain. Bgame knows the grief, and nothing will ever be the same.

The Last Letter

Jocelyn letting go of Bgame's neck with her gripping embrace, wipes the tears away from her already tear-stained cheeks. "I want them all to pay."

"I understand; we'll get the fucks," Bgame says, trying to reassure her with the fire raging in his eyes.

The grieving widow responds with matching fire. "That includes this so-called leader of men, Sgt. Parks. This is his doing. It's all his fuckin fault my Ryan is gone."

Bgame is at a loss for words, never once did he assign blame to Parks for this, and he knew Doherty and James would not want Parks to take the blame for this travesty, either. James, Doherty, and Parks all fought alongside one another to the bitter end, he knows this because the images of the videos do a hellish dance in his mind. The men would want no other way to go out than fighting for one another. Bgame can offer no amount of solace and reassurance that will sway Jocelyn during her time of extraordinary grief, she has focused her intense hate on Parks.

An Idaho State Trooper approaches Bgame, he looks up at the towering, uniformed officer, "Yes, sir, we're ready." The squad starts to approach Bgame, but he holds his hand up to wave them off, he did not want Jocelyn's anger towards Parks to be heard by the men. They will come to his defense and that will not benefit any grieving party. Bgame escorts the exhausted widow to the backseat of the elegant hearse.

Bgame heads over to Morales, Cooper, Thomas, and Culpepper. "You fellas ready?"

"Yes, sir," Cooper responds anxiously eyeing the camera crews. Following Cooper's nervous gaze, Bgame reassures the former Marine,

"Don't worry about those fucks. The state police will keep them the fuck back." Bgame looks up at the towering Culpepper and asks him, "Do you want to ride with James? I know Sgt. Parks split the squad in an unorthodox fashion, it was always you, James, and Sgt. Parks as the point team."

Culpepper looks down and rubs his beard with his large rough hand. "Team OFP. That's what James used to call us, *Team On Fuckin Point*, I hated it. Yes, I'm with James."

"Culpepper, thank you for taking that ride." Morales nods his head towards the massive man.

He looks over his large shoulders and nods slightly in return. Culpepper opens the door, lowers himself into the front seat of the hearse and gently closes the door. The driver seems nervous as Culpepper makes himself as comfortable as possible, rocking the entire hearse gently with his movements. "No fuckin questions," Culpepper states coldly, turning to the driver and eyeing him through his black sunglasses. The driver nods his head in petrified compliance and shakily starts the hearse.

"Cooper with Bgame, and Thomas with me. The rental companies are grabbing your cars from the hotel, correct?" Morales asks Cooper and Thomas.

"Roger that," Thomas responds rapidly, a little too rapid for his liking.

Cooper confirming to Morales, "Yeah, I locked that on with Enterprise last night. They were more than understandin."

Bgame gives one last look towards his rental truck and knows he is in for a tortuous ride to Boise. "Alright, men, mount up and let's get this done. Bring James home with grace and honor."

"You got it, brother," Morales answers Bgame's order. The men all exchange hugs.

Cooper walks by the window next to Culpepper, "I'll see you on the tarmac, brother. Love you, man."

Culpepper not wanting to say too much or have that bond renewed with the men of 1st Squad could not stop the words from flooding out, "Love ya too, brother." He then rolls up the window as the hearse slowly pulls behind the lead State Police vehicle.

The escort begins to pull through the gates of the compound, the news crews shouting questions at the passing motorcade. Cooper looks back as they leave Clear Creek behind them; he cannot fathom this new reality; how could this have happened. It is not possible. He tries to fight the coming words, but his resistance fails him. "We should have fuckin—"

"Don't." Bgame orders Cooper but he knows every member of 1st Squad is repeating the very same guilt-ridden statement to themselves at that very moment. Over and over again.

I should have been there.

CH. 20
DOHERTY FINDS PEACE

A tortuous week has passed since the Marines returned from escort duty of their fallen brethren. The surviving members of 1st Squad huddle together away from the larger gathering. There is a nice autumn drizzle, light enough to be relief but not heavy enough to allow discomfort. Mourners mill about, some in black attire others breaking their Marine dress out of the back of their closets. Almost all of the Bravo Co. alum are present and the others who could not make the trip are watching the service via live stream. The local Marine reserve unit has arrived to perform the ceremonial duties of a Marine burial: taps, twenty-one-gun salute and, of course, the folding of the flag to be handed to Doherty's grieving mother. A flag will also be presented to his fiancée by members of Bravo Co., although they were not married, he loved Cassie with all his heart.

"Everyone is staring at us," Del Vecchio comments, feeling uneasy among his own fellow Marines of Bravo Co.

"Remember that time we got back from our first firefight in Hiit, all of Bravo Co. out for seven days; we come back dirty as shit. The whole base of Al Asaad lookin at us like we were the fuckin walking dead." Jackson comments from the group as he, too, stares at his fellow Bravo Co. Marines, staring sympathetically upon the men of 1st Squad huddled together by an evergreen.

"Yeah, man, I remember that look." Delta answers Jackson's memory of events. The drizzle cooling his anxiety of being at the service of his former team member.

"We're getting that exact look now by our." Jackson waves politely at Cooley and Stevenson, like Jackson, dressed in their blues. They wave back fondly but everyone is reluctant to intrude upon 1st Squad's mourning.

"They don't mean anything by it, no one knows how to fucking approach us. I don't blame them," Delta sympathizes with the members of Bravo Co.

Perry starts to get anxious at the thought of the upcoming service for Doherty, he does not want this for his friend. The two shared some rough times together when they first returned home, Perry reflects, "Why the fuck wasn't I there? All because I was maybe too nervous to see everyone or just didn't feel like it. What the fuck kind of brother am I?" Perry blames himself aloud. All *Grunts* lose themselves upon returning if they experienced that adrenaline dump of *combat*; how far down the rabbit hole they go is entirely dependent on the individual Marine. The common thread, the *rabbit hole* is never healthy or beneficial to the Marine and especially the loved ones who absorb the disaster. The true unheralded lost combatants of every war: *the loved one.*

"Perry, stop that shit. We all feel like shit and all of us here had some excuse we forced upon ourselves not to go. The fact, plain and simple, none of us were fucking there. Not a damn one. Now we're stuck with that fucking eternal bullshit; *why the fuck wasn't I there?* So, for now we bury that shit. Copy that?" Delta affectionately wraps his arm around Perry's shoulder and brings him in close.

"Roger that, Sgt. Heis." Perry rubbing his bloodshot eyes to give them some much needed relief.

Delta looks about to the remainder of 1st Squad, "All of us need to put that shit to bed for the next few days. Today, Doherty, two days from now James. Until we are done, no breaking down about: *I should have fucking been there?* That's shit we will carry for the rest of our lives, but not today. Copy that?"

"Yut," the gathered respond in unison.

The remaining members of 1st Squad stand in silence, the light drizzle soothes their anger and trepidation. In fact each man feels some level of comfort standing in the group watching the onlookers pass by, all lost in their own memories of Doherty and James, but there is a collective gloom hanging over the group, depressing the air around them.

"Cash Money did a fuckin great job gettin the funeral detail from the local unit locked on for Doherty's service. Those young Devils performin this service look damn good and sharp. Shit, I remember when we used to look like that." Cooper remarks, gazing upon the Marine Reserve detachment performing the funeral detail, rehearsing off in the distance.

"You fuckin never looked that good, Coop." Thomas interjects with some light levity.

Cooper turns his gaze back to the group and finds Thomas smiling at him. "Fuck you. I have something on my chest that they don't. A CAR[48] bitch." He smiles and taps his right breast of his dress blues displaying his ribbons. The group all give halfhearted huffs of laughter in response.

"Man, Sgt. Parks used to ride your ass durin runs to get you motivated," Thomas continues to chide his old squad mate.

Cooper responds to Thomas's continued harassment, "Yeah, well fuck you. It's training, I trained. Man, Sgt. Parks realized what I was havin trouble with and worked with me instead of giving me constant shit. I also remember Sgt. Parks firing Caruso as team leader on the spot after that bridge IED and givin me the position, a LCpl. over a Cpl. So, eat shit, Thomas." He gives his friend the middle finger with his white-dress-gloved hand.

"*Dickless* also made Parks give the position back to Caruso. Remember that shit?" Jackson adds distractedly, looking at the young Marines rehearse. Cooper nods at the disappointment from the past.

"Parks was pissed, telling *Dickless 'in a fleet Grunt unit, the better Marine gets the job, regardless of rank.'* His response to Parks, *'Sgt. Parks we are not in the fleet, are we?'* We were fucked from day one with *Dickless*," Delta tells Cooper. "Parks fought for you, Coop."

Cooper looks to Delta, both caught up in the feeling of nostalgia, both wanting to be back in Iraq, once young, "Shit, I remember Sgt. Parks grabbin the 203 from Caruso, grabbin my SAW and slamming the weapon in Caruso's chest and handing me the 203. Growled at us, *'Your fuckin fired; Cooper*

---
[48] Combat Action Ribbon

you're the new team leader.' You should have seen Caruso's face. I didn't know what the fuck was happenin. Shit was fun while it lasted, all half day of being a team leader in combat." Cooper chuckling at the memory of Caruso's shocked face.

"You were the better leader and Parks knew it. Fucking micromanaging *Dickless* wouldn't let it be. That's why Parks went over *Dickless* to Gunny Hoffman and requested permission that Caruso be moved to the drivers." Delta reassuring Cooper he earned that position for as long as it lasted.

Del Vecchio moves to the side of Culpepper, which makes for a comical scene, the size disparity is humorous. "I always wondered what happened to Caruso after we got back from the bridge. One minute he's my team leader, then Cooper, then him and then *poof*, gone."

"And that put 1st Squad in *Dickless's* crosshairs permanently. That's why we were always out doing patrols and getting '*volunteered*,'" Delta recalls, trying to fill in the blanks for the men, wishing Parks were here to explain the behind-scene mechanizations better to the men. His head lowers at the thought of Parks waking to find out Doherty and James are gone. Then to miss their services, he knows Parks will lose control; Delta only hopes he's there for his old squad leader when the news hits.

Perry watches intently the Marine unit rehearse with precision, he remembers a time when he had that bearing and motivation for the Corps, "Man, I'm glad Frazier took point on gettin this organized because I know for a fact, we couldn't handle all this. He already has James' funeral locked and shit, Devils. Frazier even got a real trumpet player instead of that fake trumpet bullshit with a speaker in it. That's awesome. Doherty would have loved that." Perry starts to tear up again at the thought of his fallen friend.

Cooper looks closely at the Marine staff sergeant in the band dress uniform, "I think that's fuckin Witherow."

"Yeah, man, He went active duty Marine band when we returned from Iraq. Good to go shit," Del Vecchio informs Cooper who is looking at one of their former members of Bravo Co.

Cooper stares in disbelief. "No shit. I knew he could play instruments but damn that's cool. Only Marine band member with combat experience."

The Last Letter

The group of men stand in silence as the rest of Bravo Co. and Doherty's civilian family, loved ones, and his friends start to gather in the cemetery's cathedral. "We goin in last?" Jackson asks.

"I sure as shit don't want to go in first," Culpepper adds from the shadow of the tree, in his deep, rough voice.

Delta turns to the hulking figure, "Nah man, we'll go in last," he replies with a subdued tone.

"Good thing *Dickless* didn't show his face, that could've been downright nasty," Jackson seethes.

"Yeah, well don't dwell on that shit now. Gunny Hoffman is here and Doherty loved that man. Fucking only Gunny that mattered anyway." Cooper points to their former company guns, now a retired Master Gunnery Sergeant impressive in his Marine dress with full regalia.

Morales comes up to Delta and places his hand on his shoulder, "Do you know what you're going to say, Sgt. Heis."

"I have it ready," Delta calmly replies.

Morales looks tired beyond his pretty boy years, exhales, and glances around at the mourners. "I just can't believe this is happening. His poor mother. His fiancée. Fucking sucks." He sighs slowly, "Did you get any sleep?"

"No, not much." Delta still stares into the distant mist of the cemetery due to the weeping drizzle. He ponders how stereotypical this all seems for a funeral. It does not seem real to him, as if he is caught in someone else's depressive, somber dream.

Del Vecchio looks and sees Gunny Hoffman heading their way, undoubtedly, to order the men inside and to quit procrastinating. He has not seen Gunny Hoffman since the unit returned, but the man looks the exact same. A poster Salty Marine. His medals covering his left chest, his ribbons covering the right. "Uh-oh, I think we're in trouble." Del Vecchio signals to the group they have incoming.

The retired Marine walks to 1st Squad with a worrisome look, "You fuckers doin, okay?" He asks the men in his gruff fashion, genuinely concerned for their well-being.

They all respond in affectionate unison, "Yes, Gunny."

"Good, now you fuckers get inside." He gives them a heartfelt wink.

"Roger that, Gunny." the squad affectionately respond to him and begin to head towards the entrance of the cathedral.

Gunny Hoffman pulls Delta to the side gently by the arm, "You good to do this, brother?"

"Yes, Gunny. I'll be fine." Delta having lost fellow firefighters in the line of duty, fellow brothers, this experience is not new to him.

"Okay, Devil. Will you gather the men after the service and meet me here?" He requests of the former team leader.

Delta looks at Gunny Hoffman with dread and responds, "Of course, Gunny."

"I just want to check on y'all but now is not the time before the service," Gunny Hoffman replies, belaying the concerns Delta exhibits.

"Roger that, Gunny," Delta respectfully answers.

He pats the team leader on the back and they both head into the cathedral for the service of Ian Doherty: soon-to-be husband and father, a son, brother, Marine.

The pastor steps to the pulpit to begin her opening statements before the large gathering of mourners. She gives a soft, reassuring glance to the congregation before she begins, "There are no words for the grief that as a collective is being felt for this fallen Marine, here today. I look out upon this mournful mass and witness a sea of dress blues, a sky of black formal both adorned with the glitter of medals, promising Doherty the warrior's afterlife awaits. I found that many have a name for this, but the infantry seem to adopt the Viking lore of Valhalla. To a warrior such as Ian Doherty, they find solace in the fact that their valor for this country will be honored by fellow Marines of days past, to be reunited with their fellow brothers. It is the lore of the warrior."

Thomas, Del Vecchio, Cooper, Perry, Delta, Morales, Jackson, and Culpepper, standing along the back wall, look at each other not knowing what to expect, but their looks are of admiration for the opening remarks. "I like where she's going with this," Perry whispers to Jackson.

Jackson leans down in his form-fitting Marine dress blues, "This is goin to be rough, my friend." he slowly rubs his eyes for relief, thinking of their

The Last Letter

squad photo; his arm around Doherty, not knowing what was in store for them, like thousands of Marine infantry on the eve of that fateful day 2004.

The pastor continues, "It is this lore among you Marines in attendance to honor your fallen, that I digress from the usual sermon, for Doherty fought until a true warriors end, in battle protecting his fellow Marines with his very life. Worthy of legend, worthy of honor, worthy of remembrance, and worthy of our grief. I look out among you here, see the medals and ribbons; battle tested every one of you. You all have done something that none of us will ever know; you were willing to face an uncertain violent end for something greater than yourselves, each other, and I can see in your eyes you still are. So, as we mourn Ian Doherty, today we must recognize the sacrifice that he has made for each and every one of us in this room. Not to his fellow Marines, but his never ending sacrifice to his loved ones, each and every day of their lives. I will conclude, not with the Lord's Prayer but with a poem from Joe Carnahan, and I am sure most of you Marines will recognize it:

Once more into the Fray…
Into the last good fight, I'll ever know. Live and Die on this day…
Live and die on this day…"

She concludes with a folding of her bible and ushers her hand towards Frazier, who is standing along the wall to her left, to proceed with the itinerary. He along with the rest of the mourners are astounded but comforted by the pastor's remarks; she, to them, has epitomized the feeling among them in a tranquil sermon for Doherty. Frazier quickly nods and mouths the words *"thank you,"* knowing his words are not enough gratitude for her poignant sermon. He quickly looks to the back of the room and signals for Sgt. Heisinger, Doherty's team leader, to proceed with his speech.

Delta moves across the back of the room towards the center aisle, receiving pats on the shoulder from the men of 1st Squad aligned along the same wall. He feels the mourners and fellow Marines gaze upon him, making his way to the front of the room and up to the podium, briefly stopping in front of Doherty to spend a silent moment with his former Marine. "Thank you, chaplain that was beautiful." Delta expresses his gratitude towards the pastor, and she nods with a warm acceptance.

SSgt. Jacob Parkinson

"For those that do not know me, I am Sgt. Brian Heisinger, Sgt. Heis, or Delta as some call me. I was Doherty's team leader in Iraq from '04 to '05 with 1st Squad 2nd Platoon. I would like to take a moment to share a fond memory of Doherty:

The Smile Remains

He would moan, grunt, and complain. We all did. But Doherty did it with a smile.

The days were lean and grueling. Hostile at times. In the palm groves or on a rooftop, his smile remained.

I will tell the story of the little goatherder, the squad knows this story well.

1st Squad was on a patrol shortly after one of Bravo's, Schick, was tragically injured during an IED blast. Our CO wanted "blood" as told to us and all of Bravo was trying to be the first to get it.

After stopping at the front gate of Dulaab, giving those guys some pogey bait, we shortly encountered a young boy herding some goats; on this "outside the box" mounted patrol Sgt. Parks would take us on, that scorching hot day.

As the squad took a security halt, we witnessed this child laughing and carrying on having the best time of his life whipping the tar out of this one poor, old goat. Just relentlessly whipping this goat with a stick, laughing, and laughing, like it was his PlayStation.

Doherty looks over at the poor animal and back at us, "That kid won't be laughin so much when that goat turns around and bites his little tallywacker off."

1st Squad would erupt with laughter, and smile, covered in weeks-old dirt and sand. Much needed levity in an unforgiving environment. Through his dirt-crusted face, Doherty's smile remained.

Upon returning stateside at Bravo Co.'s first Marine Corps Ball, we all basked in the joy and revelry shared by recounting stories of hardship and exhaustion spent together. Doherty running around always with a constant "I love ya" while he wrapped his dress uniformed arm around your neck, all done with a huge, beaming smile.

Bravo Co. moved on and dispersed, fighting to stay connected with each other over the years. All of us struggled in our own ways and we were forced to abandon our hardened smiles for periods of time.

But then Doherty found his smile again through sobriety, compassion, and love. Doherty would follow the path presented before him; to help other struggling

The Last Letter

Veterans mend and heal their mental wounds. All accomplished with a smile of pride and purpose.

When I was blessed with the opportunity to communicate with Doherty again, he counseled my own guilt. His expert advocacy at the forefront of relieving my own pain. Always with an uplifting message, and I am sure with a boyish smile as we exchanged goodbyes and he responded one final time, "You too, old friend."

I had the honor and pleasure to be a part of a ragtag bunch of men in hostile territory, Doherty being one of those excellent warriors. My men are the ones that got me through Iraq, not the other way around. We formed our bonds not by combat or patrols but by our shared humor of our current situation and the men's broad sand-in-teeth smiles. As the memories fade, Doherty's smile will always remain..."

The gathering of mourners quietly applaud Delta's eulogy, he makes his way to Doherty's mother, Sandra, folds his eulogy into a small square, hugs her and passes her the piece of paper. She is in tears and holds on to his neck. Delta whispers, "I am so sorry I wasn't there." He then heads for the side door to the outer foyer to collect his thoughts, tears streaming down his face. He is not alone for long, the men from 1st Squad come piling out to support him.

Jackson strolls across the foyer in two quick strides of his long legs, quickly wraps his arms around his former team leader. "I love you, Sgt. Heis."

Delta pulls back a bit and looks up at Jackson, "Love you too, brother."

He composes himself as the others gather around him.

"That was some motivatin shit, Sgt. Heis. Doherty would've loved that." Perry wraps his heavy arms around his former team leader's shoulders.

"Thanks, man," Delta responds, hugging his troop, looking to the floor to avoid getting emotional again as the memories flood back. He was not expecting this wave of emotion upon being here, but Delta is facing the inevitable; he has buried Iraq for far too long.

Cooper seeing Delta becoming overwhelmed affectionately tells him from a distance, "That was beautiful, Sgt. Heis." Delta nods back appreciatively. Thomas, Del Vecchio, Culpepper, Morales, give Delta a quick shoulder hug as they resume mourning silently as a group, still feeling awkward around their fellow Bravo Co. Marines.

"Why do I feel on display in there?" Del Vecchio looks at the others of 1st.

Culpepper takes a long look at the squad photo that is displayed with beautiful pictures from all stages of Doherty's life plastered on a mural in the foyer. "Because they all know we should have been there. "We are the unintended walking dead," he angrily breathes. The surviving Marines of 1st Squad seem to freeze instantaneously, Culpepper's cold statement breaking the dam on their own guilt they have subdued, until now.

"Hey, big fella. Not right now. We'll get to that together." Jackson slowly approaches Culpepper and rests his hand on the man's massive shoulder.

Thomas with a slight goofy smile come over and points to a picture of Doherty with his beaming smile, "Don't do that on this day. Look at Doherty smile. Of course, he would want revenge if the positions were switched, but he wouldn't want that today."

"Come on, Devils, let's get back in there and listen to the others tell their stories of Doherty's impact on their lives. Maybe, just maybe we might find some relief and comfort from the memories of him outside of the Marines." Morales tries to get the men out of the mindset that Culpepper's harsh statement has thrown each into.

Delta snapping out of his haze instantly takes control of the situation, "Morales is right, get your asses back in there. Let's go, Culpepper, I don't feel like dragging your big ass or I can get Gunny Hoffman out here."

Culpepper turns stoically and heads towards the viewing room to rejoin the mourners. As he passes, Delta can feel the anger pouring off of the big Marine. His rage warms the surrounding environment. Delta puts his hand on Culpepper's chest compassionately halting his former squad mate, "I promise you; we will avenge this. Somehow, someway."

"Roger that." Culpepper looking down at Delta, blankly.

Delta pats Culpepper on the shoulder again to let him by as the others follow suit to resume their positions in the back of the large, cavernous viewing room. Delta files in last behind Morales, he looks over towards the front to see Bgame and Gunny Hoffman sitting next to their wives; both looking to Delta for reassurance that everything is good to go. Bravo Co.'s commanding and executive officers, Colonels Miller and Roy together in full dress uniform, also look to Delta for confirmation that all is well with the men of 1st, the weight of losing men under their command displayed in their troubled looks. Caught off guard by the officers' attendance, Delta nods to both groups, uncomfortable with the concerning stares, and acknowledges that the situation is under control. Gunny Hoffman gives him a thumbs-up to signify his thanks to the former team leader.

Doherty's fiancée gallantly makes her way to the podium, a situation made even more grim by the fact most in attendance, especially his fellow Bravo Co. Marines, did not know Doherty had a child on the way, the Marines' hearts sink. "I would like to begin by thanking all of you for being here. This is so beautiful. To see so many people touched by my Ian. To see the pageantry and display of Marine custom and tradition, Doherty would have been so honored. So, thank you," Cassie says to the gathering; she then looks tenderly at Doherty lying peacefully in the beautiful oak coffin; adorned in his Marine dress blues.

She continues, "I want to share a text message Ian wrote to me as he was at a layover in Denver on his way to Idaho. *'Cass, I just wanted to take this moment to share the wonderful feeling I have for us and our future. I was adrift but floating in the right direction and then you came into my life. You had me smiling in minutes and for once there seemed to be an end to this aimless suffering. It took me a while to work up the courage to ask you out but when you said yes and with that smile, I knew we were destined to be together forever. I found my one, and that made me the happiest man on Earth. Our time together has been brief but filled with joy, compassion, sharing, and love. To know we have a little one on the way has made my life complete. After this trip, my love, I can finally put to rest Marine Cpl. Ian Doherty and live as Ian Doherty soon-to-be husband, father, and guardian to the most beautiful souls in my world. You are my life, Cassie, and I can't wait for the next chapter upon my return. I love you.*"

The mourners release their tears down their redden cheeks, sobs of audible cries can be heard out in the ghostly, vacant foyer. Delta suddenly reminded of the cries of the women and children in Iraq as 1st Squad would snatch away their loved ones. Sgt. Parks and Delta would talk about those horrific tear-filled howls of agony after patrols; Marines were not immune to those pleas of the suffering. It is this sound that causes Delta to move politely to the foyer to gain some relief from the sobbing mourners.

"Doherty really knew how to bring the room to tears." Perry follows Delta into the foyer, a monitor displaying an endless loop of Doherty's life to music greets them.

Delta turns to see Perry coming, a tiny bit relieved someone followed him out. "Yeah, man he sure did. I just couldn't handle the crying." He returns his gaze to the screen of Doherty's life encapsulated in three-minutes forty-seconds.

"I figured. It has been a long time since I heard that amount of sorrow." Perry standing next to Delta, staring at the same media display, witnessing Doherty's life pass by.

Keeping his gaze fixated on the screen, Delta offers sadly, "Is this to be the fate of us all. To be remembered only in a short montage. Our actions disappearing, never to be recalled. This is fucking it, right here."

Perry can find no counterargument to his team leader, for he, too, sits alone and contemplates what will be remembered of him, "Yeah, Sgt. Heis, this is it."

Jackson emerges from viewing room to join alongside his fire team members, "Man, Doherty hit every emotion with that final text to his fiancée. That was crushin to listen to and then the wailin from the mourners. Holy shit." The tall Marine shudders with chills at the sudden flashback of women and children screaming as their squad would drag out the household men to be transported away, most never to be reunited with their families. But Jackson never knew the outcome, only pondered on his actions later in life.

"I had to take a breather. It's been a long time since I thought about any of our actions over there," Delta responds to Jackson. The former Marines stare at the media display, each becoming transfixed by the smiling images of their old teammate, Doherty.

Del Vecchio pushes his way through the double doors. "Hey, fellas they're getting ready to fold the flag and perform *Taps*. Colonel Roy sent me after you.", he tells the group, referring to their old company executive officer, known then to the men as Major Roy.

"That's great he showed. Only Mustang[49] worth a damn in the Marine Corps. He and Major McGinty are the only reason you and Culpepper, along

---

[49] Former enlisted Marine turned officer

The Last Letter

with Parks got those combat decorations sitting upon your chest," Delta states to the younger Marine.

Del Vecchio looks down at his Navy Achievement Medal with combat device. "Shit I didn't know that. I remember showing up to drill one month and being surprised with an award formation."

Delta pats the younger Marine on the arm, "The *'sirs'* asked Sgt. Parks to rewrite the award nominations that *Dickless* burned. He did and they got two passed by command. Yours and Culpepper's. Well fucking earned and deserved, Devils."

"Yut," Jackson and Perry echo their team leader's sentiments.

Delta, Jackson, and Perry, give one last look at the team photo they took on the eve of *Operation Phantom Fury*, flashing upon the screen, a scene repeated by thousands of Marine infantrymen on the eve of that operation 2004, cold stares and young faces. "We need to get back in there." Delta tells the other three. Jackson and Perry reluctantly follow their former team leader back into the large grief-laden viewing room.

The gathering of mourners file out of the viewing room to the adjacent cemetery, arriving at the plot prepared for Doherty's eternal rest, a procession of black and dress blue move slowly in a rolling wave to the burial site. Doherty's mom, Sandra, and his fiancée, Cassie, take their seats below a canopy erected to protect them from the light drizzle. The Marines of Bravo Co. surround the site, like an engulfing blanket of security for the proceedings. Medals and uniforms giving the ceremony the proper feel of a national dignitary being laid to rest at *Arlington National Cemetery*.

Commands for the twenty-one gun salute can be heard stoically given by the detail commander. "Ready, Aim, Fire!" The crack of weapons being fired has the Marines of Bravo Co. involuntarily jolt at the sound of the rifle report. *Taps* begins to be played by a Marine most did not recognize at first, the melody flows beautifully and effortlessly from SSgt. Witherow on an exquisitely inlaid shining trumpet to the astonishment of the gathered mourners. Two young, made of stone Marines begin to fold the flag from Doherty's coffin; methodically, precisely the one folds, while the other Marine importantly keeps the flag taut and inline. Doherty's mom and fiancée both unable to hold back the flood of tears along with their painful grief at the beautiful presentation given to their loved one.

The senior of the two Marines, kneels and hands the folded flag to Doherty's mother and recites those fateful words every mother of a Marine dreads, "On behalf of the President of the United States, the United States Marine Corps, and a grateful Nation, please accept this flag as a symbol of our appreciation for your loved one's honorable and faithful service." Sandra begins to cry once more; she never knew so many tears resided in her grieving soul.

Stevenson and Cooley, dressed in their blues as well; the lean, chiseled former Marines fold another flag and present it to Doherty's expecting fiancée. Stevenson recites the same monologue as the previous Marine had done for Doherty's mother, "On behalf of the President of the United States, the United States Marine Corps, and a grateful Nation, please accept this flag as a symbol of our appreciation for your loved one's honorable and faithful service." He then smoothly offers his salute and makes a right face, moving to the back of the gathering.

The pastor stands by Doherty's coffin and begins her closing remarks, "We are now left to our own grief, sorrow, pain, and heartache. It is inevitable. Embrace it, do not run from it. J.R.R. Tolkien once said, *How do you move on? You move on when your heart finally understands that there is no turning back.* So, let your heart mourn Ian Doherty. Let your heart grieve. But also let your heart heal and move on to the warmth Ian Doherty brought to each and every one of you here. Go with God, Ian Doherty, your place is secure. Amen," she concludes, stepping towards Doherty's mother and fiancée, the pastor offers her condolences.

Delta begins to head to the tree at the front of the cathedral that 1st Squad had gathered prior to the service. The rest of the squad follows suit, hoping to go over their itinerary for James. The drizzle still feels like a relief against the humid autumn Louisiana morning, the men's anger palpable amongst them. "What the fuck now, Sgt. Heis?" Jackson asks wondering the next couple steps the men need to take.

"Gunny Hoffman wants to talk with us and then we head to Texas. Everyone checked in at the Hilton in Grapevine in the rooms I reserved for us?"

The Last Letter

Delta looking around at each one of the men, waiting for confirmation. The instinct of being a leader in a time of crisis that the men can count on, flows over Delta naturally. 1st squad responds to his leadership now as if they were back twenty years ago in the desert.

"Roger that," Cooper answers quickly.

Perry, teary eyed responds with a nod, his fear of talking may open the floodgates of emotion, "Yeah, I'm good. The men of Bravo are gettin antsy."

Jackson stands over everyone except Culpepper, looking at his fellow members of Bravo Co. leaving the funeral service to go about their own grief of the man they once knew. They want to stop, say goodbye and offer condolences to 1st Squad, but none know the appropriate approach yet.

"They can wait." Culpepper looks over at the gathering of Bravo Co., faces he has not seen in over twenty years. Faces he walked away from long ago.

"I'm good as well, Sgt. Heis. Room 414." Morales responds to Delta.

Del Vecchio comes up next to Morales, "Roger that, Sgt. Heis. Room 418." Del Vecchio can see off into the distance, Doherty's mom and fiancée watching the funeral workers begin to lower Doherty into his final resting place. The two women hold each, for a moment of brief comfort before they must let go. "It's time to go," he offers sadly.

Thomas following Del Vecchio's gaze, suddenly the gravity of gloom washes over him, witnessing the same display of grief by the two heartbroken women. He sighs heavily, wishing there were some way to change this outcome, "Yeah, Sgt. Heis. I'm good. We still meeting for dinner?"

"That's the plan," Delta responds. He sees their former company guns heading their direction. "Master Guns is on his way over." The men all see Master Gunnery Sergeant Hoffman stride towards them in his dress blues. His plethora of anodized medals beaming even in the overcast light. The ribbons that adorn the right chest are as numerous, it is what is known as a *"salad bar"* in the Marines due to the expansive amount of colors the awards display, resembling the condiments and sides of a salad bar.

Jackson steps forward to shake Gunny Hoffman's hand as he nears the group. "Shit Gunny, any more room for salad on that chest of yours?"

"Fuck you, Jackson." He pushes Jackson's hand aside and gives the younger Marine a tremendous hug. Each of the men from 1st Squad give Gunny Hoffman some sort of hug and greeting. "Jesus, Culpepper finally good to see you again, UA motherfucker," he affectionately chides Culpepper, staring up at the big Marine.

Culpepper all of sudden feels like a young PFC in front of the almighty *Company Guns*, sheepishly answers, "Good to see you too, Gunny. I'm sorry about all that shit." His voice deep, he rubs his beard nervously. It is an emotion Culpepper has not felt since the birth of his last child.

"Don't you worry one bit about that Devil, it's just damn good to see you healthy and here." Gunny Hoffman throws an arm up and around Culpepper, who is trying to hide his awkwardness and embarrassment. "You men all heading to Texas today for James on Monday?" He asks, stepping into the center of the group.

"Yut," some of them respond in unison, the others simply nod.

Gunny Hoffman looks around at his former Marines and is saddened by the weight of burden these men seem to be carrying on their shoulders, "Listen Devils, there is nothin you could have done. This is what happened. Stow that guilt in the wall locker and mourn these two wonderful Marines. Got that."

The men slowly nod, heavy with burden, not knowing what to say to their former *Company Gunny*, standing before them adorned immaculately. It is a bittersweet vision, "Gunny, what news of Parks?" Delta asks, preventing Gunny Hoffman from continuing to uplift the men, both sides become uncomfortable, and Delta can see his men fidgeting anxiously.

He realizes why Delta asked the question and is grateful for the change of subject. Gunny Hoffman knew the men of 1st Squad shared an undeniable bond from that day it all went south outside of Fallujah. He did not want to intrude on that bond, even if he did not agree with the course of action Parks and his squad took at zero dark thirty that day.

"Parks is at the Denver Institute of Neurology. He's in the very best possible hands. From what my law enforcement contacts can tell me, SSgt. Parks is in protective custody as a potential witness. No one is allowed access to him without being vetted by DHS. I believe his mother is with him now and his

The Last Letter

children are there as well or enroute." Gunny Hoffman concludes, referring to the hospital and the Department of Homeland Security.

Perry steps forward from behind Delta, his eyes red from the tears, "What is Sgt. Parks' condition?"

"Perry, it is not the best. I'm not going to lie to you, Devils. He's in a coma, and it is not medically induced. They do not know the condition he will be in upon waking if he ever wakes. Listen, I don't want you men running up to Colorado after James' funeral and bombarding his mother with extra stress. I know you men will mean well, but let things die down," Gunny Hoffman tells the anxious Marines standing around, their eyes flash with anger.

Cooper angrily steps forward, "Let things die down, Gunny! Have you seen the fuckin news. They're callin our brothers hired guns for cartels. Both JaKL News and CRN are shittin all over our brothers' legacies! Sayin America's combat veterans are a disgrace. Fuckin Kevin Karlson talkin about Doherty, James, and Parks as failed veterans compared to Russia's combat veterans. What the fuck, Gunny?" Cooper's jaw begins to ache from the clenching of his gritted teeth.

Gunny Hoffman slowly turns to Cooper, trying to find the right words to console his rage-filled former Marine. "I am disappointed in the news coverage as well, Devil, but all we can do is ignore it. We know our fallen as honorable men, which is all that fuckin matters. You Marines got that?" He orders with his gruff authoritative tone.

"Roger that, Gunny," all this time sound off in unison.

Again, the former company guns begins to pity his men, for he knows the guilt inside must be clawing its' way to the surface. "Listen, I will keep each and every one of you posted and if it does not come from myself, Delta or Bgame then don't believe that shit. Right now, there is nothing we can do except mourn these two fine young Marines and let the authorities do their job. There will be justice, I promise you men that. Now travel safe back to Texas, and I will see you at the service for James. I love each and every one of you, Devils and if this becomes too much for you fuckers; then you better call me and that is a fuckin order. Roger that?"

"Roger that," to the man, all respond. Even Culpepper whose eyes begin to turn coal black. The Master Gunnery Sergeant in all his regalia heads off to try and comfort more of his Marines from Bravo Co.

Delta waits until Gunny Hoffman is out of earshot, "Alright, brothers, let it out. Get some of that guilt out now. We still have a job to do for James."

"Motherfuckin should have been there, Sgt. Heis. Why didn't I go. Why?" Perry utters as tears begin to fall. Del Vecchio and Jackson stand next to him and put their hands on each of his shoulders. Perry is expressing externally what they are all feeling, and they know it is only a matter of time before the guilt eats away at all of them. That is why the men cannot force themselves to witness the pain that Doherty's mother and fiancée are enduring at this very moment. They know some aspect of them will ask themselves; *I should have fucking been there.* That is another ghost they must bear for the entirety of their existence. It will never go away, no amount of counseling, no amount of alcohol, no amount of drugs, no amount of compassion, and no amount of understanding will ever let the remainder of 1st Squad forget that lone statement.

Delta looks at each of the distraught Marines, locked into their own guiltridden anguish, "Yeah, well, we weren't. And the sooner each and every one of us realizes that we can't change shit and we all should have been there, then the better we find clarity and get our job done. Leave the justice for law enforcement."

"There will be no justice. It will be forgotten and cold after a month." Jackson, standing over Perry, tells his former team leader.

"What the fuck do you propose? We go fucking rogue and solve nothing but bring more chaos to this fucked-up situation?" Delta asks the men not just Jackson. "We are not some fucking elite former spec ops soldiers. We are a bunch of former combat *Grunts*. That is all. Nothing high speed about us. So, let's focus on getting James to his final resting place and then we focus on helping Sgt. Parks recover. He will fucking need help from every damn one of us, roger that?", he barks at the Marines of his squad.

"Roger that," to the man, sound off to the former team leader.

Thomas tries to change the subject. "Hey, Sgt. Heis, maybe we should get goin. The more we sit here, the more we'll be open to questions from the rest of Bravo."

"You're right, Thomas. I don't even want to answer questions from you fellas," Delta states with trepidation, slapping Thomas's arm.

"Fuck this. Love you, brothers." Perry storms off towards his truck. Mumbling under his breath, making his way through the remnants of the mourners. All steer clear of Perry's determined walk.

Jackson about to head after him is stopped by Delta, "Let him go. He knows where to be. He has his own demons to deal with at the moment.

We all will at some point. Time to disperse. See you all at the hotel in a few hours." The team leader nods to the men he somehow inherited from this terrible, unfortunate incident. The remainder of the squad now look to him for leadership. Delta does not want the responsibility, but there is no other the men will follow, *except one*, the thought flashes before he could stop the image. *Goddammit, Sgt. Parks*.

CH. 21
JAMES FINALLY RESTS

Night begins to descend upon the beautiful flatlands of the Texas horizon. Cooper looks out from his balcony, it is a perfect autumn night and once he looks past the skyline of Fort Worth, he is captivated by the tranquility the scene begs of him. Cooper is almost at peace, almost.

He takes a long inhale of the soothing night air, to fight back the oncoming assault of guilt. He tries desperately not to bring the statement to his consciousness. It is too late. The nightmarish statement flashes before him, he inhales deeper hoping for the relief that is not to come. "Fuck you!" he yells into the emptiness of the hotel room.

There comes a knock at Cooper's door. He trusts no one and moves to one side of the door and turns out the light so it does not give him away looking through the peephole. It is Morales, Del Vecchio and Thomas, his old team members. Letting them in he catches his breath, "You fucks gave me some anxiety. Man, no one knows I'm here. I forgot I told you."

"You okay, man? I thought I heard something. You in here arguing with ghosts, brother?" Morales asks looking about Cooper's perfectly kept room.

"Man, fuck you. If you haven't been already, you will soon enough be arguing with the same fuckin ghosts." Cooper stares at Morales, who in turn looks back at with an understanding nod.

Del Vecchio takes a seat out on the balcony, dressed in a tailored black suit, finally out of his dress uniform, staring out into nothing, focused on the *nothing*, "Those ghosts have not left my side since I found out the news, then all of sudden everything just comes flooding back without my permission and against my wishes. I don't want you men to take this wrong way, but I haven't given much thought to Iraq or the squad since our return. I kinda buried that shit and moved on. Do not get me wrong, fellas, what we went through, especially that fucking day, has us bound for life. I just wanted it to go down into lore and to be uttered through rumor or at reunions, not thrust into our existence so catastrophically. I fear this is only the beginning, whether we want to participate or not." Del Vecchio talking to the air or the ghost that sits beside him, nagging at him to give it the attention it so desperately seeks.

"Yeah, thanks Mr. IED for that foreshadowin of doom. Can we please just lay to rest our brother James. Discuss the doom and gloom shit after the service," Thomas chimes in from his seat on the edge of the hotel bed, opening up a shooter of Jack Daniels. He breaks out a second one offering it to anyone, they all decline. "Hey *Mr. Doom & Gloom* can flow with spooky foreshadowin to scare the piss out of me, but I can't have some whiskey."

"Hey, motherfucker, no one said shit, damn. We're all on edge. Trust me, I will be havin a drink at dinner with everyone else. Breathe." Cooper patting Thomas on the shoulder. "Now get your ass up off my tie. It doesn't need to smell like your literal ass."

Thomas jumping up feeling relieved by Cooper's attempt to ease the tension. "Shit man, my bad."

"Dinner is going to suck. Hopefully we can rein it in. It's all of us, so that will help. How do you think Culpepper's handling this?" Morales looking around the room, tapping Thomas to give him that shooter of Jack Daniels, he obliges.

"Shit, Culpepper, James, and Sgt. Parks were the three fuckin musketeers." Cooper laughs under his breath as he adorns his tie in a perfect half-Windsor knot. The other men laugh enough to ease the anxiousness in the room for the upcoming dinner, with the hulking, silent Culpepper and the remaining members that of 1st.

Del Vecchio comes in from the balcony, looking impeccable in the tailor made suit sans the jacket, his sleeves rolled up to display various tattoos on his forearms. "I forgot what James called themselves, I will have to ask the big man at dinner."

"Sgt. Parks definitely had the squad divvied up in weird fucking way, definitely not standard for a rifle squad breakdown." Morales comments on the tactical breakdown of their squad in Iraq.

Thomas searching his pockets for another shooter and finding none, grudgingly offers, "Well our squad definitely had the biggest fuckin RO in all of Iraq. Fuckin Culpepper as RO, what a damn site."

"Motherfucker should have been a machine gunner, he damn sure should've been carrying the SAW, instead of small ass me and James." Cooper laughingly adds, putting on his two-tone black dress shoes.

Del Vecchio, smiles at the memory of Culpepper as the radio operator with the antenna sticking above his already large frame. "It definitely was a sight to see."

Morales slaps Del Vecchio on the back, "Especially when he stood next to your small ass."

"Fuck you," Del Vecchio returns with a smile.

"Where the fuck are we goin tonight?" Thomas asks, taking one last look in Cooper's mirror to make sure he has nothing hanging from his nose.

Cooper holds the door open for his fellow fire team members, "Sgt. Heis didn't say. He said be in the lobby at 1740. So down we go, gentlemen." As the men file out of the room, they are met with Culpepper and Perry in the hallway.

"Well speak of the devil. We were just talkin about your big ass and the radio, Culpepper." Thomas looks towards the two.

Perry busts out laughing with a hearty thunderous laugh, "That's hilarious, brother. We were just talkin about the same damn thing. Fuckin Culpepper and that damn radio."

Culpepper, towering over everyone, somewhat smiles and shyly looks to the ground, "I think Sgt. Parks did that as a big *'fuck you'* to *Dickless*."

"Yep, he absolutely did," Delta adds, exiting the room in his Marine dress blue uniform. He dressed impeccably, as they all are, per his instructions.

"You lucky motherfucker, Culpepper. James, Jackson, and I would bitch about that fuckin weapon every damn second, especially James." Cooper counters, pressing two of the four elevator buttons to head down to the lobby of the Hilton.

The men of 1st Squad respond in unison with huge smiles, "We know." The memory of James moaning about the SAW roars back in all their minds.

Delta smiles at Cooper's dismay at the weapon choice, "Take it up with Parks, he really had no control over weapon assignments. Which in the fleet is the opposite; squad leader has initial say."

"Oh, I fuckin will, when he wakes up and he will wake up. That motherfucker is too defiant to just die quietly." Cooper smiles at the thought of giving his old squad leader a hard time for being assigned the squad machine gun.

Culpepper moves closer to the elevator door, anxious to get the evening over with, mumbles under his heavy haze of a mood, "He better." Immediately the mood among the men changes and the jovial atmosphere is once again reduced to a fog of guilt and regret. All of them stand in silence, waiting for what seems an eternity for that annoying ping of the elevator reaching its destination of the floor. The elevators arrive seconds apart, the remaining members of 1st Squad, divide between the two and solemnly wait in the empty silence; no longer reminiscing on their fallen squad members.

Jackson, also in his Marine blues, like his team leader; is waiting in the lobby when the elevators simultaneously open and the men step out of the golden doors, "Shit you fellas look fuckin smooth. All dressed to the nines and shit. Wow." He then registers the suffocating atmosphere, "What memory was brought up on the way down that killed the mood?"

"Oh nothing, reminiscing how Culpepper ended up with the radio and you, James and Coop ended up with the SAW." Delta stepping up to Jackson to give him a hug, as *Grunts* do. "Don't worry about it, we'll have plenty of this at dinner, I'm sure."

Jackson scoffs heavily, "*Dickless* was a fuckin asshole and hated the brothers, that's why. When he ran out of brothers to give the SAW to, he gave it to James out of fuckin spite, who may I add was one of the best shooters in the platoon, if not the best and Orso, the recon kid. Come on, also how was it right for Potter to have the machine gun? That shit wasn't tactical at all."

Delta nods in agreement with Jackson's breakdown of platoon dynamics, "And that is your clinical assessment, doctorate of psychology?"

Jackson smiles coyly, "Yes."

The Last Letter

Continuing to nod in understanding, Delta adds, "I concur. What did you expect from the clusterfuck? Now let's forget that man and focus on dinner."

"Speaking of dinner, where are we going?" Jackson asks, noticing the onlookers in the lobby getting nervous at the sight of the gathered Marines.

Delta, following Jackson's gazes understands the need to depart quickly. The more the men are gawked at, the more likely it is to piss one of them off. "That's a surprise, but the limo is outside to take us to dinner and back." He then addresses the men of 1st; "We are not partying; we are going to have a nice evening together and give our brothers a proper salute. We will sit and bask in tales of days gone. We still have a job to do in the morning and that is to get James to his peaceful rest. Roger that?" Delta looking about the men for confirmation.

"Yut," the gathered circle of Marines reply in a subdued response. They then move to the outside as the limousine HMMV pulls into expansive hotel front.

"Jesus, Sgt. Heis. What the fuck, you a millionaire?" Perry exclaims, gawking at the limousine before him.

The driver steps out and politely tips his cap to the gathered men and opens the door, "Good evening, sirs."

Delta turns to Perry, "I will explain later, now shut the fuck up and get in the damn hummer." He nudges him forward to be the first into the limousine.

"What the fuck!" Perry shouts, climbing in. "Man, I'm afraid to touch a damn thing in here."

Jackson towers over Delta and peers inside the limousine, "Fuckin sweet, Sgt. Heis. It's too bad it is under these circumstances, James and Doherty would have loved this."

"I know, brother. Let's just get through this together." Delta pats Jackson on the back. The rest of 1st Squad follows suit, expressing gratitude to the former team leader and enter the beautiful stretch limousine. Delta tips the driver and enters last. "Okay, help yourself to the bar but again this is not a fucking party. We are having a nice dinner to honor our brothers, not embarrass them. Copy that."

"Roger that," all reply in unison, realizing the gravity of the situation and not wanting to embarrass their squad or Delta.

"Where are we going, Sgt. Heis?" Cooper asks, accepting a glass of Scotch from Perry. "Holy fuckin shit that's good," he admires the drink as it smoothly slides down his esophagus and warms his core.

Delta waving his hand, signaling he will not tell, leaning back comfortably almost in darkness next to Culpepper in the back of the limousine, "It's a surprise, Devil," he calmly states. The driver begins the trek to the surprise destination Delta has in store.

"Thank you, Sgt. Heis," Culpepper flatly states looking down at Delta.

Delta looks up at Culpepper who is staring straight ahead, "Yeah, man, no problem. Do you know what you're going to say for James at the service?"

"Yes," Culpepper states solemnly and continues his stare straight ahead, seemingly to understand the finality of it all, "Team OFP," he grumbles.

Delta knew not to press the issue further; he lightly pats Culpepper on his massive leg. He hopes he can keep the men focused on the final task of honoring James. Delta looks around the limousine and each Marine seems to be lost in their own thoughts and memories from their brief time together in Iraq, none of their faces expressing joy, all are of sorrow. The men quietly stare out the windows in a drained silence, no words spoken. The specter of guilt has begun to crawl its way into the consciousness of each man in the vehicle, but none will admit the guilt is tormenting their thoughts and focus.

The trip is a quiet one until the Marines reach their destination into a wide open circle drive towards the awaiting valet. Their mouths stand agape at the sight of their rendezvous.

"Dude, what the fuck Sgt. Heis? This place is impossible to get into, its only for celebrities and athletes. Like the Cowboys, Mavericks, Stars, Rangers and even then, it is only for the stars." Del Vecchio looks out the limousine's window along with the others. The men witness the standing crowd outside eyeing the extravagant limousine pull into the expansive drive, expecting a celebrity to step out of the rear doors.

Delta, already knowing where the men were going that night, is still in awe at the beauty of the place. "Hey, I only provided the funds for this excursion, Bgame had the connections through various Veteran organizations. So, make sure to thank Bgame when you see him at James' service tomorrow. We

The Last Letter

have a back room to ourselves, no one will be staring at or bothering us. Tonight, is for peaceful remembrance." Delta explains as the men begin one by one step out into the warm night air and marvel at the grand entrance to the mythical *Uncharted Lounge and Steakhouse*, Dallas, Texas.

The onlookers mystified by the incredibly dressed but grim looking Marines filing out of the back of the extensive limousine. "Let's get the fuck inside," Culpepper grumbles, moving towards the entrance, his navy blue suit stretched to its' limit due to his stonewall like build seemingly about to rip if he pushes too much. The rest of the men follow suit trying to ignore the gawking onlookers. Delta tips the driver and brings up the rear of the column of men, Jackson walks next to his former team leader and the two make an imposing representation of Marines both in their dress blues medals adorned. Once inside Delta makes his way to the host.

The host, in his sharp tuxedo, asks, "May I have the name?"

"Heisinger," Delta replies surveying the intricate and ornate beauty of the establishment he has only seen on Google. The place did not disappoint, every man is awestruck at the beauty and marvel of the *Uncharted*. Even Culpepper is looking about in wonder.

"Yes, sir. We have your room waiting. If you would?" The host gestures for the men to follow a younger as well dressed young man to their awaiting accommodations.

Delta smacks the taller Marine's back, "Look alive, man. Tally forth." He uses a somewhat British accent trying to draw Jackson's attention to the young man gesturing him to follow his lead.

"What the fuck, Sgt. Heis? You never said anything about all this." Jackson gestures with his hand to the extravagance of the atmosphere.

Delta looking at the men, "Fellas relax, everything is taken care of. Tonight, we commemorate two fallen brothers in a proper fashion, around a warrior's table. Tonight, is for Doherty and James. Let us remember and revel in their memories." He begins to usher the men to follow the young well-dressed man to their reserved lounge.

"Great speech but who's really paying for all this?" Morales makes his way to Delta as they enter the grand lounge. A large black oak round table, with black leather high back chairs sits center in the cavernous room. The lights are dim, there is a full bar with staff awaiting the men's drink orders. Private kitchen that also is standing by for the group's entrée selections.

"Don't worry Devil, it's taken care of. I'm not at liberty to disclose that information, please enjoy, brother. Look around, the men need this." Delta gestures to the bewildered but smiling Marines taking up residence in the comfortable leather chairs. Morales understands that Delta and he are needed to get the rest of 1st Squad through this tragedy on a scale they have yet experienced, never knowing the tragedy of loss in combat. Morales nods his understanding of the situation and moves to sit in between Cooper and Thomas. The eight of them make themselves comfortable in the handcrafted leather high back chairs around the exquisitely carved oak table, and immediately tear into the bread put forth before the awestruck men.

"What're we the fuckin *Justice League*, Sgt. Heis?" Jackson asks marveling at the intricate décor.

"Ha-ha. Jackson. Shut the fuck up and enjoy, that goes for everyone. It is taken care of, I mean it, order whatever you want," Delta responds, looking around at the men's wonderment and confusion. "Morales how'd you guys do escorting James home? We were worried if you four and Bgame may have trouble along the way."

Morales gives his drink order to the private wait stuff, "It went smoothly. The airline was more than accommodating. Everything went by the numbers and sadly turned James over to the funeral home. His, wife Jocelyn, Bgame and his wife were there as well to help with everything. Then we hauled ass to get back for Doherty's funeral. Fucking East Texas to Louisiana is farther than it sounds."

Looking over at the youngest member of the squad, Delta asks Del Vecchio, "How are you taking this in, brother?"

Del Vecchio gives his drink order to the staff as well, takes a deep breath, "I'm doing, just as we all are. That's about it, Sgt. Heis."

"Come on, man. Don't give me that shit." Delta still trying to get his young troop to open up to him.

Shrugging, Del Vecchio vacantly states, "Listen, Sgt. Heis, I am plagued by the same guilt we all must be feeling right now. How much of a difference

The Last Letter

we would've made out there? The guilt ridden relief we feel for not being there. We are not friends. We share no memories outside of our time in Bravo Co., but yet we are forever bound by that night outside of Fallujah." He stares at the beautiful, polished silverware, transfixed by its' shimmer.

"What the fuck, Devil?" Cooper chimes in from the other side of the table, nervously chuckling. "Man, this is bad enough without that. Holy shit and I thought Culpepper was the dark one."

Thomas grabbing his drink from the staff and nodding his appreciation, "I know, what the hell Del Vecchio? You and Culpepper say all of three words on escort duty and now your lengthy monologue is this depressin shit."

"Fuck you both, I am stating what we all feel." Del Vecchio counters, he too sips his smooth bourbon. Instantly awash with a feeling of warm comfort and relief.

"Leave him alone, he's fuckin right." Culpepper groans.

Cooper looks over at Culpepper with understanding, "I know he's right, but we don't need that shit at this moment. That shit can wait until after we put James to rest."

Culpepper nods and grabs his soda water to relieve his dry mouth. The men begin to look over the menu in silence, again it is not an awkward silence but one of familiarity. Each makes their selection of entrees and subsequent courses that accompany the meal.

"So, big man, tell us why James kept callin you three, *Team OFP*." Perry leans back in his chair with his Cognac and looks towards Culpepper.

Culpepper cannot help but pause momentarily at the recollection of himself, James, and Sgt. Parks. The ones James would deem *Team OFP*. "Shit, I don't remember the exact instance he started callin us that, but I do know why he gave us that name. It started after that three man patrol Sgt. Parks took James and I on, when all you fuckers said you were too tired to go." Culpepper mocks the men, looking sternly around the table.

"Shit, I wasn't too tired, I just didn't feel like dyin." Cooper quips back at the large Marine.

Culpepper huffs at Cooper's remark as the others laugh, "We made it back, didn't we? After that James started callin us *Team OFP*. Team *On Fuckin Point*."

Culpepper remembering that 3-man patrol through a village outside of Dulaab Sgt. Parks took him and James on trying to stir up a hornet's nest of locals.

"That's true, Sgt. Parks always took point. Never understood that shit. Only squad leader to do that. Did he ever tell you, Sgt. Heis?" Jackson wonders aloud to his old team leader, enjoying his perfectly aged libation.

Delta reflecting back to Iraq, trying to remember if Parks had ever told him why he always took point on patrol, "That's a good damn question, I know he had a reason. You will have to ask him when you see him." The table grows quiet once more as the men recollect their time together privately.

"Maybe, Sgt. Parks was tryin to die," Culpepper gruffly states. The men say nothing in return to the large Marine's cold statement. All remain in isolation, waiting calmly for their banquet of exquisite dining. Smells from the private kitchen begin to fill the room with the mouthwatering savory aroma of well-prepared steaks.

Jackson stands, grabs his glass and raises it, "To Doherty and James. Goodnight my brothers."

"Yut," the remaining Marines of 1st Squad quietly reply in unison. Again, the table grows silent; each sips their drinks and stares into nothing, transfixed by some distant memory.

Del Vecchio stands, "I'm going to go smoke this beautiful cigar out on our private balcony, since it's there. Anyone care to join me."

"Yeah man, I'll join you," Thomas replies, quickly grabbing his glass of bourbon, to join his old teammate out on the spacious marble balcony.

Jackson grabs his cognac. "Yep, I'm there with you."

"Count me in." Cooper replies, he too grabs his glass of Scotch and follows the three out on to the expansive outdoor balcony looking down on the Dallas nightlife from four stories up.

Culpepper, Delta, Perry, and Morales all remain at the large oak table in appreciative silence. The men are not bothered by the clamor of the private kitchen or the bustling of the staff. "You know James and I never got along really well, but I would have died for that motherfucker. I would die for all you motherfuckers," Perry states emotionless, staring into his almost empty glass.

The Last Letter

"We know, Perry." Delta grabs Perry's shoulder to console his former troop. Perry does not remove his gaze from his glass, his eyes grow wide with thoughts of Doherty and James' last moments, like it was a movie being played on the side of his Scotch glass. That thought creeps into his conscious; *I should have been there.*

Culpepper finishes his soda water and is promptly met with a refill by the staff without ever asking. He nods towards the nervous waitress in appreciation, "What's our plan after James, Sgt. Heis?"

"I don't really know, Culpepper. We go back to our lives as best we can. I gave Gunny Hoffman all of our info to be given to those in charge where Parks is staying to see if we can be cleared to the visitor's manifest. I should know soon enough." Delta answers Culpepper as best he can.

"Go back to our lives. Fuckin Bravo Co. looks at us like we're the walkin dead. Go back to our lives, shit. Our brothers are gettin raked through the coals in the fuckin news. Go back to our lives, fuck them all. We fuckin failed." Culpepper grinds his teeth, not at Delta's comment, but rather the inner voice that screams in his ear; *You should've been there.*

Delta is starting to get angry, not with Culpepper's reaction but that the large Marine is right, he is stating the obvious for the rest of them, "Fuck man, can we get through this dinner without that '*failure*' shit. I know I fucking failed, we all know we failed. Nothing changes that. But tonight, is fucking for Doherty and James. Not our own personal guilt bullshit. Got it?" Delta looks at Perry, Morales and finally Culpepper. They nod in agreement. Culpepper angrily finishes another glass of soda water and is promptly met with another, the wait staff sensing his rage.

Out on the balcony, Jackson leans against the stone decorative railing with his back and looks over his shoulder at the people below, exhaling on a sweet smelling La Aroma De Cuba cigar, provided by the lounge. "Man, every one of them has forgotten about Iraq and Afghanistan. Not a soul down there cares. You think they give a fuck about Marines who died over there? Fuck no. We are now relegated to a blip in history," he explains calmly.

Thomas walks over to the side of Jackson and peers over the balcony railing, enjoying his bourbon, "Nope. They could care less. None of them would sign on the dotted line to serve; I mean look at them, all trying to cock-block each other." He points at the waiting congregation of young well-dressed individuals below trying to get someone to notice them in a pathetic attempt at showing off one's class and status, trying to gain entry into the private lounge and steakhouse.

"Fuck 'em. We're here for our boys tonight. Doherty and James. Can we focus on that, please?" Cooper interjects sitting in a plush outdoor recliner, exhaling a puff of smoke of his own beautiful Ashton cigar.

"Yeah, man, we can," Jackson responds, continuing to take pulls from his cigar.

Del Vecchio, breaks out a Mayan Sicar cigar and begins smoking.

Jackson begins to laugh, "Smallest one here breaks out the most expensive cigar I have ever seen; fuckin great."

Del Vecchio not bothered by the statement exhales a puff of beautiful smoke, "Yeah and *I thought you'd be bigger.*" He quotes the movie *Roadhouse* as he inhales and exhales a large cloud of beautiful smelling smoke that engulfs the balcony for a few moments before the autumn breeze blows the cloud of sweet vapor into warm night air.

"You fuckin remember when we were in Habbaniyah gearin up for that company VCP and Captain Phillips from weapons platoon came over to James to told him take that fuckin bandana off his head. Remember what fuckin James mumbled under his breath?" Thomas, smiling, asks the men lounging, basking in warm remembrance.

Del Vecchio chuckles to himself, exhaling another large cloud of sweet smelling cigar smoke, "Yep, James said, *'who the fuck does he think he is?'* and Captain Phillips heard him and about faced right back to the hummer and scolded him, *'I am a captain in the United States Marine Corps, and I gave you a direct order, LCpl.'*" Del Vecchio gives his best impression of an officer's voice. He laughs ever so slightly, "James looked over to Sgt. Parks like a wounded fucking puppy for help."

The group laugh heartly together for the first time, it is a sincere laugh, "Fuckin Sgt. Parks looked at him and said, *'he is, and he did.'* James took off the bandana, sulking like a 4 year old. Classic." Cooper smiling broadly at the memory, leaning further back into the outdoor recliner. More subdued laughter erupts from the men.

"Well, what happened next? Sgt. Parks, before we departed friendly lines, told us to put them back on if we wanted. He knew it boosted morale." Jackson, smiles and exhales a large cloud and watches it drift away.

"Boosted morale, shit. That bandana kept the sweat out of my eyes, but it did look good," Cooper replies, with closed eyes, sipping his bourbon.

Del Vecchio stands to walk over to the balcony, "In James' defense Sgt. Parks had been letting us wear them at our discretion all damn deployment."

Jackson moves over to the other lounge chair, leans back and gently places his large feet on the coffee table that is between him and Cooper, "We all knew not to wear that shit around the rest of the company."

"Any matter, James' face was priceless." Thomas moving to the lounge outdoor sofa and follows Jackson's example of placing his feet on the expensive coffee table, has not laughed this hard since she passed, Thomas relishes the feeling for the moment, it has been long time since he has felt genuine joy. The men are tired from the past few days of dealing with the shock and grief of losing their fellow squad members. Jackson, Thomas, Cooper and Del Vecchio sit in mournful silence watching the smoke from their labored, guilt ridden exhales float into the warm, starry Texas night air.

Del Vecchio turns, breaking the somber moment states, "I hope Culpepper will be okay tomorrow, saying something for James."

"The man is an oak. He will be fine," Jackson responds still not completely out of his mournful doldrum, leaning back staring up into the night sky at all the billions of stars. He knows he will get lost in his gaze and soon be sucked into the *nothingness*; Jackson focuses his attention back inside the private dining room at the other half of their squad. He sees the men perk up as the meal begins to arrive, he sees Delta stand and turn in their direction to signal for them to return. Jackson cannot help but wonder, *what will become of them now; how will they respond?* He does know one thing; it will not end tomorrow at the service for James. Each one of them will have to face their own reality of their choice not to join the other three in Clear Creek.

SSgt. Jacob Parkinson

Gathered around the table, they eat in grave solitude, no one saying a word until the end. Delta stands, "I know the silence was welcome during our dinner. We honor Doherty and James with our remembrance of them, sitting here together after two decades. As we head into tomorrow with the service for James, let us not forget each other for another twenty years, for we will need one another to traverse the days ahead. I love you, brothers."

The limousine ride back to their hotel is filled with more emptiness, the men share an occasional nod and the raising of glasses as some continue to drink from the limousines' fully stocked bar. There is no loud boisterous tales from bygone days, nor goodbyes as they exit the lengthy vehicle upon arrival at the hotel. They ride the elevators in silence, depart each other's company in silence, and enter their rooms in silence. All of them know the sleepless night that awaits them in their lonesome hotel rooms. There is a sense of loss, unlocking their hotel rooms, to be swallowed by the engulfing dark that awaits on the other side of their door.

. . .

An uninhibited sun begins to warm the morning air, the congregation of mourners loosely gather in groups. Marine dress blue uniforms decorate the grieving, other former Marines are in all black variations of suits; some with mini-medals and ribbons adorning their chests. A Marine reserve unit of young-looking men and women at the ready to perform James' service with precision and accuracy. 1st Squad, again huddle near a tree, the rest of Bravo Co. that made the service, vacantly stare at them once more.

"Fuckin told you," Culpepper states to Delta, agitated, staring at the various groups of mourners looking their way. He never wanted to be around the Marines again, he loved every one of them, but he is done with that chapter of his life and was hoping it was behind him.

Delta turning to the direction of the mourners, "Easy, Devil. They just don't know what to say to us. I wouldn't know what to say to us either. Give them a break."

"I guess, Sgt. Heis." The bigger Marine replies in a more subdued, calm tone.

The Last Letter

Delta turns and looks up at Culpepper, which is the most emotion Culpepper has expressed since all of them were thrust into this tragedy. "You will do fine. Just say what you have to say and escape out the side into the foyer. No one is going to give you shit, brother."

In his full dress regalia Cooper heads over and gives the group a heads up, "Here comes Gunny Hoffman. Man, no matter how many times I see it, his stack is damn impressive." 1st Squad gathers around Delta, who stands at the forefront as the de facto leader of this group of worn-out men.

The retired Marine strides over to the group with military precision and purpose, "Why is there always a lone tree at these places?" He points to the tree the men have gathered around, acknowledging the same situation at Doherty's service. The Marines seem to genuinely smile, dawning on them that they have repeated the same behavior as before. "I do have some real news, not that shit out there now. You men aren't listening to that bullshit, are you?" Gunny Hoffman asks, growing irritated that his Marines are being eviscerated in the news as some *hired* guns for cartels.

"No, Gunny, we know the truth. We have maintained media silence," Delta responds for the remaining members of 1st Squad. Although the men are furious at the reports of their fallen Marines, they know not to engage with the news personnel.

The retired Marine nods his approval, "Good. Now for the news I've gathered for you, Devils. Parks is still in a non-medically induced coma. He's in critical condition but apparently recovering. Every man here has been cleared through Department of Homeland Security to visit him upon Doctor's authorization." Gunny Hoffman relays the information he has received, much to 1st squad's relief, judging by the audile involuntary sighs.

Perry begins to raise his hand out of the parade rest position, but Gunny Hoffman cuts him off by raising his own hand to signal to wait, "Yes, DHS is taking control for the time being of the investigation and Parks is under their protective custody. My guess is to determine if these men that attacked our three brothers are homegrown or breached our borders, which would make this a terrorist attack of sorts. At this stage everythin is fuckin conjecture."

Gunny Hoffman spits into a cup the tobacco juice from his mouth and continues, "Here is the private number set up at the hospital for y'all to call to schedule a visit when it's allowed. The only ones from Bravo Co. cleared are you men, Bgame, Attebery and myself for the time being. The supervisory special agent in charge, Medina, is a good man, I know his reputation through the MARSOC community. He is legend. Retired a very young Sgt. Major. If you do meet him, show him the respect he has earned, he has been there and done that several times over. Any questions?"

The men have a million questions but know not to ask any. Del Vecchio finally breaks the dreadful silence, "What now Gunny?"

"Now we lay James to rest. Then you men need to call me after the service and check in periodically. That's an order. I don't want to have to call you, fuckers. That will be unpleasant, I love you, each and every damn one of you." Gunny Hoffman looks at each of his former Marines, so they understand his urgency and care.

"Roger that, Gunny," they reply in solemn unison.

"Have you paid your respects to James' wife, Jocelyn? You need to if you haven't. She's over there with Bgame, Roca, Attebery, Lacey, and Carpenter with his wife, Major Carpenter; she is in uniform, so for those of you in blues, remember to salute. Roger that?"

"Roger that, Gunny," Delta replies for the group, looking towards James' grief stricken widow.

Gunny Hoffman looks around at the eight men and feels sorrow. He knows the guilt they are feeling, he has experienced enough over his almost 30 years in the Marine infantry field. *Grunts* are a different breed of Marine, and their experiences are like no other. He can see the regret in their dreary eyes as they look apprehensively towards James' family. "Devils, I know it's difficult, but she deserves for you to pay your respects."

"Gunny, how can we face her? We couldn't face Doherty's mother either. It's our fuckin fault," Perry states to the former company guns.

"Don't start that shit, brother You men have done nothin wrong. Get that shit out of your heads. You have no control over what happens or happened. Doherty's mom and fiancée are here as well, you men will pay your respects to both. If you cry, you cry. It's normal, what you will not do is take blame or carry guilt for somethin that not a damn one of you could have foreseen. Got that?" Gunny Hoffman grumbles, trying to motivate his former troops out from under their shared cloud of guilt.

"Yes, Gunny." They reply in unison once more but with heads lowered sheepishly.

Gunny Hoffman steps to each one and hugs them, then heads back to the group that are consoling Jocelyn and her daughters as she prepares to bury her husband. Attebery sees the grizzled Marine heading back his way and decides he will take this opportunity to talk to Parks' remaining squad without others around. Attebery knew how close the men and Sgt. Parks were, he also knows everything that happened that night outside of Fallujah. He takes his long strides towards 1st Squad.

Attebery feels awkward addressing the squad, "Hey fellas, I won't give you some speech of acceptance or this is not your fault but whatever help you need, feel free to ask. I know the bond you men have amongst the squad, but the rest of Bravo Co. is here for you. Don't forget that."

"Thanks, man." Delta gives Attebery a shoulder hug. The rest of the squad moves to shake Attebery's hand and nod. The Marines of 1st squad knew how close Sgt. Parks and Attebery became after the two squad leaders rotated over to Iraq early. In turn Attebery knew most of 1st Squad before Parks; when the unit deployed to GITMO in Cuba, 2002, watching over the captured from the newly found *War on Terror*.

"What's the plan next for y'all?" Attebery asks the group.

"Man, Sgt. Attebery, the plan is to just get through the fuckin day." Jackson replies anxiously picking the bark off the evergreen.

"Fuck, I just want to get through my condolences to James' wife and daughters," Morales states, staring off at the group Gunny Hoffman went to join.

Cooper stares at James' now widow; she is in her dress officer Border Patrol uniform; making for an intimidating figure but to see her grieve in uniform is a troubling sight. "That, my friend, will be a tough mission to accomplish."

"Listen, just go over there and pay your respects. She does not fault any of you. Not a one. She would love to hear your sympathies." Attebery explains to the eight Marines, as they fidget nervously amongst themselves.

Delta nods towards the men to head towards James' wife and pay their respects. "Thanks, Attebery."

"Hey fellas, one more thing." Attebery calls after them as 1st Squad begins its' trek from the evergreen to the front of the church at the forefront of the cemetery. "Don't mention Parks. She does however blame him." Attebery registers the confusion in their eyes. The eight former Marines stop dead in their tracks and begin to look at one another.

Each man realizes their former squad leader is the one who will take the blame for this catastrophe that has befallen Bravo Co. Sgt. Parks is about to be the boogeyman once again for Bravo. "That's not right," Del Vecchio states, moving past Attebery towards James' wife. The rest follow suit behind the smallest member of the squad, in a *Ranger file*; a column of old warriors in black and dress uniforms single file heading to give their ill-fated condolences.

Delta stays behind and looks to Attebery with concern, "Is that what everyone is saying. It's Parks' fault this happened?"

"Everyone has questions and no outlet for their anger. Jocelyn is the widow and understandably angry, hurt, and much more. The fuckin news doesn't help either. She just needs an outlet for her grief and Parks is that outlet unfortunately. We both know Parks would never want this to happen in a million years, not to his men. He loves y'all more than anythin." Attebery resting his hand on Delta's shoulder, trying to reassure him.

"It's not right. Parks just wanted a reunion. Fucking bullshit." Delta, getting visibly frustrated, takes a long inhale of the suddenly stifling morning air.

Attebery knows exactly what Delta is feeling, "I know man. Again, the company does not know the whole story, but they will. Fuckin news is makin it difficult. James' wife needs someone to point the finger at, she lost her husband and the father of her girls. It's tough all around man."

"I understand that. I do. It fucking sucks. When Parks wakes up, I don't know if he will be able to survive this go round of guilt and blame. You on the list of visitors to see him?" Delta adds, suddenly fearful for his old squad leader.

The Last Letter

"Yeah, man. His mother made sure to '*okay*' all the names she knew, and DHS vetted all of us." Attebery answers Delta, they both stare at the men lining up behind Del Vecchio to pay their respects to James' grieving widow.

Delta shakes Attebery's hand, "Thanks, man. For the words and help. Keep me posted after, on any news you hear." He leaves his card with Attebery and walks to the line that the remaining members of 1st Squad has formed to pay their respects to the grieving widow.

Each man hugs and offers their grief stricken condolences to James' widow. Perry cries, "Me and James never got along real well but I loved him. Damnit, I'm sorry." He hugs her and sobs. Jocelyn smiles politely to the emotional former Marine.

Jackson comes to her rescue, "Ok, big fella. You are holdin up the line." He gently pats Perry on the shoulder and steering him away from the widow. Perry releases his hug on James' bereaved wife, getting tear droplets on her impressive Border Patrol dress uniform.

Perry instead makes his way to finally pay his respects to Doherty's mother Sandra, "I loved Doherty so damn much. Me and him used to party too hard and I am so sorry If I embarrassed myself or him during those times. I'm so sorry we failed you." He grabs hold of her in another one of his bear hugs.

Sandra begins to cry as she remembers the times Perry and Doherty would struggle upon returning from Iraq. So many thousands of mothers of combat veterans struggle daily to help their sons but to no avail, it is a mother's unsung burden; but Doherty turned his life around and shared his experiences to help other struggling veterans, even his former squad leader Sgt. Parks, who was struggling of late, that to Sandra made her the proudest of her son, his compassion. Doherty shared everything with her, and Sandra is so grateful for the time she had with her brave son. "Perry, please stop cryin. It will be okay. We will get through this; Doherty would want you to push forward. Don't blame yourself, hon. He loved you, each of you."

"I'm so sorry." Perry still clinging to Doherty's mother.

Delta makes his way from paying his respects to the grieving widow, to his troop, "Easy Perry. It's my turn to pay my respects."

Perry releases his adorable but extended hug on Doherty's mother. She is extremely grateful for the outpouring of emotion from her son's longtime friend. Delta moves to Doherty's mother, "I'm sorry I did not stay and talk after Ian's funeral. It was honor to have served with him. I loved your son." Delta offering praise of his onetime fire team member.

"It's okay, dear. He talked about you, and the squad all the time. Even after his 2nd deployment, he still always talked about 1st Squad. I know all your stories by heart." She looks up into Delta's tearful blue eyes. "Even during his dark times, he would only smile when talking about 1st Squad's adventures. But when he turned it around, he would still smile at the stories when he decided to tell them to those that were gathered round, but the smile became one of acceptance rather than of longing. It was nice to see Ian smile at other things—his fiancée, becoming a father, and his job helping fellow Veterans, especially the *Grunts*." Delta looks at her with a quick astonishment, "Yes, I know the lingo. As mothers we listen when our sons are hurtin," Sandra offers her son's team leader, who is now the one being consoled.

Delta, suddenly overcome with emotion, hugs Doherty's mother as if he was embracing his own. Suddenly realizing what he must have put his own mother through during his times of darkness. He smiles as Doherty's mother wipes away the tears and whispers, "It will be okay," bearing the brunt of the grief displayed by those around. Trying to help James' widow bear some of the burden of mourning, Sandra returns by her side. The two forever bonded by the same tragic event that took their Marines.

The large wooden doors of the eloquent church are opened by a funeral staff member, signaling that the services are about to begin. Not a soul moves outside until Jocelyn begins her widow's trek inside to occupy the front row with her two daughters, including Doherty's mother holding her gloved hand.

1st Squad file in last, to take upon their self-isolation in the back of the modest cathedral. Delta moves towards the morose Culpepper and looks up at his hardened face. "Hey, brother, you still want to give your eulogy?"

"Do I want to? Fuck no. All these fuckin eyes on me. But James would've done it for me," Culpepper answers coarsely.

The Last Letter

"Hey brother don't mention Parks today, I know this fucking sucks." Delta notes with concern, hoping that would not change Culpepper's mind of giving his eulogy.

Culpepper breathes with a heavy burdened sigh, "I took care of it." "Thank you, Devil." Delta relaxes his stance, readying for the service.

The priest moves takes his position behind the pulpit, "Let us begin with an old prayer I hope you take solace in:

Dear Heavenly Father,

We weep with those who weep and mourn with those who mourn. Comfort these moms and dads, children, and spouses as only You can. You have collected all their tears in a bottle. Help them feel Your strong presence, see Your tender hand all around them and hear Your voice directing them in these dark circumstances. Draw them daily to Your Word to process their pain and grieve with hope. Spur the body of Christ around them to be Your hands and feet and to meet their practical needs. Thank you, Lord, that You are the defender of widows and father to the fatherless. Bind up their wounds and heal their broken hearts. You are good and You do good, and we pray that even in their pain they will see Your goodness sustaining them through pain. Restore to them the joy of your salvation and sing over them a new song. In Jesus name, Amen." The priest performs the hand gestures crossing his body upon completion.

He continues softly, "Thank you all for joining in the remembrance of Ryan James, husband, father, son, Marine. We all honor Ryan by being here today. We must find solace in the joy that he was and warmth from his loving memories. I would like to offer this opportunity for those who wish to say something about Ryan, please come forward and pay homage to a wonderful person taken from our loving embrace far too soon. Please, come forth loved ones." The priest moves aside from the podium to allow those who wish to speak on James' behalf, may do so.

Bravo Co. Marines turn towards the back of the large room, as the massive Culpepper makes his way to the front of the gathering. The eyes of the mourners turning their quizzical gaze upon the oak of man heading gingerly to the podium. Culpepper begins in his deep Louisiana drawl, "I was with James as a member of 1st Squad 2nd Platoon during our deployment to Iraq 04-05 with Bravo Co. I remember James as the fellow young Marine who would purposely annoy me with various cheesy lines from horrible movies and at the worst possible times, always while I had the radio constantly jabberin in my ear as the squad's radio operator; I know, the biggest guy with the radio. *I should've had the machine gun*, as James every day of our deployment would not let me forget. *'It's not right, I'm award winning marksman and I have the SAW,'* every day with that broad boyish grin of his and that light in his eyes. Every damn day." The Marines chuckle a bit.

Culpepper exhales and continues, "He had some very choice words when our platoon commander made it clear he was stuck with the that machine gun; but his jokes and quotes kept on comin; upliftin the morale of the entire squad, even the old squad leader. James was the buffer between of our squad leader and our platoon commander, it seemed more to me that he was like a hostage negotiator, trying to stop a war within a war. Our squad leader would reply to some asinine order with a profanity laced tirade, James would laugh and translate into acceptable terms, *'Culpepper tell higher he says, roger that.'* James loved every minute of being in 1st Squad, he would always express it through a joke or some smart remark, but the affection was always present in both his boyish smile and the glimmer in his eyes. It is true you never forget a bond formed through adversity and as I mourn my friend here today, I will never forget the unrelenting bond I was blessed to form with Ryan James, a miserable *SAW gunner*." Culpepper closes his eulogy with one last endearing shot at James, he then slowly moves to Jocelyn, leans down gives her a heartfelt hug, moves to Sandra, Doherty's mother, and gives her a warm embrace. The big man then strides to the back of the room, wishing he could leave but knowing he must stay.

"That was awesome, man." Thomas affectionately tells Culpepper as the big man takes his place alongside the back wall with the rest of 1st Squad.

Jocelyn stands and bravely makes her way to the podium, "Thank you, Culpepper. That was beautiful. You are right, Ryan loved you all without exception. He always smiled when he recollected those days and his beautiful eyes flashed brilliantly at the memories of those shared experiences. I loved seeing that smile on his face and the brilliance in his eyes. There was not a thing he would not do for those he loved, but there are times when you must

The Last Letter

let go. Ryan needed to let go, just like you all need to let go. Focus on your loved ones here and now, please. We are present. Our love is unwavering." She stares directly at the remaining men of 1st Squad seated or standing along the back wall of the church; suddenly, feeling unwanted and guilty, lined up ready for a firing squad. It was not fair to them but yet they all felt they deserved it; their heads drop slowly, shamefully.

"That love to help fellow Marines and reminisce cost him his life, needlessly. His life as a loving father, husband, son, and yes even Marine cut short for a chance to reflect, to relive. No, you all need to let go; love us that are here before you." She quietly cries, making her way back to her seat, met by Sandra who wraps her arm around the heartbroken widow. They both sit huddled and consoling one another. Every Marine in attendance suddenly felt shameful, some taking on a form of guilt, knowing she is correct. None really having thought of the ramifications of their service on their loved ones, the ones that do, it is too late to make up for the mistakes, and that regret will never waiver.

The priest shakenly moves back to pulpit, suddenly at a loss for words. The gathered mourners of Marines feel the blame, the priest registering the emotion in the room, "I will close with a prayer as we then adjourn to the cemetery grounds for the burial." The grieving congregation bow their heads and follow along silently as the priest gives his dismissal prayer. The grieving begin to file out of both of the side double doors to gather around the plot James will be finally laid to eternal rest and peace.

Jocelyn, her daughters and Doherty's mother take the front row of seats before of the cavernous, dark unearthed hole that is to entomb another loved one. Bravo Co. begins to align the pathway between the church and the plot, to salute the casket as it draws near and passes between the rows. It is a beautiful sight to behold, as the civilians in attendance stare in wonderment. Jocelyn keeps her gaze on the unearthed hole in front of her, waiting to say one final goodbye to her love. The beautifully crafted casket is placed on the lowering straps by the Marine pall bearers, awaiting its' final ceremony before being lowered into eternity.

The Marine detachment performing the burial ceremony moves into position to perform their various appointed tasks with precision. They await the gathering of the Bravo Co. Marines to find their place. It is a sight to behold once again as it was with Doherty's funeral procession.

The volley of rifle fire from the twenty-one-gun salute takes the old Marines by surprise once more as most are violently shook from their mournful gloom. Three volleys in all. A Marine familiar to Bravo Co. steps forward in his dress blues with a bugle in hand, he stands off to the side and begins to play *Taps*. It is somber, dreadful, and every loved one, service member and Veteran alike hates the beautiful, soothing, sorrowful instrumental. The familiar Marine finishes his masterful rendition of the long traditioned melody befitting James, sending him to rest in solace and peace.

"Fuckin Witherow, man, can play. That was fuckin depressingly amazin." Jackson looks down to Cooper who is standing next to him with his head bowed.

"The guy can play just about any instrument to perfection," Cooper whispers, not raising his gaze from the ground.

"It was beautiful, I have never heard *Taps* played that way. He changed it up from Doherty's," Jackson responds, watching Witherow march with discipline to take up position to the left rear flank of the mourners.

The Marines from the local unit perform the flag folding ceremony again with detailed precision. The senior Marine then kneels before Jocelyn and recites the dreaded words every loved one has come to loathe, "On behalf of the President of the United States, the United States Marine Corps, and a grateful Nation, please accept this flag as a symbol of our appreciation for your loved one's honorable and faithful service."

The Marine stands with discipline, does a slow hand salute and performs a right face and marches to the side of the congregation. The service has concluded. The widow left staring at her life being lowered into the ground, her daughters gather close as they too witness all they have known be lowered into darkness.

Bgame begins to stand, he and Roca are eager to finally get home to make sense of the past week. He moans a bit getting up, then notices a light touch on his wrist, it is the angered widow. The *Viking* looks down, Jocelyn has both her daughters weeping under her arms protecting them as any mother would.

Bgame is crushed. The remorse comes roaring out of the depths of his soul, his knees feel weak, and his eyes feel with sorrow.

Not the widow's eyes, no Jocelyn has nothing but fire in her eyes. Bgame takes a step back, her eyes as black as coal, she whispers up to him, "When he comes to, you tell him I hate him for this. Hopefully he will do us all a favor and die."

Bgame lowers his head, trying frantically to find the words, "Yes, ma'am." It is all he can fathom to say. How do you condemn a man without condemning them all. He pats her hand gently and strides off to join Roca, he wants desperately to go home.

The tired Marine is overcome with a debilitating thought, Parks will not make it through this if he survives. Not the judgement, not the blame, not the guilt and not the failure. All of it happening again. "Valhalla take that motherfucker. Do not let Parks suffer through this." Bgame avoids the pockets of Bravo Co. Marines, he wants to forget, for a few moments. Roca grabs the keys, they climb into the truck and as they pull out of the cemetery, Bgame notices Parks' squad under a tree, their heads down as Delta speaks to them. *Goddamn poor Devils*, his sympathies reaching out to the remaining Marines of 1st Squad. It is over, James is at rest.

CH. 22
GOODBYE JAKE

The petite, hard-pressed woman enters the dark, depressed hospital room. She immediately sees Parks' mother lying on a hospital bed next to her son. She had loathed that woman for years but now she feels only pity for the frail woman. Katie thinks it is touching to see a mother care that much, despite her personal feelings about Jean. She also notices a shorter muscular man sitting in a chair watching her. She does not like his presence. Katie then notices Parks deformative condition, she immediately moves to his bedside to hold his bruised hand, punctured with IVs, remembering the coarseness of his palms.

Jean stirs awake to see Katie holding her son's uninjured hand, "Thank you for coming to see him. I know you didn't have to." Jean knew her son spent his life since his marriage to Katie, trying to be the person he should have been with her, but it only provided Parks with an overwhelming since of regret and shame. Her son never moved on, silently punishing himself for all that he had done to his ex-wife.

"It's okay, I wanted to see him." Katie replies looking down upon the man that once was her husband. "Chase and Kylie are outside waiting to see you, Jean." She continues never taking her eyes from Parks bruised hand, trying to recognize the features she once knew by feel. The flood of emotions and memories from their time together hits her all at once; she does not cry, for she has no more tears left for this man, but she does feel some sorrow seeing him in this current state.

Jean rises from the bed; begins to leave the room to give Katie her time alone with Parks. She suddenly feeling guilty for the way she treated Katie during the marriage to her son. Jean victim blamed the woman for her son's arrest and abuse all those years ago, never accepting he was at fault. Jake told his mother the truth when she called on his birthday many years ago; he broke down it was awful to hear as mother, no mother wants to hear that their son is a terrible failure as a man. How does a mother cope with how much her son hurt his loved one, the guilt ravages through Jean's body, "Katie, I am so very sorry."

Katie endured ever so much during her marriage to Parks, but never did she want their marriage to end, and now she stands before her once love for the first time in years. She does not look up from Parks' hand as the older woman exits the room, "Thank you, Jean." Katie understands what Jean is attempting to apologize for but like her son's attempts at the same long ago, it is too late. Katie does appreciate the gesture, continuing to stare down at the comatose, seemingly fragile man before her, "Do you mind if I have a moment with him?" She asks the short muscular man eyeing her.

"Agent Medina, ma'am. I am afraid I cannot do that. Speak freely, please." Medina encourages her to continue, knowing his presence makes all who enter this room uncomfortable. He has no choice. Parks is a valuable witness and more importantly this incident has provided Medina with an opportunity to enact a sequence of events that will end this threat to the country, on his terms.

Katie refuses to look past Parks' hand, not wanting to see the damage done to her ex-husband's head. Her mind involuntarily remembers the horrible arguments and fights, each stubborn in their denial, Jake refusing any acceptance that the fault lies with him, the damage he had done to her and their lives. She shudders but never lets go of his hand. They truly loved each other at one point, the world was against them or so they thought, but he was always against himself, and she endured like all loving devoted spouses did of combat Veterans, silently trying to cure their warrior with compassion and love but to no avail, only to be met with resistance and anger. "Why the fuck could you not see what you had? Why, you fucking asshole? All you had to do was look at me?" she clasps his hand in both of hers, angrily. Her brilliant green eyes flash with her trademark intensity.

The Last Letter

She quickly composes her stoic presence, "I recognize your name. His mother told me on the phone you served with him, I recognize your name. Besides his squad, he talked about you quite a bit when he was drinking. How you did it the right way. All of his talk when he was drinking became repetitive over the years, he just never let go. Never saw me, only his repetitive past. I gave him my all, he couldn't wake up and move forward. Blaming me and the world."

"From what I have heard from his mother over the past week, you are the only one he sees now," Agent Medina responds calmly.

"Thank you, Agent, but that no longer matters," Katie replies heavily. She sits on Parks bed next to his covered leg. "Are you married, Agent Medina?"

"I was. Why do you ask?" he responds politely. Medina now leaning forward in his uncomfortable chair, rubbing his eyes quickly, one at a time.

Katie still not gazing past Parks' chest, not ready to bear that image in her mind, "No reason, seemed like a response of someone who is married or was."

Medina impressed with the intuitiveness of the burdened woman before him, offers, "We all carry our pack of guilt and regret. Eventually we all fall, no matter who we are. Parks always told you I did it the right way. Told everyone apparently. What is the right way? Parks fell to alcohol; I saw that at Camp Pendleton after the Osprey crash and at Camp Lejeune long before he met you. Do not take any of that on; he was gone. I fell to my career, Marines, MARSOC, DEA, DHS—all abbreviations of bullshit that will never unpack that guilt or regret I carry. I know what he feels. I see her finally as well and it is far too late. Like you said, ma'am, it no longer matters. We are unable to change our mistakes. None of us did it the right way." Medina rubs his weary eyes; the exhaustion becomes overwhelming.

This time Katie breaks hers gaze upon Parks and looks towards the man seated in the uncomfortable chair. His shoulders seem depressed, his face covered partially in the room's darkness, looks weathered and tired.

She is transfixed by the mannerisms of the man, Katie recognizes those depressive movements, it looked like Jake from years past. *The burden must follow them all*, she thinks. "That was heartfelt. Thank you, Agent Medina. I know Jake carries it all with him; some things you have to accept as your doing and live with the hurt caused to others. I will always care for him, in some way, but

I'm here to say my goodbyes one last time." Her gaze falling back upon Parks barely heaving chest, the machines helping pump oxygen into his lungs. There are no more tears to shed for this man lying before her but no hatred for him either. "I'm sorry I don't know why I'm telling you this shit. It has just been so damn long since I've seen him." Katie forcing any emotion to stay at bay, as she prepares to depart.

"I know, ma'am. It is okay to unburden yourself in the presence of a stranger. His mother has done the same, that is how I know how much torment and regret he still carries for you," Medina states standing gingerly, to make his way to the opposite side of the hospital bed from Katie. Unlike the others, all Medina does is stare at the deformity that is Parks' critically injured head. The fire rages in his soul as he ponders the justification for his plan which is never more apparent than in this moment, staring down at his once friend.

"Thank you, Agent Medina. I'm going to go let his kids know to come in and what to expect." Katie, still not looking past Parks' chest, brings his hand up to her heart. His rough, weathered, bruised hand suddenly felt weak and fragile, not the ones she remembers in hers; she lets go, and to her there is the finality she needed, "Goodbye, Jake." Katie cannot stay here and witness Parks' slow death, nor can she watch as his children become engulfed in grief; she did not have the strength to shoulder that much emotion for him anymore. Her past with Parks starts to flood her senses, Katie can barely remember the good moments, she stands quickly, making her way to the heavy hospital room door and lets in the awaiting light from the luminous fluorescent corridor, as it breaches into the dark, cavernous room.

The two behemoth guards appointed by Agent Medina do not budge at the sound of the opening door behind them. Kylie and Chase are sitting next to their grandmother Jean, consoling her. The former stepchildren both look up at Katie for reassurance, but she can find none to give for the two devastated children. No amount of words are going to prepare them for the state their father is currently in, and Katie only wishes she had the strength to offer the two support during the tragedy.

Both Chase and Kylie rise, each having to return on emergency leave from abroad, Air Force and Marines, respectively. Chase, now 22, towers over Katie

The Last Letter

and his sister Kylie, 19; she still small as ever; run to engulf Katie in their embrace. "I am so sorry kids. So sorry. Be strong." Katie consoles them as best she can, fighting back her tears for the children's pain. She waves Jean over to take the kids from her embrace, she cannot take watching the kids break. "I love you guys. If you need me just call. Take care, please." With that, Katie hugs the two lost children and releases them into the awaiting arms of their grandmother; she needs to be free of this hospital, this state, this life. Katie watches the two kids make their way nervously between the mountains that are the guards; petrified looks on their faces as they open the door into the gloom. She witnesses the darkness engulf the children, Katie then turns and walks steadily towards the elevators.

The strong willed woman eventually hears what she is trying to flee, the sound of the children witnessing the tragedy that is their father. It is a deep, painful howl from the children, it reverberates through the sanitized hallways of the hospital floor. The nurses pause; they have heard this sorrowful wail many times by loved ones on this floor of the hospital before. Katie steels herself, gripping the railing like a vice, her knuckles turning white from the tension. Listening to the pain of the children one last time emitting from the patient's room, Katie steps through the open elevator doors, resolved in knowing she will never see Parks again.

. . .

Kharkov is laying somewhat upright in a lounge chair on the back veranda of the villa, staring out at the vastness of the Gulf of Mexico. He is not enjoying what is considered a majestic view by all of humanity but nevertheless Kharkov attempts the emotion of enjoyment. He rubs his left shoulder; it will never be the same after taking two rounds in it from a firefight with the Taliban years ago. He has taken 8 total shots, even one in the head during his illustrious career, that is only mentioned by few.

"Why the long face, asshole?" the man known as *'Doc'* comes out onto the veranda to look at the same beautiful view as the Russian.

"Are you still pissed I made you bunk with me here and canceled your leave." Kharkov retorts, knowing Doc has no choice in any of this. Doc disobeys, he dies and so does his family; he runs, he dies and so does his family. Those are the rules and every man on Kharkov's team is hand selected to know the consequences.

The former SEAL medic replies candidly still staring out at the horizon line of the Gulf, "Nah, we're all goin to get what is owed to us for what we did. We crossed a line. That may not mean much to a Russian merc but to me it was a line I was not willin to cross. *Lady Death* will come for us soon, just you watch, brother." He knows Kharkov could kill him on the spot and toss his body over the cliff to the private beach down below but at this point Doc by now knows his only way out of his current employ is in a body bag.

"I crossed no line. Maybe you did but that is on your own soul to deal with. We will accomplish this mission and America will fall. Regardless of your feelings," Kharkov responds flatly, never taking his dead eyes off the blue waters that lay before them both.

Doc takes a seat in a chair that is part of the exquisite table set, takes a long drink of his fresh squeezed lemonade and lets out a refreshing sigh, "My feelins are mute. I'm here until this is done or until I'm KIA. Either way, I'm a dead man walkin."

"We both are, Doc." Kharkov finally looks over towards the medic.

Doc lets the silence hang in the salty air, enjoying their peace back at the compound before having to leave on the next assignment. He tries to remember when the exact moment he came to hate his country; he had been on so many deployments as a corpsmen with his SEAL unit, he had forgotten the point in time in which his American ideals were shattered. His unit was ordered too many times to blur the line between a true fight on terrorism or the fight designed by political corruption. He was tired of patching up bodies of friends for no clear objective, only to see the headlines back home used as political talking points for a measly vote.

No one gives a fuck about us in the dirt, fuck them back; that became the unspoken mantra of his fellow SEAL team members.Doc looks over at the Russian and wonders, *how did he know to find and recruit me*. Kharkov has told not a person in the unit how he came to find them and offer each a chance to *fuck* their country back.

"I know what you are thinking, my friend," the Russian calmly states, not moving his gaze off the horizon of the far-stretching Gulf of Mexico.

The former corpsmen continues to look at the foreigner through his sunglasses, "Yeah? And what's that, sir?"

"You are wondering how you got to this point, yes?" Kharkov asks in his thick accent, which he can change at any point flawlessly.

"Yeah, I am." Doc finally looks back out towards the ocean, sighing heavily, relishing in the boiling hatred for his country that brought him here. The lack of regard for America's combat Veterans, to be used as butts of jokes for movies and social media, the patronizing, condescending *thank you for your service*. It is probably why most of the Americans in the team are here. Doc seems to surrender to the fact he answered his own question, hatred. *Hatred* has caused him to go too far and there is no going back, he is in this plot until the very end.

Kharkov finally looks to the troubled medic sitting at the outdoor table staring into the vastness of the blue ocean, contemplating how it came to this. "I once asked myself the same questions long ago. I came to the same conclusion I am sure you have, *hatred*. Hatred for the American society taking and taking and taking. Never giving a fuck. No, it will be a pleasure to watch them tear themselves apart from within and then we come in for the carcass." He takes a drink of his lemonade as well. It is refreshing, the Russian notices how beautifully the liquid tastes in the setting he finds himself.

Kharkov is correct. Doc knew that is why all the men here have been so dedicated to this mission. *Hatred*. What Doc marveled at, is how well the Russian knew each member of the team would gel so cohesively. Kharkov, the medic realizes, is quietly a rageful genius and that underestimation has ended the lives of many men and women. "Yes, it will." The former corpsmen leans further back in the chair and lets out a deep exhausted breath. He is tired, the whole team is, and the end is getting closer; they all feel it. "Listen, I apologize for questionin you in front of the men, but I won't be a part of that again; I'm not killing anymore desperate combat vets. I'm in this because we are treated like shit, by the American government and people. I will be damned if I'm going to contribute to the destruction of struggling Veterans."

"We run into that problem again and you hesitate, I will kill you myself and your loved ones. Is that clear?" Kharkov threatens, stating it as fact or a chore.

Doc does not take it personally; he knows Kharkov would say that to all of the team members, but he also knows the Russian will execute everyone on the team if he deems it necessary to fulfill the mission at hand. It is a fact every man in the unit is willingly accepts. There is only one way out and that is to complete the objective following the Russian's exact orders. "It is," Doc replies defeated.

Both men sit in uncomfortable silence; there is no animosity between the two, only a professionalism among special operations veterans that have endured betrayal by their commands. The lemonade quenches their thirst on the hot Mexican afternoon. "What of the survivor?" the former corpsman asks of his commander.

Doc sees the Russian's jaw flex, mentioning the hospitalized survivor; every member of the team has been tracking the developing stories surrounding the survivor and as expected, Kharkov's handler has steered the narrative of blame onto the victims. There will never be a mention of a clandestine armed group of men, the news contacts on their payroll is extensive and well versed. With one word the Russian's handler can turn lie into fact and neither side of the news will dispute the authenticity of the report.

"Nothing. I am to do nothing." Kharkov does not change his expression, but Doc can see the Russian's jaw muscles clenching ever tighter.

"The news is crucifyin him, all news outlets. The contacts have done their job. This will be nothin in a couple weeks." Doc tries to reassure the Russian to some avail.

Kharkov rises and walks to the edge of the massive cliff and stares down at the private beach below, some of his men have gone down to surf and relax. "You do not join them?" Kharkov asks Doc, continuing to stare down at his team enjoy their much needed to time to rest.

"Fuck no. There are massive sharks off that beach. Take a drone up over the water and look. Fuck that. I did enough time in the water while I was in the SEALs, no more." Doc replies with a scoffs, soaking in the warm sun.

The Russian looks back at his troop, astonished his recruiting process and analytics that led him to such choices from around the globe have brought

The Last Letter

more success than originally planned. Each man is a perfect machine and due to his training and tutelage, have become more than their respective government ever could have hope for them to be. He takes the losses of his men with a heavy heart despite his exterior persona, as all true leaders would. Kharkov knows he cannot afford to have the team demoralized when the endgame is right at hand, a few more objectives and America falls. The team's next assignment comes at a perfect time, and he knows his men will be particularly motivated for this mission. "We leave in two days," the Russian states, blankly staring at some of his men in the surf on their boards, each one adept at navigating the waves.

"What's the objective?" Doc asks, staring up at the sun, hoping it is something that will free him from his guilt.

Kharkov turns to his troop to gauge Doc's response to his next statement, "Since past administration cut their losses and left Afghanistan to the wolves. The full on withdrawal of all US military personnel played out perfectly for our cause. Now after the past couple years of turmoil, we are to go back in."

The corpsmen's jaw begins to ache under the intense strain of his gritted teeth. He does not lower his head but continues to stare at the sun, "A walking clusterfuck that withdrawal was. Horseshit. Good Marines died for nothing. Par for the course with our government."

"Exactly, total abandonment of the country. It is utter chaos in Afghanistan with the Taliban in control once again, beautiful. We are to meet the other teams, seize all opium fields and to secure the distribution to Daniel's pipeline. Once secure, we will return here to ensure that it all makes its way across the border into America, poisoned of course." Kharkov explains to his troop their objective, relishing in the fact he is getting the desired effect from Doc. *Hate*.

The former SEAL sits upright in the chair and puts his face into his hands, preparing his body for the convulsion of anger that will crash over him like a tsunami impacting the coast. "Let me get this straight. The former draft-dodgin, orange fucktard president signs a peace deal with the Taliban, calling them *'great fighters'* , smiling his fat fuckin face on national TV, kissing the ass of the enemy cave dwellers. Basically, castrating all of us special forces bubbas hard work buildin up the Afghan military. Then the next shithead, ageing president seals the deal by fuckin givin a new meaning to the phrase '*hasty withdrawal*.' It was a two-part cluster fuck. Who pays the price for such fuck ups, the Marines, dying in their brother's arms for corrupt politicians. What do we expect from shitbag politicians who make it harder for an eighteen-year-old to get a six pack of beer than the weapons we use every day on the team. When will America realize, you need to be required to serve in our great military before you can hold national office of any fuckin kind, to understand sacrifice and the oath taken. It will never happen, and I'm lookin forward to watching America tear itself apart. Peace, motherfuckers." Doc gives a half-assed salute with two fingers.

Enjoying the rant of his team member, Kharkov encourages the younger corpsmen, "Yes, that is exactly right. Your America is going to implode." The warm Gulf air blows up the cliff and engulfs Kharkov in a sense of comfort. It is all going according to plan. He has been in this from the beginning in 2016, it has been almost a decade of sacrifice, the endgame is there for his taking.

Doc looks up towards the emotionless leader, his grip on the glass of lemonade growing ever tighter contemplating the frustrations brewing in his tortured soul; the glass shatters, blood oozes through Doc's grip, he does not notice the warmth of the red liquid. "It is not my America. It stopped being home long ago."

"You will have your revenge soon enough, my friend. We all will." Kharkov returns to gazing at the rest of his men enjoying the surf below. He knows he will receive the same emotional reaction from the others, and he is counting on their hatred to ensure loyalty to the mission, not him, the mission. He needs them loyal to the ideal and the upcoming objective will ensure their focus to the cause.

"All of that sacrifice and effort for nothin, for all those years. When do we leave?" Doc seethes through gritted teeth, trying to slow his heart rate.

The Russian turns back with a smile, "Tonight. I will send the alert to the men momentarily and we will meet up at the compound's *War Room* in an hour. I will brief the men as to what I just told you and then we will be *Oscar Mike*. Wheels up 2240 hours."

"Roger that." Doc answers in a subdued, accepting tone.

Kharkov looks down at his distraught American combat Veteran, sympathizing with the Doc's internal anger and conflict. America will first tear itself apart from within and their American moles will stoke the flames of rage; it is *beautiful*, he savors. Every one of his men were handpicked Veterans of the Iraq and Afghanistan wars no matter the country, he ensured this was always a part of the plan, his handler is playing the American political system like a beautiful violin, stoking the flames of his recruitment.

"Doc, take care of your hand. We need you good to go." The Russian genuinely concerned about his troop's wound.

The corpsman, still staring straight ahead out into the vastness of the blue horizon before him does not hear the Russian, he absorbs the news he is being told. *All of it was for fuckin nothin, nothin.* The only thought repeating in his head; over and over again.

"Doc?" Kharkov, trying to break the former SEAL's hypnotic trance.

Doc seeming to notice the blood gushing from his left hand, hears the Russian finally, "Yeah, I'm on it. It needs stiches, I'll be right back." The corpsman stands and heads into the villa he shares with Kharkov, to find his medical bag and begins suturing his deep lacerated wound on his left palm. *All for fucking nothin*, the statement again breaches his thoughts.

He stares at himself in the bathroom mirror, suturing his palm, he feels no pain looking at his reflection with anger and sadness, *how has it come to this?* He ponders, his reflection offers no solace or forgiving grace. His resolve to the fulfillment of the mission, is renewed and he knows this is exactly what the Russian and his handler intended. *It is masterfully played*, Doc thinks to himself, and the end result will be deservedly catastrophic for the American way of life. The SEAL's reflection again offers no solace, the dark image stares back at Doc with disgust and anger, *how have you let it come to this?*

CH. 23
HE REMEMBERS

Dr. Anand stands over his patient, who has been through a terribly horrific ordeal, and monitors his breathing. The swelling of his head, induced by the catastrophic damage inflicted upon the cranium has dissipated significantly over the last couple of months. The man before him looks peaceful, not the rogue Veteran they portray him to be throughout the news. His patient is in stable condition and improving. Dr. Anand does not hear the beeping of the machines, he has become oblivious to their sounds after decades in the profession. He can tell now by the look of a patient what their conditional status is, he is pleased with the patient's progress.

Medina sits upright. "How is he, Doc?"

"He is doing well, Agent Medina." Dr. Anand has even become accustomed to and even cordial with the straightforward agent. "Encouraging."

"Good. What are the chances he wakes?" Medina asks of the doctor.

Dr. Anand looks down at the middle aged man with concern. His patient always triggers memories of his own son and his son's untimely death; the two men almost the same age. The quiet doctor wants nothing more than to say one last thing to his son, one pleasant sentiment, and then he can say goodbye, peacefully. He stares down at Parks with concern and affection, "What will he wake to, Agent Medina? You see what the news still reports on the situation, his troubled past being exploited. You see the widow of one of his lost men blaming our patient and calling for his head. The rumblings of his men that came to see him over the weeks, all tired of the attention received from their own unit. What is he waking to?"

"I don't know, Doc. I do know he was once a good man and that is who I hope wakes," Medina responds sincerely.

"What are you going to tell him about his men in the event he remembers nothing upon waking?" Dr. Anand turns to Medina with concern and the shock of the loss will have on his patient.

Medina has been pondering that very question since the moment this incident was brought to his attention by one of his field operatives, "I will tell him the truth."

"From what I gathered from his men that came to see him, they were all concerned how their friend would take that very news. More than one expressed their concerns in private confidence, what that truth may do. One, Jackson, being a Doctor of Psychology, so I am inclined to agree. There are concerns." Dr. Anand turns back to his patient this time monitoring the machines.

Agent Medina stands, his short muscular frame aching at every joint from so much time spent in the uncomfortable hospital guest chair. "I know, his men expressed the same concerns to me as well after, doctor."

"I am still concerned with your approach to the situation, maybe it is best his mother tell him," Dr. Anand responds, again with genuine concern; he remember telling the news of his son's tragic suicide to his wife. He was direct and the fallout was devastating. His beloved still has not come to forgive him for his perceived callousness.

Medina moves to the wall of the windowless hospital room, in which he asked for in case of sniper threat, which scared the hell out of the nurses and staff. He inhales a large swath of stagnant hospital air and exhales. "She asked me to tell him. I told her I would and that is what's going to happen. Do not sabotage me on this." The agent looks sternly at the doctor.

Dr. Anand knows he will not be able to persuade Medina from withholding the news from the patient and *maybe the agent is right*, he thinks to himself. "I will not, I suppose it is better coming from someone he knows than hearing about it second hand or forbid see the news of the past few weeks."

"Yes, the news." Medina fears he cannot keep Parks from seeing the unfavorable news coverage of the tragedy that happened to him and his Marines for long. He is counting on Parks' need for vengeance to help fulfill his plan,

The Last Letter

but he needs a focused anger; not a self-destructive drunken rage and there is a fine line with Parks.

Dr. Anand sensing he is adding undue stress onto the already exhausted agent, "Agent Medina that is a bridge crossed in the future, let's just get our friend here healthy. The visits from his squad mates, and I'm speaking from a philosophical standpoint, has been beneficial."

"It was nice to hear the war stories of his squad's adventures. Brought back memories of my own Marines." Medina stands and moves next to Dr. Anand, to monitor his old, long lost friend.

Dr. Anand is taken aback at the suddenness of emotion from this hardened, experienced agent, "When was the last time you talked to any of your men?"

"Too long. All combat infantry unit leaders have that one unit or squad that will always pull at the heart strings, and it has been too long since I have talked to any of mine. The occasional tragic funeral but no real words are spoken." Medina transfixed on Parks' still bandaged head but now able to discern the features he remembers from the man.

The doctor can suddenly see the weariness of the agent; Agent Medina seems to become fragile before the doctor's strained eyes. The agent's gaze transfixed on the patient not seeing the patient but looking through time, at the moments past and opportunities missed. "Come, Special Agent, let me buy you a cup of tea in the cafeteria, I insist." The doctor trying to persuade the agent into taking a break for a brief moment.

"That would be great, Doc. Thank you." Agent Medina politely accepts the offer acknowledging the doctor is sincere in his concern. This is his last operation before he is done with his career, the toll to make everything go smoothly is beginning to take its pound of flesh from the agent's mental focus.

The two men exit the room Medina has called home for the past months. The sentries outside stand firm in their charge of guarding a potential witness, both men look up at the mountainous men on either side of the door, "Are they handpicked for guard duty because of their imposing physical stature? Is looking like a mountain a pre-requisite for protection of potential witnesses?" Dr. Anand attempting to bring humor to an ongoing stressful situation for all involved.

"I am impressed, Doc. That's a good one. No, Agents Baxter and Kineta are both the very best in several fields of tactics, forensics, and analytics. They volunteered for this operation as did the others." Agent Medina boasts confidently of his men, but Medina does appreciate the doctor's attempt to bring satire to the situation.

The exhausted agent and doctor continue down the hall to the elevators in silence, the hospital door slowly, quietly closes behind the two guards: unwavering in their posts. The resolute men's gaze solely focused on external threats, missing the movement of the patient as he slowly sits upright and awaken to his unfamiliar surroundings. The patient turns his head from side to side, trying to gauge his dark environment, he recognizes nothing but an immense empty hospital room. *Where the fuck are James and Doherty?*

Parks looks down at his hands and wrists at the various IVs pumping lifesaving fluids into his system, each spot is bruised and aches. He tries to reach up and comfort the monstrous pain in his temples by rubbing them but his muscles ache to move his arms that high. Parks slowly lowers his sore body back down on the stiff hospital bed, the catheter causing immense pressure and searing pain in his groin area. He quickly finds the button to raise the hospital bed to an incline. His mouth is dry and sore; he quickly scans for some water and is in luck there is a bottle on the stand next to the bed. Parks fumbles his way getting the top off the bottle, taking some precious gulps of water. The pain in his esophagus is immense from the cold of the liquid on his dry irritated throat; the soreness from being intubated for so long, still present. Parks coughs up the water on to his sweat stained sheets. The action sending waves of pain throughout his body, especially his injured head. It is unbearable, he begins to moan in quiet agony.

Where the fuck am I? What in the fuck happened to us? Is all that flashes before the former Marine's mind, staring up at the vacant plain hospital ceiling. He quickly scans for his phone on the stand next to the bed, it is not there. Instead, he finds a bouquet of fresh flowers and indications that his mother has been inhabiting the room. Parks frantically looks around, beginning to panic, until he spots the cards. The cards are from well-wishers lining the edge of the bed where he is positioned, he reaches out and grabs one: *Get better soon. I love ya, Sgt. Parks. -Perry.*

The Last Letter

Parks grabs another from the shelf above his head, there were dozens all with the same sentiment: *Feel better soon, Sgt. Parks. Love ya man, Del Vecchio.* Another one: *Sgt. Parks, we need you brother, don't give up. I love ya, brother. Morales* He reads a couple more. He then reaches over and grabs all off the ledge and the nightstands around the sterile hospital bed. The pain of each movement registering in his body, begging him to stop; Parks' face contorts with each agonizing movement.

You fucking bastard. I am so sorry I was not there for you. Get better soon, Sgt. Parks. Love ya, brother. -Cooper. Parks rushes through a few more cards frantically: *Fight through this you tough fuck, I still need you to lead us through this. I love you, brother. -Delta.* Family, friends, and Marines alike, all of them saying the exact same sentiment. Parks frantically tosses the read ones to the cold linoleum floor. None of the cards contain the answer he is looking for, the concern on his face turns to pure terror as he reaches the last two cards of the now extinct pile of well wishes: *Get your ass up, Sgt. Parks. We are not done yetCulpepper,* then the final card as he lets Culpepper's card fall to the floor; *Don't you quit Sgt. Parks. Our squad was the 'black sheep' of the company, you didn't quit then, do not quit now. Love ya, brother. -Jackson.* Parks lets Jackson's card fall to the floor with the rest, his terror now setting in as reality. Not one card from James or Doherty. Parks lays back down on the hospital bed, the tears dropping swiftly from his eyes. The agony is too much, the mournful moan echoes down the sterile corridor, freezing all, patients and staff alike. He remembers.

. . .

The two men sit staring at their cups of hot tea on the sturdy wood table before them, in the elegant hospital cafeteria. It is beautiful and takes on the look of a restaurant rather than a bleak hospital eatery. They say nothing to one another, it has been a trying couple of months for them both, especially keeping the status of the patient from being leaked to the press. Dr. Anand is about to broach that very subject with Medina, when suddenly the alert on his hospital pager begins to chime. He quickly checks his cell phone for the status of the alert, his face drops in shock, his gaze then falls upon the agent, who in turn is looking at his own alert.

"We gotta go, Doc. Parks is awake." Medina stands and begins to move to the elevators smoothly but quickly with the doctor frantically in tow. "Has any of your staff conversed with him?"

"No. They have express orders to contact me first," Dr. Anand answers in the affirmative as the elevator doors slide open.

"Good. Shit is about to hit the fan, Doctor." Medina's demeanor suddenly going from exhausted to alert. He is on point. These are the conditions that Medina has thrived under his whole career. It is what has propelled him to the top of his field in each and every endeavor. As the elevator cruises up to the patient's floor, Medina is flooded with memories of his own service and the fact he never acknowledged any of it and kept pushing forward, over and over moving on to the next career, "Follow my lead. Just go in, check his vitals and say nothing. Then leave. I will need a few moments alone with him."

Dr. Anand noticing the change in the agent's demeanor understands perfectly, "Roger that." He gives Medina a nervous wink. The neurologist picked up the terminology listening to the Marines tell their stories at the bedside of the patient. The stories of the squad were humorous, daring, and exciting. But most of all, filled with admiration and love for one another.

The two men arrive at the door to the patient's hospital room, they can see through the glass that Parks is in agony, tears are streaming down both sides of his face. Both men are extremely nervous; Agent Medina is trying to remember the last time he felt nervous, he cannot but this is personal. Medina pushes the door open between to the two mountainous guards, slowly and easily. Dr. Anand quietly waiting behind the special agent.

"Parks, man. It's Medina, brother," the concerned agent states clearly, softly, entering the dark room. The machines continuing their incessant beeping, oblivious to the human drama unfolding before their life monitoring functions. Dr. Anand moves earnestly checking the various readings.

"Doc, will you please get this catheter out of my dick." Parks softly demands, wiping the tears from his cheeks.

"Yes, of course." Normally the doctor would send in Nurse Bennett, but he wants to spare her the nervousness of being the one around the waking patient. The nurses have fond affection for their slumbering patient but remain highly nervous given the volatility of the circumstances in which the patient came to be in their care. "This will be uncomfortable." The doctor warns.

Parks nods his head in agreement and for the doctor to proceed. Dr. Anand puts on a pair of disposable gloves, "This will hurt momentarily." He gently as can be done removes the catheter from his patient in a flash movement. Parks groans at the sharp pain.

Medina makes his way into the light on the right side of the hospital bed. "Hey brother its me."

"I know, man. Just in too much agony to respond. What the fuck are you doing here?" Parks hoarsely replies to his concerned friend, trying to figure out why his old buddy from the Marines is here in his hospital room.

Medina moves closer to Parks, "I'm with DHS, in fact I am the director of special operations capable department of the DHS. Your encounter popped up on my radar and I responded. I am here to help you old friend." Medina waves for Dr. Anand to go prepare sedatives in the event Parks takes the news of losing his Marines erratically.

The old squad leader stares up at the off white tiles of the hospital room ceiling, "They're dead, aren't they?" Parks mutters softly, knowing he does not want Medina to confirm his fears.

"Yes. They are gone, my old friend." Medina gravely delivers the news that is the dread of the man before him. Everyone to the person expressed concern of how Parks would handle the news of his men's' fatal tragedy.

A lump forms in Parks throat. He feels as if it is constricting his airway, Parks is choking. His hands clasp his throat trying to coax the lump of grief out, but it is stuck, too large to erupt from his constricted esophagus. Medina rushes over and sits Parks upright and firmly slaps him on the back. It does the trick, and the patient begins to breathe as Medina gently lowers him back down on the unforgiving hospital bed. "What do you remember?" He asks with trepidation.

Parks does not make eye contact; he continues despondently to stare up at the horrible tile ceiling of the hospital room. He remains silent, a million

SSgt. Jacob Parkinson

last images of James and Doherty in agony desperately trying to help him with their very last breath on this Earth, crash upon his consciousness. His head begins to erupt in pain, the anger begins to build in his chest, his heart rate begins to quicken, the EKG registering the uptick in beats per minute, starts to bounce frantically on the monitor.

"Easy, friend. Breathe." Medina rests a hand on Parks' right shoulder, trying to calm the heart rate of his injured friend. The man before him shuts his eyes and begins to cry.

The tears stream down Parks face unabated, his body sears from the intense pain as each misery filled gulp of air inhaled causes a crippling headache, each exhale crushes his heart. Parks recognizes this life altering sorrow and grief; he awaits the darkness to that accompanies such loss. He has fought off the darkness before, this time it feels more powerful; his defenses have weakened over the years. The battle for his soul has begun, time is ticking down. Parks opens his eyes, sees the hideous white ceiling, *I'm so fuckin tired.*

Medina stares compassionately down at his old friend, the fleeting memories the two had together first at Pendleton and then at Lejeune, have dissipated over the years. The celebrations come back in exact detail today and Medina is caught off guard by a wave of nostalgia. The immediate avalanche of personal regret and guilt soon follow. "Parks, brother, what do you remember?"

"Everything." The tears flowing faster, Parks never breaking his gaze from the ugly, white hospital ceiling.

"What do you want to tell me?" Medina asking, not as an agent but as a longtime friend, even though the two have not spoken since Parks' meltdown in Lejeune; he still admired the man despite his flaws.

"Nothing." The squad leader replies with exhaustion.

The special agent sits in the hospital chair he has grown accustomed to over the last couple of months, like Parks, Medina is tired. Tired of the bitter, ugly, pointless politics preventing the protection of the American citizen. Yes, he too is tired of it all.

"Don't sit. With all due respect brother, please get the fuck out." Parks softly asks, his voice cracks under the rising guilt.

The Last Letter

"I understand my friend. I will make sure you are left undisturbed." Medina makes his way towards the door; he looks back hoping he is making the right decision leaving his friend alone, but he knows if he stays, the matter will only worsen, and Parks will come to resent him for trying. He has known the tragedy Parks is facing, the loss of men. Medina exits the room with a look back at his pain stricken friend and then instructs the guards to allow entrance to no one without his authorization. They nod in the affirmative with an understanding look of concern on their faces, knowing the precariousness of the situation.

Parks finally shuts his eyes, flashes of James and Doherty strobe across his waking reality, *Why the fuck not me? You, motherfucker, why did you not take me? Why! You are fuckin dead to me. You ask for blind faith, but you just take and take and take, just to keep testing that fuckin faith. It is a fuckin game to you. No more, I am done playing your game. Have faith in this, I am going to burn this country to the ground before I go. Fuck you, so called God.* This vow, Parks commits to his soul, his rage boiling beneath the surface. He wants out of this hospital bed but as he tries to move, he falls back onto his stacked pillows.

"You aren't goin any-fuckin-where lookin like that." A voice chuckles from the dark corner of the room. Parks cannot see who it is but can make out a shape of man standing in the spot . He is trying to figure out how the man got past the two guards standing alertly at the door. *I'm fuckin dreaming.* The immediate thought broaches the forefront of his mind. But the voice is unmistakable, and the dark silhouette is starting to look familiar. *He's dreaming.* James' beaming grin appears out of the gloom, like the Cheshire cat from *Alice in Wonderland*, stepping out of the corner and into the dim light.

Parks shuts and opens his eyes several times, trying to wake himself from this nightmarish visage. James moves towards Parks; he is dressed in the same Marine digital cammies and gear he wore that day the three of them set out on their joyful reunion. His smile still genuine and warm, as it was the morning setting off into the woods, as it was when James was in Iraq making *Team OFP* laugh at some movie quote or some other asinine joke, as it was over the years, he kept tabs on Parks. James' smile was that of mischief and cunning but with the noblest of intentions.

SSgt. Jacob Parkinson

"Sgt. Parks, you really do look like shit," James finally stands at his injured squad leader's bedside.

The EKG monitor begins its' uptick as Parks heartbeat begins to race with anxiety. *What the fuck, wake the fuck up.* He tries desperately rubbing his face and eyes with his hands but to no avail. His injured left hand sending waves of pain up his atrophied arm. James still stands by his bedside compassionately, boyish smile, blushing cheeks under his full sandy-blonde beard.

"Easy, old man, you're goin to give yourself a heart attack." His bearded grin pleading with Parks to slow his heart rate.

Fuckin God's sick fuckin joke, Parks acknowledges a higher power taking the hope and promise from him, even now. *Fuck you.* The squad leader stands firm in his disdain.

"Was that directed at me or the man upstairs? I'm hurt if it is directed at me Sgt. Parks, if its' him then carry on, you will have to settle that one on your own. You look better than you did. A couple weeks ago, fuckin *Sloth* from *The Goonies*. Man, you were all fucked up. But shit you bounce back fast, brother." James reaches out and gently pats his friend on the chest affectionately.

Parks shudders at James' touch; he could actually feel the sensation of his troop's gloved hand. He inhales deeply and looks up at James. The sandy beard and hair disheveled as the morning they met for their excursion; his wry smile never fading. *Fuck it.* Parks resigns himself to this nightmare; *he is being punished; he deserves this, he is in hell.* "Where's Doherty?" Parks asks, playing along with God's cruel joke.

"Doherty will be along when he sees the need to step in." James smiles, pulling up the uncomfortable hospital chair Agent Medina has called home for the last couple of months and kicks up his bloused desert boots on the end of the hospital bed near Parks' covered feet.

The old squad leader turns his head and looks at the mountainous agents guarding the room, they hear nothing. *Yeah, this is God's cruel fuckin joke.*

"It very well could be, Sgt. Parks," James, answering the old Marine's internal thought.

Parks shows no signs of shock or paranoia, he has resigned himself to insanity. "What's fucking next?" He returns his gaze to the hideous ceiling.

The Last Letter

"Well, next you will be visited by three ghosts." James looking over at Parks waiting for the corresponding reaction, he receives no reaction from his former squad leader. "I couldn't resist, sorry. Bad fuckin joke, too soon. I don't know what's next, Sgt. Parks. All I know is that I'm here, and I'm making the best of it."

Parks looks over at his fallen troop, "I'm just finally fucked. It happened; I have heard the stories but never thought it would happen. I'm fuckin crazy, everyone was right."

"Hey, motherfucker you at least acknowledge my presence, thank you. I was beginnin to think I was goin batshit, Sgt. Parks." James lets out an exhale of relief. "Hey brother, I don't know what the fuck is goin on any more than you do, you could be goin crazy, and I'm a figment of your shattered fuckin psyche, who knows. Let's just enjoy the moment, shall we." James broad smile never relenting.

"I don't want to play this game anymore. I'm too fuckin tired. Get the fuck out, Devil." Parks pleading with his lost friend.

"Right there, right there. That's probably why I'm here, to keep you from givin the fuck up. The more you keep that shit up, the longer I'm probably going to be around and that sucks. I love you, man but I do not, say again do not; want to be lingering around in your fucked up mind. I have shit to do in the afterlife, Sgt. Parks." James beams with a crooked, mischievous, grin.

"Alright fuck, I'll play along. Shut up. Shit. You're giving me a goddamn headache." Parks continues to question his reality but has no choice but to accept the warm, heartfelt image before him. The old Marine hits the television button on the hospital bed railing controls, nothing but a black screen.

He presses the button frantically a few more times. No response from the flatscreen, only black staring back at him offering nothing. *Of course.* Parks retorts in his mind.

James looks over his shoulder, back towards the small, mounted TV in the corner, "Oh man, they cut that shit when you first arrived. You don't want to know what's on the news, anyway. Nothin but pain for you there, Sgt. Parks."

Parks searches the nightstand and the ledge hurriedly. "They have that too. Your phone.", James trying to reassure his squad leader of the situation, to prevent Parks' delicate heart rate from rising again. It will trigger alarms;

the nurses will enter, and Parks is not ready to have his reality questioned at this particular fragile moment in time.

"Fuck." The patient whispers to himself, yet not truly ready to accept that this vision of James, is in fact his new reality.

James still in his jovial mood, "Yep, fuck. They probably don't want you to see the news. This situation is a clusterfuck."

"I concur." Parks finally giving in and conversing with the jovial ghost. "Why are you here, man?"

James stretches his arms above his head and yawns, "I have no fuckin clue. But I'm here, and I want to see you back on your feet, Sgt. Parks."

"Don't fuckin call me that." Parks softly speaks, turning to make eye contact with James. The tears once again stream down his cheeks.

"Call you what?" James looks over at his broken squad leader, lowering his arms back across his chest rig. Boots still propped upon the hospital bed.

Parks returns his guilt stricken gaze back to the hideous, blank ceiling. "*Sgt. Parks*. I stopped being that man long ago, I fuckin told you that already. I am nothing."

"You stow that shit right now, Sgt. Parks." James trying to help his friend with his usual form of encouragement.

"STOP CALLING ME THAT!" Parks yells, his muscles constricting; sending waves of searing, tortuous, blinding pain throughout his body. The guards immediately burst into the room.

"Call the doctor, now!" The first agent entering tells his large partner, staring in shock at the stressed patient as alarms ring on the machines registering heart rate and blood pressure.

James stands, his demeanor turns to one of concern for his former squad leader, "You done fucked up now, brother. The doc is going to sedate you and who knows when you'll wake up. Fuck, way to go, Sgt. Parks."

His gaze still transfixed on the ugly tiled ceiling, Parks roars, "Stop calling me that!"

The agent looks about the room but says nothing. He heads over to the strewn about get-well cards on the cold hospital floor and begins neatly, carefully picking them up.

"Please throw them away," Parks pleads with the caring agent.

The agent visibly shaken by the painful heart-stricken look in Parks' eyes, shivers reflexively. To the agent it felt as if he absorbed some of that guilt this man before him is carrying inside, "Sir, why don't I just stack them neatly here on the ledge and you can decide at a later time what to do with the heartfelt messages sent from loved ones." The agent trying subtlety to help Parks reconsider discarding such tender sentiments from loved ones and friends.

Dr. Anand rushes in, administering a sedative to his distraught patient, Medina, quickly on his heels. "Sir, just relax. Calm yourself." Dr. Anand readies the needle.

A heavy pressure of exhaustion hits Parks like a bag of sand lying on his chest; he suddenly sinks further into the stale pillows of his hospital bed. They engulf either side of his throbbing head and Parks shuts his eyes, "I just want him to stop calling me that. I'm so fuckin tired."

"What're you talking about Parks? Talk to me, brother. Who?" Medina asks of his injured friend, worriedly.

"It's nothing. Go ahead Doc. Make it so I don't wake?" Parks gives him a demented half smile.

Medina moves opposite the doctor, completely oblivious to the ghostly figure lingering in the background looking concerned for his former squad leader. Parks glazed stare follows the special agent as he passes right through the visage of James. *Fuck, I am crazy.* Parks thinks to himself, continuing his gaze through Medina to the desert clad James standing in the background.

"Fuck that nonsense, Parks. Push forward." Medina implores his old friend.

"Not now with that bullshit." Parks waves his friend off with a gesture of his IV riddled hand. "Medina, no visitors. Not a fuckin soul. No family, no friends, no loved ones, and no fuckin Marines. Will you please do me that favor." Parks harshly requests of his longtime friend.

Dr. Anand administers the sedative and then looks over at Medina, with trepidation. He knows the patient's mother will want to see him immediately. This will crush her. He is suddenly thrown back to his own trauma; *Is this how his son felt before he took his life? Did he feel tired? Did he give up on everyone?* He did not want the same for the young man lying before him.

"Of course." Medina reluctantly answers to the dismay of the worried doctor and even to the worry of the agent standing by the door. For the agent knows he will be the one enforcing that promise upon the patient's mother, to deny her admittance to her awakened son and the action will break the stoic agent's heart.

The men exit the room. It is quiet and filled with apprehension once again. James moves back to Parks' bedside; he lays his gloved hand on his squad leader's slowly slumbering chest and says nothing.

Parks is beginning to feel the effects of the sedative, his eyes haze, his mind numbs. He turns his head from the hideous ceiling to James, he then sees the man appear from the shadows beyond his troop. *Not now.*

He appears with that crooked, genuine smile but a smile of compassion and worry. "I am so fuckin sorry. So fuckin sorry, so fuckin sorry," Parks keeps muttering to the two apparitions standing worriedly before him.

"It's okay. Rest easy, Sgt. Parks," the new apparition states calmly, soothingly. The sedative reaching its max potency in Parks' system, his eyes begin to droop over, his vision blurred, "Please don't call me that, Doherty." He slurs as his eyes shut completely and Parks is enclosed by the darkness he has been craving long before the tragedy of his honored men.

. . .

Jean exits the elevator with a purpose, intent on seeing her injured son for the first time since she was told he had awoken 12 hours ago. She sees the two looming agents standing their dutiful post in front of his hospital room door. Over the past couple months Jean has grown close with the two detachments of agents dispatched to protect her son at all costs. Agents Baxter, Anderson, Lance and Kineta and of course Supervisory Special Agent in Charge Medina. She makes them all chocolate chip cookies, a staple from Parks' childhood, from the kitchen of the beautiful log cabin Airbnb she is renting.

Agents Baxter and Kineta both see the frail woman approaching, she has diminished since her arrival a couple of months ago and the holiday season being particularly rough. They exchange nervous glances with one another, dreading the moment she asks to see her son. A son she has stood gallantly by through the onslaught of media coverage, a son, she weeps alone at night over, the agents hearing every mournful sob. Medina ordered Kineta be the one to prohibit admittance to Ms. Parkinson. Agent Kineta has experienced trauma and has delivered the devastating news to loved ones all over the world but never has he been asked to deliver the news, a son doted upon so by this fragile but strong woman, wishes not to see her. He curses Medina under his breath, "Fuck. This is punishment for the last op, I know it," whispering towards Agent Baxter.

"You know the boss is not like that. You were the one conversing with Ms. Parkinson in Spanish, to refresh her bilingual skills. He feels she will take the news from you easier. I will call him in." Agent Baxter whispers back to Kineta, as Parks' mother fast approaches.

Fuck. One last thought passes through Agent Kineta's head as Jean looks up at him. He usually has the door wide open by now, with some quip in Spanish about the day's politics or something upbeat to lift her sprits and give her some intellectual stimulus by revisiting her Spanish, she had forgotten long ago. Though today she is puzzling why the usually upbeat agent is stalling and the harried look upon his face.

"qué está mal?" Jean asks desperately, fearing the worst. That her broken son has passed without her present. She begins to move immediately to the door.

Agent Kineta intercepts her movement and blocks entry to the shock of the mother, "Jean, Por favor podemos hablar? Por favor?" He stares down at her with such sorrow. She tries to push past him, knowing it will make no difference. "Por favor? Jean, he is fine. No quiere ver a nadie."

She looks up in bewilderment, "He said this. He's speaking. ¿Por favor déjame ver a mi hijo?" Jean pleads with Agent Kineta, tears beginning to form and drop from the corners of her eyes.

Kineta is struggling to contain his own emotions, she reminded him of his own mother who passed from COVID-19 at the age of sixty-eight, she dying alone and afraid in a hospital much like the one he stands; his mother's final moments missed due to being on an assignment. Agent Kineta always had to be in the thick of it, never wanting to miss an operation with his team, his brothers in the dirt. *What did it cost him? What did it cost them all?* Those precious moments gone forever. He could not bear this much longer.

Sensing his fellow operator's dismay, Agent Baxter swiftly intervenes, "Jean, please lets go sit. I promise to fill you in on every detail I am permitted to. Both Special Agent Medina and Dr. Anand are enroute and will brief you extensively. Please, Jean. It will be okay." Agent Baxter's soothing demeanor seems to put the distraught woman in a calmer state, she abruptly wipes the tears from her eyes and inhales deeply.

"Lead the way, Agent Baxter. Thank you, Kineta. It's okay, I understand." She puts a reassuring hand on his massive shoulder. The agent then loses a tear down the left side of his cheek; Jean quickly intercepts the droplet with her hand before Kineta has a chance to wipe it away. She turns and follows Agent Baxter, never seeing the other tears that flowed freely from Agent Kineta's forgotten pain.

Parks can hear his mother speaking Spanish outside pleading with the agent to let her in, he recognizes her shaky voice. The sedatives did nothing for his sleep. The nightmares of the forest replay over and over, a crippling loop of highlights for his body to convulse in pain after each tortuous loop. The execution of his men before him crushing his will to live. No, sleep will not be coming to Parks anytime in the near future. His eyes again transfixed on the hideous white hospital ceiling, the little spots making patterns before his eyes. Parks has no desire or intentions of seeing anyone, he wants to be left alone until he decides how to end everything on his terms. He wants no part of humanity any longer.

"Hey, brother, don't think that way. Humanity still needs a Sgt. Parks a fuckin little while longer. Right?" Doherty pulls up a chair, still in his gear from the night he fell.

Parks looks over at his friend's concerned apparition, "Not now, Doherty. Please. I cannot lose my shit now." He desperately pleads with what he can only rationalize as his fractured psyche reacting from the loss of his men horrifically.

"I appear when I'm needed and right now, I'm needed here, with you, helping you navigate this shit, Sgt. Parks." Doherty leans forward in his chair to reassure his former squad leader.

The Last Letter

"Doherty, please I am begging you; stop calling me that. I stopped being that fuckin man the moment we got back. That's what the trip was for, to gather you all and put *Sgt. Parks* to fuckin bed. Get me off this fuckin stage you men have put me on. I am nothing, I have hurt the ones I'm supposed to protect. I am so fuckin sick of *Sgt. Parks* lingering in my goddamn background. This immeasurable standard, which has long been dead. No, the purpose of the trip was to finally get rid of *Sgt. Parks* and you Marines could see me for the failure I have become. *Sgt. Parks* is dead; let him the fuck go, I have. It's over, Devil." Parks softly speaks to the vision of his former troop, pleading with the vision to leave him in peace to find the end.

Doherty only smiles and stands over the tired Marine, "No. I'm not lettin shit go and neither are the rest of the men. You need to let your mama in to see you, Sgt. Parks." Doherty motions his head towards the door to where Parks' mother stood.

"No," Parks answers with finality, continuing to stare at the despondent ceiling.

Doherty laughs slightly, "Defiant as always, aren't we?"

"Doherty's right." James appears, out of the gloom of the corner. He moves and stands next to Doherty, both exactly how Parks remembered them that morning. Suddenly the flashes of the firefight ravages his thoughts, he convulses with grief. Parks' body erupting in fiery pain as his muscles contract and tighten. Muscles he has not used in months, each muscle group screams in agony, the machines registering his quickened pulse.

James rushes to his injured squad leader's side, "Easy their little fella.", purposely talking to Parks as if he were talking to a wounded animal with that devilish smile and sarcastic tone.

It works, Parks' heart rate is dropping as the tears flow freely, "I'm so fuckin sorry. So, fuckin sorry James, Doherty. I can't do this anymore, fuckin *Sgt. Parks*, he's the cause." The broken Marine still stares at the ceiling not wanting to look at the concerned expressions on his men's faces, Parks is trying to give up.

The two will not let him, "Come on, brother, we're here for a reason so let's find out what the fuck that is, sound good?" Doherty asks, patting his old squad leader on the foot affectionately.

SSgt. Jacob Parkinson

"Oh, Sgt. Parks, to his fuckin dismay has no choice. We're stuck on this psycho fuck glorious ride until whatever conclusion God or whoever the fuck up there has in store for three hard chargin motherfuckers." James smiles, desperately trying to make light of the situation.

Parks looks over to the agent standing diligently at his post, his head constantly monitoring the surroundings, yet he notices not the two Marines in desert gear standing before his stagnant hospital bed. Parks looks at his two fallen troops standing there before him; *I am done, I'm ending this soon.*

"The fuck you are. Ending anything you fucktard. Snap out of that mindset right goddamn now, Sgt. Parks." Doherty growls at his squad leader. It is one of the few times Parks has seen Doherty cease to smile. No matter how tired 1st Squad became from doing constant patrols for their platoon and company, Doherty always smiled at Parks, letting Parks know nothing will break his drive. That smile is no longer visible, scolding his former squad leader, as if Parks were a lowly boot[50].

"Man, Sgt. Parks, what the fuck are we going to do with you? We can't have you mutterin nonsense like this the whole damn time we're together. That shit will get old fast, Devil." James hovering over Parks bedside, getting ready to position the chair to kick his boot up on the generic hospital nightstand.

Parks wipes the tears from his face and gives James the middle finger, "What the fuck do you want with me? What? What does it take for you to finally let me fuckin die?! I don't want to play any fuckin more!" He angrily asks the blank ceiling, hoping for an answer that will explain away his life's consequences, he brought upon himself.

"What the fuck, Sgt. Parks. I'm just trying to make conversation with my friend and former squad leader, dick." James, feigning a hurtful reaction, putting a gloved hand over his mag pull on the left side of his vest to cover his heart.

Parks softly whispers, exhausted by his hatred brewing throughout his body. "I wasn't talking to you, brother. I was talking to the fucktard upstairs who thought it would be fun to torture me with the visions of my fallen

---
[50] New Marines

The Last Letter

Marines. Believe me James, you two are welcome until I figure out how to end this bullshit."

Doherty stands and moves to Parks left bedside, "Come on, Sgt. Parks, don't fuckin talk that shit. You need to have some sort of faith, any faith. Which in turn will lead to some form of hope through this fucked situation." Doherty looks down towering above Parks with his 6'2" frame but to Parks, his troop seems to be looming large in the small room.

"Doherty, I love you brother but stow that fuckin hope and faith shit. I have no room for that bullshit amongst my rising hatred for this fuckin world. Let it burn." Parks never removing his gaze from the sterile white hospital ceiling, refusing to become emotionally attached to the two visions before him.

James finally finds a comfortable position with the chair and stand, kicks his boots up to their resting place, crossing his legs at the ankles. "Well, that got fuckin dark really quick, asshole. Thanks. Come on Sgt. Parks, give us a movie quote, that always made us laugh and drive Culpepper crazy. Remember that shit on *Team OFP*, when we would be out by ourselves, you and me drivin the big man crazy with stupid ass movie quotes. God, that was awesome. I miss those days. *Combat addiction*, I told you, Sgt. Parks, it's real."

Parks cringes every time he hears the men use his former title; his body tightens from the convulsion. *Fuck this, I need to get the fuck out of here.* Parks thinks to himself, reaching for the nurse's call button.

Doherty interferes with Parks' attempt at rescue, "I wouldn't do that Sgt. Parks. They will send in the agents as well as the doctors and nurses. Your poor mama will be devastated, thinkin there is a life threatenin emergency. Our poor mothers have been through enough. James back me up on this." Doherty turns towards James, pleading with him to stop their squad leader from pushing the call button. Parks, realizing for the first time the two have acknowledged one another, his shock is displayed plainly on his recovering, slightly swollen, bruised face. Parks now knows he is insane.

"You're not insane, shithead. Just listen to Doherty. Our mothers have been through enough. It's a fate that hangs over every mother of a combat veteran. When they do get that call, there are no words for a mother losing her son like this and you want to put your dear, fragile mother through that shit.

You remember the wailing and crying of the haji women. I fuckin shudder thinkin about that sound, kept me up at nights, now it has come home. Our mother's pain sits there before us haunting our waking souls." James suddenly staring off into space, no smile displayed across his face. He stares into the *nothingness*, lost in a vague forgotten memory.

Parks look over to his troop, James is crying. He keeps his hand from pushing the call button. "I am sorry. This is not what I wanted. I wanted one last gathering for 1st Squad before life absolutely takes us. I wanted you men to see that *Sgt. Parks* was no fuckin more and to reflect fondly on those times we had in Iraq that made us the *black sheep* not just of Bravo but the battalion. One long fuckin day that will forever haunt my fuckin existence. That day immortalized *Sgt. fuckin Parks* to everyone; all I did was fall from there. I wanted us to have one final time to remember before locking it all away for good. That was what the trip was about, I wanted to see you men one last time. You men were the only thing I have ever done correct in my entire life."

"What was going to happen after you saw us?" Doherty asks with his advocacy intuition kicking in on the struggle of Parks' emotional state.

"You two can read minds, you fuckin already know the answer to that question." Parks returns his gaze to the white ceiling; the tears continue to flow.

James looks over after he breaking his trance staring off into oblivion, "No, we can read only yours and that's only at times. Now answer Doherty's fuckin question, Sgt. Parks. What was going to happen after you saw us, dickhead?"

"None of your fuckin business. *Sgt. Parks*, haunting my every fuckin waking moment, staring back at me in the mirror, judging the failures. I'm tired of him." The old squad leader keeps his gaze fixed; he does not feel the pain coursing through his body anymore. He welcomes the numbness.

"Yeah, well get the fuck over it. You are not done yet and he is not done with you, Sgt. Parks." James retorts with a hint of anger rising in his throat. He is getting pissed hearing his former squad leader talk as a defeatist, giving up.

"Fuck him." Parks' anger rises at the same pace as James'.

Doherty moves to the side where James is sitting with his boots propped up on the plain nightstand. He rests a comforting hand on his friend's shoulder,

The Last Letter

"He's right, you're not done yet. You may not believe in him, but he fuckin believes in you nonetheless."

Parks suddenly erupts with a wicked smile stretching across his face, *"You got it all wrong, holy man. I absolutely believe in God, and I absolutely hate the fucker."* He erupts with maniacal laughter, his ribs blister in agony with the outburst. "There's your fuckin movie quote, James." Parks continues with the delirious laughter. Doherty rolls his eyes in dismay but smiles, knowing he set himself up for his squad leader to deliver the line.

James erupts with laughter alongside Parks, "Nice, Sgt. Parks! Vin Diesel, *Pitch Black*. Doherty you walked right into that one, blindly, douche."

"Yeah, I fuckin know. Good one, Sgt. Parks," Doherty responds with his trademark southern smile.

Parks suddenly cuts off his laughter at hearing his former title once again, but it is too late. Agent Kineta bursts through the door at the sound of the delirium. The sound takes the agent off guard, trying to pinpoint where the laughter is emitting from then realizes it is from his six o'clock position. It is the patient. Laughing to himself.

"Sir, is everything alright? Are you in pain? Would you like the doctor or nurse?" the agent asks the now still patient. "I thought I heard something, sir."

Parks keeps his gaze transfixed upward, the anger grows in his chest at the mention of his former title and his troops persistent use of it. He says nothing. Doherty looks to the agent then down at Parks, "He is just tryin to help and follow his orders, from your old friend I might add, that special agent fella. You better talk to the agent, or their will be a swarm of motherfuckers in here, Sgt. Parks."

"I'm fine, agent. No fuckin doctors. No nurses. No family. No loved ones. No anyone." Parks exhaling deeply.

"Ok, sir. Special Agent Medina and Dr. Anand are with your mother, briefing her on your wishes. Sir, if I may, your mother has been at your side without fail. Might you give her the opportunity to see you?" Agent Kineta breaks his stone adherence to protocol but in these times and the ones ahead, he knows every chance is fleeting.

Parks does not break his gaze into the *nothingness*; he breathes heavily, sadly. James picks his feet off the bed to address his old friend, "He's right,

Sgt. Parks, you need to let mama Parks in here to see you. Besides I have a million, *'I'm goin to tell your mama when we get back'* Sgt. Parks stories," James states with a broad bearded smile, his hands clasped behind his head, nodding towards the agent.

"No." Parks simply states to both men's request. His plan does not involve emotional attachment from this point forth. He desperately craves the solitude that he knows he will not receive if he stays in this hospital.

Agent Kineta seems taken aback by the tone in which Parks stated his answer. The finality of the answer, no pause for consideration, "Yes sir." The quiet agent begins to walk back out the door to go appraise Special Agent Medina of the changing situation regarding their protected witness.

"Aww. You hurt his feelings, Sgt. Parks." James continuing to enjoy the moment.

"You two, time for you to leave me the fuck alone. I don't need this shit." Parks, seemingly in a staring contest with *Death*, herself. Daring her to take him to his eternal Hell.

Doherty looks over to James and shakes his head, the two are not getting their point across to their former squad leader. "She is staring back at you but finds your defiance humorous. Sgt. Parks we both, James and I, don't know how the fuck this works but we're here, and we are here to help until this shit show ends. Roger that?' Doherty smiles down at the emotional wreck before him.

"I have no fucking choice." Parks reluctantly answers.

"There you go! Now you get it, Sgt. Parks." James chides his injured squad leader. "You're not as dumb a shit as you look right now. All still swollen and ugly. Goonies lookin motherfucker." The bearded smile continues, "Let's have a look at some of these cards you threw about earlier lookin for any from the both of us. Touching to witness and clever, I might add."

Parks groans with annoyance and misery, "No, we are not reading cards. Please fellas leave me in peace for just a fuckin second. Fuck, please." The room is silent. The two men stand, look to each other, exchange worrying glances and fade from existence. Parks slowly removes his gaze from the hospital ceiling and his pointless staring contest with *Death*, she is not answering.

The Last Letter

He looks about the lonely, dark hospital room, his men have left him to his own thoughts, much to his relief. Yet the loneliness once again sets in; a whispering in his ear that he is to forever be this way, a lone lost failed soul; destined to carry his mistakes around his neck like a weighted chain, never experiencing relief or joy; only lonely, desperate acceptance.

CH. 24
INTERROGATION

Agent Medina calmly enters the room with a pained expression on his face. The special agent weathered the storm of breaking the news to Parks' mother, that her almost dead son; one she stood constant vigil over, wishes not to see her. It was devastating, all of the agents had grown attached to the former Marine's mother over the months. "Hey, brother, I hate to do this to you. The FBI is in charge of the investigation and two agents are outside to speak with you and record your statement. What do you want to do?"

Parks scans the room for James and Doherty, waiting to see his insanity come to fruition once again in the form of his two fallen men. Nothing.

"Parks, brother. You, okay?" Medina asks, also scanning the room, looking for a perceived threat.

Once he is done looking for his men, Parks turns back to his staring contest with Death. Hoping his defiance will trigger the appropriate response from the lingering specter. "No. I want the fuck out of here, now," he responds through clinched jaws.

Medina moves to his old friend's bedside, "I know you do. I swear to you I will get you out of here as soon as I can see a clear exit strategy for your situation."

"What the fuck are you talking about?" Parks demands.

Medina looks back at the hospital door being guarded by agents Baxter and Kineta, the two FBI agents standing anxiously before them waiting for admittance. "I will fill you in but first you need to talk to these agents and tell them what you know; I'm not running point on this operation."

SSgt. Jacob Parkinson

"Medina, I just lost my fuckin men! Tell them to fuck off." Parks is getting tired, not of Medina but tired of the rising depression. He wants to be anywhere but here; currently stranded and helpless to change the situation. Parks muscles ache trying to move his extremities to see how ambulatory his body is allowing. More excruciating pain hits, his muscles tighten from the dormancy of the past couple months.

The supervisory agent gently pushes Parks back down on the uncomfortable, stale bed, "Easy, friend. Your men passed three months ago, brother. We need answers. The families need answers. I know what this is like, and you know that I do, and you have lost troops before as well."

"That was a helicopter crash, I never lost any in combat, not like this. It's my fuckin fault, it is all my fuckin fault. I couldn't lead them through. They shouldn't have been there. Not that night in the forest and not that night in Iraq; all of it boils down to me. Me, motherfucker! Just fuckin me." Parks exhausted, shut his eyes, the stream of tears flow down his slightly bruised cheeks and his still-healing jaw.

Medina looks down upon his suffering friend, flashes of the losses he has endured during his career begin to come to the forefront of his consciousness. Not now, Medina scolds himself, *now is not the time to reflect*, but the images of the losses Medina has sustained will no longer be ignored. He has pushed them away for too long and witnessing the anguish of his friend is triggering his ghosts. "Parks, we can get into all that shit later. For now, let's answer these two agents' questions and then work on getting you out of here, roger that?" Hoping the change of subject will be a relief for both the emotional men.

"Copy that," Parks whispers, wiping the tears away with his hands. "Medina, thanks, man." He exhaustedly whispers to his old friend who suddenly looks like the weight of the world fell on the agent's tired, overburdened, shoulders.

Medina moves swiftly to the hospital door, opens it to signal the FBI agents to enter the bleak room. The two FBI agents pass nervously between the guards, each one looking up as they pass between them. Medina looks past the entering agents to see Jean, tearfully waiting for a glimpse of her awakened son. He gives her a compassionate understanding look signaling everything

The Last Letter

will be okay. Agents Baxter and Kineta look down at their boss, both men pleading with Medina with their sorrowful gaze the dismay they are in, watching Jean sit there in torment and anguish; wanting desperately to see her son, if only for a brief loving moment.

"I know, I'm working on it," Medina whispers to his men as he reenters the room with the two FBI agents.

Parks does not remove his gaze from the ceiling but out of his peripheral vision he makes out the two female agents making their way to either side of his bed. "They are going to try and misdirect you with their questions on opposing sides. Classic," James explains, suddenly appearing and taking up his usual spot in the uncomfortable chair, kicking his feet up on the end of the hospital bed.

"Fuck, not now, man," Parks exhaustedly tells his old friend. The agents and Medina seem not to notice the conversation between the two Marines.

Medina looks at the two FBI agents with a shrug of his shoulders. "You agreed to talk to the agents, remember?" Parks remains motionless.

"Shit man, I wouldn't miss this for the fuckin world. I already know how this is goin to fall apart and it' glorious." James looks over the two agents and their stern demeanor and chuckles. His smile then fades, "They remind me of my wife. Especially when she would come home from a long day dealing with border shit." James closes his eyes reflecting on his beloved wife returning from a hard day and seeing his smile always made her laugh a bit after the chaotic day or rotation. *Te ves como una mierda,* " he would always say to her lovingly and she would always respond, "Fuck you" with a warm, beleaguered smile of her own. Then he would take her in his arms kiss and hug her gently; he was her teddy bear of bearded scruff. James sits, staring into void, no smile pushing his beard up, the longing for his love that will never be again. He misses her dearly.

Parks turns his gaze to James, and is witness to the suffering, "I'm so fuckin sorry. I didn't mean for this to happen. Please fuckin forgive me, brother."

Medina moves to Parks' bedside next to James propped up in the chair, he does not notice his friend staring at James mourning the loss of his life he will never return to. "We understand that, easy, brother," Medina answers the squad leader's pleas meant for James. "Parks these are Special Agents in Charge Quinn and Cortez. They are going to take your statement. They have allowed me to stay despite conflict of interest."

"Mr. Parkinson, I am Special Agent Cortez. I am going to read you your Miranda rights, you are not under arrest, but you must be made aware of them," the taller of the two agents demands. It is not a request of Parks. She is stern in her demeanor, with a cold look in her eye that you see in only long-serving veterans of law enforcement. Parks nods his head in agreement.

Agent Cortez rattles off the Miranda Rights methodically from memory without missing a beat, a task she has done more times in her career than she cares to remember. "Now, Mr. Parkinson what can you tell me about that night?" The second agent sets her phone down, beginning to record the conversation with the patient. She stands directly to Parks' left side of his head, surveying the extent of the damage inflicted and the healing process.

James snaps out of his remorse, "Oh, here we go. This is goin to be fun." His humorous smile returning. "The other one is scanning your injuries to determine extent of cranial damage. Effectiveness of testimony, also probably to see if it can be used as an excuse not to answer questions. She's good."

Parks suddenly turns his gaze to Agent Quinn, his still red ruptured eyes startling her for a brief second before she regains her composure; Parks had not made eye contact with any person in the room upon their entrance, she is taken aback by the patient's sudden movement. He slowly turns his gaze back to the ceiling and his staring contest... not with *Death*; now Parks' staring contest has superseded *Death's* chain of command, his defiance is now directed at his perceived image of God. Defiantly daring his Lord to send him to *Hell*, finally.

"Mr. Parkinson, what can you tell me about that night?" Agent Cortez asks in a sterner tone, angered at the perceived notion she is being ignored. She does not realize the game in which Parks is defiantly partaking with his God.

"Nothing. I remember nothing," He answers calmly and quietly. Medina displays no emotion or reaction to Parks' answer. He knows his old friend remembers it all, but this may work in favor. Medina knows the two agents will be registering his reactions to any words spoken by the patient.

The Last Letter

He also knows that is the only reason the two special agents allowed him in the room, is to gauge how much corroboration there is between "old friends."

"And here we go…." James now settles in to his position on the chair.

Agent Cortez shoots Medina an angry glance while her partner moves in closer to Parks. Medina displays no shock that she can register.

"Here comes the misdirection and counterattack." James points to other agent.

Agent Quinn looks down at Parks, pulling his medical chart out from behind her back. "Mr. Parkinson, we received a warrant for your medical records. Do you know what I did before I came to the FBI? Well, let me tell you. I was a neurological resident at Walter Reed specializing in traumatic brain injury. I have seen every type of injury you could imagine. I have studied thousands of charts, scans, vitals, progress, and regression. It all became too depressing, too isolating. I needed a change. First, it was the Secret Service and now the FBI, but I will never forget all of those combat Veterans and the trauma they endured. What I am getting at Mr. Parkinson is that I do not believe you have amnesia or no recollection of the events that transpired that cost the lives of two of your men and left you for dead."

"Damn she is good; I did *not* see that coming." James is awestruck at the extensive resume of Agent Quinn and her cunning. "What now Sgt. Parks?"

Parks now growing angry at the mention of his title lets out a pained moan, "Stop fuckin calling me that."

Agent Quinn moves closer to Parks. "Stop calling you what? Mr. Parkinson? I will call you whatever the fuck you want once you start fucking giving us some information. Do you understand me?" The agent gets forceful in her approach to the interrogation.

Parks keeps his gaze towards the heavens, "I apologize, ma'am. That was not directed at you." The agents both turn to Medina with puzzled looks. He simply shrugs his shoulders.

"Who was that directed towards, Mr. Parkinson?" Agent Quinn asks, calming herself.

"It's nothing. I remember fuckin nothing. That is my statement. It will not change," Parks reluctantly pleads with the FBI agent.

"What is the last thing you do remember? Let's try that approach, shall we?" Agent Cortez now asks from her side of the hospital bed.

Parks continues his despondent stare, contemplating what he should tell the agents and how much of it will prevent him from getting out of the hospital.

"They're gettin annoyed by you, Sgt. Parks. You sure you want to stick with this story?" James asks of his former squad leader, afraid the FBI agent may try to arrest his old friend, if he continues his defiance.

"Yes." Parks answers James.

"Good. What is the last thing you remember?" Special Agent Cortez demands, hoping she is finally getting somewhere with the stubborn patient. The agent is getting annoyed with his reluctance to make eye contact with either of them while answering their questions, they cannot gauge accurately if he is lying, which Agent Cortez finds she has an uncanny knack for.

Parks takes a deep breath in and exhales as the flood of memories come crashing back on his consciousness from the night of the reunion with his men. "I remember parking the truck and taking fuckin stupid selfies together. James and Doherty smiling and laughing. It was a good moment. That, Special Agent, is the last thing I remember," Parks utters exhaustedly never altering his gaze.

"I do not believe you, Mr. Parkinson. What else can you tell me? Why the fuck were you three armed to the teeth? Any ties to drug cartels, let's try that avenue? You will answer me!" Special Agent Cortez growls, annoyed at Parks lack of recollection, trying to enrage the patient.

"Fuck this turned dark, really quick and in a hurry. Shit. She looks like my wife after I have had too much to drink with the men from Bravo. Unrelenting in admonishing the guilty. Good luck, Sgt. Parks. Hopefully the other agent is the good cop," James says, joyfully eyeing the situation.

Parks winces his eyes at the sound of his title that James persists on using. It pains him each time, but he cannot stop his subconscious from playing its nasty joke on him. Parks knows he is insane. There is no other way to explain his episodes with his deceased men. He feels no different now than he did before the tragedy. *Maybe everyone is right; I have always been this way.*

The Last Letter

"You're not insane, Sgt. Parks, fucked in the head a little but aren't we all, brother?" James tries to reassure his former squad leader of his sanity with a wink and a bearded broad smile.

Special Agent Quinn leans closer to the patient, monitoring his facial movements. She notices that Parks seems to be lost in a mental dialogue that is distracting his response. She takes this as his preparing and rehearsing answers in his head, "Special Agent Cortez asked you some questions, Mr. Parkinson. Or would you respond to, what is that they call you, oh yes *Sgt. Parks.* Is that better, Sgt. Parks?" Special Agent Quinn is getting the desired effect she is seeking with her posturing and condescending tone. Parks' jaws are clenching and his eyes wince with pain at each mention of his title, he does not know how much he can tolerate. He wants desperately for it all to end.

"Good Lord. She is definitely not the good cop." James' smile disappears, growing concerned for his former squad leader.

Parks remains motionless, still clenching his jaw in welcoming agony. Medina steps in for his injured friend, "Agents, what the fuck? You told me, you were just going to ask the routine questions and take his official statement, not bring this media bullshit into what is looking more and more like an interrogation."

"It's special agents, not agents, special agents same as on your badge. We will conduct our interviews as we see fit and only extended this courtesy to have you in the room due to the fact you two served together and you are a fellow special agent. Now you can kindly step out of the room if you interrupt our questions again. Is that understood, Special Agent Medina?" FBI Special Agent Quinn commands.

"It is and it's Supervisory before Special Agent on my badge, remember that," Medina responds in a professional manner for he knew he would do the exact same given their positions. He crossed a line, and he knew he let personal experience interfere. His plan is too close to fruition and this incident has provided the path to a successful conclusion provided everything from here on out is handled properly.

Parks turns his gaze to Special Agent Quinn as she turns back from speaking to Medina. She is immediately caught off guard by his stare; it is dead.

There is no life in the patient's eyes, only emptiness. She shudders, chills suddenly traversing her spine. "Special Agent, I remember nothing after parking the truck. No ties to drugs. We are just lowly *Grunts*. Nothing special." Parks peers into her eyes. The shudder returns, she does not see malice, she sees his exhaustion.

From the other side standing next to a propped up James, who is looking more concerned for his friend as the interview progresses, Special Agent Cortez asks, "And what about your armament?"

"It's a *Grunt* thing. It's a comfortable extension of our bodies. I have never fired a round through any of them, except to initially BZO each. The weapons are just natural. That is all, there's no malice intended by our ownership of weapons contrary to stigma about Marines." Parks utters, turning his gaze to Special Agent Cortez.

She too feels the shudder of chills run down her spine, witnessing the detachment in the patient's eyes. "You mean you never fired a round through them until that night, correct?" Special Agent Cortez continues.

"Look at that, she's trying to trip you up," James comments to his squad leader.

Parks continues to stare into Special Agent's eyes. "Did I fire my weapon? I don't know."

"You know, you haven't even asked us about the events of that night or your men. Why is that? You would think for someone who does not remember, you would like the opportunity to fill in the gaps from trusted law enforcement. Why, Sgt. Parks?"

James sits up straight, now visibly annoyed, "Yep. I don't like her anymore." Shutting his eyes in desperation, Parks moans, "Goddammit, Agent, stop calling me that. You are not one of my fuckin men! I don't want to know what happened! Not now, not tomorrow, not even upon my death. I want to be left alone, for good," Parks angrily pleads with the two special agents.

Agent Quinn leans in close to Parks' ear, "It's a little late for that, Sgt. Parks."

James gets angry, his bearded smile quickly fades from his face. "Yep, I hate her."

The Last Letter

"Alright. I think that's enough for the evening, Special Agents. He told you his statement, he remembers nothing. Leave, please." Medina begins to step in and end the interrogation.

James looks over at Medina stepping forward from the shadows, "Now, him, I like."

"You pipe down there, Agent Medina. I have operational jurisdiction here and I say when my interview is over. Got that," Special Agent Cortez counters, moving to impede his progress to the door.

He looks directly at her and with sincerity, says, "It is Supervisory Special Agent. I have been more than cordial as well, letting this interrogation proceed, but it is at an end. You two will leave and then you will be receiving a call from your superior. She will not be happy. You see, she and I served together long ago. Intelligence. Marine Corps is a small world, Agent. Now as I call my Marine buddy, *FBI Director in Charge* Madeline Kranz, I will see you two escorted from the floor. Upon release from the hospital, you may interview this man again. Thank you, my agents Baxter and Kineta will see you to the elevators." With that Medina politely opens the door for the two special agents.

James all smiles once again, "Oooh, he is fuckin good."

"This is not over, Agent." Special Agent Cortez grumbles reluctantly following Medina's men out into the hall.

"Yes, it is." He calmly states to the disgruntled FBI agent.

Special Agent Quinn pats Parks on the shoulder in a hypocritical fashion, he could feel the pain tear through his muscles, but he makes no motion or noise, "Well, Sgt. Parks, we'll be seeing you." She starts to head to the door to join her partner who is fuming in the hallway.

Parks turns his gaze to the back of the FBI agent; he stares not with malice or ill intent. "No, Special Agent, you won't," he softly states; returning his gaze back to the ceiling as she turns to look back at him.

There is something in his voice that made it seem all but final, that she would not see this man again. Agent Quinn pauses because she knows the signs and the finality in the voice; she will not see this man again. The agent has lost friends and colleagues to that finality of tone, she will receive the news like everyone else, the tragedy of one taking their own life. She is too familiar with this tone of despair, of giving up, "Mr. Parkinson, you try and find peace." Special Agent Quinn faintly states, exiting the room to join her angered partner.

Medina watches the two FBI agents escorted to the elevator, as promised Special Agent Cortez receives a phone call before the elevator opens. The last thing he sees before the elevator doors shut, is her giving him the middle finger, a big "fuck you" from her to him; the last words he hears from the FBI agent are the repeated, "Yes, ma'am and no ma'am." It brings a smile to his exhausted, weathered, disheveled face. Medina turns back to head into the stale hospital room he has called home for the last few months. He moves to the bedside and takes James' position in the chair and props his feet up on the bed.

James jumps up and out of the way. "Well, excuse the fuck out of me. I guess I'm movin."

"Why did you lie to the agents? They're not idiots; they know you're lying," Medina asks his old friend.

James moves to the other side of the hospital bed in a huff. "That's a very valid question. What's your plan, do pray tell, Sgt. Parks?"

"Don't fuckin start," Parks mutters aloud to James.

"Who are you talking to, brother?" Medina looks around the room, trying to gauge the source of the conversation.

Parks inhales deeply. "No one."

"Then tell me, why did you lie to the special agents?" Medina again asks his old friend.

Parks looks at Medina with pain, "Not now. I need to leave, please Medina help me get the fuck out here. Please." He begs of his longtime Marine buddy.

"You are not under arrest and forensics indicates everything appears to be in self-defense despite the rampant misinformation. There is no money trail or unknown bank accounts hiding payroll from a cartel. You three are just ordinary Marine Veterans out on a camping trip. I will help you get out of here if you help me. Deal, my friend?" Medina asks the patient.

"What do you need?" Parks keeps his gaze on the white expressionless hospital ceiling.

The Last Letter

Medina looks over at Parks with genuine concern, "I want you to tell me what happened out there. I said this popped up on my team's radar. Well, it did for a reason. Can you do me that favor?"

"Yes, once I'm out of here. I will tell you everything," Parks plainly replies.

Medina softly taps his friend's shoulder, "Thank you, brother. Rest now, and I'll work on getting you out of here." He then stands to make his way to exit the room to begin preparations for the dismissal of the patient.

"Medina, one more thing. Do not ambush me with my mother. I mean it. I want to see no one," Parks commands sternly.

"Parks, come on. She has been here through it all. Come to your defense in the media, withstood the onslaught of the false narratives. Your mother withstood the character assassination of her son for months and I watched her little by little be destroyed each and every day. All she wants to do is see her son. Please allow her that?" Medina begs of his friend from a long ago era of Marines.

The squad leader lay motionless, except the rise and fall of his chest as he breathes heavily. "No", is all the former Marine mutters. Medina exits the room knowing Parks will not change his mind and Medina will be left to break the horrible news to the man's mother again; that her once-dying son wishes to see no one, not even her. He rubs his face in his hand; he is exhausted.

"He's a good man, that Special Agent Medina. He took my fuckin spot, though. He is right, you know, you need to let your mom see you." James moves to assume his propped up position in the uncomfortable hospital chair, his chest rig making it hard for the former Marine to get situated as he squirms to find the perfect position to sit. "Fuckin Special Agent Medina ruined my position, goddammit." The bearded smile is replaced by annoyance as he continues to get situated. "Shit, finally. There." James exhales, finding his spot once again. "Now stop fuckin around and allow your mom in here to see you."

Parks' anger begins to simmer in his still bruised chest, "Don't fuckin start with me. If you know what I'm thinking, Lance Corporal, then you know why I don't want to see anyone."

"First off, Sgt. Parks, I got corporal. Secondly, Doherty and I cannot always tell what you're thinkin. Sometimes the darkness in your mind keeps us at bay, you depressed fuck." James replies calmly, trying to ease his former squad leader with his usual mischievous banter.

"Yeah, well, I got staff sergeant and you fuckers still call me *Sgt. Parks*. The *darkness* has been there a long time, brother, spreading like fuckin cancer; I'm tired of holding it back. Tired," Parks explains with despair and futility.

James stands, stretches his arms above his head. "We told you, Staff Sergeant Parks, sounds fuckin terrible. You need to let that darkness go; there is nothing in there but pain, Devil."

"I have brought nothing but misery to the ones I am supposed to care for. You see I deserve the pain, the guilt." Parks directly looks at his saddened troop. Memories of Iraq flood his consciousness, all of his men so young, ready for anything. The weight of their gear seemingly weightless as their squad became more cohesive, fluid. The painful memory forms another agonizing guilt-laden lump in his throat constricting his breathing. He feels the slow suffocation of agony.

James looks at his squad leader with a pained expression before he fades from the room, "No. No, you don't, Sgt. Parks." With that, James leaves Parks to his depressed silence. The sounds of the hospital machines the only thing to keep the former Marine company.

The suffering patient shuts his eyes, trying to keep the tears at bay. He grabs the cards from above his bed that were resting on the ledge, he sifts through them frantically; Parks finds the first of his squad members cards, Perry's and Cooper's. He does not read the sentiments but searches for information, which he finds. They both left full contact information, he scrambles through the rest of the cards: Morales, Thomas, and Culpepper, check. All left contact information, and Parks finds some solace in the fact his squad entrusts him with that information; he continues to search the cards quickly.

I failed once again, fuckin piece of shit, Parks mumbles to himself, finding the remaining cards he is looking for, Delta, Jackson, Del Vecchio. The remainder of the squad all accounted for, he gathers those of his squad and places them in a plastic hospital property bag he pulls from the nightstand.

The rest he throws in the trash, the adrenaline flowing through his body as his strength begins to return to his extremities. Parks wipes the tears from his eyes and takes up his position staring defiantly up at God once again. *Take me now motherfucker, save everyone the trouble of what I'm going to do*, Parks projects stubbornly, angrily. Nothing happens, the former Marine is disappointed his request is not met; it has never been met over the years he has asked God to take him, never a response.

"Come now, Sgt. Parks. Don't you give up on me, not yet. Now is not the time, too many people will need you in the coming days." Doherty appears from the gloom of the corner, with an understanding grin under his beard. His gear still draped about his body, fitting him like a glove.

"Fuck not again," Parks exhales with dismay at the vision.

Doherty moves to the chair, sits, and adjusts his gear to get comfortable, as James had done before. "Fuckin chairs are not conducive to our war gear." He finally gets situated and finds his sweet spot with his equipment. "Yeah, Sgt. Parks, James and I are here for the long haul."

"Fine but don't give me that *'everyone will need you or keep pushing forward or have hope bullshit.'* You and James are dead because of my actions, my fuckin vanity. Now your families are torn apart because I wanted to have a fucked-up reunion with my squad. There is no redemption for my fuckin soul, and I want it over with. So, fuckin sit there, be a friend, and don't give me that uplifting bullshit right now. Please." Parks pleads, hoping *Death* will crash through the hideous tiled ceiling with her bony fingers and take his soul.

Doherty puts a hand on Parks shin gently, "Roger that, Sgt. Parks. Let's just sit here and enjoy the silence before the place becomes a clusterfuck with federal agents again." He alters his butt pack on the back of his flak, so he can lean back comfortably, *Oh, the sweet spot*, he relishes. Doherty watches with concern at his squad leader's defiance; this road Parks is traveling down, he has seen all too many times in his own life and those that he helps now with his advocacy work or *did help*, he ponders to himself as the reality of the situation becomes apparent to him. Doherty puts his face in his hands and begins to weep, the images and memories of his mother and fiancée cascade before him.

"God, how dare you let me fuckin live. You motherfucker!" Parks swears to the ceiling, witnessing his troop's anguish out of the corner of his eye. He cannot take the pain rising in his throat watching Doherty silently weep. The lump of guilt asphyxiating Parks; he tries desperately to breathe; the machines begin sending coded alarms to the nurse's station.

Dr. Anand and LPN Bennett come barreling through the hospital room door, between Agents Baxter and Kineta, who are busy keeping Jean from entering the room to see her now in critical despair child. Patiently, faithfully praying to her God for her son's reemergence from his devastating injuries. The agents do not let her pass much to their own heartfelt dismay.

Special Agent Medina follows suit behind the nurse and doctor. He rushes to Parks' side, where Doherty is sitting wiping away his tears, "Easy old man. This is not how you go out, Sgt. Parks. Laid up in some fuckin hospital bed, choking on unnecessary pain and guilt. Stop this shit. Come on breathe, brother." Doherty tries to ease his squad leader's constriction by talking him down; it is not working; the machines' alarms persist.

"Calm down, Mr. Parkinson. Calm down, breathe," Nurse Bennett tries to soothe Parks, placing a gentle hand on his chest, while she watches the doctor prepare a heavy sedative.

Dr. Anand gives a final glance to Agent Medina, who nods his approval as the doctor injects the needle into Parks left bicep, he offers no resistance, the sedative begins to take immediate effect. Parks' glazed-over pale eyes look over to Medina, "I want to go home," he pleads with his old Marine buddy, falling into a sedated deep slumber.

"He should be out for ten to twelve hours; I suggest you let that poor woman see her son. Now, agent," Dr. Anand orders Medina, who nods in agreement, this may be the only chance she can see him.

"Thank you, Dr. Anand." He sincerely offers his gratitude to the exhausted doctor. Medina then waves to Agent Kineta to allow Jean into see her boy.

Jean rushes over to her son's bedside opposite Doherty, who watches as Parks' grieving mother desperately clutches his hand. *Did his mother do the same? How long did she hold his hand for? Did his fiancée suffer, such as this?* Doherty stands, knowing he can no longer witness such heartache without feeling his own pain crush him, decides to fade away from the scene, leaving his old squad leader to drift off into sedation, whispering his troop's name.

CH. 25
STOLEN VALOR

Special Agent Medina comes rushing through the heavy hospital door with a large bag under his arm, a shoe box, and a wheelchair. Parks tries in agony to focus his blurred vision on his old friend frantically rushing about the dark hospital room. "Here, quickly throw these on." Medina tosses the bag with a T-shirt, a pair of dark denim jeans, socks, and ball cap in it onto Parks' lap, he also throws the shoe box onto his lap as well, sending a wave of pain throughout the Marine's body. "Quickly. Time to go."

Parks mutters not a single word, begging his muscles to cooperate, struggling to get the clothing on, each movement agony. After a few moments of tussling, he manages to get all but the shoes on. Medina quickly walks over to his old friend and helps Parks get the sneakers onto his feet.

"Aww, that is so sweet." James pops out of the gloom and takes a picture with his phone. "Yep, that is definitely gettin posted with the *#proposal* captioned at the bottom, Sgt. Parks. Nice shirt." James smirks at the choice of attire Agent Medina selected for his squad leader. Parks looks down at his black T-shirt, the catchphrase splashed on the front—*This is the way* with a picture of the Mandalorian carrying the child. "What the fuck, Medina?"

"Hey, suck it the fuck up. You want out of here; I get to pick the wardrobe." Medina smiles at his disgruntled friend.

Parks wobbly stands on his feet, holding on to the railing of the hospital bed. His legs surprisingly holding up rather well for his first use. "I have never seen the fuckin show."

"You'll like it, dickhead. Now, let's get moving." Medina brings over the wheelchair to the dismayed look on Parks face. "Oh, you're getting in this fucking chair. We don't have time for you to hobble your ass down the corridor as my agents run distraction. Your mother is also on her way here according to my team. I'm not facing your mother while pushing your ass out of here, no sir. Now sit your fucking ass down." He demands, forcibly shuffling Parks along. "You can also thank your mother for the tireless hours she spent making sure your muscles didn't atrophy. Exercise after exercise, hour after hour. She is the only reason you're mobile right now, ungrateful shit."

James laughs at the exchange between old friends. He has never seen Parks ordered around like this, and it is amusing for the former Marine. "He's right, Sgt. Parks, get your ass in the chair."

"Don't you fuckin start, shithead." Parks barks at his friend.

"I will start any damn thing I please, Marine," Medina growls at his old friend, mistaken Parks' comments were directed at him.

James amused by the moment, "I hope your mom busts in right now catches y'all two. Be like two fuckin children gettin busted for horsin around after being told a million times to go to bed." He laughs at the image of Parks' mother, Jean, barging in at that very moment.

Suddenly dreading the thought of his mother coming through that heavy hospital door, petrifies the former Marine; he instantly moves to the wheelchair as Medina heads for the door, back first, towing the patient.

"Good boy, Sgt. Parks," James smiling and waving to his squad leader as Parks is being dragged out of the hospital room for the first time in months. He flips James the middle finger. James' smile broadens farther across his bearded face, giving his squad leader a warm salute. The fallen Marine then begins to disappear into the dark gloom of the now-abandoned hospital room.

Watching James fade from view, a sense of uneasiness engulfs Parks: *Am I alone now?*

The two men make it without incident to Medina's Dodge Challenger in the parking garage. He props open the door and dumps Parks into the passenger seat like a plastic bag of groceries. Parks groans in agony as he is casually discarded. "That is for your mom," Medina quips, shutting the passenger door

The Last Letter

on Parks and swiftly moving to the driver side looking about the garage skillfully for possible threats.

"I deserve that." Parks breathes slowly, getting used to the pain of movement. "Where are you taking me, brother?"

Medina starts the ignition and heads out of the hospital entrance in a hurry, "Away from *her* for starters."

Parks catches a glimpse of his mother behind the wheel of her gray rental electric Mustang SUV, the constricting lump of guilt returns to his throat, threatening to put him in a panic state. He slows his breathing, turning his gaze away from his hopeful mother. "Thank you", is all Parks can muster through the constriction in his throat, lowering his pounding head into his hands. "How did it come to this, Medina? How?" Parks pleads with his old Marine buddy.

"I don't know, brother, but I am damn sure going to find out." Medina slams on the accelerator, tearing through the hospital garage and out into the early innocent Colorado morning.

"Where?" Parks looks vacantly out the passenger window at the predawn landscape of Colorado flowing by. It is peaceful; that is why he moved here from Rhode Island in the first place; he always hated the unknown and Rhode Island was the unknown. Parks would grow to love the beautiful idyllic summers of the small state but only stayed in Rhode Island to watch his children grow because his first wife called the place home and not to be the absent father he was left with. Another failed marriage due to his selfishness and drunkenness. *You fuckin piece of shit, you deserve all of this. You ruin everyone.* Parks rubs his bloodshot eyes wearily, continuing to stare at the beautiful landscape. It is why he escaped to Colorado, to start over, never be that person again and leave his dark, shameful legacy behind.

Parks shifts through the cards in his bag he brought with him, keeping only the cards from his squad members. The two friends sit in silence for the next twenty miles before he slowly speaks, "You're taking me home, aren't you?"

"Yes. Your official statement to the FBI has pissed off higher; you are afforded no protective status," Medina states flatly, eyeing the predawn horizon ahead driving intently, constantly scanning his mirrors.

Parks staring out the window into the encroaching *nothingness*, eyes fixated, says, "Good. I want to be left alone."

"Hey, Parks, what happened?" Medina looks over at his old friend struggling with the regrets and guilt of his past.

Exhaling deeply, Parks knows he has to tell someone, and it might as well be his old friend from 3/5, "Where do you want me to begin?" He asks slowly.

"Fuck, brother. How about what the fuck happened at Lejeune in '07? I'm training my MARSOC bubbas and next thing I know I'm getting frantic calls from Webb at the staff school you guys were at, looking for your ass. Next, I hear command is kicking you out and I'm taking you to the airport. Brother, I tried to pull every connection I had." Medina is now asking questions he has contemplated over the years from time to time wondering what became of the only man to beat him in a competition in the Marines, company honorman of boot camp.

Parks continues to stare out the windows vacantly, "Man, it all started long before then. Technically it started with the Osprey crash, Iraq, outside Fallujah, my own unit awarding medals to others for my men's actions, I was fuckin done, been going downhill ever since. Thought sobriety helped, but it leaves you facing shit alone and unprotected." Parks inhales deeply, hoping the clean Colorado air will provide him with vital energy. "I told you and Webb about what happened outside of Fallujah to my Marines and me." He keeps his gaze fixated out the window into the morning darkness rushing by.

"Yeah, brother. I remember we all telling drunken war stories at my little apartment outside Lejeune." Medina begins to recollect from his near-perfect memory the sequence of events of that time with his friends, telling hilarious stories of Iraq and the not so hilarious. His pity for Parks returning as it had all those years ago. He felt like a big brother slowly watching his little brother die from torment, guilt, and alcohol before his very eyes.

"Fuck, that was a long time ago. I know your unit was neck deep in the shit; my unit's tour was a cakewalk compared to what you and your men went through," Parks concedes, recognizing Medina and his men's combat experiences back in the '04/'05 Iraq campaign.

Medina acknowledges this homage from Parks as one warrior paying reverence to another, "And somewhere there is another salt dog saying the same

The Last Letter

about Bravo Co. We all had it horrible regardless who we were with back then and especially on that fucking operation."

"Yeah, and I carried that fuckin chip on my shoulder to Lejeune, not knowing I had one. I let it ruin my career. I never treated the Marines as a career, just another excuse to drink, start shit and be an overall fuckin waste and that is another regret to this day. Nothing but regrets, and what do my regrets cost? My regrets come at the cost of the sorrow of others. This fuckin curse. No more, Medina." Parks grits his teeth, rambling incoherently.

Medina sensing Parks going dark, tries to refocus his old friend, asking, "Parks what happened at Lejeune?"

Parks exhales with frustration, he has not thought on this in years, "All of us staff NCOs were in class awaiting our lesson from the next instructor. All instructors were Gunnies and combat Veterans. Each one, before a period of instruction, would tell some fuckin war story, most of them centered around the Fallujah operation of '04; most of us staff sergeants in the class were there for that operation; Webb was with your unit, inside. I'm not really paying attention to the asshole as he starts his fuckin rambling." Parks never changes his tone or his gaze out the window. "Halfway through his tale, I start to pick up on details of his bullshit of events. That motherfucker is telling 1st Squad's story, down to the red lens flashlight and dragging your feet for wires. Then that fucker went on to spew some sort of shit dialogue I supposedly said that night, a fuckin *Gunny* stealing the valor from my Marines. Webb and the others turn back to me and mouth the words *'what the fuck.'*

"Fuckin joke was on the instructor. I had told you guys that story in your apartment days before, so he looked like a *stolen valor* bitch that he is in front of the class. The *Grunt* world is small, the combat Grunt world even smaller.

Turns out that dickhead was a sergeant with 3rd LAR during that offensive, same unit 2nd Platoon protected that whole damn day, while they cowered in their fuckin armored vehicles. Think they would help us lowly *Grunts* during an ambush? You think they would help us lowly *Grunts* as my squad found over a dozen IEDs and I personally had to cut the wires on each with my fuckin Leatherman that day? Nope and nope." Parks jaw begins to tighten at the memory of his squad's valor being stolen right in front him.

Parks rubs his bloodshot sore eyes. "After that I was done, man. I checked out in the head; you saw me while I was there. I tried to pull it together, but I chose to drink my anger into oblivion. I showed up drunk to the mortar range with a half sleeve tribal I don't remember getting, although I did stop an idiot staff sergeant from putting an 81mm in the tube upside down. That's just basic shit. My buddy Attebery really slammed that home for me, so I credit him for that quick thinking. I lost Webb's truck while drunk the night before, missed my instruction period to teach buddy rushes after taking the top PFT. So, they hammered me. Which in hindsight I understand, but I would have handled it differently and not fry a combat decorated Marine who is obviously fucked in the head. *Grunts* take care of one another but not there. The Marine Corps was changing, and I was not a part of those plans."

Medina vividly remembers that time and he sympathizes with his old friend. "Man, I tried to rein you in, all your classmates did, brother."

Shaking his head at another long list of decisions he will never retrieve, Parks sighs, "I know, Devil. I would eventually stand before the man. He got on the phone with the CO from the unit I was deploying with, Doherty's unit. Called me a cocky, ungrateful son of bitch that showed no signs of remorse. Just because I didn't fuckin grovel and beg. I became argumentative when I ordered to speak, told the sir, *'you have three fuckin staff sergeants that couldn't pass a PFT but I'm getting kicked out.'* Especially after I took the top PFT in the class from their hero. That did not go over well, and when I wouldn't name the names of those that couldn't do three fuckin pull-ups, things only got worse.

"I asked permission to speak freely again but was denied and dismissed with extreme prejudice. The instructors and the CO were pissed that I was a reservist at an active school, fucking tried to tell them I was prior active duty India 3/5 boat company bubba but that meant shit. I'm surprised I didn't end up in the brig after the confrontation in the CO's office. The Sgt. Major pulled me in his office afterward; he helped me out with my adverse Fitrep and understood. He said in his day all Staff NCOs had bad paper; it was a rite of passage, but those times were over. I thanked him and told him I brought it upon myself; I did fuckin become a belligerent drunk, so I deserved what I got. End

The Last Letter

of career right there, no *Gunny* for me, the only rank I ever wanted." Parks shakes his head with disappointment at his past mistakes costing him so much of his future.

It was self-sabotage; Parks knows he can only blame himself. "After that, you came, picked me up, took me to eat and dropped me off at the airport. I failed and my perceived failures led to more drinking, to hurting the one I am supposed to love the most in this world, and now, James and Doherty have paid with their lives because I'm a drunk fuck that just had to have one last reunion to relive some forgotten glory bullshit. No, Medina, the death in those woods should've been mine. I should have ended this long ago." Parks' monotone voice never changes, his gaze never wavering out the car's window. His manner is that of a detached storyteller.

Medina stares straight ahead trying to remember his old friend at Lejeune. Back then it was all Medina and the other staff NCOs could do to keep him out of trouble constantly. From bar fights, to passing out drunk standing up, tattoos, disappearing; Medina was always concerned for his friend from India Co., especially after the Osprey crash. Medina had his work with MARSOC to distract him from his ghosts, Parks chose to let his ghosts betray the good he could have done.

"Medina, thank you for all you did for me back then. I never thanked you and I wanted to while I have the chance. Thank you, brother." Parks offers humbly, he knows his future is uncertain as soon as he exits the special agent's vehicle.

Medina looks over at his distraught friend. Parks head turned towards the passenger window, resting against the headrest, staring vacantly at the *nothingness*, that takes all combat Veterans periodically.

"Brother, anytime. What happened in the woods, and this is just me asking, not *Supervisory Special Agent* from Homeland Security? Your official statement as far as I am concerned is you remember nothing."

Parks closes his eyes. He does not want to remember but he remembers it all. "The woods. All we wanted was to enjoy each other's company, patrol, bullshit about life, and remember the Iraq days one last time before life takes us away permanently. After my cousin took his life, I just wanted to see everyone, one last time. You know what I mean? Make it memorable."

"I do know what you mean, Parks. I really do know where you're coming from," Medina quietly adds to convey his deep understanding.

Parks, keeping his gaze fixated on the *nothingness*, whispers heavily in return, "I know you do."

"Why those woods?", Medina asks. "Why not any place around here in Colorado?"

Slowly turning his head, he looks at his old Marine buddy, "Oh, that's right you were already FAPped out, I forgot where. I know Mitchell went to the Marine boxing team."

"I got assigned to Bridgeport to be an assault climbing instructor," Medina remembers fondly.

Parks looks back out the window as the landscape flows by at ninety miles an hour, "That's right. You missed when India got sent to Clear Creek to fight the forest fires of 2000. We were sitting idle after the Osprey crash, so they sent us to fight the fires up in Idaho. I thought it would be nice to see how the place recovered and show my men some shit Marines in the fleet did besides train and drink. That's all I wanted to do, brother. Just show my men another side of Sgt. Parks."

Medina politely asks his friend, "Why did you want them to see another side of you?"

"Man, Devil, I don't know. I'm so tired of having to live up to this image of *Sgt. Parks from Iraq*, I wanted to be something other than that. I was going to share stories from the fleet and relive some stories with my men from Iraq, of course. I wanted to tell my Marines to let *Sgt. Parks* go; I'm tired of having to live up to that ghost from the past, so they can finally see that their image of *Sgt. Parks* is no more, a fuckin fantasy. I wanted them to see me finally, for the piece of shit I eventually transformed into. I'm so tired of *Sgt. Parks*, that man has ruined my fuckin life." Parks exhales deeply, shutting his eyes for momentary relief from the strain of watching the world continue to move speedily by, the landscape oblivious to the tragedy unfolding inside the speeding Challenger.

"Have you been that same man since? Have you gotten better? Have you made amends?" Medina counters his old friend. "Parks, you are not that same person, you may want *Sgt. Parks* to die, but that man will never die in those who have served with you, and you have served with. Your men will not care as long as you return to the core values that made you *Sgt. Parks* in the first fucking place."

Parks looks over at his friend incredulously, "Nice fuckin speech. How long have you had that round in the chamber?"

Medina smiles crookedly but keeps his eyes bouncing from mirror to mirror, "Long enough. Your mother helped."

"Fuckin lovely." Parks returns his gaze to the running landscape. "I was disappointed at first that only James and Doherty could make it, you know it would have been nice to have more of the squad show but that feeling went away as soon as I saw the two of them. Their smiles beaming when we laid eyes on each other for the first time in two damn decades. Man, that was a beautiful moment." Parks reflects on the smiles of his men. "They instantly started giving me shit for my bald head and all-grey beard. I looked like an angry little gnome to them, as per James insult." The constriction in his throat grows by the second, threatening to send him into convulsions once again, clamoring for oxygen, the memory crashing down on the former Marine.

Parks stops, exhales deeply and closes his eyes. Hoping when he opens them, this will be all but an in-depth, detailed nightmare. *Please let me wake up*, he wills himself. He opens his eyes to the still rushing by Colorado landscape, much to his eternal dismay. Parks rubs the palms of his sweaty hands on his pants Medina procured for him and continues. "We hiked about four miles in and set up just off a clearing. Later that night we heard something behind us in the brush; it was a spooked elk; a few moments later the plane came exploding through the treetops over our heads, across the clearing to the opposite side and crashing inside the tree-line past the small river there.

"Instantly the three of us moved swiftly, almost like a machine again, it was chilling. Dispersion was instinctual. We arrived at the downed craft and were met by an armed survivor with a case attached to his wrist. The survivor screamed something in Spanish and fired at us. We put him down with controlled three round burst from each. Again, instinctual. The survivor was down, and James had interpreted what he said to mean *'we tried our best, leave our families alone.'* Poor fucker." Parks stops, his hands begin to tremble, his foot bouncing his knee feverishly up and down on the carpeted floorboard of the vehicle.

Medina has seen this numerous times when witnesses recall the events of trauma. "Take your time, Parks."

"Don't give me that patronizing tone, Devil. I'll make this next part brief; I don't want to fuckin dwell on it." Parks gathers his strength to continue. "We didn't touch anything, and I told James to go make a sat-phone call to the Sheriff's Office and the forestry agent. James took off up the ridge a bit, while Doherty and I discussed what the fuck was going on. James returned, told us he got through to both and it will be a minute. Immediately a helo shows up over our bivouac and we witnessed the trip flares I had set up outside of camp start popping off. Then things got frantic after that. We heard several different languages being spoken and soon they tore through our camp and were headed our way to the crash site across the clearing.

"I told James to go back up the ridge and call them back, report that we had company. He took off immediately; the helo must have spotted us because all hell broke loose after that. Small-arms fire, 16s and AKs judging from the sound, also fuckin 203s, start peppering the woods around us. Doherty and I engaged the enemy, as per SOP. I took shrapnel in the leg and Doherty carried my ass up the ridge as we withdrew under intense barrage of enemy small-arms fire." Parks takes a deep breath; he is reciting the events as best he can with the least amount of emotion, it will be impossible.

"We met James, coming back down the ridge to join us. He lost the sat-phone while engaging the helo that followed him up the fuckin ridge, but he did get a call off to his wife, voicemail." Parks continues in his detached manner. Medina not wanting to tell Parks he had already spoken to James' widow, Jocelyn. Parks didn't need that guilt during this moment.

"We immediately took up dispersed defensive positions on the ridge as best we could, given the amount of time we had. We engaged the enemy, both James and Doherty dropping bodies. I saw the helo go farther up and behind the crest of the ridge. I knew it would be a matter of time before another team would be above us and it would be over. We engaged the team as soon as it crested the peak. You remember how everything slows down and you kind of just know what to do. That feeling of *nothingness*, no fear, no excitement, nothing but instinct. Do you remember that feeling, brother, the knowing?" Parks asks of his old friend.

"I remember it well." Medina precisely remembers the feeling of *knowing*; the special agent spent his whole career in the *knowing*. That feeling Medina could not compartmentalize, driving him further into his career field and led to the loss of several what could have been beautiful relationships.

"Of course, you do. Anyway, we took overwhelming fire. James was gut shot; Doherty took one in the leg, and we eventually succumbed to concussive grenades and numbers. My men never faltered. Not once. They were instinctual machines. You make sure that's known, please brother?" Parks requests of the special agent.

Medina keeps his concentration on the road ahead and the mirrors. "That has already been taken care of by your old company, Bravo. Their relentless pursuit of defending you and your men in the media over the last couple of months has led to numerous recounting of James and Doherty's bravery in Iraq as well as on the ridge. They are now dubbing that, *the Battle of Clear Creek*. Leave it to *Grunts*, and their fucking nicknames."

Parks scoffs at the name for the place where he lost his men, "I don't care."

"Brother, I'm sorry. I know it's rough. What happened next?" Medina asks, consoling and imploring his old friend to continue.

"Their squad leader or unit leader is Russian. The rest were a mix of nationalities but there are a couple American special forces bubbas among them, Medina. *SEALs* or *MARSOC* I would guess, if they had been *Rangers* or some shit, we would've killed more," Parks explains, somewhat making a joke at the Army's expense, even now. Medina cannot help but smile a little bit. "The Russian proceeded to beat the shit out of me and then made me watch as he executed my men in front of me. You know the rest, Supervisory Special Agent." Parks clenches his fists so tight that his nails dig into the palms of his hands, producing trickles of blood, which leak onto his pants. He pays no attention to the blood droplets staining the wardrobe; he remembers the Russian's smiling face as he pulled the trigger on Doherty and James.

"Yeah, I do, brother," Medina offers in a sympathetic tone. They both sit in silence for the next forty or so miles, Parks lost in his guilt and Medina being distracted by his own life's consequences. Parks seems to be the outward turmoil that Medina has been facing inwardly over the last couple of years. His career seeming to not make a difference anymore in the protection of the American ideal. The special agent begins to question his career; was it all worth it for his men and women who served alongside him, the day-in and day-out grind of putting country and career over family. One by one the men and women of his unit would be divorced, suffer depression, battle demons, and, of course, the loss of life to suicide. He watched as it tore his troops apart from within, as the government constantly discouraged the unit's efforts and purpose.

"You do know there is a reckoning coming, don't you?" Parks abruptly asks the special agent.

Medina is awakened from his trance of the past few years and realizes Parks is speaking to him, "What do you mean?"

"That Russian is part of worldwide movement to bring America to her knees and an invasion is imminent. I can't wait to watch this country burn and all these inbred, fuckin flag flyers that never served, will shit their pants as the real threat hits their front fuckin lawn. It will be a slaughter. Then America will be begging for us combat Veterans to step up and I will fuckin break the hand America extends in peace. Fuck this country. It's not democracy, it's corruption. No Medina, I'm going to watch this country fall with a smile on my fuckin face as I go out in a grotesque military manner."

"I understand. More than you know." Medina cannot help but agree with Parks' anger towards his country, the former special forces operator and agent has seen far more than Parks could ever imagine and he is dead-on in his analysis of future events to befall the United States. The DHS agent and his operating unit have been following this theory all over the United States and across borders into Canada and Mexico. Medina only sees one option moving forward, and unfortunately, Parks and his men provide the perfect opportunity to enact that option.

The old squad leader can sense they are within a few miles of his home in Falcon, Colorado, "What now, Medina?"

The Last Letter

"To be honest, Parks, I don't know. Your official statement to the FBI is you don't remember a thing. Of course, you can always change that and tell them everything as you see fit. As far as I'm concerned, our conversation never happened and we were just two old Marine buddies shooting the shit as I relented to your request to return home, seeing as no law enforcement agency has any grounds to arrest you. So, for now, we can sit in silence until we reach your place, and say our goodbyes, for now," Medina explains the events as he sees them for the former Marine, also seeming to get his own agenda in line for the coming problematic days.

"Thank you." Parks looks towards Medina to show his sincerity, then returns his gaze to the familiar landscape as the two approach the outskirts of Colorado Springs.

Silence fills the cabin of the speeding Challenger, but it is a welcome silence that engulfs the two ageing Marines: each planning their next moves in this tangled web of guilt, remorse, anger, hostility, and pain. The special agent pulls down into Parks' neighborhood leading to his nice well-kept house at the end of the second street in the spacious subdivision. Medina pulls a card out of his polo breast pocket and tries to hand it to Parks.

"What's this?" Parks looks down at his old friend's gesture. "I won't need it, brother. Thank you for all you've done for me and my mother. I mean it."

Medina pulls the Challenger down his old friend's long, cobblestone driveway. The sun is beginning to crest over the backdrop of the mountains behind Parks' home. *I can see why he chose this house of semi-seclusion;* Medina ponders to himself. He, himself, appreciating the idea of seclusion and being finally done with life of a governmental agent fighting a losing war, that no one cares for, and politicians use as clickbait. Medina is looking forward to the solitude, but he must finish this one last crusade and needs his friend's help.

"Listen to me. You're right, the storm is coming, and it is further along than you know. The American public is too naïve, enamored with false Gods and themselves to know the real threat is sleeping beneath their very beds. I am done with this shit. I'm leaving my post effective immediately upon returning to the hospital. I need your help, brother. Once that rage inside overwhelms your catastrophic depression and your need for revenge becomes insatiable, that's when you'll need me and I you. Now take my fucking card. That's an order." Medina looks his buddy in the eye and makes Parks do the same. Medina does not see the washed-up former Marine. No, he sees the *company honorman* from boot camp, who won about every award out from under the special agent. That is who Medina sees before him.

The tired squad leader grabs the card from the special agent and stuffs it in the bag with the get well cards from his troops. "Roger that," he whispers back to his endearing friend, opening the car door to exit.

"Parks, what are you going to do now?" Medina asks after his longtime friend, rolling down the passenger window.

Parks leans on the passenger door and peers into the cabin of the sports car. "I don't know. Where are my weapons?"

Medina knew that question was eventually going to come from his wounded friend, he was hoping it would come later.

"Don't you fuckin stigmatize me, asshole. I have more inside. If I want to eat a round, I fuckin can. Where are my weapons?" Parks asks more firmly this time.

Any other person, Medina would have dropped them in their place, but he knew Parks is destroyed and needs patient answers not hinderances. "They're being held with the forestry agent in Clear Creek. I have taken her statement and read her report. I understand you are acquainted?"

"Yes. Thank you. I apologize for my attitude, brother." Parks lays his forehead onto his arm resting on the edge of the passenger car door.

"No need to apologize, my friend. I will help you get your vengeance and then you can be depressed all you want the rest of your life if you wish that existence. Deal?" Medina says, trying to motivate Parks as much as he is trying to motivate himself to see his plan to fruition. It begins here, with the enlistment of his old friend.

"Yeah, we'll see, brother." Parks shrugs off Medina's invitation and recruitment.

The special agent does not pursue the issue further, "What are the plans now, Parks? You're no longer under protective custody; I wouldn't stay here. If you're trying to avoid everyone, especially your mother. I'll

The Last Letter

be telling her the truth of where I took you when I get back to the hospital, understood?"

Parks picks his head up from his forearm and simply answers, "Roger that." He looks towards his house and the double garage. He already formulated his next moves on the ride to his home. "I'll be gone within the hour."

"Where's your phone?" Medina asks concerned.

Parks looks at his old friend cautiously, "In the hospital trash. I have a *bug out bag* with a burner in it. If I need you, I'll contact you with that."

"Good. Contact me when you come through the other side. I meant it, shithead." Medina extends his hand for Parks to embrace.

Parks grasps Medina's calloused hand firmly and puts his other on top of both. "I will, Vic. Thank you for letting me go."

"Get ahold me if you're going to head down the dark road; I do have a plan to bring you some light. Reach out, Jake." Medina leans closer to try and make eye contact, but his friend avoids the eye contact.

Parks slowly raises his head and finally looks Medina dead in the eye, Medina having the same worn, nonexistent spark in his eyes as Parks, "Answer me this question, honestly?"

"I will," Medina sincerely responds, awaiting some question about the incident Parks and his men had been through.

Parks releases his accepting handshake with Medina, looks towards his house and the young rising sun, and inhales deeply, "Who put the fuckin tarantula in my Kevlar?"

Medina did not mean for it to occur, but he burst out laughing, shocked at the sound of his own laughter. Such a surprise, Medina has not heard himself laugh in a long time, he forgot the feeling of warmth it provides. His laughter subsides quick enough, "It was Mitchell." Medina answers with a wry smile, looking up at Parks through the cab of the Challenger.

"I thought you would say that. And if I ask Mitchell?" Parks keeps his gaze to the distant beautiful horizon.

"He would say it was me." Medina's smile grows larger by the moment of recollection. He has surely not smiled like this in years, such joy has escaped him, even in the minimalist sense.

Parks looks down at Medina in the cab of the beautiful sleek sports car, sees his old friend smiling from ear to ear, and suddenly feels the beginning tug of a smile himself, due to his friend's infectious grin. "I thought so. It's been almost thirty years, and I still can't get a fuckin straight answer. You'll see me again, Special Agent Medina." With that Parks walks gingerly to his front door and punches in the code, unlocking under the proper command. Parks does not look back, instead he is eager to enter the lonesomeness of the residence.

The exhausted agent is then left awash in the glow of the interior panel lights, his old friend disappearing into his elegant home. He wonders is this the last time he will ever see Parks; *did I do the right thing by bringing him here?* "Lord, get him through the pain that will inevitably come. He's strong and we need him; he can make a difference still." With that little sentiment, Medina puts the Challenger into reverse and begins the trek back to the hospital to endure the wrath of Parks' mother. He will then retire from the agency and set in motion his agenda with the help of a few courageous agents who have volunteered to join Medina on his operation.

The Supervisory Special Agent is nervous for the first time in decades. Since the invasion of Iraq, and all subsequent tours, he moved as a machine and so did his men. No nerves, no feelings, only objective after objective which Medina has done for far too long. Now everything hinges on his successful achievement of his strategy to prevent the collapse of the United States. Yes, former Supervisory Special Agent Medina is nervous.

CH. 26
NAW THANKS, DOG. I'M STILL A MARINE.

Parks quickly shuffles to his bathroom and turns on the enormous stand up shower, with multiple jets spraying water from different directions; the steam begins to build from the scalding hot water spewing from the nozzles. One of the reasons why Parks bought the home, he knew this master shower would be amazing for his slowly breaking body and the pain that ensues. He strips down, putting on a towel and stares at himself in the mirror. Parks does not recognize the man in front of him, it is a shell, a husk. *This cannot be my true reflection*, he thinks, becoming disgusted by the empty image before him. "Yeah, you look like shit, Sgt. Parks." James appears out of the steam behind Parks, still dressed in his gear from their trip into *Hell*.

Parks puts his head into the palms of his hands. "No, not now, James, please. I can't fuckin do this anymore. What the fuck does God want with me, James, huh?" He does not raise his head from his palms; he dares not look to his troop's apparition, for that would acknowledge he is crazy, Parks does not have the time for *crazy*.

"I sure as fuck don't know, Sgt. Parks, but I do know I want to figure it out just as much as you do." James leans up against the granite bathroom countertop. He situates himself comfortably adjusting his buttpack to find that *sweet spot*. Looking over his shoulder at his reflection for the first time since their trip to Idaho, James winks at himself. "I tell you what, I look damn good in this gear. I bet Sgt. Heis would even be jealous. Right, Sgt. Parks?" he asks, referring to Delta from their squad of miscreants.

Parks clenches his fists at the mention of his title, this has to be God torturing him for the pain he has caused others; it has to be. "James, please for fucks sake, stop calling me that. I beg of you, please," the tired squad leader quietly pleads with the haunting visage.

"Shit, I would love too, but it's muscle memory to call you that, even after two decades. It's just the flow of which it sounds—*Sgt. Parks*." James continuing to smile and admire himself in the mirror, which is beginning to cloud over with steam.

Trying to ignore James, Parks moves to the shower, to soak in the spraying jets, looking for any relief he can find during this haze of despair. His shoulders drooping, his body aching with every move, Parks will make this all end soon enough, right now he wants only a hot shower.

"Nice ass for a boomer. I see you stopped skipping leg days," James comments as Parks gets in shower.

He gives his former troop the middle finger. His aching body reacts to the hot soothing water, Parks head begins to feel as if it is caught in a vise, slowly squeezing his brain together. He buckles to his knees in the shower stall and cradles his pounding head with his hands, he wants desperately for his life to end. *Is this finally it? Please let this be the end*, Parks begs with all mental acuity he can muster to get through the rough debilitating pain. *I need this to be over. Fuck! I am sorry for everything. Please end*, he continues to beg. He cares not who is listening; be it the notion of God or the Devil, he wants either entity to prove their validity by taking his soul in that very instance.

Nothing. The pain subsides, the broken Marine remains on the floor of the shower, letting the cascade of water caress his tired and battered body. Parks begins to tremble and shake as the images of James and Doherty's lasting efforts to save him before they were executed crash into his reality. The sound emanates from some deep primal place he has never experienced before. It erupts from his throat; the sound of agony, despair, futility, shame, guilt, and rage echo and reverberate throughout the beautiful quaint home.

He has lost men before, horrifically, but never in combat not on this level of violence. He never knew this pain, that of a squad leader losing his men in battle. The losses are too great for such frivolity and vanity. *This is all your fault, motherfucker*, the same thought that has plagued him for years even as he stayed sober, as the demons came unchecked, without resistance.

"Sgt. Parks, get your ass up. It's not your fault, Devil, we do not blame you. Get up, brother." Doherty appears out of the steam in the bathroom and tries to get comfortable next to James.

Parks says nothing to his old troop appearing from the haze. James looks to Doherty, "I don't think that's goin to work, you know, the sympathetic route, Devil."

"Did you do the 'boomer ass' joke?" Doherty asks his friend with a subdued smile.

James looks back at Parks crumpled on the shower floor, "Yeah, nothin. Not even a *'fuck you, James.'* Rude."

Doherty asks another question, trying to get a rise from his old squad leader. "How about the *'leg day'* one?"

James, still beaming from under his heavy beard, replies, "Nope, nothin."

"Well, he can't stay like this forever," Doherty states, sympathetically looking upon his crumpled squad leader shivering and shaking uncontrollably under the weight of his torment. The water ricocheting off his muscular, tired, aged back.

"Pray tell, what would you like us to do, ghost? We can't lift him, ass." James sarcastically answers.

"Fuck you, James. We need to motivate his ass into movin. Say somethin smartass to get him riled up." Doherty still watching his old friend shake on the shower floor, asking James to help.

James' smile gets even broader, thinking of just the thing. "Hey, Sgt. Parks, go see what the news has said about us three or combat Veterans in general."

"What the fuck are you doin?!" Doherty backhands James across the shoulder with his gloved hand.

"You fuckin said get him riled up. There you go. See, ass?" James counters Doherty's fear, both begin to see their old squad leader stir off the shower floor.

Parks raises his head, clenching his teeth so tight that his muscles begin to cramp along his jawline. He suddenly feels the hot water pounding his weathered, tired back. He sits in his kneeling position, slowly rotating his head in circles, listening to the vertebrae unhealthily pop and crunch in his neck. Parks is exhausted but the rage is boiling. It does not rejuvenate him but rather gives him the strength to slowly get up. He turns off the shower and grabs a towel to wrap around his small waist, wiping away the steam in the mirror; he looks at the six inch scar down the left side of his head from the cranial surgery. He shaved his balding head long ago, Parks does not care what the scar looks like, *If the world wants a stigma, then I will give them one*, he wipes the steam from the mirror and looks deeply at this dark reflection before him, "'Wait 'til they get a load of me,'" Parks whispers harshly the famous Jack Nicholson line to the shadowy image of himself.

"Nice, Sgt. Parks! Original fuckin *Batman*, well played." James pats Parks on his bruised back with a slight laugh. Parks can feel the worn palms of the gloves on his skin, *How can this be?*

Parks no longer fighting the images before him, deciding to embrace the stigma forming in his mind of himself, looks at James with his cruel reflection, "I thought you would like that, James." He raises himself up and looks over at Doherty. "I take it you two fellas are with me for the long haul?"

"I guess so, Sgt. Parks. Let's get rollin," Doherty offers his input to the uncharacteristic situation the three find themselves in.

Turning the lights off in the master bath, Parks heads to his walk-in closet, grabs his olive drab bug out bag and throws it on the bed. He quickly rushes to his dresser and throws on boxer briefs, a pair of olive drab work pants, opens the drawer next to it, grabs a grey Scooby-Doo T-shirt and throws it on, every movement sending searing pain throughout his body. Next his socks and Red Wing boots. He quickly checks the outer pockets of the bug out bag. He purchased fake identification in Costa Rica as a novelty from some individual making/selling them; at the time he thought *why the fuck not?* It is supposed to be an Oregon driver's license. He will now put the identification to the test.

Parks has about twelve thousand in cash and a prepaid smartphone not purchased in the state or neighboring states. He then moves methodically to his closet and pulls the lockbox from the wall safe, places his fingers on the fingerprint scanner and retrieves his .45 Smith & Wesson M&P semiautomatic

The Last Letter

pistol and two magazines. He puts the weapon into a quick-release holster and secures it in the bag.

"You sure that's a good idea?" Doherty asks Parks.

Continuing to double-check everything, then slings the bag over his right shoulder, Parks looks coldly at Doherty as he walks by, "Don't fuckin start."

"Roger that, Sgt. Parks," Doherty responding to a command from his old squad leader, like it was years ago. Doherty feels chills, he is excited for what lay ahead. It's like a rhythm is once again flowing.

Parks freezes on his way out of his bedroom but does not turn to face his men. "Please, goddammit, stop calling me that. I am no sergeant. I am no squad leader. I am damn sure not a fuckin Marine anymore."

"Never," James says with a Cheshire cat like smile. The squad leader storms off in defeat.

Continuing down his hallway, Parks grabs the keys to his vehicle he knew would eventually be used for such an occasion. He never drives the vehicle, only to get it serviced once a year, but he knew it would be his escape from this existence of sobering guilt and regret. To disappear completely, fade into distant memories of loved ones. Soon that will come to fruition, but first Parks needs to get moving, not from fear of reprisal from the armed men or the Russian. Parks welcomes his death now; no, he is running from his mother. She will be here soon and that he cannot deal with, that he truly fears.

Parks, making sure he has everything he needs, gingerly heads out his kitchen door to the garage and unlocks the vehicle next to his 2022 Bronco. The former infantryman takes a quick look behind him. He sees neither Doherty nor James. "Now you have nothing to say." He puts the keys into the ignition and the motor comes to life on his stealth black 1986 Chevy K5 Blazer. The engine is submarine quiet as well as the exhaust, which he paid extra for after a rebuilt original engine was installed; his neighbors will not hear him leave the subdivision.

As he makes his way out of the comfortable neighborhood, the memory of his mom slowly pulling his idling truck to the side of a desert road taking him back to 29 Palms, sends nervous anxiety through his body. Parks did not want her to try and sabotage his objective again, even though he knows it is out of pure motherly protection. Right before he shipped out for Iraq, he and the other squad leaders were going over a month ahead of the rest of Bravo Co. to do *right seat, left seat* with the outgoing squad leaders in their soon-to-be area of operation (AO). His command gave Parks a special weekend pass to go see his family one final time, he only got the pass because his men excelled in all areas of range and training proficiency and in turn, 1st Squad stood among the best in the company. As his mother was driving him back to 29 Palms, she purposely tried to run out of gas in the middle of the desert while her son was sleeping. To this day his mother finds humor in the tale. Parks has yet to find any:

"What the fuck, Mom!" Parks yelling, startled awake by the sound of his dying truck.

She looked over at him calmy, "I'm sorry, son. We're running out of gas."

"I fuckin know that. but there were several gas stations back that way you could've stopped at, shit." Parks in full blown panic mode.

"I'm sorry, son. I thought we could make it to the next one," she counters.

Parks looks around frantically and sees the sign for the next stop four miles ahead. He is hoping, it is open and not a deserted rest stop. "Mom, do you have any fuckin idea what happens if I miss this formation to leave for Iraq? Do you? It's fuckin desertion during a time of war. I'm going to Leavenworth for fuckin minimum thirty years. What the fuck! You did this on purpose."

"No, son, I didn't. I just wasn't paying attention; I'm losing you to the Marines." She becomes quieter, trying desperately to coast the truck the next four miles. Parks dares not tell her to pull over because that will destroy any momentum the truck is coasting on.

"Yeah, well how the fuck is losing me to prison any fucking better? This is my decision, I wanted this. Fuck! Mom, the command gave me a special fuckin pass to come see you and Jazz one last time before I left. No other squad leader got the fuckin chance and now you're fuckin me and them over. This is bullshit."

Jean now starting to understand the gravity of her actions. "Don't worry, son, we'll make it."

"Damn right we'll make it. If I have to get out and hoof it to the gas station and get us help, that's what I'm fuckin going to do. I'll asks the sheriff to give us ride back to base and to call my command. Tell them my mom purposely tried to run out of gas

The Last Letter

to keep her son out of war. Jesus. What the fuck, mom?" Parks becomes more panicked as the truck struggles more and more.

Jean reaches over, puts her hand on his shoulder, "Son, forgive me. I'm sorry."

"I know, Mom. It's okay. I'm sorry I panicked. Let's just get there or your son is fucked," he replies, shaking uncontrollably with anxiety of missing his movement to Iraq.

Parks turns out of his subdivision and heads for the interstate to begin his trek south, he recalls years later when he had returned, he asked his mother if she tried to run out of gas on intentionally.

"Of course, you are my son," she says with a motherly smile. "It no longer matters; you are here safe now to tell the story."

"Mom, I could've been thrown in prison," Parks explained to his proud mother. She sips her tea and replies, "It all worked out for the best. Besides you didn't even say goodbye to your mother before I left, just as well you didn't see me pull over and cry as I drove away, thinking I was never going to see you again."

"Mom, I had to get my shit to the parade deck, I didn't have a second, I was late, remember. I'm sorry, I didn't say goodbye, you deserved that much." Parks apologizes to his mother.

"Son of a bitch, she turned the tables around on me. Fuck," Parks scolds himself as he jumps on Interstate 25 south to his next destination. He stares ahead, the sun breaking the horizon to his east. He knows he must complete a few objectives and then he can finally be free of *Sgt. Parks*, once and for all.

. . .

The K5 Blazer pulls into a local Extended Stay America ten hours later, Parks hoping to find a vacancy. He is in luck; they have a room. Parks hands the clerk his identification he got in Costa Rica, he figures it should work for simple things like a hotel and he is not disappointed, *get the fuck out of here*, he scoffs to himself. The clerk gives Parks his keycards to the room after he pays cash for two nights stay.

The room is your basic stale mid-grade hotel room, scratchy comforter, horrible colored drapes on the self-locking window, generic space heater/cooler. Parks takes a quick look in the parking lot from his window.

SSgt. Jacob Parkinson

"What the fuck you lookin for?" James pops in from the bathroom. Parks is no longer startled by his perceived insanity and accepts his lunacy. "You're not *Jason Bourne*, Sgt. Parks."

Jaw clenching in annoyance at James once again, "Fuck if I know, I'm not a special agent. I think I'm just looking for anything," Parks answers his former troop.

"I don't think being here is a good idea, brother. We should keep movin, Sgt. Parks." Doherty appears, looking at his beleaguered and exhausted squad leader with worry.

Parks closes his eyes, "Stop calling me Sgt. Parks, he had integrity and would never have done what I have brought upon others. I don't know how it all came to this fucked up shit."

"Goddamn you are a depressin fuck, Sgt. Parks." James moves to a chair by the efficiency table, "You fuckers remember the lead up to Fallujah; the Marines were to spearhead the assault into the most dangerous city on the planet."

Doherty scoffs, "You mean good ol' *Operation Phantom Fury*. Sgt. Parks gives us the briefin, that shit has hit the fuckin fan."

"Not much of a briefing, if I can remember. Basically, we're going right down the road to the outskirts of the city and try to be engaged," Parks adds, relenting and joining his former troops in the distraction of conversation.

James erupts in laughter, "That fuckin JAG[51] officer held up a blank sheet of paper and told us *that* was our *Rules of Engagement*. Fallujah had been declared a free fire zone, *'if you see a man with a gun, smoke check him; if you see a woman with a gun, smoke check her. Fuck, if you see a goat with a gun, fuckin smoke check it,'* the officer told us. I like this guy." James keeps his smile beaming, hoping it will become infectious to his other two friends.

"Yeah, he was good to go. We would see him again in the aftermath of Fallujah, for our squad shit." Parks lays down on the bed, feeling the comfort to be off his feet. James and Doherty's eye's become wide with recognition.

Doherty snaps his fingers. "I knew he looked fuckin familiar, shit."

"Small fuckin world," James adds, seemingly answering a question he had long forgotten.

---

[51] Judge Advocate General

The Last Letter

Parks adjusts, trying to relieve his aching muscles, "Yep, and as soon as he was done with that moto speech, the body bags started getting delivered to Bravo Co. in preparation for casualties. *Welcome to the Suck*."

Again, Doherty gives the sigh of realization, "Yeah, that shit was fucked, definitely took the wind out the sails on that one."

"Yep, and we immediately had the gag order in place, so no telling the folks back home, one last *'goodbye, I love you'* bullshit." James continues trying to keep the mood of the room from taking a turn downward.

Doherty vacantly looking out the window, asks "Did you fellas ever write one of those *'if I don't make it back'* letters before that mission?"

James' smile fades at the mention of the *'last'* letter home, "Yeah man, gave mine to Culpepper. Sgt. Parks?"

The old squad leader looks to the plain, white ceiling and coldly answers, "No."

"Gave mine to Jackson. You probably should have written one, Sgt. Parks." Doherty counters sympathetically in his advocacy tone of voice. The stale hotel room grows quiet once again. All that can be heard is Parks labored breathing from the bed.

James laughs from his position after a brief depressive pause amongst the friends. "Yeah, and *Dickless* Daisy went immediately to the phone banks and cried home to his wife about where we were headed, the news spreadin like wildfire amongst the Bravo Co. family members, gettin our loved ones all riled up and shit. Fuckin asshole."

"What'd you expect?" Doherty counters, knowing there is no rationale for their platoon commander's inept decisions.

Parks answers his former troop, "Nothing much anymore, Devil." He exhales, on the verge of passing out from exhaustion.

James moves the chair towards the bed to kick up his combat boots, "Anyway, Bravo Co. is supposed to go in as a feint, draw all the goddamn enemy's fire and hold out for three to five days. Pack the basics; shit, most of us didn't even pack hygiene gear. Ammo, water, chow, in that fuckin order. Right, Sgt. Parks?"

Half-asleep Parks drearily gives an infantry response, "Yut. And it was seven days not three to five. They told us to pack for seven days."

"I don't give a fuck, five, seven; shit lasted twenty-seven," James huffs at the length of the famed operation.

"Yut," Doherty grunts, making his way to the recliner near the closet of the plain hotel room. "I think I tore the shit out of my cammies on the second fuckin day." He laughs to himself trying to get comfortable in the chair with all of his gear on. "You couldn't remember us in boots and utes, instead of all this fuckin gear. What the fuck, Sgt. Parks?"

Parks scoffs with a tired exhale, "Sorry, Devil, I don't make the rules." the tired squad leader then slowly recalls, "I fell in the shit canal on the fourth day, Devils, so I don't want to hear fuck all from you two. Try smelling like that for the next twenty-three days."

James kicks his old, battered squad leader's feet with his boot, "That shit was funny, Sgt. Parks, you have to admit."

"Fuck you, James," Parks grumbles, barely audible as he drifts to sleep.

Kicking his squad leader's feet again to keep him awake, James continues his tale of hilarity and Marine mischief. "Not yet Devil. The story is not over, dick. We spend the next couple of days runnin small unit drills, back to the numbers. There could be no fuckups on this one."

"Probably should've left your ass behind, then, huh, Devil." Doherty chides his former squad mate.

Parks chokes on his scoff of an exhale, "Good one, Doherty."

James giving Doherty the middle finger with both his hands, smiling from ear to ear, reclined as far back as the chair will allow, continues, "Fuck you. That shit kept us from thinkin about the potential hellfire we were about to walk into." He yawns, the activities over the past couple of days wearing on him as well. "The day before, Bravo Co. and some Army boys from a Bradley unit form up; gave us their Indian head army unit patches and tell us we're now honorary members of the Army's 2nd Infantry Division. Naw thanks, Dog, I'm still a fuckin Marine."

Doherty laughs, his feet fully reclined, all three on the verge of passing out from exhaustion, "Fuck them. Pissed me off 2nd Platoon got stuck rollin in with those fuckers, Bravo splits one way 2nd Platoon goes with the Army pukes. *Dickless* must have pissed someone off."

The Last Letter

James sstring to doze himself continues, "Their fuckin commander, Col. Patton, still no clue if he is related to the WWII general, gets up on top of an LAV to give his pre-battle moto speech. He's slurrin, sounds half-drunk; kept calling the LAV *'Lav-Lar.'* Pronouncing two supporting acronyms as fuckin actual words; all of Bravo and 3rd LAR Marines had their heads down tryin not to laugh their asses off. Who the fuck put *Droopy Dog* in charge of the moto speeches." He recalls the horrible speech given by the Army commander. "Major Miller gave his speech next. I don't remember the details, but I know it was chub worthy." He refers to their company commander's speech on the eve of *Operation Phantom Fury*, more commonly known as the *Battle of Fallujah*.

Parks tries to roll his aching head towards James, who is comfortably leaning back in the chair, "You don't remember much of Major Miller's speech because 2nd Platoon wasn't there for it; we were gearing up with that fucktard Bradley unit. We missed Gunny Hoffman's battle speech as well."

Doherty reacts with shock. "Shit, come to think of it, I don't remember Gunny's or Major Miller's speeches, those would've been some damn good ones to hear."

"That makes sense, Sgt. Parks. I always wondered why I couldn't remember the details of their speeches but can remember the JAG officer's." James contemplates, looking back on that day over twenty years ago.

Parks scoffs again at his former troop, "Shit, James, I'm surprised, you remember fuckin everything else."

James' smile never falters, "Fuck you, someone has to, you old ass."

"Touché," Parks says, giving up the battle of ages with his younger troop. "That last meal before rollin in, we get to go to the chow hall on Habaneya for what Doherty and I called our *'Last Supper.'*"

Doherty almost at a perfect solitary rest offers a faint, "Yut."

James keeps going, "Steak and lobster with ice cream. Yummy. The POGs were actually serving us *Grunts*, walkin around askin if we needed refills or if they could get us anythin else. They all thought we were fucked." He looks to his former squad leader, "Sgt. Parks, you thought we were gettin all cocky and shit. It may have been false bravado for some, but I truly think most of us felt like we were unstoppable at this point."

Parks looks up to the white ceiling of the hotel room, trying to make sense of the patterns of water stains, like an ugly distracted Rorschach test. "You men weren't cocky, just numb by then. We all were. You Devils had nothing left to prove by that point."

"All I know is, everyone started takin squad pictures, thinkin it will be the last photo together. Then some dickhead broke out cammie paint, we weren't supposed to wear cammie paint in country because it would scare the shit out of the locals; *win the hearts and minds* remember, Sgt. Parks. Not that night, were paintin up like a sandy version of *Braveheart*. Oorah, combat boner, right there."

The two other men quietly laugh at their old squad mate describe the events on the eve of the operation. Parks feels the pain from the slight laughter, "Stop making me laugh, Devil, fuckin hurts. You men were cammied up like boots at SOI[52], all pretty Hollywood patterns and shit. Slap that shit on and call it a day."

"Errrr." Doherty gives the customary Marine growl to his squad leader's comments. "I remember rollin in with Army PsyOps blastin, *Let the Bodies Hit the Floor*, until rounds started coming down range. Then they left us high and dry real quick and in a hurry. " Doherty kicks James' boots with his own, giving him a slight wink.

Parks sighs heavily, readying himself for a deep slumber, "That squad photo still haunts me, brothers."

"Me too, Sgt. Parks," Doherty exhales; he, too, preparing to let sleep win the battle for his consciousness.

James stretches one final time, then folds his arms across his chest rig. "Where are we goin tomorrow, Sgt. Parks?"

Doherty picks his head up a bit, interested to know their next step. "Keepin a low profile will be the best avenue of approach, Sgt. Parks."

Parks moans with the pain of age and remorse, propping himself up on one elbow, gingerly. "I'm taking you Marines home." Their former squad leader then collapses from exhaustion and passes out; missing the looks of dread spread across James and Doherty's rough, worn-out faces.

---

[52] School of Infantry

End of Part One
1st Squad Will Return,
With A Little Help From Their Friends

In memory of Cpl. Ian Doherty
12/06/1982 – 2/09/2021]

Printed in the USA
CPSIA information can be obtained
at www.ICGtesting.com
LVHW010619090924
790326LV00013B/371